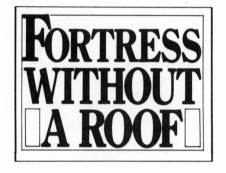

Other books by Wilbur H. Morrison

Hellbirds: The Story of the B-29s in Combat
The Incredible 305th: The "Can Do" Bombers of World War II
Wings over the Seven Seas: U.S. Naval Aviation's Fight for Survival
Point of No Return: The Story of the Twentieth Air Force

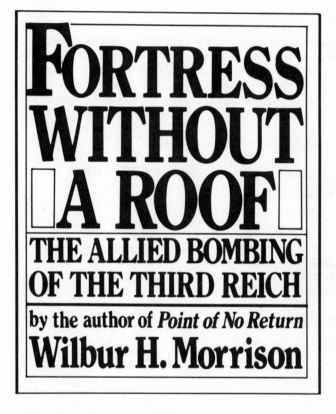

FORTRESS WITHOUT A ROOF

THE ALLIED BOMBING OF THE THIRD REICH

by the author of *Point of No Return*

Wilbur H. Morrison

ST. MARTIN'S PRESS   NEW YORK

Design by Kingsley Parker

Library of Congress Cataloging in Publication Data

Morrison, Wilbur H.
    Fortress without a roof.

    1. World War, 1939 –1945—Aerial operations.
2. World War, 1939 –1945—Campaigns—Germany.
3. Germany—History—1933 –1945. I. Title.
D785.M67   940.54′4   82-5601
ISBN 0 –312–29981–8   AACR2

First Edition

10 9 8 7 6 5 4 3 2 1

Dedicated to

Major General Haywood S. Hansell, Jr. (Ret.)

CONTENTS

A section of photographs follows p. 158

ACKNOWLEDGMENTS

The author would like to acknowledge his indebtedness to retired Major General Haywood S. Hansell, Jr., without whose assistance this book would not have come into being. Hansell's own book, *The Air Plan That Defeated Hitler,* gives invaluable insight into air operations in Europe during World War II. His reminiscences about people and events give *Fortress Without a Roof* a more human touch.

Among the hundreds who contributed recollections, retired Lieutenant Generals Ira C. Eaker and James H. Doolittle, and retired Colonel Henry G. Macdonald each provided material about the air war that enhanced the author's understanding. Eaker loaned the author a three-hundred-page transcript of taped interviews granted by him to air force historians that contained his unpublished memoirs, with permission to use the material without restrictions. These detailed memoirs gave a true and honest picture that is seldom seen in such recollections. They were invaluable to the author in re-creating events that have been distorted by constant retelling by writers who were not on the scene.

Significant assistance also was provided by James N. Eastman, Jr., chief of the Research Division of the Albert F. Simpson Historical Research Center at Maxwell Air Force Base, Alabama, and his research assistant, Master Sergeant Thaddeus E. Bugay.

The author also expresses his appreciation to the Macmillan Publishing Company, Inc., and George Weidenfeld & Nicolson Ltd., for permission to use several excerpts from Albert Speer's book, *Inside the Third Reich;* to George A. Reynolds for permission to quote from his booklet *ETO Carpetbaggers;* and to the Imperial War Museum, London, for permission to use photographs from their archives.

The author would like to express his gratitude to his agent, David Stewart Hull, whose enthusiasm for the air-war trilogy, of which this book is a part, has never wavered. He would also like to express his appreciation to his editor, Jared Kieling, for helping to resolve some of the problems in a manuscript that tells its story on many levels.

INTRODUCTION

This is a story of faith by men of conviction who believed that a country could be defeated by strategic airpower without a costly invasion by ground troops. It involves airmen of many nations, and several British and American air forces that penetrated the skies above Fortress Europe and helped to destroy one of the world's greatest military powers.

It is also a story of incredible human suffering on the ground and in the air, the likes of which mankind had never before known. This chronicle of courage and of devotion to a principle describes the actions of the men who participated in the combined bomber offensive against Hitler's Third Reich.

The fact that an invasion of the European continent was considered necessary to achieve final victory in Europe has created misunderstandings about the role of strategic airpower in World War II. Even today, few people realize that victory through airpower was possible if the Allied governments had waited until the strategic air forces reached their peak strength in the summer of 1944 and were able to launch an all-out aerial offensive. Reasons for the early shortcomings of strategic airpower are complex and can be understood only by looking at the record objectively, even though the truth reveals some of the myths of near-infallibility that several Allied leaders acquired in World War II. It is my hope that *Fortress Without a Roof* will set the record straight.

This is the second book of a trilogy about the air war during World War II. *Point of No Return: The Story of the Twentieth Air Force* was published in 1979. The final book in the series is *Above and Beyond,* soon to be published by St. Martin's Press, which describes the role of carrier aviation in the defeat of the Japanese armed forces in the Pacific.

—Wilbur H. Morrison
Fallbrook, California

Hitler built a fortress around Europe,
but he forgot to put a roof on it.

—President Franklin D. Roosevelt

1

"SEEMS TO ME YOU'RE IN A HELL OF A HURRY."

Harry L. Hopkins strode into the Government Printing Office at one o'clock one morning in early September 1942. There was a tired droop to his bony shoulders, and his light paunch sagged in baggy trousers that rode high on spindly legs. His pallid scalp shone through thinning hair, and his drawn face was wreathed in smoke as he puffed nervously on a cigarette. President Franklin D. Roosevelt's personal aide and counselor often appeared at such odd hours because his ulcers kept him wakeful. He had been in ill health for several years, and the president, who relied upon him implicitly, moved him into the White House to help him recuperate. The demands of the war forced any thought of convalescence into the background because Roosevelt needed him now more than ever.

Hopkins stopped at a table with thirty copies of a secret report labeled "Air War Plans Division-42: Requirements for Air Ascendancy." Each copy had a number, and the first fifteen copies had names stenciled in gold with Roosevelt's copy identified as number one, and Hopkins's number six. When Hopkins saw his copy, he picked it up and started to walk out.

"Sir," a flustered employee said. "That document is secret, and you can't have it."

"My identity is well known," Hopkins said brusquely. He could be blunt, almost insulting at times. He had been involved in the early phases of the report, and he saw no reason why an underling should tell him what he could do.

The employee persisted.

"My integrity in government is unquestioned," Hopkins said angrily. "Furthermore, that's my name on the document."

While the unfortunate individual continued to protest, Hopkins walked out with AWPD-42, the estimate of aircraft needed to win the air war in Europe.

Since the entry of the United States into World War II, American airpower in England had demonstrated grave weaknesses. With Lieutenant General Dwight D. Eisenhower and Brigadier General Ira C. Eaker in attendance, six light bombers of the Eighth Air Force had taken off to bomb German airfields in Holland July 4, 1942, in borrowed Royal Air Force Bostons. Before they departed, Eisenhower spoke briefly, with words of encouragement. Major J. L. Griffith's 15th Bombardment Squadron had undergone training by the British in these American-built A-20 Bostons since their arrival May 1. During the mission, only two crews dropped bombs on assigned targets. The others either failed to navigate to their destinations, or ran into such unexpectedly heavy ground fire that they couldn't complete their runs. Two of the light bombers were shot down by antiaircraft fire, and another limped home badly damaged.

The mission was not without incidents of heroism. Captain Charles C. Kegelman's plane had one of its propellers shot off by ground fire, which also damaged his right wing and started a fire in an engine. He fought to keep the airplane in the air as it lost altitude over De Kooy Airdrome, actually striking the ground once but bouncing back into the air. He spared a glance at the flak tower on his left just as German gunners swung their weapons toward him. Banking quickly, he flew directly at the tower and opened fire with his nose guns at close range. The German guns stopped firing as the bomber's guns tore the tower apart. With one engine gone, and a torn right wing, he flew across the Channel just above the wave tops, home from a mission that was not a success. It was, however, the start of an air campaign that would eventually cause more destruction in Germany and the occupied countries than anyone could have foreseen at the time. Prior to that mission, American planes had confined their activities against Germany to antisubmarine patrols. Not until six weeks later—August 17—would the first tentative heavy-bomber strikes be made against targets in German-occupied countries.

By this time—the summer of 1942—American fliers in the Pacific were already veterans. They had helped to defeat the Japanese at the Battle of the Coral Sea and defeated them decisively at Midway. After that turning point in the Pacific war, Japanese drives were brought to a standstill.

Following the Japanese attack on Pearl Harbor December 7, 1941, President Roosevelt and Prime Minister Winston Churchill agreed to meet with their aides on December 23 in Washington to plan the future conduct of the war. Before Churchill came to this Washington Arcadia Conference, it was necessary for the Joint Chiefs of Staff to agree upon a basic American position.

There had been two schools of thought in Washington about prosecuting the war. Many air corps officers, and others in the army, argued that the European conflict should have primary emphasis. Navy officials, with some support from the chief of naval operations, Admiral Harold B. Stark, had argued for an all-out effort in the Pacific, leaving the continuation of the European war to the British, if indeed that was not already a lost cause.

General Eisenhower, who was then chief of the Operations and Plans Division of the War Department's General Staff, had been asked by Army Chief of Staff General George C. Marshall to present his views in a memorandum about this fundamental dilemma. Eisenhower said he disagreed with those who suggested a pullout of troops from Australia. He said he saw no point in using scarce shipping to remove troops from Australia, which, at the time, was not even threatened. While "Asia first" advocates fought stubbornly for their viewpoints, Eisenhower used his considerable powers of persuasion to point out that the War and Navy departments had long ago agreed that in the event of a two-ocean war the United States would make its major offensive effort in Europe.

When the Joint Chiefs met for their first, formal meeting, Navy Department officials refused to concede to Eisenhower's logic. They pointed out that when a divided enemy is encountered, it is a strategic axiom that the weaker one should be attacked first.

Eisenhower said such reasoning had no validity. He reminded navy officials that military estimates are based upon relative power at a particular point of contact. Japan was then stronger in Asia than Germany and Italy were in Europe, because of her unique geographical position as an island empire and because the Russians were occupying the Germans on the eastern front.

Eisenhower's strongest rebuttal against the Navy Department's "Pacific first" position was based on the scarcity of shipping. He said that to conduct a full-scale war in East Asia would require at least three and possibly four times the number of ships required to support a similar force in England. He reminded his navy colleagues of another military axiom that, in a major effort, there should always be the shortest possible lines of communication.

The Joint Chiefs turned the problem over to their strategic committee. This committee, made up of four army officers and four navy officers, including an aviator from each service, quickly became seriously divided. Its initial position found seven members voting to abandon Europe, assume a strategic defense in the Western Hemipshere, and start a strategic offensive against Japan at the earliest possible date. The army airman was the lone dissenter. Further argument finally reversed this position and placed first priority on an air offensive against Axis Europe. The committee also recommended a buildup for an invasion of Europe, with strict economy of forces in other theaters. The Joint Chiefs accepted these recommendations and presented them to the Arcadia Conference in Washington.

During the conference, Army Air Forces Chief of Staff General Henry H. "Hap" Arnold pressed for an aerial bombardment of the European continent as called for in the Army Air Corps prewar plan. He told the gathering that he could get his first group of thirty-five bombers to England by March of 1942. He said later that his plan called for eight hundred bombers in England by the end of that year. He stressed that only through bombing could the Allies take any hostile action against the German homeland in the near future. General Arnold, like President Roosevelt, was particularly conscious of the boost such early actions would give American morale.

The "Europe first" strategy was accepted in January 1942. At last, a strategic plan to defeat the Axis powers had been recommended by the United States and accepted in principle by President Roosevelt and Prime Minister Churchill of Great Britain. Although the British had accepted the basic thesis, General Marshall now had to get specific agreement from them for an early assault on the Continent.

In the middle of March, a joint staff mission offered a plan for landing British forces near Le Havre early in the summer of 1943, but only under "conditions of severe deterioration of German military power." British officials insisted such an invasion was feasible only if the Germans had been weakened in strength and morale.

American aviators, like the British, considered such an invasion a mopping-up operation that would follow the closing and tightening of the ring through airpower. American army strategists, on the other hand, considered a cross-channel invasion as the chief method for defeating Germany. These divergent views had to be reconciled because, as the Americans well knew, any invasion in 1942 or even in 1943 would have to be primarily British. Marshall was aware that by July 1, 1942, there would be no American ground forces in England, and only 70,000 by October 1. In fact, projections indicated a maximum of 207,000 by January 1, 1943. Marshall, Eisenhower, and other top officials of the United States government knew that it would take 600,000 ground troops to divert substantial German forces from the Russian front—an impossible burden to place on the British army.

Churchill argued forcefully for operations in North Africa or Norway because, he said, the Germans couldn't bring adequate strength against invasion forces in either area. This left Marshall with a dilemma, because he had been told by President Roosevelt that American troops had to be fighting somewhere in Europe in 1942. He was aware of the pitfalls of agreeing to diversions from the principal enemy, and once involved in areas other than France, the United States would find its resources drained with small impact on the major war against Germany. He was fearful that if American forces were committed to North Africa, for instance, an invasion of France would be delayed indefinitely.

Political pressures for action somewhere began to mount. Americans and Britons alike had been served an unpalatable menu of defeat on every front, with the lone exception the defensive battle of Britain. The Germans were at the gates of Moscow, and Stalin was desperately demanding that the Allies come to his rescue. He kept saying that Soviet Russia faced a defeat that would mean the loss not only of Europe, but also of Great Britain.

With Roosevelt pressing for early action in Europe, and Churchill insisting on actions elsewhere, Marshall and Eisenhower had to convince the British somehow that a cross-channel attack against the Continent was at least feasible, even though the Germans were not yet seriously weakened. In effect, to keep the president happy Marshall had to insist on an invasion in 1942—even though he doubted it was really practicable that soon—while privately insisting upon a 1943 invasion in his talks with British leaders.

When the combined British and American chiefs of staff reviewed American recommendations in the spring of 1942, doubts were expressed that the necessary air superiority could be achieved to cover an invasion in the fall of 1942, though they believed it could be done in the following spring.

The plan was approved in principle by Roosevelt, and Army Chief of Staff Marshall went with Harry Hopkins to London on April 8, 1942, to present their views to the British. When they met with the British Chiefs of Staff Committee the next day, Marshall urged agreement on a firm decision for the assault on the Continent, as a joint Anglo-American effort. He said the American Joint Chiefs of Staff preferred an early invasion to help the beleaguered Russian army. He said also that it was important to get American troops into an active theater so that they could gain experience in large-scale operations. He admitted that, due to Pacific requirements, the United States could not build up its forces in England for such an invasion before the spring of 1943. He did recommend a more modest operation if the Russian situation worsened. This should be done, he said, only on an emergency basis. He estimated that by mid-September the United States Army could have one armored division and two and a half infantry divisions in the United Kingdom with four hundred fighters, three hundred bombers, and two hundred transport planes.

The British had been considering an emergency invasion in 1943—even sooner if the Soviets appeared to be near defeat or if the Germans themselves got in dire straits. They were not enthusiastic about any kind of a cross-channel attack in 1942, however.

The British ended up accepting the Marshall plan in principle for an invasion in the spring of 1943, with a smaller operation in 1942 if that became necessary.

Churchill wrote Roosevelt that he agreed with the provision that the Japanese and the Germans must be prevented from joining forces in the Middle East. He said a crescendo of activities against the Continent should be initiated "starting with an ever-increasing air offensive both night and day."

Crucial to the coming air war were plans made with the help of the Army Air Corps Intelligence Section, an organization born two years before with an energetic push from General "Hap" Arnold.

In 1940, Major Truman Smith, a former army assistant military attaché in Berlin, had just returned to the United States from Germany. He discussed German airpower with General Arnold, who now headed the Army Air Corps, and described in detail the progress they had made in developing military aviation.

Arnold asked Smith, "Why don't I get such information?"

"I don't know. I turn in my reports to the G-2 intelligence section in the War Department."

Arnold strode over to the office of the army's deputy chief of staff. He demanded to know why such intelligence estimates were not available to the chief of the Army Air Corps.

The deputy explained that distribution was limited to the War Department's General Staff, and Arnold's name wasn't on the list. "Feel free to read the reports in the G-2 offices," he said, "but they can't be taken out."

Arnold was furious. He went directly to General Malin Craig's office, who was then chief of staff. After explaining the problem and insisting on the right of the Air Corps to gather its own intelligence, he said, "I want permission to establish our own attachés at United States embassies around the world."

To his surprise, his request was granted.

Ira C. Eaker, who was Arnold's executive officer before the war, called in Major Thomas D. White and Major Haywood S. "Possum" Hansell, Jr., and said, "Arnold has received permission to establish an intelligence section. You two have been selected to operate it. Get on with it."

White organized the assistant air attachés, and Hansell was made responsible for strategic air intelligence and analysis.

Despite army approval, Arnold ran into strong opposition from the War Department's intelligence section. He refused to accept defeat because collection and analysis of air intelligence was essential to the success of strategic airpower. Without strategic air intelligence, on which targets vital to enemy industrial and economic structures could be selected, no sensible plans for strategic air warfare could be fashioned. He knew that miscalculations or misunderstood data from the War Department's intelligence section could be crucial.

With the help of the Royal Air Force, data collection was started immediately for Germany and Italy.

Creation of Air War Plans Division-1, the prewar plan that had been accepted by General Marshall and Secretary of War Henry Stimson on August 30, 1941, was directly related to the establishment of this intelligence section. In the event of war the plan called for six months of air attacks in Europe at full strength to destroy the will and capability of the Axis powers to sustain the war, or to create conditions under which a successful invasion could be made, if that should become necessary. The strategic air offensive could be launched in full strength in about eighteen months. In contrast, the United States Army would require about two and a half years to create, equip, train, and support necessary ground forces.

The Army Air Corps, designated the Army Air Forces after the start of hostilities, could move more quickly because they had begun partial mobilization earlier due to Roosevelt's foresight in expanding aviation before the United States entered the war. American industry had been geared up earlier to fill French and British aircraft orders, as well as those for lend-lease.

In this prewar plan, initial air operations were scheduled to start within a year of United States entry into the war. Primary targets for a strategic air war were selected on the basis of an offensive that would reach targets all over Germany and, hopefully, destroy Germany's industrial capacity. Such an offensive, however, was predicated on a strategic air command at full strength of four thousand bombers during a six-month period.

Key to the plan was the destruction of the German air force, and its supporting links. Decision-makers had to decide which ones, among many interconnecting links, would cause most impairment to the German war machine, and allocate sufficient bomber strength to destroy them.

This prewar plan pinpointed 154 targets whose disruption or neutralization would be most effective in undermining Germany's military strength. Initially, the steel industry received top consideration, but it was dropped in favor of electric and transportation industries. It was reasoned that steel furnaces relied upon electricity, and that they were less vulnerable than electric plants and transportation sites. It was known at the time that repeated attacks would be necessary to keep transportation systems shut down.

At first, it was believed that the number of air bases in England would be limited, and the plan's implementation would suffer as a result. Therefore, consideration was given to training two crews for each B-24 and B-17, and using the B-36 intercontinental bomber from Western Hemisphere bases because it had a 4,000-mile radius of action. Twelve groups of B-29 Superfortresses, then only in the development stage, were considered for Mediterranean bases, with another 12 groups in northern Ireland. The plan called for a total of 207 groups, without the B-36, for a total of 11,853 aircraft.

With the crippling of the Pacific Fleet at Pearl Harbor, all American war plans became useless—except for the air plan. Although AWPD-1 did not receive the full approval of the Joint Chiefs of Staff, it was approved as the basis for aircraft production, and since aircraft production was, in turn, based upon the operational plan, the latter received their endorsement.

A year after the first air plan was submitted by Arnold and accepted in August of 1941 by Marshall, Roosevelt again asked for an estimate of future aircraft requirements. He was still concerned about lagging airpower in the United Kingdom, so he asked Arnold to submit through Marshall, in the summer of 1942, a production plan for the numbers of combat aircraft by types that should be produced in the United States for the United States Army and its allies during 1943 to gain complete air ascendancy over their enemies.

Further, he asked Marshall and Chief of Naval Operations Ernest J. King to submit a second schedule based upon the "conflicting needs of other services for production capacity and manpower based upon the relationship of airpower to the navy and our ground forces."

By the summer of 1942, the original planners of AWPD-1 were dispersed throughout the world. Hansell, now a brigadier general, was serving under Major General Carl "Tooey" Spaatz who headed the new Eighth Air Force. He had gone to England earlier to serve on Eisenhower's staff as air planner and deputy theater air officer.

Arnold had been given an impossible deadline to meet, so he brought Hansell home to direct preparation of the new plan.

Much had happened since AWPD-1 had been prepared. The United States was now involved in a world war. Corregidor in the Philippines had fallen. Field Marshal Erwin Rommel had taken the important town of Tobruk in North Africa for the Germans. The Russians had survived the winter, but the second German summer offensive was making headway toward Stalingrad, with the possibility that the vital oil fields in the Caucasus would be captured. At home, U-boats had created havoc along the Atlantic seaboard and in the Arctic. Losses had risen to 589 ships for a total of 3.2 million gross tons. Due to all causes, shipping losses were 5 million tons, and construction was replacing only 3 million tons in the same period. The submarine war alone threatened to undermine the foundations of British life and isolate the United States from its principal ally in Europe.

Hansell went to work with the full support of the air staff. The new strategic plan had to keep in mind a worldwide situation that had changed drastically since Japan's entry into the war, and it had to be consistent with the lessons learned in combat. He had only eleven days to complete the plan, which was entitled "AWPD-42." It was an effort to determine the air requirements not only of the United States Army Air Forces, but of United States production for the Royal Air Force, and of various other Allied air units that were dependent upon the United States. Like AWPD-1, this plan called for the undermining and destruction of Germany's ability to wage war by destroying her war-supporting industries and the systems upon which her war industries and her civilian economy depended.

Uppermost in Hansell's mind was the necessity of applying strategic airpower against the interior of Germany before the Nazis achieved victory on the Russian front. If Russia collapsed, Germany's war industries and her economy would be relieved of its present tensions. Once that happened, forces and resources employed on the Russian front could be shifted to provide air defenses for the Reich to the detriment of the Eighth Air Force and the Royal Air Force. The industry and economy of the Reich would be less sensitive to air bombardment, and the Germans would have time and resources to build up the Luftwaffe. Hansell had seen reports that the Germans had decided to expand their fighter forces, and this posed a threat to the air offensive that somehow had to be countered. And if further consideration was given to the possibility of a land offensive in northwest Africa, the plan would need to make additional allowances for air support.

Hansell was also aware that the impact of the German U-boat campaign threatened all Allied efforts unless something was done about it.

Roosevelt had requested a report that dealt with precise numbers of aircraft, by type, that could be produced. The United States Navy had already approved a large aircraft production program. As a result, heavy claims were made by the navy for scarce materials and tools. The Allies also needed navy planes.

In preparing the estimate of air requirements, Hansell was surprised to find that the navy planned to operate over one thousand heavy, land-based B-24 –type bombers as patrol bombers.

For years, the United States Army Air Forces and the United States Navy had argued about land-based bombers. The navy now insisted that they needed the air force's four-engine B-24 Liberators for patrol bombers. This was an old argument, and the air force had fought for years against a navy land-based strategic air force. General Douglas MacArthur, shortly after he became chief of the army staff, and Admiral William V. Pratt, the navy's chief of naval operations, had reached agreement in January 1931 that heavy bombers should be operated by the army.

In the AWPD-42 plan prepared by Hansell, land-based bombers requested by the navy were included, but they would be assigned to air force units and deployed to meet navy requirements. When Arnold submitted the plan to the Joint Chiefs of Staff, Admiral King found it unacceptable because it dealt with navy requirements and navy personnel had not participated in drafting the document.

This was the document Hopkins took from the Government Printing Office in early September 1942. He spent the rest of the night reading it. He noted with interest that the planned air offensive would precede an invasion of the European continent by six months, or as soon as sufficient bomber strength was available to make 66,045 sorties against nine German target systems. He liked the plan because it called for a precise schedule to expand the aircraft industry. In his meticulous manner, he observed that greatest priority was given to German aircraft and engine assembly plants. He agreed that the destruction of German fighters was of overriding importance.

Hopkins had insisted that the plan should spell out strategic objectives in just such detail. Hansell had been thorough, listing primary targets in order of priority—with submarine yards, transportation targets, electric power systems, oil plants, aluminum plants, and synthetic rubber factories topping the list. Hopkins was especially intrigued by the plan's statement that 48 percent of Germany's rubber came from two synthetic plants.

At the time, it was believed that heavy bombers could penetrate into Germany's heartland because of the superior firepower of Boeing's B-17 Flying Fortress and Consolidated's B-24 Liberator. In fact, both bombers were prewar designs and already outmoded. They had acquitted themselves well in the Pacific, but modern Japanese fighters often found the inadequately armed bombers easy prey. Nevertheless, regardless of their defensive capabilities, they were the only heavy bombers available in the United States at this stage of the war.

Later, when heavy-bomber attacks over Germany produced unacceptable losses, American fighter designs were modified to give them increased range as escorts. Hansell made no reference to escort fighters for the simple reason that none had been designed for production in 1943.

The original concern that England might succumb, or would be unable to provide sufficient American bomber bases, proved unfounded. Hence the need to operate from bases in the Western Hemisphere was removed, and the B-36 was not produced until after the war.

AWPD-42 never had a formal presentation to any of the individual chiefs of staff or to Secretary of War Stimson. At the last possible moment, to meet Roosevelt's schedule, Hansell sent the edited version to the Government Printing Office for reproduction. General Arnold, of course, was aware of the general content, but he had had no opportunity to approve the final wording. In the normal chain of events, the next step would have been to present the document to him, and for him to present it to General Marshall before it was sent to the secretary of war and to the president. Harry Hopkins short-circuited that procedure.

Hopkins carried the report with him when he went to breakfast with Roosevelt that morning. He told the president, "That plan you requested for 1943 production requirements to attain air supremacy looks all right. I went over it quite carefully, and I think you ought to approve it."

Roosevelt had such faith in his adviser that he called his secretary of war. "Henry, in regard to your plan for production to achieve air supremacy, Harry Hopkins has been through it and says it's OK. If you agree, I think we should get on with it."

"Thank you, Mr. President." Stimson didn't say more because he didn't have the slightest idea what Roosevelt was talking about. He was aware that some such plan had been discussed, but he didn't have a copy of it, and he wasn't quite sure what he was asked to go ahead with.

He called Marshall and learned, much to his surprise, that the army chief of staff didn't have a copy yet either.

Marshall, his temper rising, called the operations division of the General Staff. He demanded to know what the hell was going on.

Hansell had two friends on duty with the General Staff, and they were ordered to find out immediately about this new plan that Marshall hadn't seen yet. They hurried to the Government Printing Office and procured two copies of AWPD-42. They also alerted Hansell to what had happened, saying they had only an hour to reply to the army chief of staff, and that it was impossible to read the plan in that time, let alone report on it. "What do you suggest we do?"

Hansell knew he was in serious trouble. Quickly, he outlined the nature of the plan's contents. "Tell Marshall there's no deviation from previously agreed strategy for the air war. Recommend that he endorse it."

Hansell decided it was advisable to get as far away from Washington as possible. Marshall seldom lost his temper, but when he did his wrath was something he didn't want to behold. He decided his best hope of avoiding Marshall was to return immediately to his post in England.

Three thousand miles seemed scarcely enough distance to separate him from the irate chief of staff.

He hurried over to Arnold's office and, fortunately, he was able to see him immediately. "I've finished my job, and I'm anxious to get back to my post in England."

Arnold eyed him skeptically. "Seems to me you're in a hell of a hurry. OK. Go ahead."

Hansell rushed out, his face flushed; his long nose—the cause of his nickname "Possum"—seemed more pronounced as tension strained his features.

He called his old friend Harold George, who was now commanding general of the Air Transport Command. He explained his problem hurriedly. "I've got to get out of here right away. I think I'm in trouble. I'd like to get on the first airplane headed for England."

George understood. Within an hour Hansell was on his way.

He made it just in time. Marshall had aides looking for him. Arnold (who had borne the brunt of his chief's tirade about the president of the United States approving reports before *he,* chief of staff of the United States Army, had had a chance to review them) also had aides looking for Hansell. By then, the Possum was halfway to England. . . .

In its initial summary, the requirements plan had one basic flaw. It failed to take into account the matter of spare parts. This was a serious omission, so a supplemental sheet had to be prepared and attached to the plan at the last minute.

After Arnold and Marshall calmed down, they never brought the subject up with Hansell.

2

"THE ONLY PLAN
IS TO PERSEVERE."

The England to which Hansell returned that night in 1942 had been fighting for two and a half years. Its survival was due, in large part, to the Royal Air Force, which had borne the brunt of the air war against Germany since Hitler's invasion of Poland September 1, 1939, brought England and France into the war.

Tragically, if the British and French had contested Hitler's march into the demilitarized Rhineland March 7, 1936, there might have been no World War II. Allied forces had moved out four years previously, after the Germans pledged to keep the Rhineland demilitarized under terms of the Locarno Pact. France had considered intervention, but decided against it, making a protest to the League of Nations instead. It is now known that Adolf Hitler, in tearing up the Versailles treaty, accomplished it by a token force of men armed only with rifles and machine guns. The much-vaunted Luftwaffe then not only lacked large numbers of combat planes, but most of those available didn't have guns or sufficient ammunition. Hitler admitted later that his forces would have been withdrawn with "our tails between our legs" if the French had intervened.

Hitler's bluff had worked, and with the introduction of compulsory military service and the beginnings of a modern air force, he was ready to improve on the formula that had proved so successful in the Rhineland.

While British civilians anxiously watched barrage balloons rise above Whitehall, British officers and civil servants stood silently in a room at Richmond Terrace on September 3, 1939. It was a few minutes before 11:00 A.M. as they awaited word from Berlin. The British ambassador to the German Reich had been instructed earlier, following the German invasion of Poland on the first of the month, to issue an ultimatum to

Adolf Hitler. It was a somber gathering as word came that Hitler had not yet responded. A few minutes later, the secretary of the cabinet came in. "Gentlemen," he said, "we are at war with Germany. The prime minister directs that the war telegram be dispatched immediately."

At 11:15, Prime Minister Neville Chamberlain spoke to the nation and the world by radio while the war telegram went out to all British commanders announcing the start of hostilities.

When the commander of the Royal Air Force station at Wyton received it, he immediately ordered the crew of a Blenheim bomber to fly over Wilhelmshaven and take photographs of the German fleet.

Although the photographic mission was successful, a flight of Blenheim and Wellington bombers the next day inflicted only minor damage to one German warship. Bomber pilots had been instructed, "The greatest care is to be taken not to injure the civilian population. The intention is to destroy the German fleet. There is no alternative target."

The Royal Air Force in 1939 was composed of Wellington, Whitley, and Hampden bombers, which were completely inadequate to contest the skies with German fighters. They were, however, an improvement over previous types because they were far more powerful. Now, these new and untried bombers had to bear the brunt of operations against a formidable Luftwaffe fighter fleet. At this stage, however, the German bomber fleet far exceeded comparable numbers in the Royal Air Force.

RAF bombers could carry a substantial bomb load as far as 400 miles from their bases in East Anglia, Lincolnshire, and Yorkshire, but this radius-of-action limited them in the foreseeable future to targets in the Ruhr and the Cologne area. Berlin was out of the question because it was 550 miles from these bases.

British Bomber Command had been expressly forbidden to bomb targets on land or even shipping alongside a dock, since this would risk killing or injuring German civilians. Therefore, during the first six months of the war, only ships at sea or those anchored outside of wharves could be attacked from the air.

During the winter months, Bomber Command covered the ocean areas around the British Isles in strength, ready to bomb whenever a German ship was spotted. Pilots found that their worst enemy was the weather, which limited operations on many days.

Sir Kingsley Wood, who served Prime Minister Neville Chamberlain as air minister, proved singularly inept. In following orders, he imposed so many restraints upon the Royal Air Force that there were practically no worthwhile targets that they were permitted to attack.

Bombers were sent out at night over Germany to drop propaganda leaflets, including some drops on Berlin. These missions provided valuable training for crews on night missions, but the leaflets were of doubtful propaganda value.

Sir Arthur Harris, who took command of British bombers long after this period, was particularly caustic about leaflet drops. He told superiors their only achievement was to supply the Continent's toilet paper requirements for five years.

This "phony" war, or "sitzkrieg," ended in April 1940 with the German attacks on Denmark and Norway. A month later, May 10, the Germans simultaneously attacked Holland, Belgium, and France. Yet French officials told the British government they would not approve air attacks on Germany because they feared reprisals. They made it clear that, in their views, the only use to which a bomber force should be put was to extend the range of artillery in support of field armies. French army generals called for bombing of railways, saying disruption of enemy communications was the best way the British Bomber Command could help them.

Before the war, the British government had promised the French that Royal Air Force bombers would be used to resist any invasion of France, and they would be under the direction of the French High Command. This agreement included not only the Advance Air Striking Force of short-range bombers in France, but the longer-range bombers based in England.

The British High Command had agreed reluctantly, pointing out such attacks would have only limited results. It was useless to bomb junctions and marshaling yards, because tracks could be repaired so easily. To be effective, they said, such attacks would entail repeated strikes by a force much larger than they had. French generals were unmoved by such arguments, so British bombers did their best to delay the advance of Germany's mechanized forces. Bridges were added to the list of targets, but the bombing effort was so small in comparison to the need that it did little to slow the German advance. The British frequently refused to attack some targets, knowing they would incur excessive losses without retarding German armored columns.

Spearheaded by fighters and bombers, the Germans used their superior airpower to attack ground troops and concentrated on Allied airfields, hitting eighty-one in all, as well as railway centers and factories. Next, they struck at transport ships, but were unable to prevent the British army and the French northern army from escaping from Dunkirk. On June 17 France asked for an armistice, thus effectively ending the ground war on the Continent.

After Dunkirk, the Royal Air Force hit ports, harbors, and airfields on the Continent. Until May of the following year, British bombers ranged from Stavanger in Norway to Cherbourg in France to hinder German preparations under way for an invasion of England. In general, losses remained low except for an attack August 13, 1940, against the Ålborg airfield in Denmark, which cost the British all but one of the twelve Blenheims participating in the raid.

The British continued daylight raids but changed their tactics early in

1941; due to heavy losses from flak and German fighters, they began sending a small number of bombers, heavily escorted by fighters, against German targets.

The start of a small but sustained assault had begun the night of May 11/12, 1940, when British bombers released bombs on the mainland for the first time. The München-Gladbach rail hub was the target. Flight Officer D. E. Garland and Sergeant T. Gray were the first British airmen to be honored with Victoria Crosses during the war. They were posthumously presented for actions over Belgium May 12.

Next, British heavy bombers were assigned war industries in the Ruhr, where 75 to 80 percent of all German war targets were located. The first important raid was flown May 15/16, when ninety-three heavy bombers hit a number of Ruhr targets. By June 18, 1,666 attacks by groups of six aircraft or more had been made against German targets.

During the summer and fall months, these raids continued on a small scale, but became worrisome to Hitler. The Führer told his staff September 1, 1940, "We have watched these raids patiently, and now the German bombers will answer over British towns night by night."

Sir Arthur Harris, later head of Bomber Command, was assigned as commander of 5 Group the day war was declared in 1939. Under his skillful direction, this group started a successful mine-laying campaign that, by the time war ended six years later, forced the Germans to use 40 percent of their naval personnel for mine-sweeping duties. Some 49,000 mines were laid in the waters and channels around the coast of Europe.

Harris was a disciplined man, heavyset and of medium height, and handsome. He was reserved, but his subordinates quickly learned that his tremendous energy and scathing denunciations of inadequacy made him a difficult boss. When he faced incompetence, he could be ruthless. He had no tolerance for failures if he thought they could have been avoided. Once he made a decision, his instructions were precise, and he insisted they be carried out to the letter. If they weren't, staff officers in particular received the full benefit of a voice that could cut like a whiplash.

Harris deliberately isolated himself from his pilots, but he soon became a legend. His contempt for the British army and the Royal Navy often was expressed in frank phrases. No one could stop him from criticizing those branches, and in fact few tried.

At the time, Harris's 5 Group had the Hampden bomber, inadequately armed with only a single gun on top of its fuselage, another underneath, and a third gun in a fixed forward position. Harris knew that it would take months to work his way through bureaucratic red tape to give the

Hampden effective firepower, so he went to Alfred Rose and Sons, a small family firm, and sought their help in designing and making gun mounts for the bomber to double its effective firepower. He knew that if he purchased just a few of these mounts without authorization he would be personally charged for them. Therefore, he ordered two thousand knowing that he couldn't possibly pay for that many, and that the Air Ministry could do little but chastise him. His scheme worked. He was soundly condemned for violation of the rules, but he got the mounts he wanted in time to make his bombers more effective against the enemy.

After the ground war ended on the Continent, Bomber Command continued its raids on German factories, but on a small scale. Harris used every occasion to present his views to higher-ups. He reminded them that the submarine had been the predominant weapon in World War I. Now, he said, the bomber is the new weapon, even though there were only five groups in Bomber Command—equipped, for the most part, with inferior aircraft. Harris was particularly incensed over the continued use of small bombs, which he considered useless against strategic targets. He was correct, but it took an inordinately long time to convince the Air Ministry.

Harris was most annoyed by orders to bomb marshaling yards that, at this stage of the war, he knew could not become bottlenecks. He stressed that the German inland waterways should be attacked instead, reminding officialdom that the Dortmund-Ems Canal was a true bottleneck because it was the only water link between the Ruhr and eastern Germany, or between the North Sea and the Baltic. He personally approved several attacks by his 5 Group, which succeeded in damaging both aqueducts in low-level attacks. With the bombers available at this time, heavy losses were inevitable.

While the threat of invasion faced Britain, Bomber Command did an excellent job of destroying invasion barges in channel ports, although it received little credit for it. That credit went to Fighter Command, which was fighting valiantly to protect the homeland. But Bomber Command raids also were effective in countering the invasion threat. It was Harris, again, who reminded officials that the thousands of power-driven barges in use on Germany's inland waterways could also be used to transport troops to England.

After a large part of the continental forces had been withdrawn from Dunkirk, Winston Churchill, who had replaced Chamberlain as prime minister following the German attack on France and the Low Countries, called for a bomber offensive as the only way to bring the war home to the German people. His advisers told him that the army would need fifteen armored divisions and seventy infantry divisions to invade the Continent successfully, while providing other divisions for home defense. Churchill had no illusions. England had neither the manpower nor the shipping to mount an invasion.

After the Germans bombed central London August 24, Churchill authorized the chief of the Air Staff, Sir Cyril Newall, to make a retaliatory raid on Berlin. This was executed the following night, and again on the twenty-sixth, much to Reichsmarschall Hermann Göring's discomfiture. He had assured Adolf Hitler that such a raid would never happen.

Although the raid did little damage, the Führer was aroused by its audacity and vowed to wipe out Britain's cities in retaliation.

Churchill had been urging his War Cabinet to increase bomber production. He met with them September 3, 1940, at a time when the Battle of Britain was at its height. Although the outcome was still in doubt, Churchill thought first of the future and stressed the need to expand Britain's retaliatory bomber forces so that they could make a supreme effort against Nazi Germany.

Soon after, Churchill recommended that Sir Cyril Newall be replaced as chief of the Royal Air Force's Air Staff by Sir Charles Portal. Newall was one of several military men who, many politicians believed, had not measured up to the war's needs, even though the fault lay with their parsimonious defense budgets prior to the war. Portal assumed command October 4, and immediately named Sir Richard Peirse, an exponent of precision bombing, as head of Bomber Command.

They both agreed that Bomber Command should be built up to 4,000 heavy bombers. Portal told intimates that he was expected to start a bomber offensive with only 250 medium bombers and 50 heavies. He said their efforts during the past had only served to cause insignificant damage to targets in the Ruhr.

Portal also advised the Air Staff that the concept of daylight bombing should be abolished, and they agreed. The casualty rate was ten times what the Royal Air Force could tolerate and remain a viable force. Yet he had no illusions that night operations would be any more successful, because only half the crews could identify a target at night. If the target could not be readily spotted by inexperienced crews, then night operations would also fail.

Despite his reservations, Portal was ordered to bomb railroad marshaling yards, oil plants, aircraft factories, and shipping. Nothing he could say about the inability of Bomber Command to destroy such targets carried any weight. He did ask an oil expert to assess Bomber Command's previous efforts, and his worst fears were realized. Little permanent damage had been done.

Churchill expressed the feelings of most government officials when he said, "The navy can lose us the war, but only the air force can win it. The fighters are our salvation, but the bombers alone provide the means of victory."

Portal now proposed that the Air Staff approve a plan to bomb twenty German cities indiscriminately as reprisal raids for Germany's attacks upon British cities. He issued his first directive to Peirse. Heretofore, individual oil installations had been assigned as principal targets. Although oil targets would continue to be the command's primary objectives during the eight to ten nights of each month when there was moonlight, bombing urban areas to reduce enemy morale was given equal priority.

Air Marshal Harris was transferred from 5 Group in December and assigned a mission to Washington to procure American aircraft. In parting, he reported that 65 percent of crews failed to find their targets at night, let alone hit them. In a report to Portal, photographs were enclosed following two separate attacks against the oil plants at Gelsenkirchen in the Ruhr. Two hundred ninety-six aircraft had dropped bombs on the plants, with crews reporting hits on their aiming points. Poststrike photographs, however, showed no signs of major damage at either plant. A few bomb craters were visible where there should have been at least one thousand. Portal was not surprised because he had tried to tell the Air Staff that their plan to end the war within a year by destroying strategic oil targets was wishful thinking.

Air Staff refused to concede defeat, ordering Portal in a directive January 7, 1941, to destroy the German synthetic oil plants in the next six months.

Portal appeared before Prime Minister Churchill and the War Cabinet Janaury 13, and pledged that the Royal Air Force would paralyze oil production with a series of moonlight raids. On dark nights, he said, he would continue to order attacks on cities in his secondary role of reducing enemy morale. Two days later, he ordered destruction of seventeen oil plants in the German Reich.

Portal was a fighting man in spite of his quiet and modest manner. Although he was an intellectual with a judicious mind, he had the expertise and knowledge of how best to utilize airpower. He could be quietly persuasive in his dealings with others, with an assured sense of the right words necessary to make the impression he wished to convey.

He had stopped bombing so-called bottlenecks in the German war industry because his small command was being spread too thin. Instead, he started to make attacks on a full-effort basis against industrial cities like Mannheim with one hundred bombers. In subsequent attacks against Bremen, and the naval bases at Wilhelmshaven and Kiel, Bomber Command began to cause real damage.

Although the Germans had initiated blitzkrieg tactics on the Continent, first against Poland, then against Belgium, Holland, and France, they never appreciated what a large force of stragetic bombers could accomplish, and never developed a plan to use such a force. At the start of the war, Great Britain had only about 600 first-line fighters, while the Luftwaffe had twice that many. In bomber strength, the Germans had over 2,000 bombers compared to England's 536. The German air force bomber fleet was mostly in the category of light-to-medium bombers, however.

Despite this disparity in numbers, British designers outpaced Germany during the last two years of peace, overcoming the lead held by German designers. The British Air Staff had belatedly realized their shortcomings in 1935 and had laid down specifications for medium and four-engine bombers. Not until 1941, however, did these designs show up in aircraft like the Stirling, the Halifax, and the Manchester. The latter was a disappointment, but after modifications it became the highly versatile Lancaster. Although Great Britain had failed to provide an adequate force of these bombers early in the war, and to equip them with accurate bombing aids, the balance began to shift.

When the British attacked Essen March 8/9, 1941, a new system was used to improve the accuracy of bombing at night, along with the use of marking flares. "Gee," developed by British scientists, transmitted radio beams from three widely spaced stations in England to help a navigator determine his bomber's position in the sky in relation to a target. Theoretically, this system could determine a bomb-release point that would permit bombs to be dropped on a target with an accuracy of one tenth of a mile.

Unfortunately, the flares burned out by the time the main force arrived over this largest and most important industrial city in the Ruhr. As a result, bombs dropped everywhere but on the city, with virtually no damage. In fact, no serious damage was caused by eleven subsequent raids during the next three months. It was apparent that enemy use of decoy fires diverted most of the bombers. Early hopes for successful use of Gee had to be discarded. It did prove helpful in reducing operational accidents on return to base, but as a reliable aid in blind bombing it was almost worthless.

While bombing and navigational aids developed slowly, British bomber crews continued to fly missions with inadequate equipment.

Squadron Leader R. F. Widdowson, pilot of a New Zealand 75 Squadron's Wellington, swung away from Münster after its bombs were dropped on a traffic junction in the Ruhr the night of July 7. Although searchlights had been bothersome over the target, flak had been light.

Suddenly, he felt the shock of cannon shells slashing into the airframe. The rear gunner, Sergeant A. J. R. Box, opened fire, reporting a Messerschmitt 110 on their tail.

Widdowson's copilot, Sergeant James Ward, had been watching for German night fighters in the astrodome, a small plastic bubble in the cabin roof used to take navigational sightings by sextant. He hurried to the cockpit after finding the communications system out, just as Widdowson put the airplane into a steep dive. Ward was thrown off-balance and almost tumbled into the pilot's compartment as he reported that the right engine had been hit and that there was a fire burning the fabric surface of the wing.

Widdowson pulled out of their dive, noting reports that the bomb bay doors had fallen open and that the landing gear was halfway extended. He knew this meant he was losing hydraulic pressure.

The fire on the wing continued to burn, too far out to be reached by extinguishers. The men held a brief conference. Ditching near the English coast seemed preferable to a long stay in a German prisoner-of-war camp, so Widdowson headed for home, grateful that the ME-110 had made only one pass.

Ward was watching the fire on the wing with growing desperation. He proposed that he crawl out through the astrodome with his parachute on, secured to the cabin by a line, and attempt to extinguish the fire. Widdowson and the others called such a stunt crazy, saying he would be knocked off the wing by the slipstream. But Ward persisted, finally getting his pilot's reluctant permission.

Widdowson slowed the airplane to the lowest possible speed at which it would remain airborne, while Ward crawled through the astrodome. The young copilot was shaking as he jammed his right foot through the wing's fabric to get a firmer foothold. Then, step by step, poking holes through the fabric for foot- and handholds, Ward worked his way outboard to the fire. He had brought a canvas cockpit cover with him to stuff into the burned hole, hoping it would smother the fire. Suddenly it ballooned out, almost sweeping him off the wing. Slowly, each tortuous step seeming like an eternity, he clawed his way to the burning hole in the wing. Hastily, he stuffed the cover into it, and the fire went out.

Now he had to return, with the wind howling in his ears and threatening to push him off into the darkness below them. Anxious eyes watched from the cabin as he laboriously used the steps he had broken in the fabric to walk back, teetering at times from the force of the air pressure.

Once safely back in the cabin, Ward watched with consternation as the fire flared up again. For a moment, he thought his dangerous wing-walking had all been for nothing. Finally the fire died down and went out.

A grateful crew pumped the wheels down by hand and Widdowson landed the Wellington safely at base. For his unusual heroism, Ward was presented with England's coveted Victoria Cross.

Raids over the Continent became more hazardous after the Germans built an early-warning system along the coasts of France and the Low

Countries, as well as along the coast of Denmark. Additionally, the Germans devised clever new tactics and techniques and used more modern equipment for night-fighter operations.

Despite generally disappointing operations, Portal retained his faith in the bombing offensive. He had many detractors, including officials of the British army, who kept insisting that he provide an air contingent for the army that was larger than his total front-line air strength.

Prime Minister Churchill injected a new problem for Portal when he said that now that the Battle of the Atlantic had begun, he must take the offensive against the U-boat and the Focke-Wulf aircraft wherever they could be located. "The U-boat at sea must be hunted, and the U-boat in the building yard or in the dock must be bombed. The Focke-Wulf and other bombers against our shipping must be attacked in their nests."

Portal recognized the inconsistency in Churchill's comments because he was asking for a diversion from oil attacks, which he had previously stressed. Actually, these attacks had been minimal, and the Royal Air Force had made only two raids against seventeen key targets.

In August 1941, the Air Ministry called for an analysis of night bomber raids made during June and July. The result shocked officials because only one bomber in every five was able to drop its bombs within five miles of a target. Attacks against Ruhr industrial targets were even worse.

In September, Churchill wrote to Sir John Anderson, lord president of the council, and one of the nine members of the War Cabinet. "In order to achieve a first-line strength of 4,000 medium and heavy bombers, the Royal Air Force requires that 22,000 bombers be made between July 1941 and July 1943." He said 5,500 of these could be expected to reach them from American factories.

Portal now wrote a memorandum to Churchill to press his case for undisguised area bombing. He presented a plan that, he said, would devastate "beyond all hope of recovery" forty-three named German towns with a total population of 15 million people.

Churchill said later, "I was forced to cool down the claims which some of our most trusted officers put forward in their natural ardour."

To Portal, he wrote, "It is very disputable whether bombing by itself will be a decisive factor in the present war. On the contrary, all we have learnt since the war began is that its effects both physical and moral are greatly exaggerated." He said his views were based upon the fact that "only a quarter of our bombs hit the target, consequently an increase in accuracy to a hundred percent would, in effect, raise our bombing force four times its strength. Most that I can say is that it will be a heavy and, I trust, a seriously increasing annoyance."

Portal was not easily swayed by the opinions of others, even those of the prime minister. He challenged Churchill to produce a new strategy if he was rejecting the principle of the attainment of massive air superiority.

Churchill replied that he envisaged air superiority as a precursor to "simultaneous attacks by armed forces in many of the conquered countries who are ripe for revolt. We all hope that the air offensive against Germany will realize the expectations of the Air Staff. Everything is being done to create the bombing forces desired on the largest possible scale, and there is no intention of changing this policy. It is the most potent method of impairing the enemy's morale we can use at the present time.

"Even if all the towns of Germany were rendered largely uninhabitable, it does not follow that the military control would be weakened, or that war industries could not be carried on. The Air Staff would make a mistake to make their claim too high. It may well be that German morale will crack, and that our bombing will play a very important part in bringing that result about. But all things are always on the move simultaneously. One has to do the best one can. He is an unwise man who thinks there is any certain method of winning this war or any other war between equals in strength. The only plan is to persevere."

When 10 percent of the four hundred bombers sent out over Germany on the night of November 7 were lost, Churchill ordered that for the next three or four months only small forces should be sent out, and none of them to distant targets. This order virtually banned the bombing of Germany. Such action had to be taken because Bomber Command's acquisition of new planes and crews remained almost static, and it would soon have been liquidated.

In the War Cabinet, Portal's effectiveness as head of the Royal Air Force was openly questioned. To many, it appeared he had achieved little or nothing. Peirse bore the brunt of criticism, but some of it was unfair because many of his bombers and their crews had been diverted to the Middle East.

Portal's persuasiveness won the day and Churchill obtained reluctant approval from his cabinet for a bomber command of four thousand planes equipped with the latest scientific improvements in navigational and bombing aids. While many in the cabinet objected to such a diversion of industrial capacity to build up a large bomber fleet, Churchill brusquely overrode their objections and insisted that the national effort be diverted to the building of such a fleet. It was a decision of profound significance for the future.

3

"LET 'EM HAVE IT—
RIGHT ON THE CHIN!"

In Germany, Göring was so out of favor with Hitler that he tried to shift blame to others in the Luftwaffe. He directed his anger primarily at Ernst Udet whom he blamed for failure of the Battle of Britain, for the decline in aircraft production—particularly during the summer offensive in Russia—and for not developing long-range heavy bombers.

The easygoing, hard-drinking Udet was in fact completely out of his element as technical director of Germany's military aviation because his background was flying and not the design and manufacture of military aircraft. Göring tried to develop what he thought would be a foolproof case against the war hero before trying to fire him. Even after Udet's job was given to Feldmarschall Erhard Milch, one of Hitler's most ruthless followers, Göring still dared not announce it because Udet was such a popular hero.

Udet shot himself November 17, 1941, leaving a note on his bed. "Reichsmarschall, why have you deserted me?" Göring didn't reveal the true cause of Udet's death, saying only that he had been killed testing a new weapon. At first, Göring considered a posthumous court-martial, but he was afraid to do so. Instead, he authorized a state funeral and personally led the mourners. Despite all this maneuvering, Hitler's faith in the Luftwaffe, and Göring in particular, was completely gone.

Udet's successor, Milch, overhauled the aircraft industry by improving the use of manpower and materials by eliminating duplication. He did a far better job than Udet had.

General Werner Mölders, head of the German Fighter Command, was killed flying to Udet's funeral. The strongly religious Mölders was a non-Nazi who became an ace during the Spanish civil war, and later was appointed commanding general of the Luftwaffe's Fighter Command at the age of twenty-eight. He was replaced by General Adolf Galland.

Air Chief Marshal Sir Arthur T. Harris replaced Peirse as chief of the Royal Air Force's Bomber Command in February 1942. He had been in Washington since May of 1941 as head of a British delegation to procure American aircraft.

After Harris took over, he told newsmen, "There are a lot of people who say that bombing can't win the war. My reply is that it has never been tried yet. We shall see."

The switch from precision to area bombing had taken place before his assumption of command. The idea of bombing key factories had been established before the war, but Harris knew that German air defenses made daylight raids on such targets impractical. Although he considered the situation almost hopeless until radar aids to bombing could be developed for night bombing, he established several new doctrines. First, he asked for larger bombs, because small bombs had proved ineffective. Big two-ton and four-ton bombs had been used in a few instances, but he wanted more of them, and even larger bombs. He noted that, to date, four-pound incendiary bombs dropped in clusters had proved best for destroying large industrial areas, so he planned to use more of these, despite the difficulty of aiming the clusters accurately.

After reviewing operations, Harris asked for marker bombs or target indicators to improve spotting of a target for follow-on crews. They didn't become available for another year. He also introduced trained "bomb aimers" to the crews. Previously, navigators had dropped the bombs. By the end of 1942, Harris's command had grown to an average of 261 bombers, but only 42 were heavies. The Manchester, which had proved to be such a failure in operations as a two-engine bomber, made a formidable appearance in operations rebuilt as the four-engine Lancaster. With modifications, it was later able to carry the 22,000-pound "Grand Slam" bomb, which no other aircraft in the world could carry. At the same time, British Bomber Command continued to lose trained men to other commands and to groups in North Africa. Harris complained bitterly that his units were training aircrews for other commands all over the world.

Harris had inherited an outstanding officer, and an old friend, when he took command. As his deputy, Air Vice-Marshal Robert H. M. S. Saundby was a firm supporter of strategic air warfare, and both were convinced that if bombing could be done consistently, and in force, it would have a great impact upon the war's outcome. But such forces were not readily available because Harris's crews and planes were being drained off to support the British army in North Africa, and to fight the submarine menace in the Atlantic. To add to Harris's difficulties, Sir Richard Stafford Cripps, Lord Privy Seal, spoke out in the House of Commons against further expansion of Bomber Command. He said there was a strong question in his mind whether better use could be made of the country's resources.

The British strategic air campaign began in March 1942 when 235 bombers attacked the Renault works near Paris, which was producing war material for the Germans. This first large-scale effort was successful, and the plant was knocked out of production for four months.

The Baltic supply port of Lübeck was hit by the Royal Air Force the night of March 28/29, and it proved to be easy to identify on the river Trave. It was not a vital target, but Harris selected it to prove that a first wave of bombers could light up a target for the second wave. Half the town was destroyed by over two hundred bombers, and the tactic proved successful, although thirteen bombers were lost for a rate of 5½ percent.

Another Baltic port was attacked April 23 when Harris sent his bombers to Rostock, home of a Heinkel aircraft factory. They went out in waves on four successive nights, and 521 bombers severely crippled the city by destroying three quarters of it and damaging the Heinkel plant.

When the Germans invaded Russia, the German army had been supported by over 50 percent of the entire German air force. These RAF attacks, and those yet to come, began to have their effect on the eastern front. To defend her cities, the Nazis were forced to transfer more and more fighters from the eastern to the western front.

For some time, Harris had been wanting to concentrate his command against a major city, and target analysts recommended Hamburg or Cologne. Harris liked the idea of a mass raid involving one thousand or more bombers, but they weren't available in combat units and he would have to draw upon other commands, including the training command. Each such attack would dangerously commit Bomber Command's entire reserves.

He discussed the raid with Sir Charles Portal, who gave reluctant approval.

Prime Minister Churchill backed Harris, but suggested consideration of Essen as an important target. Harris drove to Chequers, Churchill's official country residence, in his old Bentley to discuss the raid.

Knowing the limitations of Gee, Harris told Churchill that they had to have an easily identified city. He suggested Hamburg, which lay on an estuary of the Elbe River, or Cologne, which was located on the Rhine River. Although Hamburg was entirely out of Gee range, the city could be identified more readily because of its location on the Elbe.

Churchill questioned Harris about losses. When he was told that it was anticipated that fifty bombers would be lost, or 5 percent of the total force, the prime minister replied, "I am prepared for the loss of a hundred."

On May 19, the prime minister gave final approval to Portal, who told Harris that he probably could count on the Coastal Command unless they were otherwise engaged. Two days later, Sir Philip Joubert de la Ferté, chief of the Coastal Command, wrote Harris, "I can get you 250." That was the number of aircraft Harris had requested.

Harris selected Cologne as the target city. The raid had to be scheduled during the next period of full moon to aid visual identification of the city. There wasn't much time—the next full moon would be May 26–30.

Harris was told he could count on 1,081 planes if two groups of the Flying Training Command were brought in. There were risks involved in using untrained crews, particularly when bombers had to be concentrated at low levels over the target. Harris's greatest concern involved collisions in the target area.

He called upon Dr. B. G. Dickins, head of Bomber Command's Operational Research Section, to work out the details of the flight plan. After analysis, Dickins told Harris that the risk of collision was very high if only one aiming point was selected. Harris agreed, and three aiming points were chosen. Although still worried about air collisions, Harris decided that formations would be sent at different altitudes to overwhelm antiaircraft defenses on the ground as well as night fighters in the air.

The night of May 27/28 had already been selected when Coastal Command withdrew its support at the last minute, due to Admiralty orders. The British navy gave as its excuse that it didn't want to jeopardize so many bombers on one mission. There had long been rivalry between the Admiralty and the Royal Air Force, and the British navy had tried several times to reduce the scope of Bomber Command operations.

While bombers waited at fifty-three bases, bad weather settled in over the Continent. Harris worried about a security leak as the weather failed to clear; thousands of airmen fidgeted nervously for two days, waiting for the word to man their planes. The delay did provide Harris with a chance to assign more bombers to the mission.

Weathermen predicted that the weather in the early morning hours of May 30 would clear over Germany, so 1,046 crews were placed on full alert. Harris knew they had to go this last night of the moon's full phase or forget the mission for the time being. He was faced with a lonely decision. At the last minute, his weatherman, Magnus Spence, told him Cologne might clear at midnight, but the British bases might be fogged in. Now Harris had a new problem: one of arranging alternate landing sites for more than one thousand aircraft.

Like many a commander before him, he weighed the pros and cons and reached a decision. He messaged all bases, "Thousand plan tonight. Target Cologne."

Everyone was relieved once the die was cast. Planes were loaded with 500,000 incendiaries and 1,300 general-purpose bombs weighing up to 4,000 pounds each. Almost half the bombers were Wellingtons, rugged two-engine Vickers aircraft that had proved reliable, easy to fly, and often returned to base with unbelievable battle damage. Crews called her the "Wimpy" after J. Wellington Wimpy in the "Popeye" cartoon. There were a few twin-engined Avro Manchesters and redesigned four-engined Lancasters. The Short Stirling, a four-engine heavy bomber that proved to be a poor design, and that should have been retired, also participated, along with a somewhat similar Handley Page Halifax. Two obsolete two-engine bombers, the Armstrong Whitworth Whitley and the Handley-Page Hampden, completed the fleet. They were manned by 6,000 airmen from Great Britain, Australia, New Zealand, Canada, and even a few from the United States.

At briefings, each commander told the anxious, uplifted faces in flying gear, "You may have guessed there's something special on tonight. Well, this is what it is. We're bombing Germany with over a thousand aircraft."

Briefing rooms were full of cheering airmen, and their voices roared against the rafters as they pounded one another on their backs.

Each commander read a message from Harris. "The force of which you form a part tonight is at least twice the size and has more than four times the carrying capacity of the largest air force ever before concentrated on one objective. You have an opportunity, therefore, to strike a blow at the enemy which will resound not only throughout Germany, but throughout the world. In your hands lie the means of destroying a major part of the resources by which the enemy's war effort is maintained. It depends, however, on each individual crew whether full concentration is achieved. Press home your attack to your precise objective with the utmost determination and resolution in the foreknowledge that, if you individually succeed, the most shattering and devastating blow will have been delivered against the very vitals of the enemy. Let 'em have it—right on the chin!"

Gee-equipped Wellingtons and Stirlings from several squadrons of 3 Group took off as intruder forces while eighty-eight fighter-bombers and fighters headed for German airfields to help draw German fighters away from the bombers. Unfortunately, German fields were cloud covered and impossible to locate, so little damage was done and three fighters were lost. The heavy cloud cover forced many fighters to return, and some encountered icing conditions that made further penetrations foolhardy.

The first bombers lumbered off their fields at 10:00 P.M., and Harris noted with satisfaction that all were on their way within half an hour, although one hundred were forced later to return, and some crashed.

The weather cleared just as the Wellington vanguards were within sixty miles west and slightly north of Cologne. The moon shone brightly, and crews could clearly see the Rhine reflecting its light as it curled toward Cologne. To the north and south, the Rhine intersected flight paths because the bomber stream was coming from almost due west at right angles to the city. Crews could spot the Hindenburg Bridge, and a mile west they could see the center of the old city on the Rhine's left bank. This was the first aiming point.

German air-raid sirens went off at 12:17, and the city lay before them in total darkness.

Wing Commander J. C. Macdonald and Squadron Leader R. S. Gilmor approached the city from the north at fifteen thousand feet in two Stirlings of 15 Squadron. Macdonald noticed the Rhine shining in the moonlight off to his right, and even the outline of Cologne could be seen. Cologne Cathedral, begun in the thirteenth century and completed six hundred years later, was not a target, but it was less than half a mile northeast of the old city. Flak burst in the sky, but it was light and ineffective as the first incendiaries hit the old city at 12:47. It was hoped these pathfinder bombs would start fires and provide aiming points for those to follow.

The Germans lit false fires far from critical areas, hoping to fool follow-on bombers, but this time they were not successful.

Even at eighteen thousand feet, bombers were hit as searchlights probed the sky. The lights were so brilliant that pilots had to fly by instruments. Planned runs were disregarded as bombers circled Cologne. The flames on the ground were bright enough to reflect redly on the planes, while an awesome destruction engulfed the city. Here and there, midair collisions momentarily lit the sky as aircraft exploded and crews died without warning. Pilots took evasive action, not so much to avoid German fighters, but to stay clear of their comrades. German defenses were completely overwhelmed as every minute eleven British bombers unloaded their deadly cargoes.

Flight Officer Leslie T. Manser of 50 Squadron turned away after dropping his bombs. He knew his plane was badly damaged, but he fought to keep his Manchester flying. Soon it became apparent that the plane could not be kept in the air, and he ordered the crew to bail out, but declined a parachute when his flight engineer handed him one. He knew that if his men were to evacuate the bomber safely, he had to remain at the controls until the last man was out because the Manchester kept trying to stall. His posthumous award of the Victoria Cross spoke of his gallant sacrifice in saving his men's lives.

As other returning crews headed home, the city's flames could be seen for two hundred miles.

By 2:25 A.M., the destruction was so awesome that late-arriving crews were appalled. They stared with ashen faces, briefly illuminated by the flames below, at the hell beneath them while the largest bombs of all were dropped on the stricken city. Orders had been issued that bombers unable to release by that time should return to England without dropping. Flight Lieutenant George Gilpin was one of many who violated the rule. As a result, he had to fly his Lancaster partway back in daylight over enemy territory. Fortunately, German day fighters did not molest them.

The Germans were appalled by the destruction, though Göring derided British claims that one thousand bombers had been sent on the mission. The Nazis said only seventy bombers had been over the city, and that half were shot down. In retrospect, such a false claim would seem to be a foolish admission that so few bombers could cause so much visible destruction.

Once daylight photographs were available to British analysts, it was evident that about 600 acres of the city had been leveled. The raid killed 469 people, wounded 5,027, and destroyed 45,000 homes. Analysts saw that incendiaries had caused the most damage.

Harris had predicted the loss of fifty bombers. He was not far off in his estimate because forty-one bombers and three intruders were lost on the mission. The partially trained crews in the medium bombers from training command suffered the worst, with a loss rate of 4.5 percent, while the more experienced crews had a rate of only 1.9 percent. The mission was remarkably effective for the loss rate and helped to persuade Harris that Germany could be defeated by airpower if he could obtain the necessary bombers and crews to make each effort as destructive as the attack on Cologne. It also convinced Harris that such raids could be made with acceptable losses and would shorten the war. He said later there would never have been a bomber offensive if it hadn't been for the attack on Cologne. He was also aware that further one-thousand-plane raids could not be continued on a sustained basis; at least not until the American Eighth Air Force was up to full strength and his own Bomber Command could be increased many times over its present strength.

Only one more such raid was made during 1942, and that one was to Bremen on the night of June 25/26. .

Hitler screamed at Göring, demanding more protection for Germany's cities. He accused German daytime pilots of cowardice, threatening court-martials and even executions for the pilots. Göring's Luftwaffe was also blamed by Hitler for the disasters on the Russian front.

The Germans knew that if such raids continued, no city in Germany would escape damage on a catastrophic scale.

One side effect hoped for by the Allies was the continued transfer of more German fighter units from the Russian front to the west.

Göring, who had told the German people in 1939, "My name is not Göring if any enemy aircraft is ever seen over Germany; you can call me Meyer!" adopted a low profile. His credibility among the German people reached its lowest point to date in the war.

The Cologne raid dramatically increased the amount of destruction in Germany. After the Rostock raid, the total acreage destroyed had come to 780; roughly equivalent to the amount of acreage destroyed in British cities during the German air blitz. Now, on one mission, the total was almost doubled.

The Germans were so concerned by the Cologne raid that they increased their twin-engine night fighters to 530. Hitler approved top priority for such fighters, and single-engine fighters were also increased in production in anticipation of greater daylight attacks by the American Eighth Air Force.

When production was raised to 360 fighters a month, Generaloberst Hans Jeschonnek, chief of the Air Staff, protested that he wouldn't know what to do with so many new fighters. There just weren't trained pilots for them. General Milch, in charge of aircraft procurement, ignored him and sought permission for eventual production of one thousand fighters a month. The balance was slowly tipping in favor of the Germans, and Bomber Command's casualties rose sharply as fighter attacks increased.

Harris assigned Ruhr cities as first priority for his bombers. He sent out another large raid June 1/2, but bad weather prevented worthwhile damage. A short time later, a Focke-Wulf factory at Bremen was largely destroyed. The heavy raid on Düsseldorf September 10/11 was especially noteworthy because it caused about the same amount of destruction as the one on Cologne. This city had an unusually large number of corporate headquarters. Albert Speer, who later ran Hitler's armaments program, told German officials at the time that he had hoped the loss of records would lead to a temporary loosening of the ties of bureaucracy. He told interrogators after the war, "We often received a message that the administrative building had been burned out on a raid, but that production continued at full pressure."

4

"I'M TOLD YOU'RE A
MEAN SON OF A BITCH."

Brigadier General Ira C. Eaker, commander of fighter defenses on the West Coast of the United States, had received a telegram from General Arnold, chief of the Army Air Corps, shortly after war broke out. He was to report to Washington, for duty overseas.

Eaker walked into Arnold's office December 15, 1941. "What's up, boss?"

"You're going over to England to understudy the British Bomber Command and to lead our bomber forces once I get you some crews."

Eaker was surprised. "Bombers hell. I've been in fighters all my life. That shows a lack of wisdom." The square-jawed, tough-looking Eaker could be blunt despite his soft speaking voice.

He expected to hear Arnold say, "I've evidently sent for the wrong man." Instead, the Air Corps chief replied, "I know that. We want the fighter spirit in bombardment aviation."

He learned later that bomber crews needed far more courage than fighter pilots because they had to hold a steady course, despite opposition, while being exposed to continuous enemy fighter attacks and anti-aircraft fire from the ground. He learned such missions took real guts.

Eaker had grown up in Texas where his mother and father were farming people—devoutly religious, and hardworking, self-reliant people of the soil. Although today they might be considered poor, Eaker often said they never considered themselves poor because they lived simply, were almost always comfortable, and had plenty to eat. His mother and father instilled many virtues, not the least of which was a desire to make something of himself.

On his trip to England in February 1942, he and the six members of his small staff had to dress in civilian clothes and carry no official documents. Such precautions were necessary because they had to land in Portugal, which was teeming with Nazi spies.

In Lisbon, when they went out to dinner, they played a game on the Germans. Each person arranged his luggage in a certain way so that they could detect if it had been searched. Upon their return, it was quickly apparent that everything had been gone through.

A KLM Royal Dutch Airlines DC-3 flew them out of Lisbon and headed for London. To Eaker's surprise, the Dutch pilot made an unscheduled landing at Oporto, on the Portuguese coast. He explained to Eaker that the landing was precautionary, to throw off the Germans. After they took off again, they flew well out to sea to avoid interception. Civilian planes had been shot down on this route, and the Dutch pilot was taking no chances.

En route to England, the pilot called Eaker to the cockpit. Silently, he pointed to a Ju-88 streaking toward the coast of France with a smoking engine. It was obvious the German plane was in serious difficulty and bound for a forced landing in Normandy.

The blackout in London was an old experience for Eaker, who had been in England during the Battle of Britain as an observer for the United States. Eaker met Theater Commander Major General James E. Chaney and other air officers on his first day in London, and the next day called on Air Chief Marshal Harris, whom he had met while the British officer was in Washington seeking to buy American combat planes.

Arnold had given Eaker brief instructions. "Make the necessary preparations to insure competent and aggressive command and direction of our bomber units in England."

During this period, British activities were at a low ebb. Feldmarschall Erwin Rommel had denied the British army a hoped-for victory in Libya, and the German battle cruisers *Scharnhorst, Gneisenau,* and *Prinz Eugen* had escaped from Brest through the English Channel. In the Far East, Singapore had fallen to the Japanese. Eaker had to exercise patience; the Pacific had first call on emergency supplies as the Japanese spread their perimeter ever wider.

At that time, only four of Chaney's thirty-five-member staff were air officers, and most of the others were antagonistic to men of the Army Air Forces. They not only wanted to handle all air operations out of England, but were adamantly opposed to a separate Army Air Forces in the United Kingdom.

Eaker's first task was to procure air bases, which the British agreed to supply. Those selected were in East Anglia, north of London. Construction and development costs were paid by the British, who cooperated wholeheartedly. To simplify communications and operations, Eaker agreed to copy British systems.

Colonel Harris Hull, Eaker's intelligence officer, told Eaker to try and get Wycombe Abbey, a beautiful building housing one of the best girl's schools in England and surrounded by landscaped gardens and a pond on which stately swans paraded. It was located at High Wycombe near Harris's Bomber Command headquarters, and thirty miles from London. At first, Eaker was told there wasn't a chance of acquiring it. Later, the British agreed to turn the school over to the Americans and the headquarters was code-named Pinetree. Americans were surprised to find a placard in each room of the former girl's school that read, "Should you desire the services of a mistress during the evening, push the bell." There was much ringing of bells until Eaker no longer found it amusing.

He established himself in the former headmistress's office, which had a large window looking out on a beautiful garden. His aide, Captain C. C. Mason, kept the wall situation maps up-to-date. Eaker busied himself with studying the operational methods of Harris's Bomber Command and attended their briefings. Meanwhile, he drew up plans for airfields to accommodate the bomber groups he hoped would soon be coming from the States. He knew that the pressure was on him to get American crews into action as soon as possible, to back up Arnold's heavy demands on the Joint Chiefs of Staff for planes and equipment to start the air war in Europe.

Eaker formally established headquarters for the VIII Bomber Command in March 1942, but it was a command in name only because he still had no planes or crews.

After President Roosevelt ordered implementation of Hansell's 1942 plan for a bomber offensive against Germany, Eaker used it even though the United States Joint Chiefs never had approved it over the opposition of the United States Navy. In the absence of any other guidance, field commanders of strategic air forces followed the plan, but they were on uncertain ground.

Eaker believed the B-17 Flying Fortress was the best combat airplane ever built. He knew it was more sturdily constructed than the B-24 Liberator and that it could sustain more battle damage. Although the B-17 was relatively slow, bombing at only 155 miles per hour, it was tough, doing everything it was asked to do.

During his first conversation with Harris in England, the British bomber commander said, "I don't think you can do daylight bombing against German defenses. You may recall that General Arnold gave us some B-17s and we sent them out on raids and got the hell shot out of them."

"We know that," Eaker replied. "We don't plan to send individual planes out. Eventually, we plan to send a thousand out. There are ten guns on each one of them—ten automatic weapons—to cover every sphere. And we plan to send fighters with them, to take them as far as their range permits, then meet the bombers on their way home to help the cripples."

Eaker knew the main British concern was likewise to get American bombers into action as soon as possible because they were hard pressed. He realized Harris was quite right in saying that if the Americans joined the British at night, they could get their bombers into action sooner.

During this first of many sessions, Eaker thought carefully before he responded to Harris's arguments. "We must give it a try. We've been talking daylight, precision bombing to knock down individual fighter factories and other war-production centers for many years. Our crews are trained for the daylight effort, and we have bombsights that give us precision. I believe it is going to help your night effort. If you go in at night, and we go in the daytime, the German defenses will have to be on alert twenty-four hours a day. That means they're going to have to have three shifts. You tell me there are a million Germans standing on the Westwall as fire fighters, as antiaircraft crews, at fighter fields. Think how many divisions we would keep away from the eastern front."

Harris was not convinced. "I hope the hell you can do it, but I'm doubtful that you can."

Harris had earlier talked to General Arnold in Washington about the best way to use the Eighth Air Force, suggesting that the Americans be used for coastal patrol. Arnold had been adamantly opposed, saying such a diversion of precious bombers would adversely affect Britain's defense.

Following extensive communications with Arnold in Washington, Harris had sent a "most secret" cable to Portal in early January 1942.

> Arnold asked me to tell you that so far as he can he aims to get up to twenty heavy bomber units into the United Kingdom this year. He hopes to achieve at least sixteen, but this is likely to be adversely affected by certain tendencies now growing in force. In spite of lip service to the agreed grand strategy of the United States–British overall war, the Far East looms ever larger and more insistently in the minds of the highest ones in the land. Added to this, the navy has now realized the limitations of the flying boat, and covets the heavy bomber in quantity. Recent successes against Jap ships lend weight to their case, and in any event, they have always opposed the bomber plan by fair means or foul. They are concerned only with seas safe for sailors to sail on, and do not think as far as winning the war, or making land safe for landlubbers to live or fight on.
>
> Our proposal to sidetrack 250 17s to Coastal Command made the airmen here very hot under the collar. We are thereby flying straight into the navy's hands. As to what he wants to do about it, Arnold was not clear but in general he expressed an urgent desire that you should fight every proposed diversion of heavy bombers from the bomber force, and from direct action against German territory, to the last ditch.
>
> I told him that he would be preaching not only to the con-

verted, but to the very leader of the sect, but that I would nevertheless inform you. He implores your backing against the threat of diversions, and that my assurance that he has it will be backed by reiteration at the highest levels that the bomber plan still holds the field as the agreed war-winning strategy.

Harris was kind enough to offer Eaker his home April 15 for three months. It was a three-bedroom country house, with stables and gardens, located three miles from Bomber Command headquarters.

Although Eaker and "Bert" became good friends, Harris never ceased trying to convince the American that he should give up day bombing and join the RAF at night. They spent many evenings in what Harris called his "conversion" room, where he showed Eaker three-dimensional target photographs of German cities the Royal Air Force had bombed. Eaker stubbornly resisted such blandishments.

Harris talked also about the mental strain of commanding an air force. He said a naval commander might engage in a major action only once or twice in a whole war, and an army commander might have to fight a major battle once in six months, or, in rare circumstances, once a month. He reminded Eaker that a bomber commander committed his whole force every twenty-four hours. And even when weather would often be an acceptable excuse for keeping his bombers on the ground, the inevitable result would be defeat for Britain in the air war. Also, he said, even when weather aborted a strike, planes still had to be ready to commit.

Harris pointed out that the bomber offensive was the only Allied operation that was presently helping the Russians, who had already lost half their country and might well lose all of it if the anticipated German drive in the summer was successful.

In defense of his night bomber raids, Harris said they were forcing Hitler to keep many of his fighters and antiaircraft guns on the western front, thereby providing direct assistance to the beleaguered Russians. Destruction of war factories, he said with emphasis, will help immeasurably when American and British soldiers invade the Continent.

Eaker remained steadfast in his views because, he said, a daylight bomber offensive would cause greater destruction of industrial targets due to the greater accuracy of American bombers. He noted that, by Harris's own admission, British bombers had frequently bombed the wrong cities, or no cities at all because they had been misled when the Germans set up dummy cities with lights in the middle of fields. This was a familiar tactic, he knew, which the British themselves had used during the blitz.

When Harris replied that new radar equipment would improve accuracy, Eaker said he was not convinced radar bombing would ever be as accurate as visual bombing.

In what he hoped would clinch the argument, Harris said, "You destroy a factory, and they rebuild it. In six weeks they are in operation again. I kill all their workmen, and it takes twenty-one years to provide new ones."

This argument proved no more successful than the others in changing Eaker's views.

Generals Arnold and Portal respected each other, and eventually became close friends. Arnold admired Portal's agile and remarkable mind, although he found him somewhat taciturn and frequently differed with his theories on strategic bombing. Arnold always found the British air chief perceptive and cooperative. Arnold had a basic gospel about daylight strategic bombing, which he literally tried to force upon everyone, so it is no wonder the two disagreed at times.

After the war, Portal said he still believed that Arnold's theories were wrong in respect to 1942 and 1943, but he was convinced that viewed in the context of the entire war, Arnold's theories about use of bombers to attack precision targets was correct. Portal's friendship with Arnold was important because the British air chief actually was the number-two man on the Combined Chiefs of Staff. He had powerful friends, including Winston Churchill.

Those who knew Arnold intimately realized that his petulance was often due to the fact that he was under enormous pressure. His genius was particularly noticeable in adversity. While commands all over the world demanded more and more airplanes and crews, Arnold established a new bomber or fighter school every week during 1942, an incredible achievement under the circumstances.

Soon after Major General Spaatz came to England to take over the Eighth Air Force, the British gave him a formal dinner party attended by the top brass of both air forces, plus Winston Churchill.

Spaatz was a taciturn individual, not gifted in small talk—one of the least outgoing officers in the United States Army Air Forces. At the dinner, he was seated next to Air Marshal Sir William Sholto Douglas, head of British Fighter Command. The seating arrangement was deliberate. The hosts hoped that these two great air strategists would become good friends. Unfortunately, they had overlooked one important mutual characteristic. Douglas was even more closemouthed than Spaatz. As one course followed another, each sat stiffly without exchanging a word.

When the decanter of port wine was passed to the left around the table,

Spaatz—uncharacteristically—decided to break the ice. He turned to Sir Sholto and said, "I'm told you're a mean son of a bitch, and I'm going to have trouble with you."

Sir Sholto was so shocked that he almost dropped his glass of port. He turned to Spaatz with dismay. "I say, old boy, I trust this isn't so."

From then on, they got along famously.

General Marshall visited England with Harry Hopkins April 8 to press for a 1942 invasion of the Continent the following September, and not wait until 1943 or the following year. Fear of a Russian collapse was mounting—a fear deliberately fed by Stalin, who was demanding a second front to relieve pressure on his Red armies. Marshall was received politely by Churchill, who considered such an invasion impractical but did not definitely turn it down. The American army chief of staff understood Churchill's position, but he wanted to get the British thinking positively about an invasion sometime in the future.

Marshall had luncheon at Air Marshal Harris's home on the twelfth, with Portal in attendance, and expressed his appreciation for Portal's support of the buildup of the Eighth Air Force in England. That afternoon, Marshall sat down for a briefing by Eaker at his VIII Bomber Command headquarters. He told Eaker that the plan for a strategic air force in England was still in effect, and he was anxious to find out when Eaker's command could start operations.

Marshall was one of the defense establishment's finest strategists and administrators, a no-nonsense officer who could be tough in getting to the heart of a matter. Eaker knew his characteristics and took special care in his presentation.

When he was done, Marshall said, "Eaker, I do not believe it will ever be possible to invade the Continent of Europe by crossing the English Channel until the Luftwaffe is destroyed. Do your plans provide for the destruction of the Luftwaffe?"

"Yes, sir. That's our primary objective. One of the reasons we plan to conduct a bomber campaign is to assure German fighters will come up so that we can fight them, and destroy them. They will only come up if we are destroying vital targets. If the Combined Chiefs of Staff supply the forces we've indicated in the bomber offensive plan, I'm sure that a year from now the Luftwaffe will not jeopardize your plans for cross-channel operations."

Marshall was satisfied. He told Eaker and his staff they should strive for an understanding of the British viewpoint, and not let irritations affect their relationship. "We are laying cornerstones. Forget yourselves. Rise above your own views." In parting, Marshall assured them of his support in building up a large-scale air offensive against Hitler.

Eaker had no illusions about what his Eighth Air Force bombers would face on the Continent of Europe. Reportedly, the Germans had two thousand fighters and twenty thousand antiaircraft guns. To go against such defenses with a small force of bombers, Eaker knew, would be sending men to their death.

Upon his return to Washington, Marshall wrote Portal May 8 and gave some of his reasons for pushing for a second front in 1942.

> Until and unless we actually initiate combined operations, ground as well as air, the pressures from other fronts for more matériel—the planes and shipping involved—will be constantly increasing. Therefore, we must accept calculated hazards and accordingly resist the attrition of the forces that must be concentrated as quickly as possible for our major purpose. You, personally, have been struggling with this problem for many months, but I do not believe you can accurately picture the destructive diversions constantly pressed upon me from a number of directions. Unless a determined stand on this issue is taken now, I am convinced that we will bleed ourselves white instead of gathering the strength necessary for the leadoff toward a knockout blow.

Within two months of Eaker's establishment of Bomber Command, eight former British bases had been improved and were ready for use. The British had prepared the bases in record time, but still there were no bombers for them.

Churchill was so disturbed by the lack of bombers that he wrote to Roosevelt March 29, seeking to learn when Arnold would send the first groups. "Can you not manage to expedite this? Never was there so much good work to be done, and so few to do it. We must not let our summer air attacks on Germany decline into a second-rate affair. Everything is ready for your people here, and there are targets of all kinds from easy to hard. Even a hundred American heavy bombers working from this country before the end of May would list [sic] our air effort to the proper scale."

Arnold had his own battles in Washington with the United States Navy and the Pacific commanders, who kept demanding more air support. He just didn't have the bombers available to send, but he did reaffirm to Portal April 6 that he was doing everything humanly possible to meet his July schedule. He cautioned, however, that a force large enough to equitably share the burden of the air war against Germany during the summer months could not be expected.

The British also pressed for American production and use of the

Lancaster bomber, which they considered the best bomber either side possessed. There was no question that it could carry the heaviest bomb load. (When modified, it later carried bombs in excess of ten tons.) But Arnold refused to consider the Lancaster, knowing it was inadequately armed to withstand German fighter attacks in daytime. He reaffirmed his intention that the United States would pursue daylight precision bombing.

Harris, meanwhile, intensified his campaign to convince Eaker that the Eighth should join the RAF at night.

Eaker finally said, "If you fellows keep this up, we Americans will all be in the Pacific."

Portal cautioned his commanders that such pressure was counterproductive. Arnold had told him in no uncertain terms that the "Europe first" strategy was not popular in many circles in the United States because the United States Navy and General Douglas MacArthur were waging a continual campaign against the strategy.

At this stage of the war, the British had far more experienced crews than planes, so Portal suggested to Arnold that American planes be turned over to the Royal Air Force until American crews could be trained. Prior to America's entry into the war, Arnold had agreed that England would receive ten thousand combat aircraft of all types in 1942. Such deliveries were impossible if the Eighth Air Force was to be built up quickly, and demands met for more and more aircraft for Pacific operations.

Although both Churchill and Marshall knew that an invasion in 1942 was impossible, the British prime minister had agreed with reluctance under pressure from Marshall. Arnold now had a ready excuse for not delivering more planes. He told Portal April 16 that all available planes would have to be saved for the invasion, and that the British would have to carry the brunt of the air war until the fall of 1942.

With Rear Admiral John H. Towers, head of the United States Navy's Bureau of Aeronautics, Arnold met with Churchill and the British armed forces chiefs and Eisenhower in London May 26. They quickly learned that while Arnold had a frank disposition, he could turn on the charm to get his way. He used all of his personal magnetism to convince the British that they'd have to accept strict allocation quotas for combat aircraft.

For the British, this news was bad. Arnold was saying that the Royal Air Force would receive five hundred fewer heavy bombers, and one thousand five hundred fewer medium bombers than he had originally told them. Meetings lasted four days, and the British were shocked by the news.

Churchill said it was his understanding that American factories intended to produce sixty thousand aircraft in 1942, and he wanted to know why Britain would receive only five thousand. His plans to hit hard at German industries in the near future would now be impossible, he said, and he stressed the importance of dropping large numbers of bombs on the enemy this year, and not the next.

Arnold maintained his composure. He knew that there were no American crews available right away to send to England. If he gave the British heavy bombers, then he would be depriving the Eighth Air Force of any chance of starting operations in 1942. He was frank in expressing his views, and those of President Roosevelt, that the United States would soon have exceptional young aircrews available. He called them the "cream of the crop." Diplomatically, he tried to explain that he believed American youngsters could fly American planes better than those of any other country.

Churchill agreed that, in general, it was advisable for American crews to fly American planes. He stressed, however, the importance of exerting maximum force against the enemy now.

Churchill invited the American military officials and Ambassador John G. Winant to dinner at Chequers May 30. Churchill had a sly purpose behind the invitation, which he extended to Portal and Harris also. This was the night his first one thousand-plane mission was scheduled to attack Cologne.

Churchill announced the raid as they sat down to dinner, and he relayed details all evening.

Arnold had to admit that he was impressed with the raid, knowing this was hardly the time to press the merits of daylight bombing, but it didn't change his mind.

At a dinner with the mayor of High Wycombe and the town council June 5, Eaker was asked to speak briefly to the British soldiers and sailors in attendance. He said, "We won't do much talking until we've done more fighting. I hope that when we leave, you'll be glad we came."

Eaker moved his quarters from Harris's home to Wycombe Abbey July 14. He left Lady Thérèse Harris a note. "Very few abodes have I left during my twenty-five years of military service with the lump in my throat I had this morning as I carried my effects from that comfortable room. If I spent the rest of my life I could not repay you and Bert for your many kindnesses to me."

5

"YANKEE DOODLE
CERTAINLY WENT TO TOWN."

In June of 1942, Eaker wrote Spaatz that the British had cooperated 100 percent in every regard. "In addition, they have made available their most secret devices and documents."

Eaker still had no combat unit in England. He had hoped to have twenty-one heavy units by April 1943, but he knew he wouldn't reach that goal the way things were going.

The first units to arrive were the 97th Bombardment Group, July 1, 1942, and the 1st and 31st Pursuit groups. Arrival of the 97th had been delayed because it had been sent to the West Coast of the United States during the Battle of Midway.

The pursuit groups' planes had traveled via Presque Isle, Goose Bay, Iceland, and England, using bombers for navigation, and the loss was only 4 percent.

The air strategy that had been agreed to on April 14 —that a full-scale air offensive should be prosecuted to a successful conclusion prior to a landing on the Continent—began to come apart shortly thereafter.

Once it became apparent that the main Allied thrust against Germany might be transferred to the Mediterranean as proposed by Winston Churchill, a reexamination of Army Air Forces' needs in Great Britain was needed in light of available trained units and equipment. Arnold and Portal had agreed in principle earlier that priority of aircraft allocations should be based upon the need for planes in the strategic air offensive against Germany. Now combat aircraft for England would be diverted to support an invasion of the continent of Africa if such a plan were approved.

The Royal Air Force initially asked for greater transfer of P-40 pursuit planes to the Middle East. In return, it would equip American fighter units in England with Spitfires. This request came at an inopportune time because American plane losses in the Pacific during the first half of 1942 were substantially higher than predicted. Furthermore, the American home front was clamoring for American crews to fly American planes.

Arnold had discussed the problem with Churchill in the meeting on May 26. Afterward, he reviewed aircraft needs with his own commanders. Along with demands from China and Russia, these needs far outran the quantity available from American production lines. Arnold stressed Roosevelt's wish that every "appropriate American-made aircraft be manned and fought by our own crews."

The British understood this ticklish situation. They were willing to cooperate if the Americans agreed, at the earliest possible date, to train and equip the largest possible air force, contingent upon available production resources.

Arnold faced a dilemma. He found it difficult to agree with principles advocated by both governments. The British were counting on American aircraft, which had been promised. The Americans also needed aircraft to equip their own forces, which were needed for the fulfillment of agreed strategic plans. Production schedules could not meet both requirements, at least initially. Arnold was forced to compromise. In a memorandum to Portal back on May 10, he had outlined the American position. He had told the RAF chief that he had to consider the British desire for aircraft reinforcements in the Middle East; the Royal Air Force Coastal Command's request for long-range bombers, which he believed was a responsibility of the United States Navy, and not the Army Air Forces; and the continuing demand for light bombers. The latter were produced almost entirely in United States factories.

After final negotiations in Washington, an agreement satisfactory to all was reached June 21. Arnold agreed, in conjunction with United States Navy Chief of Operations Admiral King, and Portal, that the combined strength in each theater would be maintained or increased according to the combat situation.

After Spaatz assumed command of the Eighth Air Force in London June 18, he learned quickly that the strategy agreed upon earlier—a strategic air offensive to precede any invasion of the Continent—was in danger of being overturned by Prime Minister Churchill because of drastic changes in the battle fronts. Tension had eased in the Pacific theater after the Japanese suffered severe losses in the battles of the Coral Sea and Midway. Onset of the monsoon season had lessened the Japanese threat to India. On the Russian front, the German offensive during the summer months was in full stride as Feldmarschall Erich von Mannstein conquered the Crimea, and his armies were at the inner defenses of Sevastopol. Russian Marshal Semën Timoshenko's winter campaign below Kharkov had failed, and now the German armies were driving toward the Caucasus with its strategic oil fields. Churchill feared such a drive might continue on to the Middle East and cut off Britain's land link with India. Feldmarschall Erwin Rommel had opened his North African offensive in May, driving the British back, and defeating them at Knightsbridge June 13. After Tobruk's large garrison surrendered June 21, the British Eighth Army a week later dug in for a last stand at El Alamein, only seventy-five miles from Alexandria.

Churchill was deeply concerned about the German threat to the Middle East. Loss of the area's important oil resources alone would have a drastic impact on the British war effort. His concern went beyond resources because loss of the area would cut the southern lend-lease route to Russia, as well as the British link with India and the southwest Pacific. Finally, it might lead to the collapse of the Russian war effort. In private, he and his war staff were pessimistic about Russia's survival. The need for a second front to ease the pressure on Russia was crucial. But Churchill was equally opposed to an invasion of France at that time. Memories of staggering losses of British men in the mud of Flanders in World War I, of the quick defeat of French and British forces in northern France, and of the narrow escape of Allied forces at Dunkirk were all fresh in British minds. They recoiled from an early cross-channel invasion in force and searched for alternate strategies. They considered an attempt to establish a foothold at Brest or Cherbourg, or a raid on Dieppe, as gestures of desperation.

Roosevelt, however, was anxious to get Americans involved in large-scale ground operations before the end of 1942. He bore the double burdens of Stalin's threats and appeals, and of domestic dissatisfaction with American inaction. Churchill pleaded with him to forgo a continental invasion of any size in 1942 and to help the British in the Middle East.

After much discussion, and listening to staff advisers, Roosevelt and Churchill approved plans June 21 that a cross-channel invasion would be considered for 1943, with emergency invasion operations kept under active consideration for 1942.

Americans thought they detected a lack of enthusiasm among their British counterparts for an invasion even in 1943. The American Joint Chiefs discussed among themselves the possibility that unless the British would wholeheartedly support an invasion in 1943, they would recommend to President Roosevelt that he change his decision to make the major effort against Germany and instead commit American forces to the prior defeat of Japan.

These views were presented to the president July 10.

A week later, General Marshall, Admiral King, Harry Hopkins, and a small staff flew to England to make a last effort to persuade the British to agree definitely to an invasion no later than 1943.

The British refused. Actually, a major invasion would have been impossible because American buildup of ground forces could not be made in the time available, and American airpower still didn't have the strength to start the required six-month bomber offensive originally agreed to prior to an invasion of the Continent. The British cited their experiences at Dunkirk again, and their defeats in North Africa. They said they had a healthy respect for the German army and that commitment to any kind of an early invasion would be suicidal. Instead, they proposed an invasion of North Africa.

The Americans agreed that there should be no second front that year, but the American Joint Chiefs were, in turn, bitterly opposed to the North African venture. General Marshall contended that such a thrust would be tangential to the true objective—Germany—and that an African invasion would absorb vast resources without being decisive. General Arnold concurred and pointed out that the air offensive against Germany would suffer. Admiral King contended that any resources not directed against Germany should go to the Pacific. President Roosevelt listened to the military arguments of his chiefs of staff, weighed them against the forces of political reality, and overrode his advisers.

On July 22, agreement was reached that if by September 1942 an invasion in the spring of 1943 appeared impracticable, a combined attack should be launched against North and Northwest Africa prior to December 1. These decisions were approved by Roosevelt and Churchill and passed along to the Combined Chiefs of Staff.

An American commander for the operation was selected August 7 with the appointment of Lieutenant General Dwight D. Eisenhower, who had been sent to England earlier to replace Chaney as commander, European Theater of Operations. He had participated in all the London conferences and was agreeable to the French, whose sensibilities would have been offended by a British commander warring against French colonies in North Africa.

When the Combined Chiefs of Staff officially rejected Marshall's plan for an early invasion of the Continent during a July 24 meeting, all previous plans had to be reconsidered. Eisenhower passed the word to Spaatz and Eaker that, instead, North Africa would be invaded in late fall, and he would command the forces. He called it the "blackest day in history."

Spaatz and Eaker agreed, pointing out that the heartland of Germany was the principal target, and that the Allies should not go off on a tangent that would reduce the Eighth Air Force's effectiveness.

In July, the British reiterated a contention they had first brought up April 1, that an intensified bomber offensive over Germany was, in fact, the second front that the Americans wanted. They pointed to the success of their own one-thousand-plane raids against Cologne and Essen as examples of what could be accomplished from the air to alleviate Russian problems in the east.

The Eighth Air Force at this stage was outnumbered many times over by the Royal Air Force, but it was treated by High Command British headquarters on the same level. The relationship between Spaatz and Portal was excellent, particularly after Spaatz received Arnold's agreement that air commanders of both services in the theater should solve their problems on their own. Additionally, there was an equally close relationship between Eaker's VIII Bomber Command, and Harris's RAF Bomber Command.

The Eighth Air Force under Spaatz included bomber, fighter, and service commands. Fighter units were assigned to the Eighth to perform direct bomber support and, at Spaatz's insistence, were not integrated with British fighters for defense of the United Kingdom, or into the British Fighter Command. By agreement with the Royal Air Force, British fighters provided direct escort coverage on short-range missions, and also performed fighter sweeps in conjunction with bombing raids.

General Arnold had made it clear shortly after American entry into the war that United States bombardment operations must be guided by American doctrines and principles. His insistence helped to clear the air later because American doctrines were entirely different from those of the British.

The United States Army Air Forces had long emphasized daylight bombing of precision targets. When Mr. C. L. Norden, a civilian consultant to the United States Navy, developed the Norden bombsight that was used during World War II after earlier models had been in use by the navy since 1920, accurate bombing from high altitudes became possible. The Army Air Corps had secured twenty-five improved Mark XVs in 1932, and improvement in bombing scores was dramatic. The Norden sight was extremely accurate in the hands of a skilled bombardier, but few such bombardiers were available in the early days of the war.

By prior agreement, and according to plan, Eaker's first missions would be assigned to docks and ports in France in which the Germans were operating submarines. Aircraft factories and key munitions-making plants were given next priority. Lines of communication were listed in third place.

Eaker hoped these missions would prove his command's capability of destroying pinpoint targets by precision daylight bombing. He knew their success would be determined by the ability of bomber crews to ward off German fighters and evade antiaircraft guns. Initially, operations were to be supported by British fighters to the extent of their limited range.

Eaker set a date of August 10 for the Eighth's first mission of its heavy bombers to attack the Sotteville railroad marshaling yards near Rouen in occupied France. It was an important traffic center for shipment of German supplies and personnel, and within range of British Spitfires for fighter support. Colonel Frank A. Armstrong, commander of the 97th Group at Polebrook, was assigned to lead the mission.

Spaatz announced that he would fly the first mission, and that Eaker would fly the second. Eisenhower approved so long as they didn't fly the same mission. He asked Spaatz who should replace him if he was shot down, and the Eighth Air Force commander designated Eaker. The latter, in turn, selected Colonel Newton Longfellow, his chief of staff, who had recently arrived in the theater, to head Bomber Command if he was lost.

The British expressed their strong disapproval, reminding Spaatz and Eaker that they knew all of Britain's secrets, and if they were captured, or killed, it would take months to bring new leaders up to the same point of knowledge. Harris told Eaker, "It took me many years to get to know the things I should know to be a bomber commander. Portal and Sir Archibald Sinclair would relieve me if I contemplated flying missions."

Spaatz agreed, but Eaker planned to go because he believed it was his duty to lead the first mission.

One delay followed another. Arnold wired, "Why are Eaker's bombers still on the ground? There is pressure in Washington for the Eighth Air Force to get going. It will be easier to get appropriations in Congress." He cited other reasons why the Eighth's first mission should be flown as expeditiously as possible.

August 14 Eaker wrote Arnold that the theory of daylight bombing was about to be tested with men's lives at stake, and that he still had faith in the concept. He said his bomber crews would prove to be the toughest air fighters in the theater.

Air Marshal Harris viewed the raid with misgivings. He was resigned to the fact that the Americans might suffer heavy casualties, but that they had to learn for themselves.

Finally, the crews, who had been waiting for the weather to clear for a week, took off at 11:00 A.M. August 17 with twelve Flying Fortresses. The forty-six-year-old Eaker, an outstanding pilot in his own right, flew in *Yankee Doodle* in the second element of six aircraft.

Four squadrons of British fighters met them at the coast.

Eaker spotted the small town of Sotteville, three miles north of Rouen, just beyond a bend in the Seine River.

Just before bombs away, Eaker looked down through the bomb bay to watch the bombs hit. He noted with satisfaction that half the bombs landed in the target area causing damage to tracks, and that some railroad cars were destroyed. He was concerned, however, when he noticed bombs bursting in the village of Rouen.

After return to base, he told Spaatz, "I'm fearful we've killed French civilians. The marshaling yards are only a few hundred feet from that little town. All bombs obviously didn't fall on the yards."

Eaker and Spaatz were so concerned about French casualties that they got in touch with General Charles de Gaulle who was in charge of the Free French forces in England.

De Gaulle replied, "We're delighted you've begun operations, and we know that there must be casualties if you're going to kill Germans. Our purpose is to aid you in any way we can to kill Germans. We want to get the devils out of our country. We don't blame you at all."

Arnold forbade Eaker to fly more missions. In effect, he was acting because of what General Marshall had told him following the deaths of several top-ranking aviators: "I'm not going to select any more airmen for senior commands if they're just going to go off and kill themselves."

Spaatz announced the first raid publicly and, mindful of British criticism of daylight attacks, extolled the merits of the mission far beyond its worth. In saying the bombing exceeded all previous high-altitude attacks in the European Theater, he added that he would not exchange the B-17 for any British bomber in production. This propaganda may have been needed in America at the time, but it served no useful long-range purpose in England.

The mission taught Eaker several things. It was apparent, he realized, that formations had to be tighter to afford better protection against fighters, and navigators had to improve their skills. He knew targets farther inland would not be as easy to identify. He was also aware that bombardier training needed improvement, as did gunnery training.

In a letter to Spaatz August 25, Eaker said that tighter formations would be mandatory in the future, because stragglers could be picked off so easily. Crew comfort, he said, must be improved, and he recommended that the B-17 not be used above twenty-five thousand feet because of the cold, which could reach minus 44 degrees Fahrenheit. Such extreme temperatures froze oxygen masks, he said, and reduced crew efficiency by 50 percent.

Harris sent Eaker a wire following the raid. "Congratulations from all ranks of Bomber Command on the highly successful completion of the first all-American raid by the big fellows on German-occupied territory in Europe. Yankee Doodle certainly went to town, and can stick another well-deserved feather in his cap."

To his staff, Eaker's assessment of the mission was not as ecstatic. "The raid went according to plan, and we are well satisfied with the day's work. However, one swallow doesn't make a summer."

In support of ground troops who struck Dieppe in a hit-and-run raid August 19, B-17s hit the airdrome at Abbeville to help pin down the

German air force. This first assault on Fortress Europe by British and Canadian troops who attempted to break through German coastal defenses at Dieppe was ill advised, although it was part of the emergency procedures deemed necessary to relieve the Russians in the east. It did have some practical value in testing equipment and tactics.

Stalin had long pressed for a second front, although he knew that at this stage of the war a full-fledged invasion was impossible with the Allied resources available. Stalin never understood strategic airpower, believing like many American and British generals that wars were won only on the ground. The Dieppe raid brought no relief to the Russians, and unfortunately half the force was either killed or wounded.

A mission to bomb the docks near Rotterdam started off badly and got worse. A small formation of Flying Fortresses was sixteen minutes late to a rendezvous with its escort of British fighters, and three out of the twelve bombers were so low on fuel that they had to return. As the depleted formation neared the Dutch coast without Spitfires for protection, Eaker sent out a recall order. While turning back, they were jumped by twenty Focke-Wulf 190s and Messerschmitt 109s, and the Fortresses met their first stiff resistance over the Continent.

Lieutenant Richard F. Starks, pilot of one of the B-17s, suffered such severe burns to his hands as the cockpit caught fire that he was unable to fly the airplane. Copilot Lieutenant Donald A. Walter was wounded severely in the savage blasting of the cockpit; he was incapacitated and later died as the Eight's first heavy-bomber casualty.

Once the fire was put out, the bombadier, Lieutenant Edward T. Sconiers, who had washed out of pilot school, took over the controls and flew the plane on two engines back to England where he crash-landed at the first RAF base he could find.

Despite the complete fiasco of the mission, Eaker was heartened by the fact that his Flying Fortresses could fight it out alone over enemy-held territory if need be, and survive.

Eaker set up the first September mission on the fifth to hit the Avions Potez aircraft factory at Meaulte near Rouen. This time he included the newly arrived 301st Group. Each group lost a plane—the first heavy-bomber losses suffered by the Eighth in the war.

The fall campaign reached a new threshold when Eaker was able to send 108 bombers, the largest number yet, to Lille October 9. Lille's heavy industries were vital contributors to the German war effort. The most important target was the steel and engineering works of the Compagnie de Fives-Lille, and the locomotive and freight-car plant of Ateliers-d'Hellemmes.

The Germans contested every mile as bombers dropped 147 tons. Bombing accuracy was unbelievably bad, with only nine bombs falling within fifteen hundred feet of the target, and some bombs were released miles away. Although German attacks were fierce, only four bombers were lost.

Eaker was unhappy with the results of the mission, but he took some consolation in the fact that his bombers proved they could withstand heavy attacks. He refused to believe claims that fifty-six fighters were destroyed, and another twenty probably destroyed, because such a loss would have amounted to 15 percent of the total German fighter strength in western Europe. He was right. The Germans actually lost only one fighter, with another damaged.

Eaker had told Spaatz that a force of ten groups could destroy enemy aircraft factories to the point where they would be unable to supply the Luftwaffe, and submarine activity would be completely stopped within a three-month period by destroying their bases, factories, and docks. Further, he said that he considered ten missions a month feasible, despite the bad weather. He said that his bomber command could use a larger force than the ten groups contemplated for 1942, but that such a force would be adequate only if it was reinforced by an additional ten groups in 1943.

In conclusion, he said, "Coupled with the British night-bombing effort, it is possible to dislocate German industry and commerce, and remove from the enemy the means for waging successful warfare."

Spaatz agreed, referring to the extreme accuracy of American bombers. How he could justify such a statement after the combat record to date is difficult to imagine.

Arnold was not convinced. He believed that fair accuracy had been achieved according to European standards of area bombing, a factor that Spaatz later recognized. Arnold did accept Eaker's estimates of future accuracy and force requirements, and the bomber buildup was predicated upon these figures.

President Roosevelt's comment that "Hitler built a fortress around Europe, but forgot to put a roof on it" was not yet true at this stage of the war. In the coming epic air battles, Allied fliers faced German combat veterans in superior airplanes, which made each mission a life-and-death matter.

The delay in the start of operations by the Eighth Air Force can be directly traced to events dating back to the 1930s. The worst setback to American strategic airpower came when the secretary of war issued a memorandum to the chief of the Army Air Corps, Major General Oscar Westover, that experimentation and development for the fiscal years of 1939–40 would be restricted to aviation designed for the close support of ground troops, and for the production of that type of aircraft such as pursuit, and light and medium bombers.

Westover had been appalled by the order because it spelled the death knell of the heavy bombardment program, and the B-17 Flying Fortress in particular. The memorandum threatened to kill the B-29 Superfortress program also. It said, "No military requirement exists for the procurement of experimental pressure bombers in the fiscal year 1939 or 1940 of the size and type described."

Fortunately for the free world, men like General Arnold, with the backing of General Marshall, got such orders rescinded prior to the outbreak of war. If he had not been successful, Nazi Germany could well have won the air war that was about to be unleashed. The fact that she did not is due primarily to the caliber of men in the Allied Strategic Air Forces and not to the outmoded airplanes that their shortsighted countrymen had given them. The margin of victory proved to be too thin for comfort.

6

EPIC BATTLES

Eaker's greatest concern in the fall of 1942 was the decision by the Combined Chiefs of Staff to build up air and ground forces simultaneously. Eighth Air Force priorities for men and airplanes would suffer. This was a battle he fought and lost at the highest levels because most Allied army and navy officials refused to believe that Germany could be defeated by airpower alone.

Spaatz was equally adamant during the infighting that went on in Washington and London. He told Secretary of War Stimson that European strategy had been originally conceived as involving the use of airpower supported by ground troops. Now, he said, it's a matter of airpower supporting ground forces.

In the first fourteen missions against Nazi-dominated Europe, American bombing accuracy improved slowly. Eaker was encouraged that his bombers seemed to be able to hold their own during the first nine missions. Although German fighters became more aggressive, and more inclined to tangle with the much-vaunted Flying Fortresses, he still believed they could fight their way through to targets with a minimum amount of assistance from escort fighters. Up to this time, antiaircraft fire had not proved a serious threat. After the tenth mission, bomber losses rose due to increased fighter attacks, but American losses still remained far below those suffered by the Royal Air Force in night attacks. The comparision, however, could be misleading. Most British Bomber Command strikes were deep inside Germany, whereas Eighth Air Force attacks were against targets in France and the Low Countries.

Allied bombings had accomplished little in target damage of key German industries during the summer of 1942. Albert Speer knew that worse was yet to come, but he was the only German leader to warn Hitler in September that tank production at Friedrichshafen, and the ball-bearing facilities at Schweinfurt, were vulnerable to air attacks, and that their loss would be crucial to Germany's war effort. Hitler agreed to increase protection for industrial sites and German urban areas.

Despite growing concern in Germany, British criticism continued. Sir Archibald Sinclair, secretary of state for air, in a memorandum dated September 25, voiced the opinions of many British leaders when he said, "What are the Americans doing? They have not dropped a single bomb on Germany."

Persistence began to pay off. British officials now admitted that the Army Air Forces strategy showed promise, and Eaker wrote air force headquarters: "The British acknowledge willingly and cheerfully the great accuracy of our bombing, the surprising hardihood of our bombardment aircraft, and the skill and tenacity of our crews."

The British Air Ministry, after reviewing the results of the Eighth Air Force, said, "The damage caused, commensurate with the weight of the effort expended, is considerable. Complete destruction of any of the targets attacked with forces at present available could not have been expected." Its conclusions, however, indicated there had been no change in their opposition to day bombing. The Air Ministry said it wished that these Fortresses could be employed at night to increase effectiveness of the area-bombing program.

The British press, which had belittled American bombing efforts in the past, now softened its criticism.

Eaker was convinced that once he had a force of three hundred heavy bombers with trained crews, he could attack targets deep inside Germany by day with less than a 4 percent loss. He was aware that a smaller force suffered increased losses on a mission because of its inability to defend itself to the fullest extent. He told Spaatz and Arnold, "Daylight bombing of Germany with planes of the B-17 and B-24 types is feasible, practicable, and economical."

For the present, Eaker knew he had to proceed with caution. If he committed crews and aircraft over heavily defended targets prematurely, he said, "We will not only incur crippling losses but ruin forever the good name of bombardment."

In a letter to Arnold aide Brigadier General George Stratemeyer, he wrote, "Please do not let anybody get the idea that we are hesitant, fearful, laggard, or lazy."

Eisenhower dropped a bombshell on the Eighth by telling Spaatz that the air offensive had to be stopped in the near future because all bombers would be needed in the forthcoming North African invasion.

Arnold protested. He told Eisenhower that he didn't want the Eighth's bomber offensive stopped, although he recognized Eisenhower's need for bombers in North Africa.

Eisenhower backed off, realizing that Arnold must have had Marshall's backing before he wrote.

Inconsistently, Churchill now sought Roosevelt's assistance in building up the Eighth Air Force even though he had been responsible for the diversion of most of its strength. He wrote the president September 16:

> In spite of the fact that we cannot make up more than thirty-two squadrons of bombers instead of forty-two last year, we know our night bomber offensive is having a devastating effect. If we can add continuity and precision to the attack by your bombers striking deep into the heart of Germany by day, the effect would be redoubled.
>
> To do this effectively and without prohibitive loss, they must have numbers to saturate and disperse the defenses. I hope you may consider it wise to build up Spaatz's strength.
>
> We must make the North African invasion a success, but I am sure we would be missing a great opportunity if we didn't concentrate every available Fortress and long-range escort fighter as quickly as possible for the attack on our primary enemy. I cannot help feeling some concern at the extent to which the program for the buildup of American air forces in this country is falling behind expectations.

On September 25, he asked Air Marshal Sir John Slessor, assistant chief of the Air Staff, some blunt questions about the American air effort.

"What are the Americans doing? As far as I know they haven't dropped a single bomb on Germany. Is it true they have not dropped a bomb outside the range of our single-seater fighter cover?"

Slessor replied the next day. He was the most considerate of all British commanders in regard to the United States Army Air Forces and its policies. He told the prime minister there were six American heavy bombardment squadrons operational, but that only three had seen combat. It should be noted that the British squadron was identical to an American group. Actually, Slessor's figure was not correct. At this time, there were seven groups in England.

Slessor reminded Churchill that a number of these groups were being readied for a "certain operation." The North African invasion was so secret that no mention was ever made of it in dispatches. Slessor added that Spaatz was faced with the problem of training new crews who had arrived from the States without adequate training, particularly in gunnery proficiency.

In a later report to Sir Archibald Sinclair and the prime minister,

Slessor said he was convinced that the Americans would be successful in daylight strategic bombing once sufficient bombers were available. He said that the B-17 had proved it could defend itself and take an enormous amount of punishment, but it had yet to be shown that it could carry the air war deep inside Germany without prohibitive losses. He hastened to add, however, that he personally believed that it could.

In response to criticism that American bombers had not yet bombed beyond the protective custody of British fighters, he said the Eighth Air Force was still in Phase 1, which didn't call for such attacks, and that American bombers had fought beyond such fighter protection and had given a good account of themselves. He described American crews as fine material and said their bombing had been reasonably accurate.

He told Sinclair that it was dangerous to push the Americans too far away from what he called their "cherished" policies. He advised that if day bombing failed, he was not at all certain that the Americans would turn to night bombing. He said there was a very real danger that the Americans might send their bombers to the Pacific war fronts.

Portal, who still believed there was a question about day bombing versus night bombing, also sought Slessor's comments. In Portal's view, a good night-bombing force could quickly be trained as a day-bombing force, but it would be difficult to do the opposite. He said such a change would involve modifications in American factories to equip the bombers for night operations, along with extensive retraining of crews.

"Perhaps I am unduly optimistic," Slessor replied, "but I've always felt that when we get large numbers of bombers we should be able to go in by day. I think that if the Germans in the Battle of Britain, even with the same number, had had aircraft with the performance, armament, and precision bombsights of the B-17, the answer might have been very different. I have talked about this a great deal with Spaatz and to others of my American friends. They are, I think, unwarrantedly cock-a-hoop as a result of their limited experience to date. But they are setting about it in a realistic and businesslike way. And, making all allowances for their natural optimism, I believe they will do it."

Slessor failed to convince Portal, who replied, "It is quite easy to pick off small targets by day when you are not seriously opposed. It is an entirely different matter when you are being harassed all the time by fighters and flak. Secondly, there is a question of their ammunition range when unescorted.

"I do not think they will ever be able regularly to penetrate farther than the Ruhr, and perhaps Hamburg, without absolutely prohibitive losses. On the other hand, I have no doubt that if by the end of 1943 we had a force of three thousand American heavy and medium bombers, properly trained for night flying to our standards, we and they together could pulverize almost the whole of the industrial and economic power of Germany within a year, besides utterly destroying the morale of the German people."

Eaker was aware of these British beliefs, and he knew that they would never be convinced until the Americans could bomb German targets and return without prohibitive losses.

Although Eaker had received four other bomber groups from the States in the last three months, he was about to lose the 97th, 301st, and 93rd groups to North Africa. For the most part, these were experienced combat crews.

When the American bomber campaign was halted for five days in early October due to bad weather, Spaatz told Eisenhower on the seventh that weather was still the greatest weakness in the American bombing program. Actually, only one mission had been flown since September 7.

Lieutenant Henry A. West was awakened at 4:30 A.M. and slowly came to life as he dressed for the October 9 mission to Lille in occupied France.

During the specialized navigator's briefing at their 301st Group base at Chelveston, he learned they might be opposed by one hundred FW-190s, and that the antiaircraft fire would be moderate to heavy.

Later, on the flight line, they took off six minutes late, and formed on Group Commander Colonel R. R. Walker's plane.

At Felixstowe, West noted with relief that their escort fighters had joined them, and he found it comforting to see three squadrons of British Spitfires, and an equal number of American P-38s, flying above them.

Despite some inaccurate flak, the mission proceeded to Lille without incident. There were a total of 108 B-17s, and some B-24s from the 93rd Group. Their target was the locomotive carriage and wagon works of Chemin de Fer du Nord at Lille.

At first, Walker's plane had difficulty locating the target, and their group made 180-degree turns, much to West's dismay because he knew they were inviting trouble and giving the German fighters a chance to get up.

He breathed a sigh of relief when Walker's plane straightened out and headed on their run. Just as Lieutenant Arthur L. Carlson started to synchronize his bombsight, a formation of B-17s cut in front of them, and he had to quickly switch his cross hairs to a nearby railroad terminal.

No sooner were bombs away than black flak surrounded them and German fighters struck savagely at their squadron. Several planes were hit, and three of them had to feather engines.

West watched with growing concern as two engines in a nearby B-17 were hit by flak and creeping flames started to cover the bomber while eight crew members hastily bailed out. He watched anxiously for another, but evidently one crew member couldn't make it. With relief he noted that all those who had exited the bomber were floating safely to earth. Suddenly, some FW-190s attacked the Americans who, tugging at their shrouds, tried to collapse their chutes momentarily so they could drop under the machine-gun shells swirling toward them.

Meanwhile, another plane in the formation had taken so much punishment that it fell away from them. West noted later that it managed to rejoin the squadron as they headed home.

Over the Channel, West watched anxiously as another B-17 circled to the left and headed down for a water landing. He learned later the crew was saved by the Air-Sea Rescue Service.

Only nine bombs fell within one thousand five hundred feet of the target's aiming point, and Eaker's Eighth Air Force failed to live up to his expectations. Four bombers were lost, and the British press expressed incredulity about the fifty-six fighters claimed by the Eighth's gunners, even though the raid was called a great victory. To make matters worse, there was a heavy loss of life among French civilians, who bore the brunt of the falling bombs.

Lieutenant West flew only two more missions out of England before the 301st was transferred to North Africa November 24, and the Chelveston base became the home of the 305th Group.

Churchill also expressed disbelief at the number of German fighters claimed to have been shot down on the Lille raid. He wrote a personal memorandum to Portal three days later. "American newspapers are naturally elated about the unprecedented feat of the Flying Fortresses and Liberators in last Friday's daylight raid on Lille in northern France when the bombers shot down forty-eight Germans and probably destroyed thirty-eight others." The original American figures had been adjusted downward. "The New York *Mirror* says that the Lille raid established American Flying Fortresses and Liberator bombers as veritable battleships of the air, self-sufficient for both offense and defense. The pursuit ship is becoming obsolescent and will be replaced by the many-gunned air cruiser.

"Is there the slightest truth in these American claims? What is the Air Ministry's view?"

The Air Staff, pointing out that there probably were no more than sixty German fighters in the area at the time of the raid, didn't believe the claims either.

Postwar records show that only ten German fighters were lost that day, and four were shot down by Allied fighters.

During the first nine months of 1942, German U-boats had increased from 90 to 196, and in August 108 Allied ships were sunk.

After losses increased the next month, Churchill sent Harry Hopkins a telegram. "I am oppressed with the heavy U-boat sinkings and the biting need for more long-range aircraft." He asked for another fifty Liberators so that U-boats could be under constant attack as they went out from their Biscay ports and patrolled between Iceland and the Faroe Islands. If these packs could be struck in the mid-Atlantic, he told Hopkins, it would be the greatest possible help.

Eisenhower gave the Eighth Air Force two directives in response. October 20, and again on the twenty-ninth, Spaatz was advised that submarine bases on the west coast of France should have first priority. He was told that the major portion of German Atlantic U-boat activity against shipping bound from the United Kingdom to North Africa with huge amounts of men, supplies, and equipment was possible because of these bases. The directives gave second priority to aircraft factories, repair depots, and airfields in occupied France.

These directives delayed the strategic bombing of industrial targets in Germany. Such orders were frustrating to strategic air planners, although they were aware of the dire need to reduce the submarine menace in the Atlantic. Otherwise all plans for Europe and North Africa would come to naught. Eisenhower had told Spaatz bluntly October 13 that he considered the defeat of submarine operations "one of the basic requirements to the winning of the war."

It was hoped that the use of American bombers to make precision attacks in daylight would reduce French civilian casualties, which were a cause of growing concern. Prior to the October 7 raid, the British Broadcasting Corporation had warned the French people that American bombers would strike only at German forces, and those industrial targets in France and occupied countries that supported the German war effort. The broadcast advised all French citizens within two kilometers of factories supporting Germany to vacate their homes. They warned that bombing of small targets from high altitudes might result in some bombs falling outside target areas.

French civilian losses at Rouen, Lille, and Lorient had been heavy at times. The Nazis kept French bitterness alive by using the controlled press to great propaganda advantage. Spaatz considered such losses tragic, and he issued orders that intentional bombing of civilians would not be tolerated.

The Eighth's antisubmarine campaign began October 21 when thirty high-explosive bombs, each weighing a ton, were dropped on German bases. Although accuracy was high, not one bomb penetrated the roofs of the submarine pens. The surrounding areas were hit hard, but there were few French casualties. Opposition by German fighters was heavy.

Some groups later carried two five thousand-pound "Disney" bombs mounted on external racks. These armor-piercing bombs were designed to penetrate the roofs of submarine and E-boat pens. Those who dropped them soon learned, as one pilot said, that their ballistics were "about as consistent as a fart in a windstorm." Another pilot said that flying a B-17 with these monstrosities under the wings was like trying to tap-dance on a billiard ball resting on an ice cube. Such tactics were quickly discontinued because even these large bombs could not penetrate the submarine pens.

Spaatz wrote Arnold October 31, "Whether or not these operations will prove too costly for the results obtained remains to be seen. The concrete submarine pens are hard, maybe impossible ones to crack. The bombing of the surrounding installations should seriously handicap the effective use of the bases."

Spaatz was less than enthusiastic about his diversion of bombing efforts from the principal task of hitting strategic targets. It was clear, he told Eaker, that new tactics must be devised other than high-level bombings.

To increase bombing accuracy, altitudes were lowered by the end of October. Spaatz was aware that bombing such targets at lower altitudes would cause higher crew casualties, but he had noted that antiaircraft fire had been ineffective. The targets were outside the range of escort fighters, however, and German fighter resistance had increased.

Churchill became concerned about the refusal of Americans to use more of their bombers to keep the sea-lanes open to North Africa. In a policy statement he sent to his chiefs of staff October 22, he said, "The utmost pressure must be put upon the United States authorities here, and in America, to utilize their Fortresses and Liberators to support our sea communications during Torch [the invasion of North Africa]."

He returned to his favorite subject about American persistence in preparing for deep penetrations by day into Germany, saying such attacks would be disastrous. "We must endeavor to convince them to turn to sea work in support of Torch, including bombing of Biscay ports and to night work."

Actually, Spaatz and Eaker were not against attacks on submarine pens. They considered such attacks suitable because they could be conducted by relatively small forces. Earlier, Eaker had told Spaatz that the best way to destroy the submarine menace was to destroy them in their factories and pens, not at sea.

Churchill wrote Harry Hopkins again October 16, insisting the United States must turn to production of night bombers and produce P-51 Mustang fighters with British Merlin engines: "Such a fighter, in Portal's view, should be far ahead of anything in the fighter line you have in hand." In the case of the P-51, equipped with the Merlin engine, his words proved prophetic. The Allison engine in the original P-51 designed for the Royal Air Force lacked sufficient power.

Churchill went on to caution Hopkins that he shouldn't believe all that he had been told about the B-17. "I must say to you for your eye only, and only to be used by you in your high discretion, that the very accurate results so far achieved in the daylight bombing of France by your Fortresses under most numerous fighter escort, mainly British, does not give our experts the same confidence as yours in the power of the day bomber to penetrate far into Germany."

Spaatz and Eaker, as well as Harris and Portal, were concerned about the trend in Churchill's thoughts, particularly regarding diversion of the bomber effort to assist the North African invasion. The British Air Ministry disapproved of the North African invasion because it would take forces away from the strategic bombing of Germany. Slessor warned Churchill that any attempt to divert the Americans away from daylight bombing would only play into the hands of those Americans who were pushing for a "Pacific first" strategy.

Harris was equally forthright, believing many things the prime minister had said recently were counterproductive. "My American friends are despondent," he told Churchill. "They foresee the success of efforts by the United States Army, and particularly the United States Navy, to keep them off bombing France and thereafter to keep them from bombing Germany.

"You'll please excuse frankness in this matter. My information is that unless you come down personally and most emphatically on the side of throwing every bomb against Germany, subject only to minimum essential diversions elsewhere, the bomber plan, insofar as United States assistance is concerned, will be hopelessly and fatally prejudiced within the very near future for an unpredictable period, if not for keeps."

Eaker had supplied some of these arguments to present to Churchill, but the prime minister considered the Eighth just a paper air force. He was so concerned about the effect U-boats might have on the North African invasion that he could think of little else.

Oddly, Churchill never went directly to President Roosevelt to complain about American air operations. Eaker always assumed that he would tell the president that the Eighth was playing too small a part in the war.

Until now, the Eighth had flown 1,540 bombing sorties during four and a half months since their first raid. Their loss rate was less than 2 percent for a total of thirty-two aircraft. This was better than the Royal Air Force's loss at night of approximately 4 percent, but the latter were flying missions over Germany.

Portal sent a memo to the British chiefs of staff November 3, seeking their approval for a bomber offensive. "I'm convinced that an Anglo-

American bomber force based in the United Kingdom, and building up to a peak of four thousand or six thousand heavy bombers by 1944, would be capable of reducing the German war potential well below the level at which an Anglo-American invasion of the Continent would become practicable.

"With such a force at their command," he said, "six million homes would be destroyed, along with a proportionate number of industrial buildings, sources of power, transportation, and public utilities. It is my belief," he said, "that twenty-five million Germans would be made homeless, and such raids would kill an estimated nine hundred thousand Germans, and another million seriously injured."

Sir Alan Brooke, chief of the Imperial General Staff, refused to believe Bomber Command's estimates of destruction. He said that experience had shown that built-up areas could withstand far more "knocking about" than had been originally thought.

Eaker now believed that his command was ready to bomb targets in Germany, weak as it still was in numbers of bombers and crews.

Spaatz, who had been in England during the Battle of Britain, had been impressed by the Royal Air Force's efficiency and fighting abilities and warm in praise of their operations. As a result, the British revealed their best-kept secrets to him. He had noted that Germany's failure to destroy British radar stations was crucial in that battle.

During a visit by General Arnold, Spaatz told his chief, "The British still have a lot to learn about bombing." He added hastily that he was not being critical, because his command also had much to learn, and he was aware that they all could learn much from the Royal Air Force, which had been bombing for two years in a real war.

Arnold nodded agreement. His normal cheeriness, which had earned him the nickname "Hap" at West Point, was subdued. He knew the task facing his air forces in Europe was formidable, but he had every confidence in Spaatz, whom he had known since 1917. He often picked subordinates whom he did not particularly like personally, judging them on their ability to do the job handed them. This wasn't true of Spaatz, because he had long admired him and progressively gave him increasing responsibility in high-command positions.

General Hansell, upon his "escape" from Washington in September 1942, was first named deputy theater air officer for Spaatz, who functioned as both commander in chief of the Eighth Air Force and the theater air officer on General Eisenhower's staff. Hansell thus performed a liaison function between Spaatz and Eisenhower while heading up

Eisenhower's Air Plans Section. During this period, he frequently discussed the air support that would be required for the contemplated invasion of the Continent, and both were in agreement that the first step was to defeat the German air force.

Spaatz gave Hansell the job of determining what units of the Eighth Air Force should be assigned to the Twelfth Air Force in the Mediterranean in support of the coming invasion of North Africa. This new air force, commanded by Major General James H. Doolittle, was to be created by carving up the Eighth Air Force. For Hansell, it was a most unwelcome duty. He was told to pick the best units because the Twelfth would be in a very trying situation. Hansell selected two groups from the limited number in England, and Eisenhower later borrowed two more and kept them longer than originally envisaged, much to Eaker's dismay.

Hansell found Eisenhower cooperative about strategic air plans against Germany. Still, Ike made it clear that he wanted maximum air support for his upcoming Mediterranean operation. In effect, draining off bomber groups from England for support of the North African invasion denuded the Eighth Air Force of its heavy-bomber strength.

Eisenhower frequently referred to his role as one of bringing disparate military people together. He was aware that the tradition of coalition armies was that they tended to fight one another more than the enemy, and he believed strongly that one of his most important tasks was to acquire a staff of personnel who could get along. The fact that he achieved this goal in North Africa, and later as Supreme Allied Commander for the invasion of the Continent, proved to be his greatest asset as a commander.

The veteran 97th and 301st groups were transferred to the Twelfth Air Force prior to the November 9 raid on the U-boat base at Saint-Nazaire, so most of the crews available for that attack were not seasoned veterans. The training of gunners with the new crews was particularly inadequate.

Eaker had authorized the lowering of bombing altitudes for the raid on Saint-Nazaire. The twelve B-24s that were assigned 18,000-foot altitudes suffered little damage from ground fire, but the thirty-one B-17s at 7,500 and 10,000 feet were mauled. For the first time, flak from both light and heavy guns was not only intense but extremely accurate, causing the loss of three bombers and another twenty-two damaged. The bombing was the worst yet—only 75 out of 344 bombs released over Saint-Nazaire could even be plotted.

Eaker and Spaatz now were convinced that operations against the sub pens were futile, although they had to be continued. Altitudes were raised to 17,500 feet and 22,000 feet, to reduce losses from antiaircraft fire, and six more attacks were launched against submarine bases in the

Saint-Nazaire and Lorient areas, until January 3, 1943. Some missions ran into stiff opposition, but the overall loss rate of 5 percent for the 199 bombers used on these missions was within reason.

Throughout these bombings, accuracy remained poor, and the submarine shelters suffered no permanent damage. U-boat activity actually increased during this period. Target specialists decided that heavier armor-piercing bombs would not even help, yet even to keep the surface structures destroyed called for more frequent attacks.

Prior to the war, United States Army Ordnance experts had said that a four thousand-pound bomb, properly placed, could destroy any known structure. They hadn't counted on the ingenuity of German engineers, and higher headquarters eventually realized that attacks against German submarines at sea proved more effective. Grand Admiral Karl Doenitz, commander of the U-boat fleet, said after the war, "Not only were the pens themselves impervious to anything but the heaviest type of bomb, but they housed virtually all necessary repair and maintenance facilities. What slowed turnaround most effectively was the necessity for repairing the damage done to hull structures by aerial bombs and depth charges by air and surface attacks at sea."

Albert Speer, who replaced Dr. Fritz Todt as head of Germany's ministry of armaments and war production after Todt died in an aircraft accident in January 1943, felt that Allied attacks against German shipping and shipbuilding facilities in coastal cities did considerable damage. However, he too credited long-range aerial reconnaissance over the Atlantic sea-lanes as most effective in hindering German U-boats.

In the closing months of 1942, the Eighth Air Force flew five of the last fifteen missions against the German air force and enemy-operated transportation facilities in occupied countries. Three missions were against Lille, and they accounted for almost all the damage inflicted upon transportation targets.

Only the single raid against aircraft plants at Romilly-sur-Seine was worthwhile. Romilly's aircraft repair depot, near the Seine River sixty-five miles southeast of Paris, held reserve aircraft for the German air force in France and the Low Countries. The Eighth made its deepest penetration yet; seventy-two bombers stirred up a hornet's nest in early December as formations received the full brunt of almost every German fighter in northeastern France. It was an epic battle that would long be remembered by participants. The FW-190s attacked just as Allied fighter escort had to turn back, making head-on attacks in wave after wave. The contest continued on the way home as German fighters managed to knock down six of the heavies and cripple two others, which had to crash-land in England.

In the past, German fighters had made most of their attacks from the rear. Once they learned that American bombers, which lacked nose turrets, were more vulnerable to head-on attacks, they took full advantage of a basic weakness in these early American bombers. Claims of fifty-three German fighters destroyed were completely out of line. The Germans admitted the loss of two fighters, but three others lost that day could have resulted from the battle.

Although the Eighth's accomplishments fell short of Eaker's expectations, he believed his command had proved that daylight bombers could survive over Nazi-occupied Europe. He was confident that once the trickle of replacement crews became a flood, the American strategic air effort would have an overwhelming impact on the war's outcome.

7

A MATTER OF FAITH

The decision to postpone an invasion of Europe in favor of North Africa caused problems for the Eighth Air Force beyond the loss of men and planes to the Mediterranean theater. The United States Navy decided it was time to press for its earlier demands for greater efforts against the Japanese in the Pacific, saying that emphasis should be shifted from Europe to Asia now that Russia seemed likely to survive. The navy viewed the bomber offensive in Europe as something to support a continental invasion; many top officials of the army felt the same way. Arnold, of course, fought any contention that airpower's primary role was in support of ground and sea operations. As far as the North African invasion was concerned, he considered it a regrettable but temporary diversion from a combined bombing offensive against the heart of Germany. Eisenhower tried in September to bring all bombing operations from the United Kingdom to a complete halt if that should be necessary to prepare for his coming North African invasion.

Arnold refused to tolerate such a total diversion, pointing to the Army Air Forces doctrine of establishing complete air ascendancy over the enemy agreed to by President Roosevelt. The air force chief pointed out that the European war was ideal for use of massed strategic airpower because most of the vital targets were within range of available heavy bombers. In the Pacific, he said, the impact of very heavy bombers like the new B-29 Superfortress could not be made until early 1944, when the first of these bombers would start coming off the production lines and America would have acquired bases within striking distance of Japan's home islands.

Arnold's great worry was that America's airpower would be dispersed throughout the globe to meet local needs and would never be decisive in any one theater. He advised commanders of the smaller war theaters that they must get along with minimum air resources so that major theaters could have the overwhelming number of aircraft they needed to be effective.

To his staff in Washington, Arnold said, "We have an education job as well as an allocation job. Successful air operations depend upon the continuous application of massed airpower against critical objectives."

The doctrine of concentration of force was a fundamental element in all strategic planning. As earlier plans indicated, concentration was especially applicable to the air war in Europe.

Spaatz was told to enlist the aid of key commanders in his theater to advance this Army Air Forces theory. Arnold was aware that without their support, there was a chance that air strength would be "so dissipated by diversions elsewhere as to be only a token effort."

Fortunately, Spaatz and Eisenhower had developed a good relationship. They had gone to West Point together—Spaatz graduating in 1914, and Eisenhower in 1915—and were personal friends. Spaatz had written Eisenhower September 5 that strategic air attacks launched against the heart of Germany would contribute support to ground operations in North Africa. In urging Eisenhower to capitalize upon these advantages, he said maximum continuity of action could be achieved through cooperation with the Royal Air Force. Spaatz said he would use the entire air forces of the United States in the United Kingdom to support the invasion of North Africa if that should become necessary. He said, however, that air operations over western Europe would tie up a large part of the Luftwaffe, which might otherwise be shifted temporarily to African bases.

In a letter to Arnold, Spaatz requested that a strong force of heavy bombers and fighters be maintained at all times in the United Kingdom. Specifically, he sought ten heavy-bomber groups and five fighter groups by October 15. By January 1, 1943, he said he would need twenty heavy groups, ten medium, and five fighter groups.

Spaatz's persuasive powers were used to good advantage with Eisenhower, who agreed to rescind his September 12 order terminating bombing operations in favor of vigorous air force participation, both from England and from Mediterranean bases, in the invasion and subsequent conquest of North Africa.

Pacific commanders such as Admiral Chester Nimitz and General Douglas MacArthur—neither of whom had ever agreed to the "Europe first" strategy—kept insisting that their needs also be met. They urged that the central, south, and southwest Pacific should have parity of priority with Europe. Spaatz claimed that such priority would operate to place the needs of the United Kingdom in fifth place, or the lowest priority.

It was a classic example of neither Pacific commander viewing the world strategy objectively and agreeing that forces should be allocated where they would do the most good. Local commanders naturally think in terms of local objectives and local needs. It was a problem for the Joint Chiefs and the president.

Arnold armed himself with facts and figures for support of his convictions. In maintaining that Germany was still the chief enemy, he also pointed out army intelligence estimates that there were five thousand planes assigned to the Pacific, including those on carriers, and that American combat air strength already outnumbered the Japanese, who would not reach a total of four thousand before the spring of 1943.

Under this barrage from all angles, Admiral King capitulated. He agreed that North Africa and the Mediterranean should have priority, but that their combined needs should not exceed those of the central and southwest Pacific. King and Admiral William D. Leahy, chairman of the Joint Chiefs of Staff, remained opposed to precedence for bomber forces in the United Kingdom over operations in the Pacific.

When the military situation in the South Pacific became critical on October 24, Roosevelt sent a memorandum to the Joint Chiefs. In it, he said that it was necessary to hold Guadalcanal at all costs. "We will soon find ourselves engaged on two active fronts, and we must have adequate air support in both places even though it means a delay in our other commitments, particularly to England. Our long-range plans could be set back for months if we fail to throw our full strength in our immediate and impending conflicts."

The decision about whether to divert additional forces from the United Kingdom was postponed. Actually, nothing was done, and once the Guadalcanal emergency passed, navy officials never again brought the matter up with such vehemence. When the subject of diversion of assets did resurface, it involved only Mediterranean forces.

Allied plans for the invasion of Morocco and Algeria, under Eisenhower, were finally completed on August 13, 1942, when the relatively unknown American general was given a formal directive. The decision to move into the Mediterranean as the next major step of Allied forces meant that Pacific commands would be forced, for the time being, to hold the Hawaii-Midway line, which preserved the lifeline to Australia.

Marshall had fought for a cross-channel invasion of France, but when the president and the prime minister agreed upon North Africa, he dropped his opposition and gave full support to the Mediterranean venture. Churchill, in particular, was convinced that Hitler's armies, which were making spectacular advances against the southern flank of Soviet Russia, should be stopped lest they join up with Feldmarschall Erwin Rommel's forces in the Middle East.

Eisenhower's deputy, Major General Mark W. Clark, and some specialists were sent secretly to Algeria in an Allied submarine to be briefed by Robert Murphy of the United States State Department. Murphy had established, on Roosevelt's orders, an intelligence network throughout North Africa. Eisenhower needed to know the true sentiments of the area's French leaders, whose loyalties were divided three ways. Some favored General Charles de Gaulle; some backed General Henri Honoré Giraud, who had just escaped from a German prison camp with the assistance of a United States submarine; while still others were loyal to the Vichy puppet government headed by Marshal Henri Pétain. Roosevelt, who didn't trust de Gaulle and feared he might leak what was going on, didn't tell the French general about the conference. General Giraud had been selected to head the French in Africa, and he and de Gaulle were rivals and bitter enemies. When de Gaulle learned what had taken place, he voiced bitter anger and never forgave the American president for what he considered a betrayal.

Secrecy paid off, because more than eighty American and British navy ships and transports were able to land troops on the shores of Morocco and Algeria on both the Atlantic and Mediterranean sides November 8 against only light opposition. The few casualties were at Oran and Casablanca where the embittered Pétain ordered French North African forces to resist.

The French had fourteen divisions in North Africa, and extensive bloodshed would have resulted if they had continued to follow Pétain's orders to fight. To counter such a possibility, the Allies relied upon Giraud, whom they had smuggled out of France to Gibraltar, to assume command. But when the French general insisted upon command of the entire expedition, Eisenhower refused.

Admiral Jean Louis Darlan, who had been a Nazi collaborator, was caught in Algiers where he had gone to visit an ailing son. Much to Eisenhower's surprise, Darlan changed sides once more and agreed to assume command of all French forces. Darlan issued orders November 10 that French commanders should cease all resistance. Eisenhower, anxious to establish order in North Africa, made Darlan the political chief for North Africa because he assumed his authority would be more acceptable with Giraud in charge of the French army.

Darlan was assassinated by a French royalist on Christmas Eve, and chaos threatened to engulf French North Africa. De Gaulle managed to outmaneuver the politically inept Giraud and established himself in command of all elements of Free France.

During the Tunisian campaign, British Squadrons 142 and 150 of 330 Group played an important part in night operations. Formerly, they had been a part of Bomber Command's 1 Group in England.

From their first base at Blida, thirty-five miles southwest of Algiers, crews had more than their share of hairsbreadth escapes in their Wellington bombers. One night, Flight Lieutenant Ronnie Brooks's wireless operator had to be held by his heels over the bomb bay to try and release a hung-up bomb with an ax. He wasn't successful until they were over their target—the port city of Bizerte.

Another night, January 18, 1943, Squadron Leader J. F. H. Booth led his crew on a raid of the Bizerte docks. The first two sticks of bombs were dropped without incident, so they circled offshore to observe the other attacks in the bright moonlight. Suddenly, a Ju-88 night fighter attacked. Booth winced when shells struck his starboard engine, knowing the flames shooting out from it would make them an easy target.

The German pilot headed in for the kill, making three more attacks on the crippled bomber and knocking out its hydraulic system and some of its instruments. Booth blanched when he heard a crew member report that a portable oxygen bottle was on fire, knowing it could explode any moment.

But when the Ju-88 came in for another attack, the top turret gunner scored hits, and the German pilot broke away.

With the Wimpy in a crippled condition, Booth ordered the crew to bail out before the oxygen bottle blew. Instead, Leading Aircraftsman J. Skingsley, acting as flight engineer, tried to smother the blazing bottle. When this proved impossible, he picked it up with his bare hands, wincing as the heat shriveled his flesh, carried it quickly to an escape hatch, and tossed it out.

Skingsley's selfless act undoubtedly saved the crew.

Lieutenant Jack Ilfrey led a Twelfth Air Force P-38 flight from the 94th Squadron to the Bizerte-Tunis area the day after Christmas 1942. When he saw FW-190s attacking a crippled American bomber, he latched on to the tail of one of the German fighters. The enemy fighter turned away, flying over Lake Bizerte, but Ilfrey hung on his tail, firing every time he was lined up. The 190 started to smoke, and then plunged into the lake. Ilfrey was so intent watching the German fighter crash that he failed to notice another German fighter on his tail until shells from the German pilot's fighter whizzed past him and kicked up the waters of the lake in front of him. Kicking hard right rudder, he swung his P-38 around so quickly that the German pilot found their roles reversed, and Ilfrey clung to his tail despite everything the enemy pilot could do to shake him off. It wasn't long before the P-38's blazing .50-caliber guns tore the 190 apart and it nose-dived into the lake.

This double victory brought Ilfrey's total to five, and he was now the

The Germans were not long in recovering from their initial surprise, and Eisenhower's inexperienced troops were soon fighting for their lives. The North African campaign wasn't finally resolved until the summer of 1943.

Arnold was upset when Eisenhower did nothing to implement an agreement he thought he had with him about control of American air forces. He had written Spaatz and Eisenhower November 15, "Unless we are careful, we will find our air effort in Europe dispersed the same way we are now dispersed all over the world." In his opinion, he told them, European air operations must be planned and controlled by one man, and he recommended Spaatz for that role.

When Eisenhower finally acted, it was to transfer Spaatz to North Africa as his air adviser and place Eaker in command of the Eighth Air Force. Action for one overall air commander for both theaters, which Arnold had proposed, was not taken.

December 10 Arnold wrote Sir Charles Portal. "The recent air operations in North Africa have confirmed my opinion that the United States air effort against the European Axis should be unified under the command of one supreme commander. At the present time, we are carrying on an air war against Germany and Italy by more or less unrelated air efforts from the United Kingdom, North Africa, and the Middle East. Our efforts are being opposed by a very efficient air force, integrated by a very capable supreme air commander, Göring."

He also wrote Spaatz about the strategic air offensive. "By appropriate unification of command the North African bases made available to Torch may be used to substantial advantage in the prosecution of our basic strategic plan for offensive air action against the European Axis. Without such unification, the North African front is apt, I believe, to prove a seriously deterring factor in the effective employment of our air arm as a striking force."

Privately, both Eaker and Arnold knew that strategic air attacks so far had done little to destroy important targets. Daylight bombing was still a matter of faith until more escort fighters became available.

When General Jacob Devers replaced Eisenhower as commander of the European theater, Eaker went to London to pay his respects. Major General Idwal Edwards, Devers's chief of staff, said, "You've never met Devers, have you?"

"No, I haven't."

"Well, be very careful because he's eating air force officers for breakfast these days."

"What's the burr under his saddle?"

"The crew flying him over here landed him in Ireland. He was almost interned, and would have missed the war. He's going to tell you that story, so feel forewarned."

Edwards brought Eaker to Devers's office. "Sir," he said, "this is General Eaker, commanding the Eighth Air Force."

Eaker looked at Devers with trepidation. There was no sign of welcome or greeting. "Eaker, I want to tell you what your air people did to me." He repeated what his chief of staff had already said about being landed in southern Ireland instead of England with the possibility of being interned.

"I can sympathize with you, general, because that's what they did to me about six months ago."

Devers walked over and put his arm around Eaker. "Well, we'll survive it, won't we?"

"Indeed we will. The first thing I want you to do is come down to my headquarters and let us brief you about what our prospects, plans, and programs are. Then, I'd like you to go with me to Bomber Command and Fighter Command headquarters and meet the principal division and wing commanders. We are carrying the combat burdens for the air force at the present time, and we are very anxious to show you what we are doing. Without your support, we can't accomplish our mission."

Devers agreed, so the next day Eaker put on a parade for him with his headquarters troops. It was well done, and Devers acknowledged that they had done as well as any infantry outfit he had seen in recent years. In the following weeks, Devers flew with him to Eaker's various commands.

They developed a relationship that was invaluable to Eaker later because Devers often took Eaker's side against Arnold, Spaatz, and Eisenhower. It soon became known that anyone who disagreed with Eaker had to reckon with Devers.

Air Marshal Harris frequently took Eaker up to Chequers to visit Churchill. These opporunities gave Eaker a chance to observe the prime minister in his relationship with British war leaders and to meet visiting delegations from the United States.

He was present when Lieutenant General Joseph T. McNarney and an administrator stopped off in England en route to Russia to brief Joseph Stalin about Allied war plans. After they took off, Churchill invited the assembled representatives of Britain's services and Eaker to join him for dinner. Now that Eisenhower and Spaatz were gone to North Africa, and Devers wasn't able to attend, Eaker was the ranking American military officer.

It was after 11:00 P.M. before the meal was served and cigars and brandy were passed around.

Churchill decided to play a game. He gave each member of the group at the table a name of a member of the German High Command or one of Hitler's principal subordinates.

When he got to Eaker, he said, "You are Göring."

Then, he pulled a small lock of hair down on his forehead and twisted it into a curlicue. He beat his chest and loudly proclaimed, "I am Hitler! Now, gentlemen, what do we do?"

When it came time for Eaker to speak as Göring, Churchill berated him for not being able to overcome the pitiful little British Fighter Command in the Battle of Britain.

After each had told Churchill as Hitler what should be done in order to win the war against the Allies, Churchill pushed back his chair. It was now 4:00 A.M., and an old butler drew aside the blackout curtain to let the first light drift in with the fog.

"Well, gentlemen," Churchill said, "if I have been correctly advised, we now know what the devils will do so we can circumvent them. Thank you very much."

These sessions were invaluable to Eaker in maintaining relationships with his British counterparts. He considered Churchill a genius because he could get the most out of his subordinates. His personality was such that he created confidence even under the direst circumstances. Eaker could never understand how he could work sixteen to eighteen hours a day and still be able to get to the heart of a matter.

He also got to know Portal better during these sessions. He considered him one of the truly great minds of the Combined Chiefs of Staff, with a rare ability to get along with others.

Portal's plan for a bomber offensive, which he had submitted to the British chiefs of staff November 2, was strongly endorsed December 31. The recommendations called for a joint American and British bomber force of three thousand medium and heavy bombers to operate from bases in the United Kingdom by the end of the new year of 1943.

8

A DRASTIC CHANGE
IN THE WAR'S DIRECTION

The Eighth Air Force started 1943 by organizing into a Bomber Command, a Fighter Command, an Air-Ground Support Command, and a Service Command.

Bomber Command consisted of three wings: the first with B-17s, the second with B-24s, and the third, which originally had been a B-26 medium-bomber wing and was now equipped with B-17s.

When Major General Ira Eaker had succeeded Spaatz as commanding general of the Eighth Air Force the previous November, Brigadier General Newton Longfellow moved up from head of the First Bombardment Wing to take over command of Bomber Command, and he was replaced by Brigadier General Laurence Kuter. Brigadier General James Hodges was placed in command of the Second Wing, and Brigadier General Haywood S. Hansell, Jr., was named to head the Third Wing.

Kuter soon realized that single groups lacked adequate defensive firepower in penetrating Germany's air defenses and that a full wing with four groups was too cumbersome to fly formation on a single leader. Therefore, he proposed a "field" organization of combat wings, consisting of two to three groups each, and Eaker gave his approval.

On his first mission to the submarine pens at Saint-Nazaire, on the third of January, General Hansell flew with a crew from the 91st Group. In order not to disrupt the combat crew, he stood between Colonel Stanley Wray and his copilot so that he could observe what was going on. He was distressed by the poor organization of the four groups, particularly because the formations did not relate to one another, and each was different.

Spitfires covered the bombers up to their fuel limits and then had to leave for home. German fighters, which stayed away from the formations until the escorting British fighters had to depart, then drew ahead, turned 180 degrees, and made head-on level attacks.

Hansell watched with concern as German fighters bored in where the B-17 defensive firepower was weakest. At times, the fighters seemed bent on head-on collisions, and Hansell watched the FW-190s and ME-109s come in with yellow blinking lights on their wings as German pilots fired cannons.

As German fighters tore through their formations, Hansell noted that his gunners had opened fire too soon and fired with extremely poor accuracy. It was apparent the Germans knew that the top turret guns on the Fortresses could not be depressed below the horizontal, so they made their attacks at the same level or slightly below the bombers. Once a Flying Fortress was crippled, fighters pounced upon it. Despite the savage attacks, the bombers never faltered, even when seven out of eighty-five B-17s over the target plummeted to earth. Hansell's lead flight caught the brunt of the attack, and two of his wingmen were lost. Unfortunately, courage was not sufficient to achieve bombing accuracy, which was too erratic for serious damage to the target.

Hansell went along on a second mission to Saint-Nazaire, flying this time with Colonel James Wallace of the 303rd Group, a former classmate at flying school. This mission was even worse because they lost two bombers in the lead flight, and two more in the next flight. While German tactics remained the same, there was no improvement in performance by the American groups. They persisted in operating separately, so the entire operation was ragged and exposed the bombers to ground and air attacks too long. This time, there were more German fighters in opposition, and the flak was intense. Hansell felt one shell strike their wing. On the ground later, they saw where it had passed through the wing but failed to explode.

The two raids were a painful experience for Hansell, and he called a meeting of the group commanders and set up a procedure that was followed for the next seven months. Hansell knew standard tactics had to be devised—and quickly—from which no deviation would be tolerated, in order to control a bomber force that could stick together for mutual defense and accomplish its mission. At the same time, he realized, combat commanders had to keep learning from experience. They simply could not afford to make the same mistake twice. Hansell reviewed tactics of his wing and discussed procedures with his group commanders after each mission. When changes were necessary, they were made quickly and Eaker supported him. Once changes were agreed upon, they became mandatory until after the next mission.

Hansell realized that his first task was to approve a standard formation. On the Saint-Nazaire mission, each of the four groups had flown a different formation. After heated arguments, a basic formation was adopted, which was a compromise of the one used by the 305th and 306th Groups. This standard formation was a "javelin" type—later called a "combat box"—made up of three squadrons of six airplanes each. Squadrons were echeloned in altitude; one squadron flew higher than the lead squadron, with the third underneath. On turns, the high squadron simply slid across the top of the lead squadron, and the lower squadron slid under. This formation provided excellent maneuverability and assured good firepower to the rear and to the flanks. It also improved firepower for frontal attacks. The most vulnerable position was that of the lower squadron during attacks from the front, since the B-17's forward turrets could not fire below the horizontal. Another consequence was that the higher squadron could not provide supporting fire for the bottom element.

A number of different formations were tried in combat before this one was adopted. On one operation, sixty B-17s had actually flown in a single formation on one leader, but such a formation was much too unwieldy. It was found that a more satisfactory solution was to make up large formations in units of combat boxes, each under its own leader.

Another tactical requirement was for standardization of control for forces larger than a combat wing. At Saint-Nazaire, the groups had been so widely separated that there was no mutual advantage for defense.

The "trial by combat" of the standard formation indicated that it was sound. Later, as the Eighth Air Force grew in size, the "combat wing" was increased to three boxes of eighteen bombers each. These boxes were arranged by altitude in a wing of fifty-four aircraft that formed on a single leader for mutual defense. The great offensive formations that were assembled later were columns of these combat boxes, which flew at altitudes of twenty-one thousand to twenty-seven thousand feet.

Hansell's next major problem was to improve bombing techniques to assure greater accuracy. Only the lead bombardier used his bombsight, and all other airplanes had to drop their bombs in salvo with the lead airplane. Hansell ordered all sights removed except in the lead and deputy-lead planes, and gun mounts were improvised that mounted twin flexible .50-caliber guns in the nose of each B-17 without bombsights. This was a drastic field modification, which would not have been approved by Wright Field specialists, but Eaker agreed to it.

At the initial point, combat wings divided into boxes of eighteen aircraft. Bombing runs were made straight in to the target from this initial point regardless of flak or fighters, a maneuver suggested by Colonel Curtis E. LeMay to improve bombing accuracy. At the rally point, after the bombs were dropped, combat wings reassembled to fight their way home.

Automatic flight control equipment had been standard on all bombers.

When it was connected to the bombsight, the bombardier actually flew the airplane on his run to the target. Each time he made a correction on his bombsight, the equipment automatically moved the bomber's control surfaces.

Hansell learned that it was difficult to force pilots of lead aircraft to submit to this procedure. Early automatic pilots were sluggish at high altitudes, where the extreme cold often stiffened the equipment's lubricants. In some cases, gyros would precess and start to throw the aircraft out of control. Pilots did have an override system, but they weren't happy with the procedure until the equipment was installed with better lubricants and heaters for the autopilots.

Hansell well understood a pilot's reluctance to turn his airplane—and in fact an eighteen-plane formation—over to a bombardier who was not a pilot. A bombardier's main concern was getting bombs on the target, so he viewed his surroundings through the restricted field of his bombsight's telescope and often was oblivious of the formation's bombers fighting their way through intensive German fighter attacks. It took all of Hansell's disciplinary power to get pilots to agree to use their automatic pilots. When they did, bombing accuracy was greatly improved. During the first nine months of 1943, only 24 percent of all bombs were dropped within 1,130 feet of their aiming points. That error was reduced to 820 feet during the period from October 1, 1943, to March 1, 1944.

Colonel LeMay proved to be the most successful of the early group commanders because he was a stern taskmaster. His 305th Group got more bombs on target than the others, and they came home with fewer losses.

He insisted that a tight formation be flown at all times so that guns could be brought to bear on enemy fighters. If his group flew a ragged formation on a mission, he often made them fly again as soon as possible and hammered away at their weaknesses.

After Hansell left England in October 1943 to become the air member of the Joint Plans Committee of the Joint Chiefs of Staff, he learned that Frank Armstrong, one of his combat wing commanders, had told members of the wing that Hansell had supported suicidal missions that had resulted in unnecessarily high losses. Armstrong implied that if he had been in charge he would have opposed such tough missions until a sufficient force was available.

Hansell felt that the "fatal weakening" of Nazi Germany could not be achieved by attacking unimportant targets, nor could the Eighth be fashioned and tempered into a decisive, war-winning tool without tackling vital and dangerous missions. Eaker, in carrying out the strategy of the Joint Chiefs, attacked tough targets. Hansell lent his full support to Eaker's decisions. He felt that Armstrong's job, as a combat-wing commander, was to do the same, and not to undermine the determination of the combat crews.

Kuter was transferred to North Africa January 1 to become deputy to Air Marshal Sir Arthur "Maori" Coningham, commander in chief of the Allied Tactical Air Forces.

Hansell then was transferred from the Third Wing to the First Wing, which was also equipped with B-17s. Under Hansell were Colonel Frank Armstrong and the 101st Combat Wing and his 306th Group, and Colonel Stanley Wray's 91st Group. Colonel LeMay commanded the 102nd Combat Wing, plus his own group, and Lieutenant Colonel John de Roussy's 303rd Group.

Creation of the Twelfth Air Force had stripped some of the Eighth's best groups; those left behind in England were too small in number to have a significant impact upon primary targets in Germany. They did develop the basic tactics and doctrines for air combat in the heat of battle. When the promised flow of new groups began to arrive later, they were fortunate to have battle-tested tactics and uniform doctrines already established.

Eaker permitted his early combat commanders great latitude in the field. He reserved only the right to approve those tactics that had been proved in combat, and authorized the successful ones as rigid standards for his entire command.

The tactics, techniques, and standard operating procedures that Hansell and his group commanders developed and proved in combat during the first half of 1943 later permitted control of large forces during penetration of German air and ground defenses.

About every two weeks, Churchill visited Harris's Bomber Command, and Hansell and other members of his staff were occasionally invited to these "morale" sessions. The climax of each of the prime minister's visits was a dinner in a big hall with a roaring fireplace at one end. Churchill had a special table with a bottle of scotch in the center. After dinner, he would talk about the progress of the war, pacing back and forth, while his audience watched spellbound. At times, he seemed to be having a conversation with himself. There would be long pauses while he sought just the right word to express his thoughts. Hansell was enthralled by these sessions and grateful that he had a chance to participate.

Eaker now realized that American claims of German fighters destroyed by bomber crews were unintentionally inflated. On January 5 he issued new regulations so that a more accurate appraisal of German losses could be made. Henceforth, he said, an enemy plane would be counted destroyed only if it was seen to go down in flames, not if flames were just coming out of an engine. Since the Germans were flying over their own territory, he knew that many partially crippled fighters could still make safe landings. A claim would be approved, however, if a fighter disintegrated or the pilot was seen to bail out. This rule was not fool-proof, and claims continued to be too high.

It was learned after the war that German reports to Hitler of Ameri-can and British bomber losses were often inflated. Actually, many of such reports were not deliberate and were due primarily to conflicting and overlapping claims. Göring insisted that each fighter commander report claims within two hours of a battle. Inasmuch as German fighters often landed at fields all over Germany, it was impossible to report an accurate count in such a short time.

German defenses against British night attacks improved slowly. At first, a belt of searchlights was set up along typical approach routes, but they failed to illuminate the bombers so night fighters could attack them successfully. Later, early-warning stations along the coast improved the Nazi defense system, but the equipment in use was so limited in range that British bombers merely climbed to higher altitudes before they reached the coastal defense zones, and dove through them at high speeds to reduce the time German fighters could attack. When the British introduced bomber streams, even German ground control found it im-possible to direct a fighter to a particular bomber. German fighter pilots found rear attacks on bombers deadly because 50 to 70 percent of such attacks resulted in their being shot down. After German fighters were equipped with airborne radar sets in late 1942, British bomber losses started to increase.

Day and night, Allied fighters were almost immune to attack by German fighters because Göring had ordered his fighter pilots to attack bombers only. Time and time again German fighter pilots insisted that they be given a chance to attack Allied fighters, but their requests were always denied. As a result, as the war went on, and German fighter losses increased, pilot morale plummeted.

One of Hitler's gravest mistakes in 1942 was to ignore requests from some of his commanders to place Germany on the defensive, and admit that the Russian invasion had failed. If he had done so, the fighter arm could have increased its 1,000-to-1,200-fighter command to 4,000, and there is little doubt that such a defensive force could have inflicted catastrophic losses on Allied air fleets. The American and British air offensive would have been canceled, thereby precluding an invasion of the Continent.

Air Marshal Harris at first had resisted formation of pathfinder groups for his Bomber Command, and when he finally agreed to establish them he chose Group Captain Donald Bennett as air officer to command 8 Group. Most crew members didn't like this aloof young Australian and criticized Harris's choice because Bennett had no administrative background, but he was an outstanding pilot and navigator.

Five pathfinder squadrons were operational by the start of 1943 after extensive special training. Harris had set forty-five missions for a tour of duty because pathfinder crew training was so expensive. Selected to command 5 Group was Air Vice-Marshal Sir Ralph Cochrane, a superb pilot who had already flown two bomber tours and was known for his feats of courage. He would become a wing commander at the age of twenty-six. As leader of 617 Squadron, he had pioneered precision marking and understood the techniques of bombing better than other British airmen. Now he was given an assignment where his skills were vitally needed.

A drastic change in the war's direction was noticeable in early 1943. A year before, the Axis powers had been able to dictate the time and place for each battleground. Now, the situation was reversed; Germany, Italy, and Japan were on the defensive.

Such a change was not due to the efforts of the United States Army, which had less than one field army in contact with the Axis powers throughout the world. The United States Navy had won important battles in the Pacific, such as those in the Coral Sea and at Midway, but the stalemate of enemy forces was due primarily to the efforts of the British and Russians whose victories at Stalingrad, El Alamein, and in Tunisia helped to turn the tide. This was no fault of the United States because it was still in the throes of a rapid expansion of its armed services, which were far from being totally mobilized.

Churchill, still upset with the Eighth Air Force because it had not yet dropped bombs on Germany, wrote Sinclair for an appraisal. Five days later, Sinclair replied for the British Air Ministry, saying he did not know when the Americans would start their bomber offensive on the Reich. He reminded the prime minister that the demands for United States Army Air Forces planes were heavy throughout the world, but that once large numbers of American bombers were available they would intensify their daylight bombing campaign. In his opinion, Sinclair said, day losses then would be no heavier than Royal Air Force losses at night. "The results, combined with night attacks, should be doubly effective."

Churchill found Sinclair's reply unacceptable, saying that words were meaningless without proof. "What I am going to discourage actively is the sending over of large quantities of these daylight bombers and their enormous ground staffs until the matter is settled one way or the other. It is much better for them to work in Africa."

These behind-the-scenes actions would have disturbed Eaker had he known about them. As it was, he suspected that Churchill was working constantly to force him to change over to night operations.

That winter in England, mud conditions were worse than ever. If a bomber wandered off a taxi strip the landing gear would sink to the wheel hubs, and it took a long time to get the plane out. If the lead plane got stuck, or one of the first in line for takeoff was mired, everyone behind was stranded because there was no way to turn around on the narrow taxiways.

One morning at Chelveston, the fog was like pea soup as LeMay prepared to take off for a mission with Lieutenant Russell Schleeh in the copilot's seat. He had told Schleeh to bring a flashlight so that he could spot the right-hand edge of the runway as they taxied out, explaining that if the plane was kept within two feet of the right side, there would be no trouble staying on the narrow strip.

Schleeh called out directions as they moved along, being careful to do just as LeMay advised. The colonel had said for months that any lead crew that ran off the taxiway, thereby aborting the mission, would catch hell from him.

Schleeh felt confident of his directions, and they seemed to be staying on the tarmac. Suddenly, the plane sank to its oleo struts.

LeMay started to chew Schleeh out because the mission had to be canceled.

"Damn it all, colonel," Schleeh said, "you ran off on *your* side!".

LeMay didn't live that one down for a long time.

On another occasion the weather was equally bad. Normally, if there was a half-mile visibility, the mission was approved. The practice was to send the most-senior pilot off first after jeeps were placed at the end of the runway with their lights on. A pilot then could set his directional gyro and fly a straight line at the lights, making his takeoff on instruments. This particular morning, the lead pilot called back after takeoff, "OK to take off here. Visibility at least five hundred yards."

In the tower, a voice was heard to say over the radio from another of the bombers, "I don't know what runway he took off on, but I can't even see my goddamn copilot."

Weather conditions such as these were bad enough for takeoffs, but even worse upon return in a shot-up condition, often with low fuel. Many times crews were more concerned about getting back than they were flying over Germany. With groups flying every which way over England, there was always the danger of collisions. A typical crew comment was that they'd rather get shot down over Germany than get killed over Great Britain. At least, they said, they'd have a chance of winding up in a prisoner-of-war camp.

When LeMay's 305th Group first had arrived in England in the late fall of 1942, he had told them they were not to fly across the Channel if anything on their plane was inoperable. "Don't try to be heroes. Abort." On the first two missions, a large number of crews turned back with one malfunction or another. When another mission was flown to Lille, and an exceptionally large number aborted, LeMay told the group, "I told you I'd court-martial you guys if you tried to be heroes, but now I'll court-martial the first guys who turn back without a damned good reason."

The crews thought this was funny and laughed appreciatively. Aborts dwindled after that, however.

9

BOMBING

AROUND THE CLOCK

President Roosevelt and Prime Minister Churchill met January 14 at Casablanca with the Combined Chiefs of Staff to decide what the next major steps should be against Italy and Germany. In the east, the ground situation had stablized with the Germans stopped before Stalingrad, and Marshal Rommel had been defeated at El Alamein in North Africa.

Among the decisions reached at the conference was the elevation of Eisenhower to Supreme Allied Commander, Mediterranean. General Devers was replaced as head of the European Theater of Operations by Lieutenant General Frank M. Andrews, a highly respected airman who —but for his untimely death a few months later in a Greenland air crash —might well have been Marshall's choice over Eisenhower as Supreme Allied Commander in England for the invasion of the Continent.

At the Casablanca Conference an Allied Air Forces, Northwest Africa, was formed under Lieutenant General Spaatz. Luftwaffe forces, although much smaller, had defeated Army Air Forces units because the Luftwaffe was centrally organized, while the United States Army Air Forces in the area were decentralized. United States Army ground forces had suffered unnecessarily because of inadequate American air support. Marshal Bernard Montgomery, who had earlier learned the value of unified air control in tactical support of ground troops, recommended unified command of available air forces. Improvement was noted almost immediately.

The previous November, Churchill had argued in favor of an attack against Italy, which he called Europe's "soft underbelly." Eisenhower, having just arrived in England, had been unsure of himself. Now he was no longer afraid to disagree with Churchill. At times, their disagreements were almost violent, but Eisenhower had learned one thing about the prime minister that was to stand him in good stead later on. He had developed a friendship with him, despite their disagreements, and found that once a decision was reached, Churchill forgot their previous disagreements.

Eisenhower considered Churchill a worthy adversary, one who never gave up until the final argument was laid to rest. Although he had a cherubic face, Churchill could be forbidding. His jutting chin and bulldog head—and ever-present cigar—made him a formidable-looking opponent. His moods could change quickly because he was an accomplished actor who, by words and gestures, had won many a tough political round long before World War II.

General Arnold spoke strongly against further expansion of the war in the Mediterranean. He told the conferees that the way to win the war was to hit Germany where it hurt most, where the source of her strength lay—in other words, right across the Channel from England, which Arnold considered the shortest route to Berlin. He said that the United States would soon have the airpower to destroy Germany's factories, communications, and supplies, as well as to defeat her air force; that airpower could isolate the coastline of Europe anywhere for a landing of Allied invasion troops; and that once command of the air was assured, any threat from the German air force would be minimal.

Portal agreed with the chief of the American air forces, having said much the same things since the start of the war. Admirals of the British and United States navies, however, rejected any such plans.

Churchill also was opposed. He spoke of a channel filled with the bodies of British soldiers. He often referred to the heavy casualties the British had suffered during the First World War in land battles on the Continent, and reminded his listeners what had happened during the Battle of France. He seemed haunted by the frailty of massed men against tanks, aircraft, and artillery.

Although Arnold and Portal were in agreement at Casablanca about the best way to attack Germany, they were in total disagreement about the best use of bombers. Portal thought day raids were suicidal, while Arnold continued to press for precision daylight strikes, believing that they were far more effective in destroying vital targets and that they could be accomplished without intolerable losses.

Arnold refused to recede from a strategy based upon a maximum effort by the Allies along the shortest possible route to the heart of Germany. He warned that further attacks in the Mediterranean, against Sicily and Italy, would stalemate the Allies against one of the hardest "underbellies" in the world. Inevitably, Arnold lost that argument because the American airpower buildup had barely begun and had not yet demonstrated the potential it would later.

Arnold continued to press for command unification of all strategic airpower in the United Kingdom and in the North Africa–Middle East theaters. He pointed out that bases in these areas would form an encircling "horseshoe" from which Allied airpower could strike at Axis Europe from whichever area had the best weather on any particular day for bombing a specific target. Arnold believed the plan would provide true strategic mobility, posing strains on the Italian and German air forces that would prove insurmountable in the long run. He found little favor for such a doctrine.

The Combined Chiefs went along with the British view that an overall air commander just for the Mediterranean should be established, and Sir Arthur Tedder was selected. A suave, handsome officer with strong prejudices that he never hesitated to express, Tedder proved intensely loyal to Eisenhower, and they became close friends. Associates could always tell the amount of emotion Tedder was feeling by the quantity of smoke rising from the pipe that was constantly in front of him. Under Tedder, Spaatz was named air commander for Northwest Africa, and Air Chief Marshal Sir William Sholto Douglas was named commander for the Middle East. Spaatz's command included the Western Desert Air Force, the Twelfth Air Force, and the Eastern Air Command.

The Combined Chiefs insisted that Spaatz divide his command into three major subcommands: a heavy and medium bomber force with escort fighters; a coastal air force for port and shipping protection; and a tactical air force or air support command. The last two would work in conjunction with General Sir Harold Alexander to help in the destruction of the Axis in North Africa.

The decisions reached at the conference reflected lessons recently learned in battle. Shortly after Eisenhower's forces entered Algiers, he had called Spaatz to his command post. He reminded him that, by the day's intelligence reports, Rommel had five hundred planes. "You have four hundred American planes, the British have two hundred, and the French another one hundred. That's seven hundred. Why is it every time Rommel attacks us we get the hell beat out of us?"

"I thought I had explained that to you," Spaatz said. "Every time Rommel attacks, I'm outnumbered five to four. Every time he attacks the British, he outnumbers them five to two. When Rommel attacks the French, he outnumbers them five to one. That's all wrong. The air forces should never be partitioned. They should be kept together."

"I get the message, Tooey. From now on, every airplane we have in the theater is under your operational control."

It was the last battle Rommel ever won in Africa.

At the start of the Casablanca Conference, Churchill had spoken to President Roosevelt about stopping daytime bombing and joining the

Royal Air Force in night attacks. Arnold was upset because he had always considered the Royal Air Force and the Eighth Air Force as complementing each other. He never considered them as competitive. He was concerned, therefore, to learn that Churchill's arguments had found a receptive ear with the president, and that Roosevelt was inclined to discontinue daylight bombing.

A few hours later, in England, a motorcycle courier came up to Eaker's house with a message. When decoded, it turned out that it was from Arnold. "Meet me in Casablanca." Eaker had not even known that there was a conference under way, due to the strict secrecy.

He called in his bomber commander, Newton Longfellow. "I have to go down to Casablanca. Give me a B-17 crew that is not standing by for a combat mission to take me down there. I'll be at Bovingdon at midnight." In the cold of a late January night, Eaker met his pilot, Captain William Smith, at the headquarters field, warming up a noncombat B-17. . . .

Eaker's plane was met the next morning at Casablanca at 10:00 A.M., January 19, by Arnold's aide, Colonel Gene Beebe, who took him to a villa.

Arnold was shaving when Eaker walked in. He greeted Eaker by saying, "I've got bad news for you, son. Prime Minister Churchill has talked President Roosevelt into having the Eighth Air Force discontinue daylight bombing and join the British in the night effort."

"General, that makes no sense at all. In the first place, we've been trained to do daylight bombing. We'll lose more people coming into that fog-shrouded island at four o'clock in the morning than we lose over Germany in the daytime. Number two, our airplanes shoot a flame out of each of their four engines that can be seen for a hundred miles at night. The night fighters will knock them out. It will take months to make the necessary engineering changes, and crews will have to retrain for night operations. Bear in mind, also, that we are keeping German defenses up twenty-four hours a day. There are a million men standing on the Westwall just to defend themselves against these one hundred bombers."

Arnold turned to him. "I'll tell you what I'll do. I will make a date for you, if I can, and I think I can, to see the prime minister. I've heard him tell the president that he has a high regard for you. If you can't get him to change his mind, we're sunk."

The next morning, Eaker went to Churchill's villa, which was an attractive part of the Anfa House compound. He waited nervously for the prime minister in a large living room that had a tall glass window looking out on a beautiful orange grove.

Promptly at ten o'clock, Churchill came down a stairway with the sun shining through the windows illuminating his air commodore's uniform.

Eaker thought this was a good omen, knowing that Churchill usually wore the uniform of the branch of service of the man he planned to interview.

The prime minister immediately came to the point. "General Arnold tells me that you are unhappy about giving up daylight bombing and joining us in night bombing."

"Yes, sir. In my year of service with your forces, I have heard that you always hear each side of a case before you make a decision. I've set down here, on one page, the reasons why I think it would be unfortunate for us to give up daylight bombing. All I ask is that you read this."

Churchill took the paper, sat down on a couch, and motioned Eaker to sit beside him. He said that he was concerned because so few American missions had been flown, and that the Americans had been operational for five months and had not yet dropped a bomb on German territory.

Eaker replied that only one convincing argument had ever been advanced for night versus day bombing, and that was that it was safer. "In point of fact," he said, "the Eighth Air Force's rate of loss in day raids has been lower than that of the Royal Air Force on its night operations."

Eaker emphasized that day bombing, regardless of safety, could do things that night bombing could not. He pointed out that day bombers could hit small, important targets such as individual factories that cannot be found, seen, or hit at night.

He said he estimated that American accuracy was five times better than the best night bombing due to the excellent bombsight in the American bombers. As a result, he said, day bombing tends to be more economical than night raids because a force of only one fifth the size was needed to destroy a given target.

In his considered judgment, Eaker said, Eighth Air Force operations by day would be most economical in reducing German air strength because Nazi leaders would have to use more and more of their fighter strength to defend vital objectives.

Churchill then fired off a series of questions. Why had there been so many abortive sorties? Why had there been so few missions? Why should United States bombers and those of the RAF not be given the same directives and the same targets? Why had United States bombers not bombed Germany?

Eaker explained patiently. He said there were many reasons for the Eighth's limited operations, including inexperienced crews, loss of planes and crews to support the North African invasion, bad weather during the fall and early winter months, diversion of his command to attacks against submarine pens and bases, and lack of escort fighters. He assured the prime minister that these were temporary problems that would be overcome. He said the Combined Chiefs could resolve many of the problems faced by the Eighth Air Force—by relieving his command from nonproductive strategic operations against the submarine menace, for example.

He sought Churchill's support for an *intensified* bombing campaign in daylight against Germany. He told him that if high priority was given for such missions deep inside Germany, her defenses would be scattered. By alternating day attacks with RAF night raids, the Allies could cause the German civilian population such hardships that Hitler's war effort would be undermined. He said that if he was given a force of one hundred heavy bombers and one hundred fighters, he would carry the war to Germany by February 1. He said further that if Eisenhower no longer needed the entire strength of the Eighth Air Force, a directive should be issued that was more in line with the strategic situation in northwestern Europe. It was his belief, he said, that Eisenhower now had an adequate air force for his operations, so target directives henceforth should be issued by the chief of staff of the RAF or the Combined Chiefs instead of Eisenhower.

Eaker reminded Churchill that day-bombing raids imposed a severe strain upon the Luftwaffe, despite American losses, because the accumulation of German losses would eventually decimate the German air force.

He concluded by saying that conversion of a trained daylight bombing force, such as the Eighth, into a night force would be so time-consuming that the war's outcome would be affected. Such training, he said, undoubtedly would cause more casualties than his command would otherwise suffer in combat on daytime missions.

Churchill remained silent as he perused the paper Eaker had given him. Eaker kept quiet, knowing he had said all he could in defense of the American concept of strategic bombing.

Eaker noticed the prime minister was reading half aloud. When he came to where Eaker had written, "If the RAF continues at night, and the Americans by day, we shall bomb them around the clock, and they will get no rest." He repeated "bombing around the clock," and reread Eaker's words, wherein he said, "Bear in mind that by your intelligence estimates, a million men are standing on the Westwall to defend against our bomber effort. These defenders—fire fighters—can be greatly reduced if we stop daylight bombing." He paused, and then read those last words again slowly.

Churchill put down the paper and turned to face Eaker. "General, I want you to know that the reason I have taken this position is because I have been heartsick because of your tragic losses. My mother was a United States citizen, so I'm half American. Marshal Harris tells me you are sometimes losing ten percent on a mission, while his losses are only two and a half percent. You've made a strong case here. While you have not convinced me that you are right, you have convinced me that you should have further opportunity to prove your case. When I see your president at lunch today, I shall tell him that I withdraw my suggestion that you discontinue your daylight bombing, and that you will not be joining the Royal Air Force in a night-bombing effort. I suggest that your Eighth Air Force continue this daylight-bombing experiment for a time."

Eaker breathed a sigh of relief. In more than one sense, he couldn't have asked for more.

The meeting with Eaker cleared up several points that had been troubling Churchill. Prior to this meeting, he had thought the Eighth Air Force had five hundred bombers and twenty thousand men in East Anglia. Actually, the bomber force was less than a hundred, because so many had been sent to North Africa.

Following the meeting, Eaker reported the results to Arnold, who replied, "You apparently have accomplished the purpose for which I sent you, and I suggest that you get back to England and prove your case."

Arnold turned now to an equally important matter: the search for agreement among the Combined Chiefs of Staff on the strategic conduct of the air war. Sir John Slessor wrote the directive to govern it, after hours of discussion with American aviators. Known as the "Casablanca Directive," it stated that the purpose of the air offensive against Germany was "to bring about the progressive destruction and dislocation of the German military, industrial, and economic systems, and undermine the morale of the German people to a point where their capacity for armed resistance is fatally weakened."

It was specifically approved by Prime Minister Churchill and President Roosevelt.

It should be understood that this was a war-winning concept, no longer just a plan for preliminary bombardment of Germany to make possible an invasion. Nothing was said about a cross-channel invasion of the Continent. In fact, at this point Churchill was strongly opposed to such an invasion. It appears that his support for a stepped-up air war was in fact given because he was against such an invasion and hoped that a successful strategic air offensive would make one unnecessary.

A few days after Eaker returned to London from Casablanca, he got a call from Commander C. R. "Tommy" Thompson, Churchill's naval aide, who said the prime minister was giving an address the next day in the House of Commons about the results of the Casablanca Conference. He said Churchill thought he might care to hear it.

Eaker told him he would be delighted, and Thompson advised him where to meet him the next morning.

Thompson guided Eaker to a seat in the visitors' gallery of the House of Commons. He watched with growing excitement as Churchill strode to the podium.

It was a dramatic moment for Eaker as the now familiar voice held everyone's attention. At one point, Churchill said, "It was there decided that our gallant RAF shall continue their effective night bombing, and the courageous Americans will continue their daylight bombing. We shall bomb the devils round the clock 'til they get no rest." As he mentioned the words "round the clock," he looked at Eaker in the gallery, as if to say, "If this is plagiarism, you must admit I acknowledge the author."

Eaker could now feel certain that his arguments at Casablanca had not been in vain. Churchill had saved the daylight-bombing campaign. Soon, with the long-range fighter escorts he knew were being readied, their bomber losses would come down. Now, more than ever, Eaker realized that the Casablanca Conference had been not only critical for the American air effort, but the turning point in the air war.

Eaker authorized the first attack against Germany January 27.

Colonel Frank Armstrong led the B-24 attack along a North Sea route to hit the submarine plants at Vegesack, thirty miles up the Weser River. He found the primary target covered by clouds and diverted the formations to the port of Wilhelmshaven, where little flak was encountered, but fighters attacked on their way home. One B-24 was shot down in a rather inauspicious beginning for the Eighth over Germany.

On another mission, Eaker became upset with Brigadier General Robert Williams. Americans had been told repeatedly they would be court-martialed if they dropped bombs on civilians. During a diversionary attack by fifty bombers on fighter fields at Brussels, the formation flew over the city and mistakenly dropped bombs on a residential area. While the main force hit the harbor at Saint-Nazaire, the first Wing used the best approach to the airfield on the edge of Brussels by flying directly over it. (This decision was made because there were fewer antiaircraft batteries along this flight path.)

An investigation was held by Eaker to determine if any action should be taken against General Williams for the bombing of a residential area. After it was determined that the area was occupied solely by Germans, and that no Belgiums were either injured or killed, Eaker decided there was no necessity to pursue the matter further.

After the Vegesack mission, Harris sent his congratulations to Bomber Commander Longfellow. "This opens a campaign the Germans have long dreaded. To them, it is yet another ominous sentence of the writing on the wall. To Bomber Command, it is concrete and most welcome proof that we shall no longer be alone in carrying the war to German soil."

Harris's words were sincere. He had never criticized the Americans for their late start in bombing the Reich. To intimates, he said they should not have "short memories," reminding them that it had taken British Bomber Command two years to become effective, and that Eaker and his small staff had arrived in England only the year before without either crews or bombers.

Arnold, in Washington, was not as considerate. He continued to demand better performance by the Eighth Air Force, angrily telling Eaker there were far too few missions and too many aborts.

Eaker tried to explain February 26, reminding Arnold that his command had only received twenty-four crews and sixty-three replacement aircraft during a period when his command had lost seventy-five planes and their crews. In defense of the number of missions, Eaker said he felt obliged to save planes until weather conditions were such as to permit maximum operations.

While Curtis LeMay was head of the 305th Group, he named Major Henry H. Macdonald as commander of the 364th Squadron.

Typically, he imparted the news to the new squadron commander in an unorthodox manner. While Macdonald was sipping a drink at the club's bar, LeMay walked up behind him and kicked him in the behind so hard it made his eyes water.

"That's just a warning of what I expect from you when you're the new commander of the Three-sixty-fourth." In other words, he intended to kick ass until the squadron was straightened out.

They had both been concerned by the inaccuracy of firing hand-held guns, knowing that gunners were liable to shoot down their own formation's planes. Neither blamed the gunners for their inaccuracies because they knew they had had so little practice in training, including the firing of computing gun turrets. It had become all too apparent that gunners were unable to control the size of the reticles on their gunsights so that proper distances and lead angles could be computed.

Macdonald decided to give them some practice. Every day his squadron wasn't on a mission, it was roused out of bed early to make bomber attacks against a target towed by the group's A-20 light bomber. He flew the airplane himself after a gunnery range halfway across the Channel was set aside. Each time Macdonald circled ahead and turned toward the bomber formation. Then, he flew right through it in order to involve the gunners in the toughest speed and tracking problems, just as German fighters had been doing to such deadly effect against their bomber formations.

The second time up, Macdonald's tow operator reported that the reel had jammed, so the target was out only four hundred yards below the A-20, instead of the usual one thousand yards. Macdonald had no radio to call the bombers, so he decided to go ahead with target practice. He believed four hundred yards was a sufficiently safe distance and that gunners couldn't possibly miss that much.

On the sixth pass, a gunner on one of the bombers sent a burst right through the A-20; one shell hit Macdonald in the back, while his windshield exploded in front of him.

In excruciating pain, Macdonald flew back to England and landed at the first available base. He was proud of himself for getting the airplane safely on the ground, despite the facts that he was about to pass out and that the accidental gunburst had blown one of his tires.

While they were putting him in an ambulance, a young American driver, unfamiliar with the British car, put the gearshift into reverse instead of forward, and the ambulance smashed into the back of the airplane, wrecking most of its tail section.

Despite his pain and shock, Macdonald was furious. Wounded by his own men, he had landed the plane safely, only to have it seriously damaged by an incompetent driver on the ground.

At the Casablanca Conference, agreement had been reached to invade Sicily and to delay the cross-channel invasion of the Continent until 1944. Of these decisions, Roosevelt said, "Germany will be given Allied priority until the Allies beat them into unconditional surrender."

Although Arnold had lost his bid to get a unified air commander for his "horseshoe" attacks against Germany and Italy, he considered himself fortunate that a combined bomber offensive had been approved: Eaker's Eighth Air Force no longer would be required to support operations in the Mediterranean. The separation of theaters was not formalized until February 4 when the Mediterranean Theater of Operations was established under Eisenhower and American forces in England were placed under Lieutenant General Frank M. Andrews, who was transferred from the Middle East. Responsibility for the air offensive against Germany fell to Sir Charles Portal who, as agent for the Combined Chiefs, directed it for the rest of 1943.

Target priorities were established, with German submarine construction yards given top priority, followed by the aircraft industry, transportation, and oil fields and plants.

The American Joint Chiefs of Staff were offense-minded and had opposed further operations in the Mediterranean after the North African invasion. In their opinion, steps such as the invasion of Sicily, and later Italy, would do little to advance the destruction of Germany's military might, and would prove costly. Events later proved the soundness of their judgment. The Joint Chiefs believed that Allied efforts should be used to attack the heart of Germany by air and land. The British resisted. They believed, at this stage of the war, that a viable alternative to a cross-channel invasion in 1943 was the Combined Bomber Offensive, supported by further amphibious landings in the Mediterranean.

Arnold, Eaker, and Spaatz were pleased that the Americans had been successful in getting the heaviest possible bomber offensive against the German war effort. They were dismayed, however, that continued advances in the Mediterranean would divert resources from the Eighth Air Force and delay United States implementation of its part in the bomber offensive until June.

The American Committee of Operations Analysts (COA) had been endeavoring to draw up priority target lists since Arnold had given them the task December 9, 1942. Their biggest problem had been constant changes in overall strategy for the conduct of a two-front war. With varying viewpoints, and conflicts between the United States Army, Navy, and Air Forces, analysts in the past had never been certain whether target selection should be based upon aerial destruction of German war capability as a primary goal, or air support for an invasion. Now, the Casablanca Directive gave them specific guidelines, so there no longer was confusion as to the ultimate objective to be achieved by the Allied powers.

In March 1943, the COA submitted its initial report. They listed sixty targets, the destruction of which, in their opinion, would gravely impair or paralyze Germany's war efforts. The targets were listed in priority from the standpoint of effect. Military strategists would have to consider the feasibility of destroying each, the size force required, the probable losses, and the influence of time. From this list they would have to select their primary targets. The report minced no words. "Only the most vital considerations should be permitted to delay or divert the application of an adequate striking force to this task."

Arnold ordered Eaker to prepare plans for the American part of the Combined Bomber Offensive (CBO). The head of the Eighth Air Force found his task much easier because now he didn't have to argue every point with army and navy officials. Despite little cooperation from the army and navy, neither of which understood the plan or fully supported it, Marshall and Arnold approved it.

On March 23, Colonel Charles Cabell, one of Arnold's special advisers, brought Eaker the list of potential targets that had been prepared by the Committee of Operations Analysts. Eaker's own planning teams used them to prepare a strategic operational plan within the capabilities of the Eighth Air Force.

Eaker assigned Brigadier General Hansell, commanding the First

Bombardment Wing, to direct the planning team. Brigadier General Frederick Anderson, commanding the newly arrived Fourth Bombardment Wing, was assigned to Hansell to assist him. Air Chief Marshal Sir Charles Portal provided Air Commodore Sidney O. Bufton, the able director of the Air Ministry's bomber operations. These were the key people, but there were others who played roles in drawing up the plan for the Combined Bomber Offensive for the United Kingdom. It differed from the American AWPD-42 plan because this was a capability plan drawn up with the resources then available in England. In other words, the CBO plan was specific in its instructions as to what could actually be accomplished to achieve objectives with available forces, and those that would be committed later.

With two important exceptions, the original American air plan was followed in the new one. The exceptions included the addition of antifriction bearing plants to the list of targets and elimination of electric power plants, which had been dropped to thirteenth priority on the list provided by the COA. Transportation and synthetic petroleum targets were retained.

The British Ministry of Economic Warfare endorsed the targets, giving the German aircraft industry and ball-bearing plants first and second priority before attention could be switched to other industrial targets.

The British had learned an important lesson after the devastating German attack against the city of Coventry. A major aircraft engine factory there had suffered only superficial damage, but most of the glass windows were blown out, and before they could be replaced, it rained heavily. Ball-bearing trays were soaked and immediately started to rust, making the bearings unusable. To the consternation of the factory manager, there were no reserve bearings in stock, so engine production had to be discontinued despite minimal damage to the factory.

The production halt was only temporary, of course, but economic experts at the Air Ministry speculated what might have occurred if *all* ball-bearing factories had been destroyed. It was an intriguing thought, and one that led air planners to consider such German targets as a top priority. They were aware that factories in Sweden and Switzerland might be able to supply some of the lost bearings if German factories were destroyed, but they didn't believe such assistance would be substantial.

The plan Hansell and his committee drew up was in four phases. The first, with 800 Allied bombers available in July, had to be limited to the range of escort fighters—with one exception. The ball-bearing factories at Schweinfurt were considered so important that attacks were planned despite the fact that the targets were beyond the range of escort fighters. For the second series of attacks starting in October, when it was hoped to have 1,192 bombers, targets were selected that were within 400 miles of English bases. On January 1, 1944, with an anticipated 1,746 heavy bombers available, the depth of attacks would be increased to 500 miles. In the fourth phase, the available 2,702 bombers would be limited only by their operating radius, which should encompass practically all targets in Nazi-occupied Europe.

Hansell assured Eaker that if these numbers of bombers were available on the dates indicated, and were not diverted to other tasks, it would be possible to carry out the mission prescribed by the Casablanca Directive by the spring of 1944. If they were not available, the mission could not be accomplished until mid-1944 or later.

Eaker liked the plan and Lieutenant General Andrews, European theater commander, gave his endorsement.

Simultaneously, the Royal Air Force members of Hansell's committee submitted their recommendations to the British Air Ministry.

Cabell, Arnold's adviser in Washington, told Eaker that regardless of who drew up the plan, Hansell was not to present it to the Joint Chiefs of Staff for final approval. Cabell said Hansell had been persona non grata to the United States Navy ever since he had taken a thousand bombers out of the original navy plans despite navy insistence they be included.

Eaker called Hansell into his office. "I want to give this plan precisely as you have given it to me and General Andrews." Hansell had presented it orally. "Sit down, and write it out, not just what's in the plan, but your explanation of every point in it, and I'll study it."

Hansell underlined the items in the plan, and also presented the arguments he had used for their adoption.

Eaker memorized everything on short notice. When he appeared before the Joint Chiefs, he did so without notes. His presentation was so thorough that he was commended for it.

Arnold said afterward, "Evidently you were convincing because I can see we are going to approve the new plan."

It wasn't adopted by the Combined Chiefs until May 18, 1943. Unfortunately, a sentence was added to the original Casablanca Directive that led to considerable confusion. The original had referred to the "progressive destruction and dislocation of the German military, industrial, and economic system, and undermining of German morale to the point where their capacity for armed resistance would be fatally weakened." To this, someone had added, "This is construed as meaning so weakened as to permit initiation of final combined operations on the Continent."

By itself, the change didn't seem at the time to do more than clarify the original statement. In effect, however, it raised doubts as to the basic purpose of the Combined Bomber Offensive. To understand the meaning, one has to keep in mind that "undermining the morale of the German people" was considered by the RAF's Bomber Command as the significant clause that gave meaning to "the point where their capacity for armed resistance would be fatally weakened." In other words, the RAF considered such a statement as strengthening their case for area bombing at night.

The United States Strategic Air Forces viewed the words in an entirely different light—namely, the light of day. To them, the "progressive destruction and dislocation of the German military, industrial, and economic system" was the path to the "fatal weakening," which could best be achieved by destroying selected targets in Germany. "Fatal weakening," in the views of American airmen, meant collapse of the entire German state.

The final addition to the directive left the question, "Is this a decisive war-winning objective, or is it simply a preliminary bombardment to insure success of the invasion?"

Their disagreements were tactical ones. Actually, airmen on both sides agreed on strategic objectives. They were almost alone in their belief that airpower could be decisive against Germany. Army and navy men on both sides, including Churchill and Roosevelt, believed that airpower's basic objective was to prepare the way for an invasion of the Continent. For them, the term "fatal weakening" meant disruption and dislocation of German military might to reduce its effectiveness in opposing such an invasion.

After the Combined Chiefs approved the plan at the Trident Conference in Washington May 18, 1943, Sir Charles Portal was told to proceed with the Combined Bomber Offensive. However, it wasn't until June 10 —six months after Casablanca—that the coordinated efforts of the Eighth Air Force by day and the Royal Air Force by night could launch their parallel efforts.

10

COMBINED BOMBER OFFENSIVE

Despite the great goals established by the Casablanca Conference for the Combined Bomber Offensive, the daily necessity for routine harassment of Germany's U-boat fleet continued to make excessive demands on the limited number of bombers available for all operations.

British Bomber Command was ordered by Harris to lay mines with all groups, and not just 5 Group, whenever weather prohibited attacks on the Continent. Although such mining had been conducted throughout much of 1942, the most important phase was undertaken the previous November, before and during the invasion of North Africa, and frequently delayed U-boat sailings. Harris was convinced that minelaying helped to destroy more U-boats than did the attacks against their bases. Mine-laying, however, became an extremely hazardous occupation after the Germans placed large numbers of antiaircraft guns near important channels.

Industrial cities in northern Italy had been attacked to assist the North African invasion in late 1942. Bomber crews were able to bomb in daylight because Italian defenses on the ground and in the air were far inferior to German defenses on the rest of the Continent. The effect on Italian morale was enormous, and Mussolini called for nightly evacuation of all civilians in the affected areas.

The RAF attacked German U-boat shipyards in Germany whenever weather permitted, and fast Mosquito bombers raided a number of small targets in occupied countries, including one in Berlin by three planes that interrupted a speech by Göring and panicked the populace.

The first of a series of attacks authorized by the Casablanca Conference as part of the Combined Bomber Offensive had been made the night of March 6/7. The Casablanca Directive had given Air Marshal Harris full latitude to attack cities of one hundred thousand or more. He selected the Ruhr because it was the most important industrial area in Germany, and the first attack was set for Essen because it was the largest industrial center in that region.

Four hundred and forty-two bombers took part, with a pathfinder force of heavy bombers and eight Mosquito bombers equipped with an electronic device nicknamed Oboe because it emitted a bass tone. Bombers tuned into ground stations that transmitted a continuous signal so that navigators could plot their positions in the sky relative to a predetermined bomb-release point. Stations could transmit only up to 350 miles, so only the central Ruhr targets could use Oboe.

The large force crossed the Dutch coast and flew to a point fifteen miles north of Essen. Meanwhile the twenty-two heavy-bomber pathfinders moved into the target area and marked it with green markers on the ground as guides for the main force, and Mosquitoes marked with red indicators.

When the bombers swept in at the rate of eleven per minute, the weather was clear, although haze covered some of the factory areas. Bombardiers found the red indicators easier to spot, even though they were fewer in number. The bombing was good, and fires spread without a break until they covered an area two miles in diameter.

Harris called the mission a success because there were below-average losses of fourteen aircraft, and he saw no reason why such attacks could not be repeated against other Ruhr cities.

Lieutenant Jack W. Mathis, lead bombardier for the 303rd Group, studied the Bremen Vulkan shipbuilding yards as his formation approached Vegesack March 18, 1943. He was keyed up to a high pitch, knowing that so many counted on him to get their bombs on the target and make the mission worthwhile.

"Bomb bay doors open," he called, noting the heavy flak that burst around them. As he neared the bomb-release point, he noted nervously that the Germans were scoring hits, and *The Duchess* shuddered as flak blossomed so close he could see the red centers as each shell exploded.

While Mathis carefully synchronized his bombsight, a heavy piece of flak tore through the bombardier-navigation compartment, smashing a right window. He was hit and thrown violently against the navigator, and both men slammed into the bulkhead. Despite a shattered arm and mortal abdominal wounds, Mathis painfully crawled back to his bombsight, noting thankfully that it was not damaged. His seat, however, had been blown out of position. Bleeding terribly, he knelt over his sight, made quick last-minute corrections, and released his bombs. The navigator heard him say, "Bombs . . . " and that was all.

The navigator saw Mathis reaching for the bomb bay door retraction lever and, thinking the bombardier's intercom had merely been out, completed the call " . . . away."

Mathis failed to complete the call because he had died just after releasing the bombs, which landed on target. For his bravery he was awarded the Medal of Honor.

Mathis's brother Mark, who had been serving in medium bombers, requested transfer to his late brother's squadron, hoping to avenge his death. He flew in *The Duchess,* using his dead brother's bombsight, but was listed as missing in action on his fourth mission.

Following the early March raid, Essen continued to come under heavy attack by the Royal Air Force's bombers during the spring of 1943. Five more attacks were made—one with seven hundred bombers—until the important Krupp works and Essen were in ruins. Perhaps the last attack on the night of July 25/26 was the most successful because the largest Krupp building, used for construction of locomotives, was never successfully repaired despite the high priority given to the job. Also, Krupp production of shells and fuses stopped entirely, and production of guns was cut in half. Despite the large number of German night fighters, the bomber loss, compared to 1942 attacks, which were largely unsuccessful, was well below the previous year.

The Krupp losses were serious, particularly because of the demands of the German armies in Russia and the Mediterranean. The plants of the Krupp Corporation were in the heart of Essen, which was unusual; most German plants were on the outskirts of cities. Therefore, the Essen works were more vulnerable to British bombers because, with the marking equipment available at the time, the aiming point had to be on the center of the city. The Krupp installation at Essen, covering hundreds of acres, was an ideal target. When Gustav Krupp von Bohlen und Halbach visited the ruins of much of his factories, he suffered a stroke from which he never recovered.

Other Ruhr cities came under attack in the spring of 1943, and most of them were heavily damaged. Some were not in the Ruhr itself, but adjacent to it. Cologne and Düsseldorf, which were badly damaged the previous year, were hit again. This time the damage was much more severe, and crucial, because the previous damage had been repaired.

The Skoda Armament Works at Pilsen, Czechoslovakia, which now became more important to the Nazi defense effort after the destruction of Krupp, was twice attacked unsuccessfully; once in April, and again in May.

British scientists now had developed a new radar device called H2S.

Pathfinders were equipped with these primitive radar sets, which scanned the ground and transmitted a picture of land-and-sea contrast on cathode-ray tubes inside the pathfinder aircraft.

The great part of Düsseldorf was destroyed the night of June 11/12, following an unsuccessful raid in late May that failed because of bad weather.

Now that Harris's bombers were able to use the new and more efficient Mark XIV bombsight, which he had long sought, shorter bombing runs were possible. Great fires were started in many cities by four-pound incendiary bombs dropped in clusters.

Since Harris took over Bomber Command, he had tried to get his bombers equipped with .50-caliber machine guns. Their .305 guns were too light for use against German night fighters, which were protected by armor plate and had heavier, longer-range guns. He believed the original British turrets were badly designed, but it took him three years to overcome the lethargy of the British Civil Service. In complete frustration, he turned again to Alfred Rose and Sons of Gainsborough, who offered to help when he needed their assistance so desperately. They quickly developed a revolutionary new turret that could use the .50-caliber guns.

Despite numerous shortcomings of equipment, Harris was convinced that attacks on the Ruhr had proved that the industrial resources of Germany could be completely destroyed if he had more bombers. He was aware that such destruction was impossible with the average of seven hundred bombers then available to him.

Other targets farther inland than the Ruhr had to be bombed by June of 1943 despite the fact they were beyond Oboe range. These targets produced aircraft parts, and he now joined the Americans in attacking them.

The former Zeppelin plant at Friedrichshafen, on the shores of Lake Constance, was set for attack on the night of July 20/21. Harris selected an experienced officer from his old 5 Group to direct the force by radiotelephone. Because of the limited hours of darkness available, he advised the formations to fly onward to North Africa after bombing the plant that made radar devices, and then return to England after refueling.

This time H2S was used on a limited scale in pathfinders because so little equipment was available. It was not as precise as Oboe, but it had the range the latter lacked. On the average, only three out of fifteen later missions with H2S proved successful.

On the Friedrichshafen raid, Harris had ordered target maps made to represent how the target would appear on H2S tubes. Unfortunately, available target maps of the area were not up-to-date, and the town did not appear on the H2S tubes as it was represented on the target maps.

Despite the long flight, the loss rate was only 4.6 percent, and the plant was heavily damaged with half its equipment destroyed.

When pathfinders were first proposed, Harris had objected because it would mean taking the best men from each squadron. When they proved their effectiveness, he insisted these men should get quicker promotions and wear a distinctive badge. Group commander Donald Bennett led one of these elite groups until he was shot down while attacking the battleship *Tirpitz* in Norway.

General Arnold was intrigued by the H2S system, but the British were reluctant to supply units, except on a trial basis, because so few sets were available for their own bombers.

Arnold went to the Radiation Laboratory at Massachusetts Institute of Technology and they agreed to supply equipment of this type. The first units were available by September 1943, and they were designated H2X to differentiate them from the original British sets.

That autumn, twelve B-17s used both systems effectively when they bombed the port of Wilhelmshaven successfully. The target was easily identified because it lay on the coastline near an estuary of the Weser River. The shipbuilding facilities were severely damaged, with hits on the aiming point. Although these systems improved blind-bombing techniques, they fell short of accomplishing what could be done by visual means.

The British had every right to be skeptical of American air operations because their success so far had not lived up to claims made by America's air leaders. Weather was always a problem in England and over targets on the Continent. And because of the increase in German fighter opposition, the British still believed American losses would be prohibitive.

General Marshall, in recognition of command responsibilities between the Army Air Forces and the Royal Air Force, had earlier stated the position of the Joint Chiefs: American bombers in England would be under the operational control of the RAF, which would prescribe targets and timing, but procedures and techniques would remain the prerogative of the American commanders.

At this stage of the war, the Allies sought two main objectives for a combined air offensive. The submarine still remained the principal threat to Allied operations, and the German air force had to be defeated prior to any invasion of the Continent. Therefore, agreement was reached that submarine bases and construction yards must have an intensified bombing campaign by the combined efforts of the Royal Air Force and the Eighth Air Force, with particular attention focused on the Bay of Biscay bases.

It was believed that the German air force was in a critical state, particularly in regard to reserve crews. Although the morale of German pilots was low and the training of new crews inadequate, there was no shortage of fighter planes. The Combined Chiefs were of the opinion that decisive action should be taken before the German air force could recover, and that North African bases were ideal for intensified attacks. American and British aviators argued that German aircraft factories, for the most part, were out of range of African bases and could be hit more effectively from the United Kingdom.

American airmen continued to express confidence in precision attacks on what they referred to as "bottleneck" industries, which they believed would be most productive for sustained attacks. The British, however, still believed that massive night raids against populated areas were more productive because of their impact on enemy civilian morale.

Allied air commanders had to relearn a hard-earned truth: It takes years to assemble and train a combat air force. Although they had helped to draft the Casablanca Directive for the Combined Bomber Offensive, they knew there was not time to train their fliers properly. Whether the directive's goals would be achieved depended upon one basic fact: Can a few thousand partially trained aviators defeat one of the world's most experienced combat air forces? For men like Spaatz, Eaker, Portal, and Harris, it was an awesome responsibility. How the men of the Combined Bomber Offensive met the challenge will remain a monument to their courage and devotion to duty.

11

THE CATASTROPHE
STAGGERS THE IMAGINATION

Prior to the official start of the Combined Bomber Offensive, one of the most successful missions had been one flown on April 17, when 107 planes seriously disrupted production in the Bremen Focke-Wulf plant. Losses were exceptionally high with 16 bombers down, and another 46 damaged. The loss was not in vain because the Germans were forced later to move the plant to Marienburg to get it temporarily out of range of the Eighth's bombers.

Dr. Joseph Goebbels wrote in his diary, "The day raids by American bombers are creating extraordinary difficulties. If this continues, we shall have to face serious consequences that in the long run will prove unbearable."

Such expressions of concern by Hitler's propaganda chief and other high officials of the Reich were unknown to Allied leaders at the time, and British and American officials were even considering whether the bomber offensive was worthwhile. They received only one indication, when the RAF intercepted a message from Göring to his Luftwaffe, saying that the Fortresses must be destroyed, "regardless of everything else." He even threatened to court-martial pilots who were less aggressive than he thought they should be.

After the series of RAF raids on the Ruhr, particularly when the community of Wuppertal was damaged heavily by seven hundred bombers that wiped out five of six factories, Goebbels publicly denounced the raids. He called them "a kind of aerial terrorism . . . the product of sick minds of the plutocratic world-destroyers." His denunciation reached the point of hysteria. "A long chain of human suffering in all German cities blitzed by the Allies has borne witness against them and their cruel and cowardly leaders, from the murder of German children in Freiburg May 10, 1940, right up to the present day." Goebbels had adjusted his facts. The Freiburg bombing was done mistakenly by off-course Luft-waffe He-111s lost in a weather front, causing the deaths of fifty-seven civilians, including many children.

The most effective bombing was done during the last phase of the Battle of the Ruhr, and the Air Ministry viewed the results with more satisfaction. They hoped the Germans now knew how the people of Rotterdam and Coventry felt after similar terror bombings of those cities.

During the first three months of 1943, due to the loss of trained units to North Africa and the difficulty of getting new crews from the United States, Eaker's command averaged only seventy-four crews and bomb-ers. His fighter strength was not much better because only one American fighter group was available consistently for operations until April 8.

Head-of-theater Andrews joined Eaker in urging the War Department to get more planes to the United Kingdom so that three hundred heavy bombers could be used in a mission. That meant that six hundred bomb-ers had to be available to keep half of them operationally ready for a mission. Andrews pointed out that German fighter strength in the west was increasing because of transfer of German units from the Russian and Mediterranean fronts. He told the War Department that unless continu-ity of replacement aircraft and crews was assured we can "only nibble at the fringes of German strength."

The RAF's Portal wrote to Arnold, expressing his own concerns, telling the air force chief that further replacements were needed immedi-ately if the Allies were to continue the day and night bomber offensive. Arnold, of course, already shared those views, and the dispatch was meant really for the Joint Chiefs of Staff who were still permitting diversion of bomber units to the Twelfth Air Force. Despite repeated requests for a speedup of men and planes, Eaker had only one hundred heavy bombers on hand by the end of April.

Many attacks against important industrial targets had to be scrapped during the first half of 1943 because of the raids on submarine installa-tions along the French coast. During a meeting of the German Central Planning Office May 4, Grand Admiral Doenitz said, "The Anglo-Sax-ons' attempt to strike down the submarine war was undertaken with all the means available to them. You know that the towns of Saint-Nazaire and Lorient have been rubbed out as main submarine bases. No dog or cat is left in these towns. Nothing but the submarine shelters remain."

It was all too true. Once the Germans started to repair submarines beneath heavy thicknesses of concrete, attacks by anything but six- or seven-ton bombs proved ineffectual. And these big bombs were not used until late spring of 1943, when the submarine menace had been checked by Allied use of improved detection methods, convoy techniques, and joint sea-and-air attacks on the high seas. Doenitz agreed after the war that air attacks at sea ended the Battle of the Atlantic. According to the official United States bombing survey, "Strategic bombing can at best be considered only an incidental contributing factor."

Vital aircraft plants, which should have had top priority, were neglected through necessity; only 15 percent of all air attacks were directed against them during this period.

Raids against German submarine installations in France, unfortunately, still caused heavy French casualties, and officials of the occupied countries protested bitterly about the high loss of life and property. Fortunately for the Allied cause, the people in these countries remained predominantly pro-American and pro-British.

When Eaker visited Arnold in Washington during April, his chief had been blunt in criticizing Brigadier General Newton Longfellow, who headed Bomber Command, and his chief of staff Colonel Charles Bubb. Arnold said that he had long been concerned by the caliber of some of Eaker's staff members, and pressed him to make some changes. He accused Eaker of letting friendship cloud his judgment.

Eaker defended members of his staff, particularly Longfellow whom he had known for years and whom he admired. He failed to convince Arnold.

Longfellow had many admirable qualities, but he had incurred the dislike of some group commanders because he frequently lost his temper. Behind his back, they called him the "Screaming Eagle."

After Eaker returned to England, General Jacob Devers (who had replaced Andrews as head of the European Theater of Operations following the latter's death in an air crash) told Eaker he had heard criticism of his staff during his recent visit to Washington. Eaker replied angrily that these were gross slanders about some mighty fine officers who had done excellent work. He suspected that Arnold was the source of the comments, though, and realized that eventually he would have to make some changes.

He tried another tactic first with Arnold, sending him a cable on May 13, 1943, asking for maintenance and supply specialists. The Eighth Air Force, he said, was short on talented individuals in both categories, particularly because mechanics sent to Europe with new groups were largely untrained. Eaker reminded Arnold that the European theater was different from all others because of the heavy battle damage suffered by his bombers on raids over the Continent. He blamed inadequate repair facilities as of equal importance with bad weather conditions in keeping so many of his bombers on the ground.

He later wrote Arnold a letter that the present position of the Eighth Air Force was not a credit to the American army. "In sixteen months of war, we still are unable to dispatch more than 123 bombers toward an enemy target. Many crews have been in combat for eight months. They understand the law of averages. They've seen it work on their friends." He asked Arnold again to redeem his promise to send more planes and crews.

Eaker had cause to be furious. Although Arnold had made no firm promises, he had told Eaker he would try to have nineteen heavy groups in England by June 30 and a total of thirty-seven by the end of 1943. Eaker was still waiting for the three groups Arnold had promised him in March.

Eaker commiserated with Portal, complaining that the Eighth Air Force was serving as the training ground for other theaters. Portal was sympathetic; the same thing had happened to the British Bomber Command.

Arnold responded to Eaker's letter with words of praise and little else. He called them pioneers, saying he wished he could send them more planes.

In May, the Army Air Forces chief of staff managed to find more crews for Eaker, and he sent Brigadier General Fred Anderson to command the Fourth Combat Wing. Major General George Stratemeyer, a top Arnold aide, told Eaker that Anderson was highly regarded in Washington. "There's no finer officer in the world. When and if you get into any kind of a jam and need some good, straightforward, fine-looking advice, don't hesitate to call on this fellow. He's got it."

Anderson's ground crews were coming by sea, and some of his bases were not yet ready, so the flight echelons of his Fourth Wing were temporarily superimposed on the groups and bases of the First Wing. It was a fortunate burden because Hansell and Anderson were old friends. Hansell selected a seasoned squadron commander from one of his own groups, and transferred him to Anderson, where he was made a group operations officer. Anderson's crews received their baptism of fire as passengers in Hansell's bombers. Most important of all, Anderson's groups were steeped in the standard operating procedures of the First Wing, thus assuring uniformity.

Eaker wrote Arnold again May 13. "This is a great day for the Eighth Air Force. Our combat crew availability went up in a straight line today from 100 to 215. That's because the five new groups have finished their training and are off this afternoon on their first mission."

Robert A. Lovett, American assistant secretary of defense for air, had been in London that day participating in a series of conferences to find out what the Eighth was doing, and what its problems were. Upon his return to Washington, he wrote Arnold two memos. In the first, he said it was evident that bombers must be escorted on as many missions as possible to protect them. He said the Germans had established a fighter defense in depth and that P-47s could serve as top cover for the bombers once satisfactory belly tanks were available. For longer escort duty, he recommended the P-38 because it had two engines, which, he said, made it less vulnerable and easily identified by Allied crews. He conceded it was not as maneuverable as German fighters, so the P-51 Mustang was also needed.

The second memo said new crews should receive better training in gunnery and formation flying at high altitudes. He also cited the need for more replacement crews and greater forward fire power in B-17s. It was his opinion, he concluded, that there was an immediate need for long-range fighters, and that once his recommended changes were carried out, operations would increase by at least 50 percent.

The British had long recommended P-51s equipped with Merlin engines. To intimates, Arnold admitted that it was the United States Air Forces' own fault that it had not got the fighter into production sooner. He blamed the Matériel Division for its indifference to the Mustang when it was developed by the British with their own Merlin liquid-cooled engine, which Wright Field specialists, he said, believed was too vulnerable to fire. They couldn't have been more wrong, as time was to prove. Meanwhile, precious months were lost.

Failure to develop a prewar escort fighter proved tragic. Such a fighter was considered and rejected by Claire L. Chennault while, as a captain, he was chief of the Pursuit Section at the Army Air Corps Tactical School. Chennault was an outstanding fighter pilot who performed near-miracles with outmoded aircraft while leading the Flying Tigers volunteer group in China prior to America's entry into the war. He was passionate in his view that a fighter should be used for air combat only, and certainly not used to escort bombers. At the time, experts at Wright Field agreed with him, saying if greater range was given to a fighter, it would in effect no longer be a fighter but a bomber. Adding range to fighters then in service, they said, would reduce performance.

Chennault was an apostle of air-to-air combat of the kind fought between fighters since World War I. To win a dogfight, Chennault argued, one had to have a high-performance fighter, with as small a load as possible, a minimum of structure, and the lightest amount of fuel for maximum operational effectiveness. He contended that it was impossible to build a fighter with sufficient escort range and still have a good fighter. Chennault was not an engineer, so he was clearly out of his element.

He was not solely to blame. The chief of the Army Air Forces Matériel Division should have had better liaison with engineers at Wright Field. But when Chennault became head of the Pursuit Board he continued his attacks against all those who urged development of escort fighters. When an escort fighter was proposed at Langley Field by bomber commanders, Chennault opposed it violently, and he prevailed over such early precision-bomber experts as Colonel Harold George and many others.

Eaker was anxious to replace General Hunter who commanded the Eighth's Fighter Command, even though this particular move had not been suggested by Arnold. Hunter was a good fighter commander, but he disagreed completely with Eaker—himself a former fighter pilot—about the most effective tactics to protect bombers. Eaker wanted Hunter's fighters to stay close to the bombers to protect them to and from the target. Hunter wanted his fighters to sweep the bomber route independently and destroy German fighters wherever they found them. (Actually, toward the end of the war, this was the tactic that proved most successful in protecting bomber fleets.)

Eaker would have removed Hunter long before, but he had no satisfactory replacement in England. When he asked Arnold for one, Arnold suggested Barney M. Giles, an Arnold aide, or William Kepner, who had a reputation for being a good fighter pilot and a tough commander.

Giles responded to Eaker's request on behalf of Arnold. "General Arnold has been much concerned, and, as you know, has sent you two or three cablegrams reference the small number of heavy bombers reported ready and actually used for combat. I pointed out to him that a large number of your groups are very new, and a number of your combat crews have recently arrived in your theater. General Arnold believes you are especially weak in your chief of staff and your bomber commander."

This was not what Eaker wanted to hear. It was obvious that Arnold hadn't made up his mind what to do about the fighter situation.

Then another Arnold aide, Colonel Emmett O'Donnell, returned to Washington after spending some time with Eaker's command and listening to the arguments between Eaker and Hunter. On June 12 he wrote Arnold a memorandum entitled "Ineffective Fighter Support to Bombardment in the United Kingdom," saying that fighters were not very helpful to bomber operations. "The people in the P-47s haven't suffered many losses but, on the other hand, they haven't shot down many enemy planes. If the P-47 actually doesn't have the ability to escort on fairly deep penetrations, we have been badly fooled and our planning is extremely faulty. The large number of fighters we have allocated to the United Kingdom are not paying their way if they are providing escort across the Channel only. This, in effect, delivers the bombers safely into the hands of the wolves."

Arnold, armed with this lack of evidence, continued to procrastinate.

12

"TOUGH IT UP! CAN THOSE FELLOWS WHO CAN'T PRODUCE!"

Arnold aides reported to him each morning what the Eighth had done in Europe the previous day. Eaker had waited thirteen days between missions before he sent 252 Flying Fortresses to Wilhelmshaven June 11. Arnold was caustic. He told his aides that after such a long hiatus, a greater number of airplanes should have been ready. He was convinced the maintenance problem was basically a matter of management, and he blamed Eaker's staff.

He expressed his dissatisfaction the following day in a cable to Eaker headed: "Further relative to the low percentage of airplanes your organization has been able to keep in commission." He told Eaker a clear-cut supply-and-maintenance plan was needed, as was an air service commander with sufficient initiative, force, and executive ability to carry it out.

Eaker replied three days later with the usual excuses describing his difficulties in England, saying they were of a size and character that no other combat units had ever experienced.

The details of the raid to Wilhelmshaven had been forwarded to Arnold by the time he received Eaker's letter. The lead plane, hit on the bombing run by antiaircraft fire, almost collided with several other bombers. As a result, the formation was scattered so widely that bombs hit everything but the target. The raid on the Kiel shipyards was also a fiasco, due to heavy German fighter attacks. Only sixteen planes bombed the harbor, and twenty-six bombers were lost—many of them on the return flight when crewmen of the 94th Group, believing they were safe from further fighter attacks, were caught cleaning their guns by a last wave of German fighters.

Arnold minced no words in a letter June 15. He had earlier in the month dispatched two cables saying he believed too few of Eaker's bombers were being used in combat. Now, he said,

I realize full well the necessity for having a period to acclimate the crews, and the necessity for having a period of time to get them ready for operations. I also realize there are certain modifications that we on this side will never be able to put in to meet your desires, so there must always be a delay if your planes are to have all the changes made. On the other hand, I am not sure that all these changes are absolutely necessary, and in certain circumstances somebody may be leaning over backward trying to get 100 percent perfect planes when 90 percent would do the trick.

All reports I have received have admitted that your maintenance over there is not satisfactory, yet you have not taken any steps to recommend removal of those responsible, nor have you attempted to put in men who could do the job.

Such comments irritated Eaker. He understood the enormous pressures Arnold faced in Washington every day, justifying the buildup of heavy-bomber forces in Europe, but he felt that Arnold didn't completely understand conditions in England. For one thing, there were not enough depots to keep pace with the heavy repair work needed after each mission. Once while visiting a combat group, Eaker had stood on a ladder, stuck his head and shoulders through a hole in a B-17 wing, and had his picture taken. He had sent the photo to Arnold with the inscription, "Here's one of the planes that wasn't able to go out today."

Eaker had learned early that if he sent a pilot and his crew out on a mission shortly after they arrived from the States, chances were that the crew would be lost. He had set up operational training units for gunnery training and formation flying; as a result, new crews often did not fly for some time after their arrival. It was therefore difficult for Eaker to be understanding when Arnold's letter told him, "I'm willing to do anything possible to build up your forces, but you must play your part. My wire was to get you to 'tough it up,' to can these fellows who can't produce, to put in youngsters who can carry the ball. I will send Kepner, but I cannot let you have Giles. In any event, a definite change seems in order, but you have to be tough to handle the situation."

In his letter, Arnold mentioned there were 851 bombers in the Eighth Air Force. This puzzled Eaker. He realized that Arnold must have reached this conclusion by subtracting the total number of bombers he had sent him from those reported lost. It was evident that Arnold wasn't considering the bombers that were disabled due to extensive damage. Actually, he had only 275 heavy bombers available on July 4.

Averell Harriman, President Roosevelt's personal representative to the United Kingdom, arrived at the end of June and told Eaker that Arnold was not unfriendly toward him personally or officially, but there was no doubt but that he was critical of some of Eaker's methods.

Although Arnold had never sought Hunter's removal, now that he finally had authorized Kepner to replace the Eighth's Fighter Command head he wanted it done immediately. He wrote Eaker again on June 26, blaming him for waiting so long to replace Hunter.

Robert Lovett also wrote Eaker from Washington and said many of the same things Harriman had said during his visit to England. Eaker decided to write Arnold to clear the air, even if it cost him his job. He told Arnold in a five-page letter that he had removed Longfellow and Bubb effective July 1, and replaced them with Fred L. Anderson as bomber commander and Colonel John A. Sanford as his chief of staff.

> I will never agree that there has ever been in this command a better qualified man who was available to me to take Longfellow's place. Anderson had to be brought along very fast to be ready for July 1. This bomber commander job is a man-killer. It will break anybody down in six months unless he is a very unusual fellow.
>
> Regarding the fighter commander, Hunter was definitely the only man I had for that job. I believe Kepner will be a good man in Fighter Command, but I cannot put him in without some indoctrination and experience in this theater.

He also took a dig at Arnold for his failure to get the required long-range fuel tanks that were needed if escort fighters were to be truly effective.

> Averell Harriman talked to me today about his two conversations with you. His conversations, and your most recent letters, lead me to the following comment quite frankly and after the most careful consideration. Regarding our personal relationship, I have always felt the closest bond of friendship between us as two individuals. I have never thought you placed quite the confidence in me officially as an officer as you did as a friend. I sometimes thought you were tough on me officially in order that nobody got the feeling that I got the positions I held through our personal friendship. And, to make doubly sure that you did not allow that friendship to influence you unduly toward me officially. I shall always accept gladly, and in the proper spirit, any advice, counsel, or criticism, but I do feel, however, that my past services, which have come under your observation, indicate that I am a horse that needs to be ridden with spurs. I think you know that I will do my best not only for you, but because I realize the importance of this war, and to our

air force, of the job I have to do here. Naturally, I am working pretty hard and under considerable strain. We have been through a very dark period and we are not entirely out of the woods yet. But I think we will make the grade in one of the toughest spots imaginable if I can maintain your confidence and backing.

Arnold replied July 7, saying he would never have built him up for the job if he had not had confidence in him, and that he should keep that thought firmly in his mind. "I give you full credit for having the inherent ability, the knowledge and judgment that goes with the command that you now hold. That being the case, I see no reason in the world for fears or suspicion as to our relationship entering your mind. But you must know me well enough by this time to know that I am very outspoken. I say what I think, and do what I think best, so when you hear these rumors, comments, criticisms, or what have you, always remember that if there is anything serious you will be the first one to hear it. It will come from me direct."

It was a vote of confidence, but Eaker knew that if he failed to deliver, friendship wouldn't save him.

"GONER,
FROM 'G' GEORGE."

Earlier in the spring, British Wing Commander Guy Gibson had led a raid May 16 against three Ruhr dams with nineteen of his 617 Squadron Lancasters. They had been training for weeks to drop new barrellike, counterrotating, 9,500-pound bombs specially designed by British scientist Dr. Barnes Wallis. To drop them precisely against the wall of each dam, a 240-mile-per-hour speed had to be maintained at exactly sixty feet above the water. Spotlights were attached beneath each bomber in such positions that when the aircraft was sixty feet above the water, their beams converged on the surface.

The Möhne Dam was first on the target list. Not only did it provide water for four million Germans, but its adjacent electric plant helped to power the huge Ruhr industries.

After release of his bomb, Gibson flew back and forth over the lake while other Lancasters dropped their bombs until the dam was finally breached. For Gibson, it was an awesome sight as the lake emptied like "stirred porridge" into the valley below for fifty miles, engulfing cars as drivers frantically raced ahead of the tumbling waters. Most didn't make it, and as the avalanche of water inundated each car, its lights flickered uncertainly until they were extinguished.

He wired home base at Granthorn, "Goner, from 'G' George," indicating the dam had been breached.

Gibson led the next wave to the Eder Dam. It was quickly blown open and two hundred million tons of water cascaded into the valley below, flooding coal mines and factories for 50 miles downstream.

The dam at Sorpe was next, and Gibson went along to guide the last wave. Heavy fog and low clouds prevented release of the bombs effectively, so they turned for home.

Of the nineteen bombers dispatched on the mission, only ten returned, and 56 out of 133 young men were reported missing, three of them ending up in prisoner-of-war camps.

A total of 1,294 people drowned in the raids, including many Russian and German slaves and prisoners of war.

Gibson, who received the Victoria Cross for the mission, was later killed on another raid. The special squadron he founded, however, went on to win enduring praise for using a variety of Wallis's special weapons. They were the only British squadron to adopt American-style bombing techniques of precision targets, and they were astonishingly successful.

The breach in the Möhne Dam was closed September 23 before the rainy season, and the power plant repaired. The Germans diverted hundreds of antiaircraft guns to the dams for their future defense, so the raids could not be repeated.

Flight Officer Constance Babington-Smith, a British Women's Auxiliary Air Force (WAAF) photo interpreter in London, noticed a peculiar black shadow on a photograph of Peenemünde in the Baltic in May. She correctly interpreted it as a ramp with a cockpitless airplane on it. She noticed another such shape at Watten on the coast of France.

British Intelligence had known of the existence of secret weapons for some time, but now they realized how serious such new weapons might be. Allied officials were aware that such pilotless aircraft might postpone, even disrupt, an invasion of the Continent. They immediately initiated strong air attacks against these and other installations as they were identified. They knew that massive flying bomb attacks against the British Isles could easily result in a stalemate in the west, so the Allies were forced to curtail other air operations in favor of attacks against their bases.

Many days during the spring of 1943, operations of the Eighth Air Force were limited because of bad weather. Crews returning from rough missions, some with planes badly shot up, frequently found bases socked in by dense fog. The limited hours of darkness meant a 9:00 A.M. takeoff and a return at dusk six hours later to bases in middle England. Eaker constantly faced the nightmare possibility that all of the Eighth's planes might be lost in a single afternoon. In his opinion, bad weather was a greater hazard than the German air force.

Spaatz and Eaker were most concerned about the poor training gunners still received in the States. With land at a premium in England, and every available space needed to grow food, it was difficult to establish a gunnery range. Hansell eventually established a school and borrowed an instructor from Curtis LeMay. Turrets and hand mounts were set up along a beach; a war-weary B-17 was stripped and a reel was mounted in the tail so that it could tow a practice target past the gunners. The instructor LeMay sent down was tough, often using his size 12 combat boots to reinforce his sharp criticism. General Hansell, believing that a critical situation called for extraordinary efforts, supported the instructor and kept him from being court-martialed for his "unmilitary" behavior.

There seemed no substitute for experience, and unfortunately most gunners got their first experience in combat, with German fighters shooting back at them.

Eaker worked closely with VIII Fighter Command to extend the range of the P-47 with belly tanks, but it was a year before adequate escort fighters were available for deep bomber penetrations into the Reich.

In the Mediterranean, the heavily defended island of Pantelleria, between Tunisia and Sicily, had to be eliminated before Sicily could be invaded.

Eisenhower approved plans for its assault in the spring of 1943, and advisers told him that the coastline was so rocky that assault boats could come ashore only in the small island's tiny harbor. In advance of the invasion, he ordered the air force to bomb the island, concentrating on the harbor and on the island's east end.

After three weeks of bombing, the Italians showed no signs of quitting. Field Marshal Sir Harold Alexander protested that Pantelleria was a miniature Gibraltar, and that casualties of his invasion forces would be awful.

Eisenhower insisted that the invasion proceed, but he called in Professor Solly Zuckerman, one of Churchill's scientific advisers, to draw up a precise plan for the air force to follow, designating specific points to bomb and the type of bombs to use.

Under Zuckerman's direction, bombings went on with more precision and intensity. June 11, the stunned Italian commander agreed to surrender just as Allied invasion forces were en route.

Eisenhower was so pleased with the bombing that he wanted Sicily bombed the same way before his troops landed. Air force commanders believed the Pantelleria case was setting a bad precedent. Eisenhower, they said, did not realize the bombing had been successful because the island was small and the bombers faced only limited opposition.

Eaker's worst fears about penetrations into Germany's heartland were realized when he dispatched sixty bombers to Kiel, a port city on the southeast coast of the Jutland Peninsula. Forty-four planes bombed the

U-boat yards in mid-June, while the others struck targets in the harbor. Although hailed by the British and Americans as a great victory, it was a sobering defeat because twenty-two bombers were lost. Crews fought with great courage and continued their bombing runs despite heavy fighter attacks.

While Kiel was under attack, the main force of heavies bombed Bremen with only slight opposition. Damage to targets in both areas proved insignificant.

The Eighth Air Force made its first large raid into the Ruhr June 22 to attack the synthetic rubber plant at Huls. Unlike the Kiel and Bremen raids, this attack against one of Germany's most important synthetic rubber plants was a success. The entire plant was shut down temporarily, and full production wasn't attained at the Buna plant for another six months. The Reich's ministry of armaments and war production was told, "Practically all manufacturing buildings are in difficulty." Not only was the damage severe, but the attack reduced Germany's total reserve of rubber stocks to an amount equal to a one-and-a-half-month supply.

The first large-scale daylight mission into Germany's industrial center surprised the Nazis. Eaker's plan to confuse them as to his real intentions, with diversionary attacks on other cities, worked perfectly. As he knew very well, it wasn't often you could surprise the Germans, and it only worked once. At Huls, the Germans were caught so flat-footed that the alarm didn't sound until bombs started to fall. With Germans crowding the streets gaping at the large formation of bombers at high altitude, panic seized civilians and foreign workers alike, and the latter got completely out of control. The resulting civilian loss was high with 186 killed and more than 1,000 wounded.

The German genius for quickly recovering from such an attack was demonstrated again when I. G. Farben Industries reopened the main plant after a one-month shutdown. If the Eighth Air Force could have followed up the attack with three or more raids in the months ahead, the plant at Huls would have been eliminated permanently. Unfortunately, the next attack was delayed until March 1944.

When attacks were resumed the following spring, particularly against petroleum targets, synthetic rubber production was reduced appreciably due to the integrated nature of the German chemical industry.

The Eighth was grounded for the rest of June because of unfavorable weather conditions over the Continent. During the first half of July, attacks were limited to targets in France, including U-boat installations and aircraft factories.

Lieutenant Ralph D. McKee put aside his navigation instruments and grabbed the .50-caliber machine gun mounted over his worktable. For the moment, his job of directing his crew to the target was done. Now it was time to stay alive. He scanned the sky anxiously, noting the 305th Group's formation was tight as it headed July 4 for an aircraft factory at Nantes. Only a handful of ME-109s had come up to challenge the bombers, and they were not aggressive. In the nose with him, the bombardier was hunched over his sight, centering the cross hairs on the aiming point. A few powder puffs of exploding flak appeared in front of them, but it was too far away to do any damage.

McKee waited tensely, knowing that in a minute tons of bombs would rain down and the target would erupt in death and destruction. During the last anxious seconds, the formation seemed to hang motionless. Then their B-17 shuddered and fell back as a piece of flak hit a turbosupercharger, reducing power on one engine.

In the cockpit, Lieutenant William Wetzel increased power on the other three engines while his copilot, Lieutenant Charles Cockrell, anxiously watched the instruments.

"Bombs away."

They stayed with the formation as it began a gentle turn to a westerly heading to take them over the Bay of Biscay.

Despite Wetzel's efforts, their Fortress continued to fall behind and lose altitude. McKee knew that one of the other engines must be damaged. He was not worried at first, knowing that B-17s often limped home on two, sometimes even one, engine.

Suddenly, McKee was shocked to find the air around them filled with tracers as German fighters concentrated on their lone aircraft. Shells tore the outer skin of the bomber like paper, while McKee and the other gunners fought back savagely.

A gunner shouted, "I got one! He's on fire!"

Wetzel realized that it was going to be impossible to keep the crippled Fortress in the air. One engine was burning fiercely, and there was a fire in the bomb bay. He sounded the bail-out alarm, knowing the Fortress couldn't hold out more than a few seconds longer.

McKee quickly checked his parachute. For the first time he noticed cuts on one hand. As he prepared to exit the B-17, he noticed one of the German fighters flying alongside with his landing gear extended, exultantly surveying the doomed bomber.

McKee unfastened his oxygen mask and crawled back to the escape hatch. The door had already been jettisoned, so with his right hand on the rip cord, he tumbled out.

As he fell free, his back hit something, then he was falling faceup staring at the flames licking back from the wings toward the tail. For a moment he feared that he was losing consciousness. In a panic, all he could think of was pulling the rip cord, but he knew he had to wait until he was free of those flames.

His next conscious moment was of gently swinging below a canopy of parachute. The D ring, attached to the rip cord, was still clutched in his right hand.

In the distance, he could hear the formation heading home, and it was difficult to face the reality of a hostile environment where he would be at the mercy of the enemy. For some reason, his first thought was that he would miss the steak and ice cream his group would have that night. It had been months since they had had such a treat.

Beneath him there was a neat patchwork of fields, pastures, roads, and fence rows. As he swung gently back and forth, suspended only by yards of nylon, he felt alone and powerless.

With the assistance of the French underground, McKee and Wetzel evaded capture for six weeks. Finally they reached Spain, where they were interned for another two weeks before they were permitted to return to England.

Two of Wetzel's crew died in the plane before it crashed, and the other six who parachuted out were quickly captured on the ground.

Other strikes against factories at Villacoublay and Le Bourget were outstanding. On July 6, at Nantes, the bombing was especially good, with direct hits on the aiming point from twenty-five thousand feet. This was pickle-barrel bombing at its best. The bombing at Le Bourget and the German airbase at Villacoublay was almost as good, but not quite as spectacular.

Crews appreciated missions over France because the opposition was considerably less than encountered over Germany.

A few YB-40 gunships, converted from B-17 bombers, flew on these missions, but they were of little value. They were so heavily loaded with extra guns and ammunition that they had difficulty in maintaining formation with the faster, more maneuverable bombers—particularly after the latter had dropped their bombs. They were soon dispensed with by Eaker as a good idea that didn't work.

In July 1943 there was a reorganization of VIII Bomber Command. The old wings became bomber divisions, and a new bomber division, the Third, was created, with Curtis LeMay as its commander. Brigadier General Frederick Anderson became bomber commander, and Hansell became American deputy to Sir Trafford Leigh-Mallory, commander in chief of the Allied Tactical Air Forces. Brigadier General Robert Williams took over the First Bombardment Division.

Early in the month, LeMay attended a debriefing at First Division Headquarters when Brigadier General Frank O'D. "Monk" Hunter, the head of VIII Fighter Command, and First Bombardment Division commander General Robert Williams argued heatedly about fighter support.

At the time, Hunter had P-38s and a few P-47s. Williams was upset; P-38 pilots had been ordered that if one of their number lost an engine, another P-38 should escort him home.

LeMay had been getting madder by the minute. With biting sarcasm, he said, "Every time one of my boys loses an engine, he has to go home alone. There's no one to cover him."

While the argument swirled around him, LeMay used up several pipefuls of tobacco, smoke curling around his squarish face and black hair and his hazel eyes storming with emotion. He stalked angrily back and forth, banging his pipe so hard against a glass ashtray that he shattered it.

He was aware that the twin-engined P-38's Allison engines weren't reliable and that the fighter didn't perform well at high altitudes, but he still thought Hunter was not using his fighters as effectively as he could.

Finally, LeMay could contain himself no longer. "When you guys suffer the kind of losses we have, then I'll talk to you."

In the past, bomber crews had considered the numbers of fighters available for support so inconsequential that they ignored them. When it was announced at briefings that P-51 Mustangs were assigned to the theater and were able to escort them to and from the most distant targets, crews cheered.

Later P-51s, with large belly tanks for long-range escort, at first fell for a German trick near the Frisian Islands. German fighters would jump them, forcing them to drop their belly tanks, and then refuse to fight.

Crews admired LeMay for fighting for them, although they found him aloof. Though he played poker with a select group almost every night, he avoided intimacies. He had seen too many commanders "go bananas" when they became attached to men just in time to see them go out and get killed.

During the last week in July 1943, the weather over the Continent opened up for the first time in three months, and the Army Air Forces and the Royal Air Force took full advantage to make large and continuous attacks.

Norway came under Eighth Air Force attack for the first time July 24. Unfinished magnesium and aluminum plants at Heroya and U-boat installations at Bergen and Trondheim bore the brunt of these attacks.

Air operations were intense during the raids of July 24–31, when sixteen major industrial targets were attacked. The main emphasis was to eliminate the Luftwaffe as a factor in Germany's war efforts. The all-out onslaught against Germany was finally under way.

Hamburg, Germany's second city after Berlin, was an important shipping and shipbuilding center with numerous U-boat production facilities.

It had been a prime target since the start of the war. It was out of effective range of Oboe, so it was decided to use H2S. The city was believed to be an ideal target for use of this equipment because it was fifty miles inland from the North Sea on the Elbe River.

For added protection from radar-guided antiaircraft guns on the night of July 24/25, British bombers planned to drop metal strips called "window," which confused German guns by reflecting radar beams. Ground controllers found it difficult to detect which blips on their screens were bombers and which were masses of "window."

British and German officials had long known that the use of metallic foil would upset radar sets, but both held back for fear of encouraging the other side to use it. Since the summer of 1942, Harris had fought for the use of countermeasures because he knew that up to two thirds of all his losses, which averaged 5.6 percent, were caused by radar-assisted antiaircraft guns and night fighters equipped with radar equipment. Although it proved difficult to get priority for millions of tiny strips of aluminum, and to get the plants ready to manufacture them in quantity, approval came before the Hamburg raid.

After the war, Harris said that hundreds of aircraft and thousands of airmen's lives could have been saved in the first months of 1943 if "window" had been available. Improved bombing accuracy would have been an added asset, he said.

The British had also developed the Beaufighter with special radar equipment that could spot German fighters at night and shoot them down. They were able to accompany RAF bombers on six-hour missions and were very effective.

On the first night of the Hamburg raids, approximately eight hundred Lancaster, Halifax, and Wellington bombers started fires that swept the city, creating a fire storm the likes of which the Germans had never seen.

American Eighth Air Force B-17s attacked dock areas in daylight on the twenty-fifth, losing nineteen Flying Fortresses, and again on the twenty-sixth to add to the havoc.

The night of July 27/28, 787 RAF bombers returned to Hamburg, where fires still burned from earlier attacks. Adding to problems faced by the people of Hamburg was loss of most coke and coal stocks stored for the winter months. Shaken fliers said the attacks created a sea of flames. Despite extensive air-raid shelters, thousands died due to heat from the fires. Searing winds uprooted three-foot-thick trees as further fuel for the raging flames.

High-explosive bombs tore roofs off houses, while windows and doors were blown in, often trapping occupants otherwise unhurt. Incendiary bombs were heaped on top of the debris, and fire storms spread through whole sections of the city. There was complete failure of the municipal water system, and the alternate dropping of high-explosive and fire bombs made fire fighting impossibly hazardous.

Within a half hour that night a howling fire storm completely drowned out the cries of the dying. The city of Hamburg had large blocks of flats in narrow streets built back to back, with inner courtyards between them. These courtyards quickly became deathtraps as flames rushed through the narrow streets and occupants of the homes tried to save themselves in their yards. In these areas, it seemed as if giant bellows continued to fan the flames, while in other areas fierce fires created suctions that drew everything into their fiery embrace. Before long, area fires merged into one huge hurricane, the likes of which no one had seen before.

For those on the ground, it was a hellish four days. As air was sucked from the center of the city by superheated updrafts, flames and debris whirled inward, creating a zone with temperatures ranging up to 1,000 degrees centigrade. As the fire storms spread outward, winds up to one hundred miles per hour swept everything before them, and fire fighters could do nothing but flee to the few remaining shelters. Even these became deathtraps as thousands were cremated underground.

Frequently, fire fighters were surrounded by flames and died in the streets. Throughout the city, men and women momentarily left shelters to continue the hopeless fight against a sea of flames, but were forced to retreat. Many were suffocated by the intense heat, while others, horribly burned, rushed blindly back into the fires like moths attracted to a flame. Some tried to protect themselves with wet blankets as they ran for shelters. For most, the intense heat quickly made the blankets tinder dry, and their hopes for survival vanished as the blankets themselves caught fire and they became human torches.

Others hesitated to leave their shelters, believing they were safe, but thousands either died of carbon monoxide poisoning or were crushed as flaming buildings crumpled over them.

A few made it to safety, but they had to flee red-hot streets while flames licked hungrily at their legs. Those close to canals and waterways fared better because they either swam or stood in the water with only their faces exposed until the heat died down. Even these people were showered by sparks and flaming debris, and they had to continually avoid nearby structures as they collapsed. Even those who survived emerged from their ordeal with badly burned faces to survey canals cluttered with hundreds of bloated bodies swirling gently in wind eddies.

Many victims' bodies were completely destroyed. Doctors later had to estimate a death total for one large shelter because so many of the three hundred or so people had been reduced to ashes.

Up above, while fires raged, parents continued to cling to their children's hands as they desperately sought shelter. All too often, the raging winds would tear a child from its mother's grasp and hurl it into the fire.

Unless one could reach shelter quickly, heat alone was sufficient to cause instant death. And still they fled the center of the city as the bombs fell day after day. The strong rushed across the bodies of the dead and dying, while the old and sick were left behind.

German officials were stunned by the magnitude of the disaster. Their city of two million inhabitants, with the most modern fire-fighting equipment, had been rendered helpless. In all, 50,000 people died. Hamburg's loss almost equaled the total of 51,500 Britishers who were killed in all German aircraft raids on England.

Once the raids were over, shaken survivors emerged to a deathly silence. Their huge city was lifeless, without sound of people or birds, and on the faces of the still-living was etched a horror that time would never erase. Smoke hid most of the ruins, giving the atmosphere a yellowish look as it merged with the dust from the shattered city. Summer heat quickly aggravated health dangers as the stench of decomposing bodies wafted over the stricken city.

Rescuers found some bodies hunched in death, but unscarred, indicating they had succumbed to carbon monoxide poisoning. Other faces still bore the looks of horror when they realized there was no escape after trying to claw their way out of their entombments.

Everywhere the city lay in ruins, and the streets were covered with corpses. Some mothers clutched the hands of their dead children as both lay on the blistered pavements. Almost all were naked, with waxen features like undraped department-store mannequins.

Gauleiter Karl Kaufman, Hamburg's mayor, told Nazi headquarters that "the catastrophe staggers the imagination, and the entire city must be evacuated except for small areas." He was in a state of shock as eight hundred thousand people roamed the city's littered streets completely bewildered and not knowing what step to take next.

The alternate dropping of four-thousand-pound high-explosive bombs and incendiary bombs made it impossible for the Germans to fight the fires. Hundreds of thousands had to be evacuated, and only defense forces remained after the second raid.

The city was attacked again the night of August 2/3, but bad weather prevented any major new damage, and bomber losses were heavy. For those on the ground, the ceaseless downpour of rain, thunder, lightning, and cascading bombs created an unreal atmosphere that drove some people out of their minds.

In the first three main attacks by American and British bombers, Hamburg, with a population of two million, was destroyed. A total of 6,200 acres was burned out, representing 74 percent of the city. Its four main shipyards, which produced a large number of U-boats each month, were severely damaged.

Use of "window" proved a spectacular success. These thousands of metal strips confused radar controllers on the ground, and German night-fighter pilots had similar problems of identification. Defensive fire was almost wholly inaccurate. One Allied crew member, listening in on the German radio frequency, heard a controller say, "I cannot follow any of the hostiles. They are very cunning." Fifty-seven British bombers were lost for a rate of 2.4 percent—far below the average of 6 percent on previous missions.

Albert Speer told Hitler that if the Allies attacked other German cities in a similar fashion, particularly those devoted to war production, it would bring "a rapid end to the war." He told the German Central Planning Office July 29, "If the air raids continue on the present scale, within three months we shall be relieved of a number of questions we are at present discussing. We shall be simply coasting downhill, smoothly and relatively swiftly. We might just as well hold the final meeting of Central Planning."

Three days later he told Hitler that armaments production was collapsing, and warned further that a series of attacks of this sort, extended to six more cities, would reduce Germany's armaments production to half its present level.

"You'll straighten all that out again," Hitler told him.

The Allies were unable to continue such raids, so the chance to bring about total destruction in Germany had to await a buildup of strategic American forces.

Hitler lashed out at Göring when he tried to get fighter production increased. The head of the Luftwaffe had fallen to such a level in Hitler's esteem that he refused to listen to him.

Göring now spent most of his time at Karinhall, roaming his country estate in exotic robes ornamented with precious jewels.

Hitler demanded terror raids on Britain. "Terror can only be broken by terror!"

Next year, when a few token German raids were made on England, which did little damage, the war-hardened British laughingly called them the "baby blitz."

Airpower pioneers like Lord Hugh Trenchard and General Giulio Douhet had advocated bombing of cities to destroy the morale of an enemy populace so that it would force its government to capitulate.

Arnold, Spaatz, and Eaker held a contrary doctrine. They believed that civilian morale could be reduced by depriving them of the resources to continue resistance, not by killing them. Therefore, the Eighth Air Force did not join the Royal Air Force in bombing the city, concentrating instead on dock areas in daylight, although some American bombs were jettisoned on the city by crippled bombers.

The British must accept responsibility for the destruction of Hamburg, although there were no voices raised in protest at the time. Memories of the German terror bombing of Rotterdam in Holland, and of Coventry and London in England, were too fresh in the minds of the British people to leave room for remorse. Their attitude is understandable. The German campaign of terror bombing from the skies reaped more in return than its architects bargained for.

ABOVE AND BEYOND
THE CALL OF DUTY

Flight Officer John C. Morgan, who had served a tour of duty with the Royal Canadian Air Force, now was assigned to Colonel James S. Sutton's 92nd Group. July 26 he flew as copilot in Lieutenant Robert Campbell's *Ruthie II* as it headed for Hannover to bomb the Continental Gummiwerke A. G. rubber plant.

Navigator Keith J. Koske saw the first FW-190s as they made a pass at their formation. He and the others were shocked when they felt a terrific explosion rock the bomber. A second later, top turret gunner Sergeant Tyre C. Weaver fell into the nose section and collapsed on the deck. Koske saw with horror that the gunner's left arm had been blown off at the shoulder; he was covered with blood. He tried to inject morphine into Weaver to dull his pain, but the needle of the syringe was bent. Undoubtedly, the bent needle saved the sergeant's life because he needed his wits about him for what was to follow. When Koske tried to fasten a tourniquet to Weaver he saw it was impossible because his arm had been torn off too close to his shoulder. Koske acted quickly, knowing the terribly wounded gunner must have immediate medical attention if he was to survive, and that he couldn't possibly live the four hours it would take the plane to get back to England. He adjusted a parachute on the gunner, opened the escape hatch, and placed the chute's rip cord in Weaver's right hand. In his agitation, the gunner pulled the cord, which opened the pilot chute in the bombardier's compartment. Koske gathered the billowing pilot chute, tucked it under Weaver's right arm, and positioned him in a crouch with his legs through the hatch. Once he was certain Weaver's good arm was holding the chute folds together, Koske toppled him out.

He noted with satisfaction that ball-turret gunner James L. Ford reported Weaver's chute had opened.

Incredibly, Weaver survived after falling twenty-four thousand feet and landing twenty-five miles west of Hannover, where he was picked up and given immediate medical attention by the Germans. For him, the war was over; he was incarcerated in Stalag Luft IV until 1945.

Koske went back to man the nose guns, but there were no more frontal attacks. The German fighters were concentrating on the tail.

Copilot Morgan had taken the plane off from its English base, and now the pilot, Lieutenant Campbell, took over. The first fighter pass had knocked out the oxygen system for the waist, tail, and radio sections. Now, cannon shells smashed the windshield on the copilot's side, hitting Campbell in the head and splitting his skull open. Campbell fell forward over the wheel, with his arms wrapped around it in reflex, causing the bomber to nose down.

From his side, Morgan grasped the controls, using all his strength to pull the plane out of its steep dive. The semiconscious pilot was a six-footer weighing 185 pounds, and Morgan had a hard time pulling back the controls because of the weight of the pilot's body on them. He couldn't call for help because the intercom was out. What he didn't know at the time was that with the aft oxygen system out, the rear gunners were suffering anoxia at twenty-four thousand feet and were losing consciousness. Morgan thought they had parachuted. He was frantically trying to maintain control of the bomber by brute strength as the pilot, barely alive, tried instinctively to grab the wheel. They were still in formation, and Morgan fought these efforts because they were weaving crazily in and out of formation. He expected a collision any second. The windshield in front was shattered, and his visibility was so limited by the blinding inrush of wind that he didn't dare leave the formation. He knew that once he did, they would be a sitting duck—and a wounded one at that.

Somehow he stayed with the formation to the target, holding back the pilot with his left arm while trying to fly one-handed.

Bombardier Asa J. Irwin released the bombs, and the navigator crawled into the pilot's compartment to see how bad things were. Koske was shocked to learn the true situation.

"Get Campbell out of his seat!" Morgan yelled.

Koske asked the bombardier to help him and it took the two of them thirty minutes to get Campbell out of his seat and into the bombardier-navigator compartment, where Irwin had to hold him to keep him from slipping out of the open hatch.

Morgan miraculously brought his B-17 across the English coast with fuel gauges showing empty. The plane had been so riddled that much of the fuel from ruptured tanks had been lost en route home. Once the plane was down to a lower altitude, tail gunner John Foley revived and managed to crank the wheels and flaps down by hand.

Morgan's heroic efforts to save Campbell proved futile because he died shortly after they landed. Morgan's courage received due recognition later when he was given the Medal of Honor for his heroism. (A year later, Morgan's luck ran thin when he was blown out of a bomber over Berlin and ended up in a German prisoner-of-war camp.)

Besides the raid against the Hannover rubber plant, the submarine yards at Hamburg and several targets of opportunity were attacked the same day in northwestern Germany. In all raids, the loss of twenty-four bombers was considered excessive despite generally good results. This time target analysts proved too conservative. Actual production loss amounted to a quarter of the normal rate in these various plants during the following month.

Losses were so high during July that the Eighth was down to 275 heavy bombers. During the last week, the command had lost 88 bombers, or 8.5 percent of those attacking German targets.

While Sicily was being overrun by Allied troops in July, and Benito Mussolini's government was about to be overthrown, the Mediterranean air forces prepared to bomb the Ploesti oil refineries in Romania. These refineries had always had top priority in the Combined Bomber Offensive, but they were out of range of bombers in the United Kingdom. The Allies knew that bombers from North Africa could reach them. Eisenhower wasn't too enthusiastic about the operation, even after it was pointed out that Ploesti's refineries supplied one third of Germany's total supply of oil.

Marshall also expressed doubts about the raid. July 19 he told Eisenhower to cooperate with the British-based Eighth Air Force and attack fighter factories in Austria, even if such a raid was at the expense of the proposed Ploesti operation. In addition, he urged Eisenhower to release the three B-24 groups that he had borrowed from the Eighth and never returned.

Tedder and Spaatz were consulted by Eisenhower. After discussion, they agreed that the raid on the Ploesti refineries was important, but that it should follow a raid against the Austrian fighter factories. They justified their decision by saying that the Ploesti raid would be the more dangerous and costly in losses, so it should come later.

Eisenhower reported their decision to Marshall. He also took the opportunity of discussing the possibility of withdrawing more bombers from England for use in the Mediterranean. Eisenhower told his boss that he could understand Eaker's desire to get his bombers back, but that the Ploesti and Austrian operations by his Ninth Air Force would have a direct effect upon the entire European military situation. Both these operations, he argued, were in support of raids now being carried out in the United Kingdom, and it merely happened that his command had the more practical bases to execute them. He asked permission to retain the borrowed groups until after the Ploesti operation. He warned that one raid probably wouldn't be sufficient to destroy the refineries.

He assured Marshall that he was not trying to retain forces in his theater at the expense of the buildup for the invasion of the Continent. He reminded the army chief of staff that neither the Austrian fighter factories nor the Romanian oil refineries were specific objectives of his theater.

Marshall gave his permission to fly the Ploesti raid, saying it must be flown first and followed up by attacks against the Austrian fighter factories. Then, he said, Eisenhower must return the three B-24 groups to Eaker.

Although Marshall had refused to accept his strategic arguments for retention of the two hundred borrowed B-24s, Eisenhower continued to fight for them and even asked for more bombers.

Tedder pointed out to Eisenhower July 28 that the Germans were rushing bombers and fighters to Italy, along with ground divisions, and their availability would make the proposed landings at Salerno risky because these landings would be at the limits of Allied fighter range.

When Mussolini was overthrown July 25, Eisenhower wrote the Combined Chiefs of Staff that everyone now expected bold action to take advantage of the situation. He said he could do so only if he had the strength necessary to assure a reasonable chance of success at Salerno. He said he and Tedder believed that if the borrowed bombers could be kept three or four more weeks so that they could use them in Italy, the German air effort would be practically paralyzed in southern Italy, and that such attacks would practically immobilize all German ground units.

Eisenhower added that if the Combined Chiefs would send him three or four more Eighth Air Force heavy bombardment groups, then the chances of achieving a decisive success in the invasion of Italy would be tremendously enhanced. He conceded that such action might be construed as reducing the bombing effort against Germany, but that he considered his request strategically sound.

He recommended that if such approval was forthcoming, Eaker should personally lead his men on the scene so that he would have no apprehension about the temporary use of his bombers.

In England, when Devers saw Eisenhower's request, he filed a bitter protest. He told the Combined Chiefs that such a diversion to North Africa would be a mistake for many reasons. He reminded them that the Eighth was already too small to carry out its bomber missions, and that the months of August and September were critical in maintaining the objectives of the Combined Bomber Offensive. The Royal Air Force, he wrote, was counting on a maximum effort by the Eighth Air Force, and that maintenance crews and bases were already established in England.

He summed up his arguments. "I must be guided by the greatest damage to the German enemy, and I must never lose sight of the imminence of Overlord [invasion of France]. The German High Command would be delighted if the shift were made. The Eighth should never be diverted from its primary task."

Eisenhower disagreed when he read a copy of Devers's letter. In a cable to Marshall, he said his comments were unconvincing. Privately, Eisenhower was furious with Devers, telling aides that the much-vaunted mobility of our air forces had been exposed as talk rather than action.

Marshall replied to Eisenhower and sent Devers a copy. "Devers is right, and the heavy bombers have to stay in England."

The army chief of staff did ask Devers if he could spare four groups of medium bombers, and in a parallel cable he asked Eisenhower if he could use mediums instead of heavy bombers.

Eisenhower replied that mediums would not answer the requirements of his theater, but that he could use them.

Devers refused to part with any bombers, including mediums.

General Lewis Brereton, commander of the Ninth Air Force at Benghazi, Libya, received reluctant approval from General Eisenhower to make a low-level attack on Romania's nine major oil refineries. Bomber Commander Brigadier General Uzal G. Ent and Chief of Staff Colonel Richard Sanders had drawn up a highly secret plan in early July, under Brereton's direction, and increased the size of the special staff July 25 to include members of the Royal Air Force. Tedder, commander of Eisenhower's Mediterranean Allied Air Forces, had tried to get the mission canceled because he believed the Ninth's bombers could be put to better use by bombing targets in central Europe. He almost convinced Eisenhower because the theater commander's staff advisers also expressed doubts that one raid would be effective because 40 percent of Romanian refining capacity was not in use for the Nazis at any one time.

Brereton had argued forcefully, believing that destruction of the nine major refineries would shorten the war. His staff made the decision to bomb at treetop level because it was believed the refineries were not heavily defended, and that low-level attacks would catch the defenders by surprise.

In an attempt to ensure thorough indoctrination of the Ploesti area, a replica was outlined in the sands near Benghazi and repeatedly attacked by Brereton's bombers during training missions.

When the plan was first considered months before, defenses were light, but they had recently been strongly reinforced. A large number of antiaircraft guns now protected the area, and machine-gun emplacements covered every conceivable axis of attack by low-flying aircraft. Furthermore, there were 120 HE-111 and ME-109 fighters manned by German pilots, plus elements of the Romanian air force equipped with German-built fighters. And, along the route selected by Brereton's staff were two hundred Italian fighters.

Barrage balloons caused some concern because of the low altitude at which the bombers would make their runs. Crews were told that even if a plane did hit a trailing cable, it would snap without damage to their bomber. Few crewmen were convinced.

Only two of Brereton's Ninth Air Force groups, the 376th and the 98th, were available because the others had been assigned to the Sicilian invasion. Therefore, he was given two experienced groups from England, the 44th and the 93rd, plus the 389th, which had recently arrived in the theater but had yet to fly its first mission.

Brereton set the raid for August 1 and assigned 178 B-24s to the mission. There would be no fighter escorts despite the 2,700-mile flight because, he said, the mission would be flown at low altitudes over the targets.

The nine refineries were divided into seven general targets. Five of the refineries were located in Ploesti, one at Cîmpina, and the other at Brazi. Each plane would be equipped with a low-altitude bombsight and would carry two-and-a-half-ton bombs, including high explosives and incendiaries.

The first and second waves of bombers would have their bomb fuses set for delays up to six hours, while bombs of the last wave would be fused for forty-five seconds. Such fusing made it mandatory that the mission be flown as briefed, and group commanders were told to stress the importance of timing by telling crews that chaos would result if a precise schedule was not adhered to.

Colonel Keith K. Compton's 376th Group was scheduled to take off first. At dawn, August 1, Major Brian Flavell's plane was first in line to make its takeoff roll at 7:00 A.M. The heavy load of fuel and bombs made Flavell's B-24 Liberator seem sluggish, so he held it to the runway longer than usual before he pulled back and they were airborne.

Flavell glanced back just as a following bomber blew up on takeoff, and he turned away quickly, appalled by the sudden disaster. As he headed over the blue Mediterranean, he began to have serious forebodings about the mission. When another plane from his group caught fire, and the pilot fought to keep it in the air, he was even more convinced that the mission was starting off badly. Crew members to the rear of Flavell's plane reported that this second plane crashed on landing, and they saw only two crew members run away from the wreckage.

More planes started to turn back, and by the time all five groups were in the air, eleven planes had to return due to one malfunction or another, cutting the force to 163.

For a time, things quieted down as the strung-out formations crossed the Mediterranean. Suddenly engine trouble developed, and Flavell's plane plummeted into the sea off the island of Corfu. Confusion reigned momentarily until Group Commander Compton, with General Ent on board, hastily took over the lead as they crossed the border of Greece into Albania and turned northeast.

Close to Yugoslavia, heavy clouds built up over the mountains, and General Ent viewed them with misgivings, knowing his groups would be scattered even more.

To make matters worse, Colonel John R. Kane's 98th fell behind schedule because he had ordered his group to fly through the clouds at a lower level where unexpected head winds slowed them down.

Colonel Jack Wood's inexperienced 389th Group, which had flown higher than the two lead groups, now was in danger of overflying Compton's 376th Group and Lieutenant Colonel Addison E. Baker's 93rd. In jockeying back into position, Wood's group now fell behind schedule.

General Ent anxiously scanned the sky as they crossed the Danube and the clouds became scattered. At two thousand five hundred feet, the groups started to form for their runs into Romania.

Compton's and Baker's groups did so quickly, but the other three were twenty minutes behind schedule. Kane's group, which was supposed to lead the mission from this point, had ended up over Bulgaria and finally came in from the south. Therefore, the first two groups to arrive at the rendezvous had to wait for the late arrivals in order not to spread the formations too far apart. Ent was exasperated at the delay because he knew that any chance of surprise was now lost, and that the carefully planned runs would be impossible.

While the late groups were still forming, Ent impatiently ordered Compton and Baker to head for their initial points.

The other three groups finally headed for their targets in shallow dives, hoping to gain some of the lost time by increasing their air speeds. At Pitesti, the 98th and 44th groups dropped to treetop level, while the 389th split off to make its single-group attack upon Cîmpina.

Up ahead, Compton's lead 376th group headed for its initial point at Floresti. Ent and Compton both mistook Targovista for Floresti, and despite strong protests by the plane's navigator who knew better, they ordered the new heading, which, unbeknown to them, placed them on a course for Bucharest instead of Ploesti.

To compound the error, Baker's 93rd Group followed them. Before long, Ent realized his mistake and ordered a turn to the south, which would bring them to the target but on a different axis of attack than the one briefed. Until now there had been no opposition, but the ground suddenly seemed to explode as they neared their target and B-24s blew apart around them. Three bombers simply disintegrated as ground fire caught them at point-blank range, one of them cartwheeling into the ground as if it were a giant pinwheel, spraying flames in every direction while crumpled bodies were hurled grotesquely out of hatches.

Compton's and Baker's group had been scheduled to drop their bombs on the Romana Americana plant, but they never found it in the hellish antiaircraft fire erupting below them. These battered groups now headed for Ploesti in tight turns as Compton led his men in a semicircle around Ploesti, hoping to come in from the north. Such a run would conform somewhat to the original flight plan, which was designed to route them over the least-defended ground area.

Inexplicably, General Ent got on the radio as they neared their target and told them to select targets of opportunity. Compton's group did as the general ordered, and each formation tried to spot the most likely place to drop their bombs.

Major John L. Jerstad, who had completed his missions with the Ninth prior to the raid and had volunteered to fly one more, quickly found his plane caught in a withering cross fire three miles from the aiming point his crew had selected to bomb. He knew they were badly hit after his Liberator caught fire, but he ignored an open field that would have served as an emergency landing area and continued to the target. After his bombs were released, he tried to make a forced landing but his wings were on fire and he lost control. The bomber crashed with no survivors.

Baker's 93rd Group, which had followed Compton when he turned toward Ploesti, refused to heed General Ent's instructions to bomb targets of opportunity. Instead, Baker brought his group of thirty-five surviving bombers in from the south, but he never did find his assigned target, the Concordia Vega, which, fortunately, had already been bombed mistakenly by a formation led by Major Norman C. Appold. They fought their way through exploding flak to strike at the three refineries assigned to Kane and Johnson's groups.

During Baker's final run, his plane was struck by a shell that killed his copilot and severely wounded him. In shock, Baker noted that the whole forward section of the pilot's compartment was on fire. Despite flames licking at him, Baker held his course until his bombardier could synchronize on a single large building. After bombs away, he tried to gain altitude so that they could bail out, but it was too late. The B-24 went out of control and ripped itself apart as their formation mates stared in consternation, knowing such a fate might soon await them.

Baker's plane was one of eleven lost by his group, and the tragic toll took only a matter of minutes.

At first, Jack Wood's group had flown up the wrong valley, trying to locate their assigned target at Cîmpina. Realizing their mistake, Wood directed them up the correct valley. En route, flak of all kinds lashed at their planes as they headed for the Steaua Romana Refinery.

Lieutenant Lloyd S. Hughes's bomber met especially heavy concentrations of machine-gun fire, which ripped open his left wing and ignited the gasoline in a tank. He fought desperately to maintain control even though sheets of flames poured out of his wing and bomb bay. Once bombs were released, he tried to land but his bomber exploded on contact.

One squadron from Compton's 376th Group had joined the attack with Wood's group, and the refinery was smashed.

Colonel Leon W. Johnson's 44th Group and Kane's 98th now faced an exploding hell on all sides as they came in late. If they had abandoned the mission, no one would have faulted them. Instead, they chose to continue even though it meant flying directly into a maelstrom of enemy ground fire and—even worse—the exploding bombs of the group that had mistakenly come first with their forty-five-second-delay fuses instead of the long-delay fuses, which still remained to be dropped. Explosions on the ground grew in such intensity that six bombers blew up in midair, sending further shock waves through formations of bombers relentlessly continuing to the target.

Colonel Kane, leading the 98th, stared with disbelief when he saw Compton's group leaving the target and flying underneath him on the wrong heading while his group made its approach.

He watched tensely as machine-gun emplacements on the ground fired at point-blank range, while gunners in the bombers responded with every gun they could bring to bear. At the height of the battle, an engine was shot out, and Kane quickly ordered it feathered. With bombs bursting beneath them from earlier attacks, fuel-storage tanks erupting in smoke and flames that reached higher than their altitude, the ground fire increased and the full horror of exploding bombers became a nightmare that Kane did not expect to live through. It was an awesome sight and he knew he need never fear any other man-made hell if he survived this one.

Miraculously, Kane led the survivors of his group through to the bomb-release point, and then they were in the clear. A quick recount of planes still flying almost threw Kane into shock. Of the thirty-eight that had followed him on the run, only seventeen survived.

The Phoenix Orion target was hit well, Kane noted, and he hoped that the other formation had been equally successful at the Astra Romana Refinery.

Colonel Leon W. Johnson's 44th Group was also mauled badly; coming in last, with gaping holes in his own lead plane, Johnson led them through an exploding maelstrom that included guns of all calibers. There was no thought of turning back, only to press on until their bombs were added to the unbelievable destruction that lay before their eyes. The rolling fires beneath created enormous heat, and pilots of the 44th had to strap themselves to their seats as their scorched and crippled bombers were tossed by extreme turbulence like toy airplanes on a windy day.

Two B-24s slammed into trailing cables from barrage balloons that slashed brutally at their leading edges, cutting wings to the front spar. Other bombers wheeled around tall chimneys in maneuvers that pilots themselves would have thought impossible at such altitudes, but desperate actions were necessary to escape disaster.

Incredibly, the heat continued to intensify the closer the last bombers came to their bomb-release points. Flames shot above them, so hot that the surfaces under their wings and fuselages were scorched.

Johnson's own plane was so hot that he expected it to explode any moment. Further adding to the horror of the scene, one of his bombers reared straight up, seemingly standing on its tail, as heavy flak ripped it apart.

At last, mercifully, it was over. Although Johnson didn't know it at the time, eleven of his bombers had gone down. As they headed for home, many B-24s were flying with one or more engines out, and most planes had wounded aboard. Crews watched with a feeling of helplessness as German fighters circled overhead. But their treetop altitudes, which had caused so much havoc to their formations over the targets, now protected them. Enemy fighters tried to dive on the bombers flying just above the ground, but many that made the attempt found it impossible to pull out and crashed. At last, fighter attacks ceased, but flak in certain areas continued to take its toll, and three more Liberators were lost en route home.

During the approaches to the mountains, some badly damaged airplanes threw everything out that could be spared to lighten their crippled bombers. One B-24 was so stricken that the pilot ordered everything thrown out that wasn't a permanent part of the airplane. George R. Miller threw his personal possessions, including a pocket New Testament encased in bullet-resistant steel, out a window. These efforts were insufficient to keep the bomber in the air, so they all bailed out over Hungary, and the nineteen-year-old Miller was taken prisoner.

(In 1977, Miller, then fifty-two years old and living in La Canada, California, was close to death following brain surgery to remove a blood clot. Much to his astonishment, a Hungarian woman had found his New Testament and, seeing his name and address on the flyleaf, had returned it to him. His wife said that before recovery of his New Testament he had been morose and negative. "When the book came back into his life," she said, "he became a happy, well-adjusted man." He died a year later.)

Others of his comrades were not so lucky at the time. One formation had to drop to a low altitude over the Adriatic, and they were promptly attacked by Italian fighters from Foggia. Five aircraft were lost because gunners were trying to help wounded comrades instead of manning their guns.

For their outstanding bravery Baker, Jerstad, Kane, Johnson, and Hughes won Medals of Honor.

This second raid against Ploesti was a far worse disaster than Colonel Harry Halvorson's raid June 11, 1942: Fifty-four out of 163 B-24s were shot down. On that first raid, only 13 bombers participated, and most survived, although many landed in neutral countries. Such losses were too excessive for the limited gains achieved on the mission.

Tedder immediately ordered Brereton to postpone future strikes against Ploesti and to direct his efforts to the Italian campaign. Eisenhower commented, "As usual, mathematical calculations could not win over unexpected conditions."

Although 40 percent of Ploesti's refining capacity was destroyed in the raid, the Germans quickly made up their losses by activating idle units. When no follow-up was made, the mission had to be adjudged a failure because it did not meet its objectives.

On August 4 Marshall formally rejected Eisenhower's earlier request for transfer of more bombers from England.

Eisenhower tried again to retain the three B-24 groups that had taken part in the Ploesti raid. On August 12 he wrote the Combined Chiefs that he considered every available force should be brought to bear against the enemy.

Devers protested again, and Marshall backed him up, insisting the bombers be returned.

Eisenhower had persisted because he wasn't accustomed to turndowns from his boss. He wrote Marshall, "I'm not submitting any detailed argument on the point because I'm sure you understand that we are not asking, from this theater, for anything we do not believe to be absolutely necessary to carry out our mission." Again he took the opportunity to describe to Marshall the situation he faced prior to the Salerno landings. Hostile bomber forces, he said, jeopardized the success of these landings.

General Arnold responded for Marshall. He told Eisenhower that the Eighth Air Force was engaged in a critical battle for air supremacy over Germany and that the three borrowed groups would provide Eaker with enough long-range striking power to account for perhaps an aircraft factory a week. He reminded Eisenhower that increased actions by the Eighth Air Force would help his Mediterranean forces as much as those preparing for the invasion of the Continent.

Arnold's message neatly turned Eisenhower's arguments against him.

In a major behind-the-scenes victory for strategic airpower, Eisenhower returned the three groups the following week.

Bombers were joined by P-47 Thunderbolts with jettisonable fuel tanks for the deepest-ever penetration when a plant at Oschersleben, ninety miles southwest of Berlin, was bombed. American fighters caught sixty enemy pilots by surprise as the Germans were casually picking off stragglers from the bomber formations. Before they could recover, the Thunderbolts shot down nine of the enemy and drove the rest away. Despite the good support, twenty-two bombers were lost, but only one P-47 failed to return.

The P-38 Lightning had appeared to promise greater protection over German targets as escort fighters. Earlier, despite protests by General Hunter, former head of the Eighth's Fighter Command, his best units had been transferred to the Twelfth Air Force in the Mediterranean. Prior to the transfer, Hunter's problems were compounded by engine deficiencies with the P-47 and serious radio shortcomings. Through the efforts of the Rolls-Royce Company, these problems were resolved, and the fighter's range was extended through the use of droppable fuel tanks. Although similar tanks had long been used by the British and the Americans, there were none available earlier in the war for the P-47. The fighters were equipped with resinated tanks for ferry purposes, but these were not pressurized and therefore useless above twenty thousand feet. Belly tanks were ordered on a crash basis, but they didn't become available until August 1943.

Before he was relieved, Hunter had improved the range of the P-47s so that they had a radius of action up to 375 miles. This range gave the fighter the ability to escort bombers as far as Emden.

Although Italy was not considered the most dangerous front in the air war, British Sergeant A. L. Aaron proved that it could be when he gave his life in support of air operations August 12 and was given a posthumous award of the Victoria Cross.

That same day Air Marshal Harris wrote Portal, "It is my firm belief we are on the verge of a final showdown in the bombing war. The next few months will be vital. Opportunities do not knock repeatedly and continuously. I'm certain that given average weather and concentration on the main job we can push Germany over by bombing this year."

Both men were aware that Churchill had lost interest in the bombing campaign. To them, it appeared that he no longer believed bombing could be decisive, although he still applauded the destruction of cities like Hamburg.

A surprise raid on the V-1 and V-2 launch sites at Peenemünde on the night of August 17/18 shocked Hitler. The Royal Air Force used Mosquito bombers to drop flares on the target. Damage to installations was not extensive, although two important rocket scientists were killed and forty British bombers were lost. Following this raid, however, Luftwaffe Chief of Staff Generaloberst Hans Jeschonnek committed suicide. In a note, he said, "I can no longer work with the Reichsmarschall. Long live the Führer!"

Jeschonnek had been one of Hitler's toadies, abjectly following orders that he must have known were militarily wrong and that led to serious shortcomings in preparing for the aerial defense of the Reich. He had earlier told Hitler that the Germans had to win by December 1942 or they would never do so. He shot himself August 18 out of despair over the setbacks at Stalingrad and in North Africa, and raids over Germany, which his Luftwaffe couldn't seem to stop. His death, like Udet's, was hushed up. Germans were told he died of a stomach hemorrhage.

V-weapon production was delayed by the raid, and certain production facilities and testing installations were moved elsewhere. Hitler appointed General Gunther Korten, an incompetent sycophant, to succeed Jeschonnek. Korten was killed less than a year later, on July 20, 1944, by a bomb intended for Hitler.

15

A BOLD
STRATEGIC CONCEPT

Eaker's Eighth Air Force had lost some of its best units to the Twelfth Air Force for Mediterranean operations, so his command was still extremely short of crews. Now, as a further complication, some of the early crews began completing their twenty-five missions and returned to the United States. Major Robert K. Morgan's *Memphis Belle* crew was first to leave. Major Morgan later flew B-29s against Japan during a second combat tour.

Sergeant Maynard "Snuffy" Smith peered out of his cramped ball turret, where he was curled up as his B-17 turned away from Saint-Nazaire after bombing the submarine pens. This was his first mission, and the ground below had such a sameness that he was unaware that, due to navigational error, his formation had made a wrong turn. Instead of returning to England, the group was starting to let down over the coast for a landing in occupied France.

When they were jumped by German fighters, "Snuffy" was too preoccupied firing at attackers to pay much attention to the excited chatter on the intercom, and when it went dead, he wasn't concerned at first.

The plane was in a bad way as the pilot headed out toward the English Channel. Fighter attacks intensified. Copilot Robert McCallum took one look into the radio compartment and recoiled. All he could see were flames. It was like looking through the door of a furnace. He knew fire extinguishers were useless.

In panic, the radio operator and waist gunners bailed out into the Channel. The tail gunner was stuck, seriously wounded by fragments from a 20 mm shell, and the navigator and bombardier were also too wounded to bail out.

In his ball turret, Snuffy wondered what was going on inside the cabin, why the guns were so silent, and why he could hear no conversation on the intercom. He decided he'd better find out, so he cranked his turret to the position that enabled him to crawl up into the cabin. He first saw the painfully wounded tail gunner and gave him first aid. Seeing the radio compartment was in flames, he jettisoned the oxygen bottles and ammunition because they would explode if the fire reached them. He was desperate now—the fire was gaining on him. He tried everything to stamp out the flames, including urinating on them.

When fighter attacks were renewed, he rushed into the waist to man the guns and ward off some 190s.

When these attacks ceased, he returned to the radio compartment in his desperate battle to get the fires out, and finally managed to beat them out with his bare hands.

Despite the lack of fully operable pilot controls and loss of its tail wheel, the B-17 made it across the Channel with its fires out, thanks to a scrappy sergeant who refused to give up the battle.

Hansell recommended the Medal of Honor for Smith. His heroic actions could be confirmed by crewmen of another bomber in the formation. The fuselage of Snuffy's plane was so full of bullet holes it looked like a sieve, and they could see everything that Snuffy was doing.

When Secretary of War Stimson came to England, he went up to First Division Headquarters to pin the Medal of Honor on Snuffy, who had to be taken off KP to attend the ceremony. Able hands quickly pressed his uniform and shined his shoes, barely in time to meet the secretary. (He had violated some ground rules and was being punished.)

LeMay prepared his Third Air Division for takeoff the morning of August 17, 1943, to bomb the Messerschmitt plant at Regensburg, sixty miles southeast of Nuremburg in southern Bavaria. He knew this plant produced two hundred ME-109s a month—nearly 30 percent of Germany's single-engine fighter production—so he was anxious to destroy it.

Bad weather had canceled this two-pronged strike at Regensburg and the ball-bearing plants at Schweinfurt for several days. Now, the weather still was bad, but if LeMay's division was to land in North Africa in daylight according to plans, the decision had to be made quickly.

It was an anniversary mission. Just a year before, the Eighth had flown its first raid against German-occupied territory. In this mission, five combat wings of the First Air Division, totaling three hundred B-17s, would take off after LeMay's Third Air Division, which would lead the assault and as a consequence absorb the brunt of German fighter attacks. It would proceed from Regensburg on to North Africa. It was hoped that the First Air Division, attacking Schweinfurt, would benefit from the fact that German fighters would be refueling from their attacks on the Third Division. For further protection, eighteen squadrons of Spitfires from the Royal Air Force were assigned to protect the bombers to the limit of their fuel capacities. Meanwhile, Typhoons from the RAF and B-26s were assigned airfield strikes to keep German fighters on the ground as much as possible along the bomber routes. These plans, which revolved around precise timing, had been drafted with care, but they started to come apart right at the start.

At Bushy Park Eighth Air Force Headquarters, Eaker kept constantly in touch with his Bomber Command at High Wycombe. He had the utmost confidence in Fred Anderson despite the fact that the thirty-eight-year-old West Point graduate had been in command for less than two months. Still, Eaker fussed about the delay in ordering the Third Air Division to take off. He had requested permission to lead the mission, but General Devers had warned him that if he did so, his next trip would be back to the United States. Arnold had made it clear that he didn't want Eaker to fly any more missions because of the danger he might be killed or captured.

Fog on the First Air Division bases held their bombers on the ground. It started to lift at the 91st Group's base at Bassingbourne, although other East Anglia bases were still shrouded. LeMay's Third Division was finally given the word to leave. It wasn't until the division passed over Woensdrecht at 10:17 A.M. that it encountered its first flak.

"Fighters at two o'clock, low!" The familiar cry alerted Captain Thomas F. Kenney's 96th Group's crew with whom LeMay was flying as copilot.

At 10:25, a pair of 190s drove through the first formation, hitting two bombers, and then half-rolled over the lead group.

LeMay had noted prior to this mission that German fighters had developed a new strategy of employing fighters in depth rather than in mass. Earlier, Göring had tried to meet Allied bombers over France or the Low Countries without success. Now, he ordered his fighters to concentrate along a 150-mile corridor, so fighters took off only upon approach of the bombers. When they were out of fuel and ammunition, they landed and another group took over, deeper inside Germany. In this way, earlier groups could attack American bombers again on their way home. Bomber crews enjoyed a grim joke that the Germans escorted them all the way.

Kenney happened to glance once at LeMay, just as he took off his oxygen mask, filled his pipe, and, when it wouldn't start, squirted pure oxygen from the demand system until it flamed up. While the pilot gaped at him, LeMay took a couple of puffs, knocked his pipe out, and put his oxygen mask back on.

While his Third Air Division crossed Holland, LeMay was aware that the Schweinfurt force was still on the ground because of fog. Although his bombers had managed to get off despite fog, he knew that fog was worse inland. He was still not satisfied that this was a justifiable excuse for the First Division to remain on the ground. His own crews had been practicing instrument takeoffs for weeks, so they were prepared to take off from socked-in airfields.

LeMay was also disturbed by the failure of two P-47 groups to put in an appearance, to give them protection for at least the first one hundred miles into the Continent.

Actually, Major Loren G. McCollum's 353rd Fighter Group's thirty-two P-47s had overflown LeMay's three combat wings at 10:00 A.M. and had taken up an escort position at twenty-three thousand feet as they approached the Dutch coast. LeMay simply hadn't seen them.

(At Bushy Park, Eaker was filled with doubts whether he should recall LeMay. He knew that unless the 230-plane force for Schweinfurt didn't get off the ground soon they would be too late to take advantage of LeMay's diverting German fighters away from the ball-bearing plants.)

Lieutenant Colonel Beirne Lay, Jr., a member of the Eighth's head-quarters staff, had volunteered for the mission and was in *Piccadilly Lily,* a 100th Group plane piloted by Lieutenant Thomas E. Murphy. They were fifteen miles behind the lead 96th Group. His plane was flying at seventeen thousand feet, the lowest and most vulnerable position of all. He watched with approval as the group's twenty-one B-17s tucked close for protection as they crossed the Dutch coast, with the 95th Group led by Colonel John K. Gearhart leading the 3rd Combat Wing.

Eight minutes after the first flak at Woensdrecht, Lay watched nervously as 190s swept through the 2nd Bombardment Wing—Colonel Elliot Vandervanter's 385th Group and Colonel Frederick Castle's 94th. He noted over the city of Diest that two B-17s started to smoke after they were hit, but they remained in formation. One German fighter also was hit, smoke pouring from its nose and metal flying off as it was hit by the massed guns of the formation.

From twenty-five thousand feet, fighter commander McCollum had seen twelve 190s dive toward the bombers, but he knew it was impossible to intercept them due to their speed and distance beneath his American fighters. Fifteen minutes later, McCollum spotted a 190 and, in a screaming dive, tore the German fighter to pieces with his eight heavy .50-caliber guns.

Now, his fighter group had reached its maximum range and had to return. Meanwhile, Colonel Hubert Zemke's 56th Fighter Group arrived to escort the bombers another fifty miles, as far as Eupen near the German border city of Aachen. Then, they, too, would have to turn back. Both fighter groups had new pressed-paper auxiliary tanks whose fittings had proved hopelessly inadequate. The tanks themselves broke apart easily. In addition, the 56th had flown its first mission only five days earlier, and they were still green.

Zemke was frustrated by the tactics of the German fighter pilots, who refused to engage until the American fighters were forced to turn back. Although he spotted fifteen or so fighters near Hasselt, ten miles from the Belgian-German border, the Germans avoided contact, knowing that soon they would be able to attack the bombers without Allied fighter interference.

Near Diest, Zemke watched in horror as a B-17 exploded, plummeting to the ground in a huge ball of fire without a single crewman able to bail out. At 10:30, another bomber started going down near Maastricht. This time six airmen dangled from their chutes. Now, he, too, had to turn back, leaving the bombers without fighter protection.

The Germans struck savagely as 109s and 190s darted through the groups firing 20 mm nose cannons and machine guns.

Lay listened with growing apprehension to gunners no longer able to call out individual attacks because there were so many of them. He could hear radio calls from commanders, advising gunners, "Lead 'em! Use short bursts!" The Germans now coordinated their attacks. Some came head on, either slightly above their altitudes or slightly below. Others attacked the rear as the sky was crisscrossed with orange tracer bullets and puffs of smoke from ground antiaircraft guns.

Just as LeMay's 2nd and 3rd Bombardment Wings received the brunt of the fighter attacks, twin-engined 110s joined the fray, often diving out of the sun, knowing gunners would be blinded.

Meanwhile, the five combat wings of the First Air Division were still on the ground in England.

At High Wycombe, Anderson faced a grim decision. The coordinated strategy had already failed. He hadn't dared to call LeMay's Third Division back once it was airborne because it would have had to drop its bombs in the English Channel with the danger of hitting Allied ships. With fog still hugging many of the First Division's bases in East Anglia, he had to decide whether to dispatch them more than three hours late to Schweinfurt. He knew that by the time they reached Germany, Nazi fighters would have refueled and would be waiting for them.

At Bassingbourne, Brigadier General Williams waited impatiently to get the word from High Wycombe to take off. He was so self-disciplined and calm in a crisis that he was not upset by the delay. Despite the loss of an eye during the Battle of Britain, where he had served as an observer, the mustachioed Williams had been given the overall responsibility to lead the Schweinfurt mission. A disciplinarian himself, he was fully aware of the tough decision Anderson faced as he strode around 91st Group Operations swinging his swagger stick.

From High Wycombe, Anderson ordered the Schweinfurt groups to depart at 10:40 A.M. He felt he had no other choice because the weather over the target was the best it had been for two weeks.

Eaker, at Bushy Park, was relieved when he heard the decision. He had not interfered, respecting Anderson's judgment and knowing there was greater loss of morale if a mission was canceled once it was all set to go.

At 1:26 P.M. Williams's force crossed the English coast and headed for Schweinfurt by way of Eupen, Aachen, Wiesbaden, and Darmstadt. It was now three and a half hours late. Worse than that, a third of his force had to abort; he led far fewer bombers than he had anticipated.

No sooner had the First Air Division cleared the English coast than the Germans alerted their fighters to repell what they suspected was an attack on Schweinfurt.

The division was divided into two task forces, with the first under Colonel William M. Gross. Each force was almost ten miles long—one with 116 bombers and the other with 114—and flying in the clear while clouds still covered their bases in England.

Meanwhile, with LeMay's Third Air Division over Germany, Lay in *Piccadilly Lily* watched German fighters press attacks as close as fifty yards. Once, a fighter misjudged his distance and plowed into a B-17; the impact shattered both planes, and the combined wreckage plummeted to earth with no survivors.

The worst attacks on the rear wing began ten minutes after the last Allied fighters departed for home. About twenty 109s and 190s came in low at the rear of the formation; then, making 180-degree climbing turns, they attacked head-on. Some fighters were hit, but a B-17 in the 95th Group and three in the 100th Group fell in flames.

Lay watched with disbelief as a copilot from one of the crippled planes somehow crawled out on the right wing of his bomber through a shell hole in the fuselage. Lay gazed at the man in utter horror because he did not have a parachute. Then, as he watched, the copilot clung to the shattered fuselage with one hand while he reached into the nose section with his other hand to get his parachute. He almost made it, but he lost his grip and his body was swept against the tail and he was hurled to his death.

While Lay continued to watch the plane ahead for possible survivors, the nose of the Fortress rose into a tight stall and it exploded with a force that rocked the rest of the formation.

Murphy, pilot of *Piccadilly Lilly,* saw that Lay looked numb from the shock of airplanes plummeting to earth as clusters of parachutes followed them at a more leisurely pace, the German yellow chutes mingling with the American white in an incongruous setting below the bloody battle up above. He let Lay fly the airplane to get his mind off the tragedies unfolding around them.

Lay had lost all hope the attacks would diminish as they got deeper into Germany. He knew that the German Fighter Command had recently been reorganized to counter the growing American bomber threat. He had seen intelligence reports that the Germans had even withdrawn two fighter groups from the Russian front to use in defense of their cities and factories.

LeMay's 1st Bombardment Wing, in the lead, had not received the heavy attacks suffered by the rear wings. The lead 96th Group was flanked by Colonel Edgar Wittans 390th Group in the high position on the right and Colonel William B. Davis's 388th Group in the low position on the left.

LeMay's 95th and 100th groups of the 3rd Bombardment Wing continued to undergo persistent attacks, and German fighters swarmed around them. Stragglers, forced for one reason or another to leave the protection of their formations, faced almost certain annihilation as German fighters pounced upon them.

In *Piccadilly Lily,* Lay felt trapped by the pairs of 109s that swarmed around them. He jerked upright as a piece of metal flew past their right wing, narrowly missing one of their props. He quickly realized it was the main exit door of the Fortress ahead of them. As his throat constricted, he watched in horrified fascination as a man, with his knees up to his head, hurtled through the formation, barely missing several propellers before his parachute snapped open.

German fighters lobbed rockets now, which exploded with blinding flashes in their formation, incredibly not appearing to do any damage. A quick glance up showed Lay that other German fighters were flying above, dropping bombs fused to go off at their altitude. The sky seemed filled with debris as Flying Fortresses exploded and pieces of airplanes blew throughout their formation, while bodies continued to tumble out of crippled Fortresses, some dropping sickeningly to the countryside when their parachutes failed to open. Lay knew the target was still a half hour away, and with the 3rd Bombardment Wing so threatened, he seriously doubted any of them would get through.

Below *Piccadilly Lily,* Major Gilbert Cleven, commanding officer of the 350th Squadron, noted that his plane was one of only three survivors in his entire squadron. His second element had been completely wiped out as fighters bore in relentlessly, shooting more accurately than he had ever seen.

The Third Air Division fought its way to the initial point after fifteen bombers were shot down, but the 131 survivors maintained their formations and refused to admit defeat. As planes were shot out of formations, others moved in to close ranks and provide a solid front of firepower for those remaining.

LeMay's 1st Combat Wing, leading the Regensburg raid, had suffered least with only two losses. He did not realize what had happened to the following wings because they were under strict radio silence. The full extent of their losses would be known later, and he was appalled when he found that most survivors of the following wings were shot full of holes with wounded aboard. The other wings were smaller than his 1st Wing and had borne the brunt of the attacks.

As they turned on the initial point, LeMay could see for twenty-five miles in all directions, and the mile-square cluster of buildings of the Messerschmitt plant at Regensburg shone clearly.

Lieutenant Dunstan T. Abel, lead bombardier for the 96th Group, synchronized carefully on the target, grateful that the fighters did not attack and that there were only two bursts of antiaircraft fire.

"Bombs away!" Abel cried.

The entire wing dropped their bombs as they saw the bombs release from the lead plane at 11:45 A.M. Leaning over his bombsight, Abel watched anxiously for the bombs to hit. When they covered the plant, he let out a whoop, telling the crew that it appeared that nearly every building had been hit.

LeMay's division turned south after they all had dropped their bombs, losing another three aircraft before they reached the Swiss Alps, bringing their total losses to eighteen. The Germans turned back, and the Americans headed for North Africa.

Colonel Stanley T. Wray, Bomber Command's assistant operations officer, had been sent along by General Anderson to help direct the mission to Schweinfurt. Over German-occupied territory, Wray was grateful there were no enemy fighters in sight, and he still had ninety-six Spitfires to protect his bombers almost to Antwerp where two American fighter groups would take over protective custody until Aachen.

With the 91st Group in the lead, the formations started their climb to bombing altitude shortly after they crossed the Dutch coast. No sooner had the Fortresses reached bombing altitude than German fighters hit them. Major Thomas P. Becket's 384th Group, lowest and most vulnerable in the entire division, was immediately set upon, even though Spitfires engaged many of the German fighters. British fighters were still engaged ten miles north of Antwerp until they had to return home because of a shortage of fuel. They took a toll before their departure, downing nine German fighters, with no loss to themselves.

Major James J. Griffith's 96th Group was first to encounter German rockets, but here again they did no damage.

The 92nd Group ran into a flock of 109s shortly after crossing the coast that tore at the group with cannons firing at those in the rear.

Griffith stared with dismay when a large flash appeared in the center of a German fighter formation, and he found himself staring at three-inch rockets coming at them so slowly that he could see them. Black bursts appeared throughout the formation as they detonated. So powerful were their explosions that shrapnel caused extensive damage to two of the group's Fortresses.

The 91st and 381st groups in the lead ran into more fighters between Antwerp and Eupen. One plane headed earthward and seven bodies exited their doomed bomber, but two parachutes failed to open.

Lieutenant David Williams, chief navigator for the mission, fought off fighter attacks with nose guns as the lead formation met constant frontal attacks near Eupen.

General Williams, in a nearby plane, watched restlessly as his one good eye counted up the number of attacks. Noting their mounting losses, he hurried to the bombardier's compartment and grabbed a gun that wasn't in use, squeezing off shots at oncoming fighters.

He was concerned because he hadn't seen any friendly fighters. Lieutenant Colonel Donald Blakeslee's 4th United States Fighter Group had escorted them from Diest to Eupen, but had already broken off for lack of fuel. Some P-47 fighters had such trouble with their pressed-paper auxiliary tanks that they arrived just about in time for their scheduled departure. German fighters withdrew each time Allied fighters came along to support the bombers, knowing they would find easier pickings once the Allied fighters turned back.

The 78th Fighter Group took over from the 4th now, but they were eight minutes late at rendezvous, and seven fighters out of forty-four had to abort due to belly-tank failures. The remainder, led by Lieutenant Colonel James F. Stone, escorted one formation safely past Eupen and then turned back without even spotting a German fighter.

Between Koblenz and Frankfurt, the First Division lost its eighth Flying Fortress, while the 384th Group, in the lowest corner of the 2nd Combat Wing, fought off fighters coming from all directions.

General Williams spotted the factories at Schweinfurt at 2:50 P.M. They were only fifteen miles away, but with fighter attacks increasing and losses now up to twenty-one bombers, he knew it would seem an eternity before they could drop their bombs. He noticed that the city appeared small against a greenish-gold background. For some reason, he was surprised that it looked exactly as it had on the plaster mock-up back at headquarters. In the foreground, he noted the curves of the Main River, with hills rising away from the water's edge. He spotted the Würzburg railroad track that led unerringly to the center of the five factories of the ball-bearing complex.

Williams was confident that despite their heavy losses the Germans could not stop them from dropping their bombs. The target lay clearly exposed, and he could see how the railroad tracks converged into a marshaling yard with a passenger station and freight depot. He was proud of the way his men had fought their way through to the target against the worst opposition any bomber force had ever faced.

In Lieutenant Colonel Clemmons L. Wurzbach's lead plane, Lieutenant Sam Slayton made final adjustments on his bombsight, not knowing until later there was an unexploded German shell in their left fuel tank.

Five miles from the city, heavy flak slashed at their airplane, but soon they were through it and the bombs were away while the entire formation dropped on the leader. When they turned left to head for home, following crews could see the first cluster of bombs strike the factory, but later formations did not drop so accurately because of smoke spewing from factory buildings already hit.

Only eighteen B-17s of the 381st Group survived to reach the initial point. Now, another was hit by flak on the bomb run, falling out of formation with three engines out and dropping steeply in a low glide toward earth.

The 384th, in the coffin corner of the 2nd Wing, limped toward the target. Major Becket led his battered group into the target with only eleven bombers out of his original eighteen. Lieutenant Joseph W. Baggs found it difficult to bomb through the smoke and flames, and his formation's bombs hit to the left of the target despite a last-minute correction.

Colonel Howard M. "Slim" Turner's 40th Combat Wing was composed of the 305th, 306th, and 92nd groups and was led by Major William S. Raper. The wing found the target covered by smoke and flames, but they added to the destruction.

Colonel Henry Macdonald, deputy leader of the 40th, was shot out of formation on his return and crashed at an RAF emergency fighter strip along one of the camouflaged beaches. His boss, Slim Turner, gave him a well done for saving his crew, but the RAF station commander gave him an ass-chewing for tearing up his wire-mesh and tar-paper camouflage material.

When Colonel Maurice Preston's 4th Combat Wing arrived, the destruction was so heavy that his bombardier, Captain Joseph Brown, had difficulty spotting the aiming point. He finally did so and the formation's bombs added materially to the damage as the ball turret gunner reported the bombs were all on target.

The 303rd Group was the last to approach Schweinfurt and found that the defenders had added a protective smoke screen. Major Curt Mitchell's bombardier, Lieutenant Lawrence McCord, knew it would be difficult to locate their aiming point, the Kugel Fischer plant, despite its huge size. When McCord found they were coming in off course, he made a broad turn to line up with the factory, and he had only ninety seconds before bombs away.

A minute before bombs away, McCord was hit in the stomach by a piece of flak. The navigator, Lieutenant R. F. McElwain, quickly removed McCord from the sight. It was too late for accurate bombing, and the bombs dropped on the city of Schweinfurt. Tragically for civilians in the city, the bombs were dropped on them because their own antiaircraft fire had been accurate.

Lieutenant Rothery McKeegan, flying in the most vulnerable corner of the tightly knit 101st Wing, was exultant after they pulled away from the target. There hadn't been much flak directed at their formation and few fighters.

He called the crew. "We've made it. Old Dad will get you home."

He spoke too soon. Thirty seconds later a piece of flak cut the fuel line to his number-three engine. He tried to feather the propeller but it started to windmill. He felt as if everyone had their feet hanging out, dragging his B-17 back as they fell behind the others.

He called the formation's leader, asking him to slow down. The speed was reduced to 150 miles an hour, but now flak knocked out another of his plane's engines and they fell even farther behind.

McKeegan called Lieutenant Merlin D. Fetherolf, Jr., in the navigator's compartment. "Which is closer, fighter cover or Switzerland?"

"Fighter cover."

Near Frankfurt, McKeegan noticed little black dots growing more numerous on the horizon, and they were all headed in their direction.

Just as it didn't appear possible things could get any worse, a fire developed in the number-three engine, though it was forward of the fire wall, where he hoped it would be contained.

Desperately, McKeegan held to his homeward course, as dozens of calls announcing fighter attacks came over the intercom system.

Someone said, "Let's head for Switzerland."

Another replied, "Hell, we came here to fight. Let's take this bird home so she can bring another load of bombs next week."

McKeegan said, "We're headed for England. Come on, gang, keep those damned fighters off old Pappy's ass."

The enlisted men were flying with McKeegan for the first time, and he thanked God for the job they were doing, with his B-17 under constant fighter attack and claims of enemy fighters shot down rising by the minute.

Staff Sergeant Frank E. Williams, manning the left waist guns, was getting a free hair singe every time he tried to shoot from his side as cascades of shells ripped the fuselage around him.

Once, as he stepped back from the window, he saw Staff Sergeant Robert McLain stumble out of the tail section. The whole top of his helmet was ripped open and blood flowed down the sides of his face. Williams marveled that a man could walk in such a condition. Somehow McLain managed to get to the radio compartment, but he died soon afterward. Technical Sergeant Charles L. Murray quickly grabbed a walk-around oxygen bottle and headed for the tail guns to replace him.

Williams's attention had been distracted only a moment because another Nazi fighter was boring in with all guns firing. Carefully he took aim and watched with satisfaction as the enemy fighter disintegrated, giving him his second kill of the day.

He had concentrated so much on this first fighter that he failed to see the one behind it. A 20 mm shell from the second fighter exploded at the top of his window, showering him with fragments that slashed his face. At first, he thought he had lost a thumb that was around his gun's butt. Upon inspection, he found his thumb was bleeding but still wiggled.

Before he could get back in action, another shell exploded in back of his feet. A glance down showed him the heel of his right boot was gone.

In the rear, Murray called out his third kill after taking over the tail guns. Now, however, he was out of ammunition.

Fortunately, they had a breathing spell and there were no more fighter attacks for fifteen minutes. Williams was grateful because his gun would only fire four or five rounds at a time before it had to be recharged manually.

Although fighter attacks had ceased, the airplane was doomed, with flames pouring out of the second engine. McKeegan, slumped behind his armor plate after 20 mm fragments had slashed his arm, knew they had to bail out. To his consternation, the alarm bell wouldn't work, so he told his engineer, Technical Sergeant Albert E. Peach, to clear everyone out of the waist. To his copilot, Lieutenant Frank J. Sulkowski, he said, "Get Marty and Buck out of the nose!"

McKeegan fought to keep the stricken bomber level as Fetherolf and Lieutenant Baxter F. Harris hurried out of the nose to the escape hatch. The gunners had reported eight kills, so McKeegan figured that was a fair exchange for a B-17.

In the waist, Williams bailed out first, followed by Staff Sergeants James M. Prehart and Claude M. Davis.

Once he was sure that everyone had left the aircraft, McKeegan dropped his legs out of the escape hatch to tumble out, but those extra pounds he had recently acquired were almost his undoing. His shoulders stuck to the sides of the hatch, and he had visions of his knees plowing up acres of Kraut soil when the airplane hit.

After struggling for ten seconds that seemed like an eternity, McKeegan climbed back to the flight deck. One look at the mess there convinced him that he *had* to get out—and quickly. Hastily, he dove headfirst through the hatch, this time clearing all sides.

While he swung beneath his parachute, a German fighter circled a couple of times, and McKeegan got an empty feeling in the pit of his stomach. He feared the worst, but the German fighter pilot broke away without firing.

For months, the Belgian underground kept McKeegan safe from capture, but he was finally betrayed and ended up in a prisoner-of-war camp. Williams also evaded capture, with the help of the underground, but he was located later by the Germans and also was sent to a German prisoner-of-war camp.

One hundred eighty-two Flying Fortresses had dropped 420 tons of bombs, but the cost was high. Three cripples failed to make England, bringing total losses for the Schweinfurt force alone to 36. German fighters attacked the formations on their return until Allied fighters met them along the coast and fought them off. Among the bombers that returned, 122 were damaged, 27 so seriously it was thought they would never fly again.

While Williams's shattered First Air Division was landing in England, LeMay's Third Division was starting to touch down at two air bases in North Africa at Bône one hundred miles west of Tunis.

Before the mission, Brigadier General Lauris Norstad, Spaatz's chief of staff, had told him the fields at Telargma would provide them with supplies, extra mechanics, everything he needed because it was not only a depot but a combat base. When LeMay found the base virtually deserted, with only a skeleton crew because the war in Africa had moved eastward, he was livid.

After Beirne Lay arrived in *Piccadilly Lily,* he too was astonished at the condition of the base, appreciating LeMay's caustic comments about Norstad's incompetence.

For the first time, LeMay learned how badly his Third Division had been mauled. In the lead, frontal attacks hadn't been bad, and the 96th Group, with which LeMay flew, hadn't lost an airplane. As Lay briefed LeMay as to actual losses, describing the heavy attacks on the rear elements, the division commander was shocked. He had insisted on radio discipline so as not to aid German fighter pilots, so he learned only now how bad things had been several miles behind his lead formation.

As one heavily damaged airplane after another limped in, LeMay knew he had a critical situation on his hands because there were no adequate maintenance facilities to repair them. He wondered how they could complete their shuttle bombing by getting ready for another mission en route back to England.

He wired Eaker and told him that he had lost twenty-four of the 146 planes with which he had started out, and that the condition of his command was not good.

Eaker had already got the sad news about the heavy losses on the Schweinfurt raid, and with LeMay's losses added to them, it appeared that it was the worst day the Eighth had ever suffered. He decided to fly to North Africa to appraise the situation.

LeMay greeted Eaker soberly the next day when he arrived in North Africa.

"Curt, when will you be able to go back?"

"As soon as we hang some bombs and put some fuel in these crates."

In talking with Eaker, LeMay said he was convinced the Regensburg plant was destroyed. He said the destruction was due to skilled bombardiers at the head of tight formations. He admitted losses were sobering. He told Eaker that in addition to the twenty-four bombers that failed to reach Africa, another six had gone down in the Mediterranean or Italy. At least twenty others, and possibly more, he said, would never fly again. And, not sparing the bad news, LeMay said, "Perhaps twice that number are so badly damaged that they need repairs."

Despite his losses, LeMay insisted upon bombing a target en route to England. Eaker refused. "We'll see that you fly across North Africa and the Bay of Biscay at night."

In England, Eaker noted that in addition to the sixty bombers shot down on the Schweinfurt mission, forty to fifty others would never fly again, and one hundred more would need significant repairs. Eaker had not expected to lose so many.

General Williams, who led the mission, told him that four of his First Division groups were so badly depleted that he could put only six combat boxes in the air for another mission in the immediate future. LeMay's division was in even worse shape due to the lack of repair facilities in North Africa.

These raids demonstrated again the dire need for long-range fighters. They did hasten the day of long-range fighter availability, and later, at a critical time on the Russian front, the Germans had to recall many of their fighters to protect the industrial heart of Germany.

After the mission, Eaker told his staff, "It was a bold strategic concept and one of the most significant and remarkable air battles of the Second World War."

After losing 147 bombers and fifty-five crews in one day, Eaker was forced to keep his planes on the ground for ten days while his command rebuilt its strength.

Albert Speer claimed in his book, *Inside the Third Reich,* that the Americans made a mistake by dividing their force, sending half to Schweinfurt and the other half to Regensburg. He said ball-bearing production at Schweinfurt dropped 38 percent, whereas there was only negligible damage at Regensburg. Industrialists resisted relocation, he said, because production would have been held up three to four months.

He said armaments production would have been crucially weakened after two months, and after four months would have been brought to a complete standstill if attacks had been continued. Such attacks, he admitted, would have had to have been made against all ball-bearing plants at Steyr, Erkner, Cannstatt, and in France and Italy as well as Schweinfurt, and been made every two weeks regardless of what postattack photographs showed.

At the time, however, the German High Command viewed the raids with consternation, and attacks against Göring increased in number and maliciousness. Germany's armaments chief, Feldmarschall Erhard Milch, told Speer, "We're no longer on the offensive."

16

A CLASSIC EXAMPLE
OF PRECISION BOMBING

It was clear to Eaker that the German air force had to be destroyed before sustained day bombing of Germany could be feasible. He was still pressing hard for development of long-range escort fighters before deeper penetrations into the Reich were undertaken.

He wrote Arnold August 30, thanking him for promising long-range fighters, even though Arnold still hadn't specified when they would be available.

The air force chief of staff arrived in England September 1, and Eaker reminded him again of the escort fighter problem. Arnold cabled Marshall, endorsing Eaker's plea. "Operations over Germany conducted here during the past couple of weeks indicate definitely that we must provide long-range fighters to accompany daylight bombardment missions."

Later, Arnold sent Marshall another cable. This one dealt with the diversion of more fighters from England to North Africa. Eisenhower had requested them earlier, and evidently Arnold had unthinkingly approved his request. After listening to Eaker, Arnold realized that he had made a mistake. Eisenhower needed all the fighters he could get because his forces were invading Italy in two days, but Eaker's problem was equally acute.

When Italy surrendered on September 8, the war in the north of the peninsula was continued by the Germans, but thirty Italian divisions were eliminated from the Balkans, and the first wedge was taken out of Fortress Europe. With the Italian fleet out of the war, Allied naval units were available for use elsewhere. The loss of Italy to the war effort was a blow to German prestige but, most importantly, Hitler had to disperse his ground and air efforts even more to take over from Mussolini's armies in the north of Italy and the Balkans after Naples was captured October 1.

The United States Army Air Forces gained airfields near the Adriatic, which opened up important targets in the Balkans, Czechoslovakia, Austria, and eastern and southern Germany. There were many vital targets in these areas, including the Danube supply route, the Wiener Neustadt industries, and the Ploesti oil fields. For the first time, Allied air forces could directly assist the Russians in their drives toward Romania and Bulgaria.

During the Quadrant Conference in Quebec in late August, while Italian leaders were negotiating their country's surrender, Arnold expressed doubt that strategic bombing from bases in occupied Italy could accomplish much if operated independently. He was more than ever convinced that an overall command should control all United States bomber operations. He argued that such control would permit movement of bomber forces between England and Italy as weather permitted and the choice of targets dictated.

At Quebec, he said he had his doubts that heavy bombers could be used to maximum advantage prior to the 1944 invasion of the Continent, then tentatively set for May 1, if they were confined to operations from English bases.

Portal agreed, but he was equally concerned by the slow progress being made in reducing German air force activities. "Unless the fighters are checked in the next three months," he said, "the battle might be lost."

Portal said all of southern Germany would be within easy range once northern Italy was occupied. (In fact, it took until the end of the war before all of Italy surrendered to the Allied powers.) He reminded Churchill and Roosevelt that two of Germany's largest aircraft factories, which produced 60 percent of the enemy's fighters, as well as the Ploesti oil fields were all within easy range of such Italian bases. Portal cited other pluses, such as removal of half of Germany's fighters from the western front to the southern front to protect vital industries. In conclusion, he said that bombers flying from Italy would find the Alps a useful shield against Germany's early-warning network.

About a month after the Quadrant Conference, Eisenhower and Spaatz approved Arnold's plans to use Italian bases. Eisenhower reminded Marshall, however, that new airfields must be built, runways extended, and additional steel matting made available before such operations could begin.

Eisenhower had always assumed that General Marshall would be assigned as Supreme Allied Commander for the invasion of Europe in 1944. In a memorandum to his chief October 5, he told Marshall that he would need a top air leader under him—one who had served his schooling in all phases of air employment, particularly in supporting armies in the field. He said the greatest danger lay in selecting an air commander who was wedded to strategic bombing.

Before and during the assault, he advised Marshall, you will need every plane you can get. Without the right top man, the supreme commander would find airmen scattering their efforts in strategic raids inside Germany, making no direct contribution to victory on the battlefield.

He strongly recommended that Air Chief Marshal Tedder be given the job because he was an expert in air-ground coordination. He said also that Tedder had the complete confidence of Chief of Air Staff Portal, and during critical periods, Tedder would be able to get every last British airplane from Portal without procrastination.

Eisenhower described Tedder as a personal friend, but said that he was willing to release him from the Mediterranean in favor of giving Marshall the utmost advantage as Supreme Allied Commander.

In a memorandum to the Joint Chiefs October 9, and later to the Combined Chiefs, Arnold submitted a plan for dividing the Twelfth Air Force. He said that two air forces should be created: one for tactical support of ground troops, the other for strategic bombing, in line with decisions made at Quadrant. He said Italian air bases could be used to attack targets that were beyond the range of bombers in the United Kingdom, thereby helping to destroy them and also to divert German air and ground defenses from the western front. He said that with strategic bases in England and Italy, it would be possible to shuttle from one country to another, bombing targets en route. One of the advantages of bases in Italy, according to Arnold, was to increase the number of operations against the enemy by using either country's bases at times when weather was a factor in one of them, and not in the other.

His recommendations were approved, despite objections from Eaker, who viewed shuttle operations with some misgivings, based on his own recent experiences with North Africa.

The Twelfth Air Force, which would be responsible for tactical support of ground operations, and a new Fifteenth Air Force, which supposedly would be used as part of the Combined Bomber Offensive, would both take orders from the theater commander, and the Combined Chiefs would issue directives for its strategic employment. Eaker predicted such an arrangement would jeopardize the air offensive as well as the cross-channel invasion. Later events proved him correct. As he prophesied, the weather in Italy wasn't all that good in comparison with English weather, and construction of the needed airfields caused delays. The

Fifteenth had continual problems with facilities to maintain its heavy bombers.

James H. Doolittle, who had won a Medal of Honor for leading a squadron of medium bombers on the first raid over Japan June 9, 1942, now commanded the Twelfth Air Force as a major general. He had been sent to the Mediterranean by Arnold when the Twelfth was created shortly after the Tokyo raid. General Marshall, the army chief of staff, recommended to Eisenhower that Major General George S. Patton, Jr., be given command of ground operations, and Doolittle of air operations.

At first, Eisenhower was not happy with Doolittle's performance, but Doolittle slowly gained Eisenhower's confidence and, in a unique action, Ike wrote on the citation for Doolittle's second Distinguished Service Medal, "This man, during the period he has been in my command, has improved more than any other senior officer."

When Doolittle assumed command of the Twelfth Air Force in the fall of 1942, his case was unusual. He had never commanded anything larger than a squadron, so he had a lot to learn. While he had been out of the service during the 1930s, many tactical and strategic ideas had been developed by others, and he was now at a serious disadvantage. Eisenhower's original criticism was based on his belief that Doolittle was not a professional military airman. At the time, Doolittle privately agreed with him.

In his dealings with other high-ranking officers, Doolittle had a major problem. He was the only reservist in any of the services ever to achieve three-star rank, as he did later in the war. Many regular officers resented the fact that he had left the service, taken a lucrative job in industry, and made much more money than if he had stayed on active duty. Many of his subordinates resented his quick promotions and told him bluntly they would not work for him. In each case, he abided by their wishes—and transferred them.

When it came to the question of division of the Twelfth Air Force in late summer of 1943, Doolittle sided with Arnold and Spaatz.

Procedures were quickly set in motion to transfer six groups of heavy bombers from the Twelfth to the nucleus of the new Fifteenth Air Force. Eaker's worst fears were realized when fifteen more groups were withdrawn from the allocations for the Eighth Air Force and sent to Italy. Foggia was selected for a cluster of airfields because weather supposedly was better there in winter, and it was believed that heavy bombers could operate on fifty-five days from November 1 to May 1, compared to an average of thirty-one days in the same period from the United Kingdom.

Spaatz met several times with Eisenhower's chief of staff, Major General Walter Bedell Smith, to iron out details. Arnold's plan was approved October 16, and Eisenhower had a new air force in his Mediterranean theater.

Eaker had opposed the plan all along, and Portal, who earlier had favored such a plan, now joined Eaker in opposition. Both were concerned that the Combined Bomber Offensive and the invasion would be jeopardized by the splitting of the bombing effort. They were in the minority. The Fifteenth was activated November 1 with Spaatz as commanding general of the Army Air Forces in the Mediterranean theater, and Doolittle was named to head the Fifteenth Air Force, with headquarters at Foggia. The Fifteenth would build up to a total of twenty-one heavy groups, seven fighter groups, and a reconnaissance group by March 31, 1944. It would serve under the Mediterranean commander and would operate under guidance of the Combined Bomber Offensive plan, but would also be available for emergency needs of the ground forces.

Arnold still was not satisfied with such an arrangement. The problem wasn't resolved until November at the Sextant Conference at Cairo. The British disliked Arnold's plan for establishment of a European-wide United States Strategic Air Command, but they were overruled. Henceforth, operations of the Fifteenth in Italy and the Eighth in England were linked in an organization called the United States Strategic Air Forces in Europe under Spaatz.

At this conference, Eisenhower was selected to lead the Allied Expeditionary Forces in the cross-channel invasion to be launched from England in the spring of 1944.

The problem-plagued P-38 was finally able to extend its radius of action to 450 miles in October 1943, although it still had difficulty attacking German fighters at high altitudes because it was less maneuverable.

General Hunter's early efforts, before he was relieved, at last brought results. In November, the P-47 groups had destroyed 273 German fighters for the loss of 73. Bomber losses dropped sharply, although German use of rockets, air-to-air bombing, and long-range cannon fire caused increasing concern. Air-to-air bombing was more psychological than destructive. It was disconcerting, to say the least, for formations on their way to the target to sit almost helplessly while tons of bombs were dropped on them from far above. Returning crews were most shaken by twin-engine ME-110s, which attacked from the rear with 20 mm and 30 mm cannons, staying safely out of the range of the bombers' .50-caliber guns.

The first B-17Gs had arrived during August and September with chin turrets, so crews now could fight off head-on attacks more successfully. It had been all but impossible to do so with hand-held guns.

VIII Bomber Command strength rose to 373 bombers after the B-24 units, which had been detached for the August 1 Ploesti raids, returned to help with the bombing of central Germany.

Losses rose as the Eighth penetrated ever deeper into the Reich, including missions as far as Danzig and Gdynia in Poland. Except for missions to Anklam and Marienburg, where the Focke-Wulfe plants were almost completely destroyed, the results were poor. Weather proved uncooperative throughout most of September, and clouds obscured the whole of Germany for eighteen days.

The successful raid on Marienburg on October 3 so impressed Sir Charles Portal that he wrote Churchill, "This is the best high-altitude bombing we have seen in this war. All but one building of the factory was destroyed, and that was damaged. It was a magnificent attack."

Reich officials were profoundly disturbed by these attacks against Polish and East Prussian targets because they knew now that no part of the Reich was immune. Perhaps Göring was the most surprised of all because he had gone to Marienburg to dedicate a new runway. Just before noon, he had to run for his life along with everyone else to escape a cascade of American bombs.

Eaker called the raid a classic example of precision bombing.

The Eighth had the strength to go out again the following day against Münster's rail junction. On this raid, against a key transportation center in the northern part of the Ruhr, German fighters ganged up on the 100th Group in the lead. At the time, rumors were rife that this was an act of revenge because a 100th pilot allegedly had deliberately fallen behind his formation as German fighters approached. By mutual informal agreement among pilots, this was a signal the bomber was surrendering. But when the Germans closed in to escort the bomber to the airfield, the story went, United States gunners opened fire at point-blank range. There is no evidence that this story is true. It is more likely that the 100th, the first B-17 group to have shiny aluminum airplanes instead of the camouflaged early models, stood out more clearly than the others, or that someone's landing gear had dropped as a result of battle damage.

In any event, the massed firepower of German fighters broke the 100th's formation apart in two minutes, destroying all but one bomber in seven minutes. Although other units of the Third Air Division did not suffer such catastrophic losses, they were still heavy, with 29 bombers out of 119 failing to return. Allied claims of 183 German fighters were greatly exaggerated; the Germans actually lost 22 fighters, with 5 damaged.

Morale plummeted at the 100th's home at Thorpe Abbots as the "bloody" 100th licked its wounds.

Arnold wired Eaker that he was pleased with these multiple attacks, which were, he said, hurting the enemy. "As you turn your efforts away from shipbuilding and cities, toward crippling the sources of the still-growing German fighter forces, the air war is clearly moving toward air supremacy in the air. Carry on."

He was too optimistic, as events were quickly to prove.

The loss of eighty-eight heavy bombers in three days undermined morale, and the strain of almost-daily operations began to take its toll.

Eaker noted that German fighters now waited until bombers turned from their initial points for the run into the target before attacking. They flew parallel to the bombers, out of range of their guns, in groups of twenty to forty. Then, singly, or in pairs, they peeled off to make frontal attacks.

Eaker, who had recently been made a Knight Commander of the Most Excellent Order of the British Empire by King George VI, was deeply concerned by the losses. He appreciated, however, the fact that bombing accuracy had improved so much in the last three months. He knew it was due to better crew training in the States and increasing discipline in formation and bomb-aiming over the target. Strong discipline, he knew, was essential because German fighter pilots were concentrating on lead formations, one group at a time, to split them and shoot down the stragglers.

Anderson and his Bomber Command staff had completed a new plan October 12 to attempt the total destruction of the ball-bearing plants at Schweinfurt. When he sought Eaker's approval, the head of the Eighth Air Force came to High Wycombe to discuss the mission. He listened carefully as Anderson outlined plans for the new strike, meeting in the underground command post. Eaker approved the strike for all available bombers to hit the Schweinfurt factories on the fourteenth.

Casablanca conferees. Seated, President Franklin D. Roosevelt and Prime Minister Winston Churchill. Members of the Combined Chiefs of Staff, standing *(from left)*, General Henry H. Arnold, Admiral Ernest J. King, General George C. Marshall, Admiral of the Fleet Sir Dudley Pound, General Sir Alan Brooke, and Air Chief Marshal Sir Charles Portal. *Courtesy of United States Air Force*

Walking with RAF Air Chief Marshal Sir Arthur T. Harris on his estate are *(left)* General Henry H. "Hap" Arnold, commanding general, United States Army Air Forces, and *(right)* Major General Ira Eaker, commanding general, Eighth Air Force. *United States Air Force photo*

Boeing B-17H Flying Fortress. *United States Air Force photo*

B-24 Liberator. *United States Air Force photo*

British Lancaster Mark III. © *Imperial War Museum, London*

With the aid of instruments, a Ninth Air Force B-26 Marauder Bombardier releases eight 500-pound bombs through heavy clouds onto a German railroad yard. *United States Air Force photo*

RAF Wellington Bomber. © *Imperial War Museum, London*
Side view of the deadly Focke-Wulf 190D. *Courtesy of United States Air Force*

A deadly adversary. The German Messerschmitt 210 caused the loss of many Allied bombers. *Courtesy of United States Air Force*

Messerschmitt 109G. One of the most versatile German fighters, the ME-109 went through a series of configurations. *Courtesy of United States Air Force*

The Ruhr, the industrial heart of Germany, was bombed repeatedly by the Royal Air Force and by United States Army Air Forces. Dispersal of bomb craters indicates how frequently important targets were missed. *Courtesy of 305th Group Memorial Association*

Pinpoint bombing. This raid against plants at Vegesack was one of the few times that such accuracy was achieved. *Courtesy of United States Air Force*

Cologne marshaling yards, frequently attacked by Royal Air Force and American bombers, show extensive damage. Miraculously, city's cathedral, upper right, remained nearly intact. *Courtesy of 305th Group Memorial Association*

Submarine pens at Saint-Nazaire. Flying Fortresses, in one of their heaviest raids, failed to damage the sub pens themselves. *Courtesy of United States Air Force*

B-17 Flying Fortresses head away from Schweinfurt after the August 1943 bombing. Target was clearly visible for early attackers, but smoke from burning plant prevented accurate bombing by later planes. *Courtesy of United States Air Force*

Royal visit to Bassingborne, an American base in England. Queen Elizabeth and King George VI *(second from right)*, tour the flight line. Other officers *(from left)*, Brigadier General Haywood S. Hansell, Jr., Brigadier General Fred Anderson, who was head of the VIII Bomber Command, and Colonel Stanley Wray. *Courtesy of Major General Haywood S. Hansell, Jr.*

Remarkable reconstruction efforts by German work crews were started immediately after each raid on the ball-bearing plant at Schweinfurt. Note machinery protruding from rubble, and neat stacks of pipes and lumber for rebuilding the vital plant. *Courtesy of United States Air Force*

Battered marshaling yards at Foggia, Italy, were still out of commission eight months after American B-17s and B-24s bombed them in February 1944 to prevent German resupply of the Anzio and Cassino fronts. *United States Air Force photo*

Bombers struck the Renault motor vehicle and armaments plants near Paris on April 4, 1943. *Courtesy of United States Air Force*

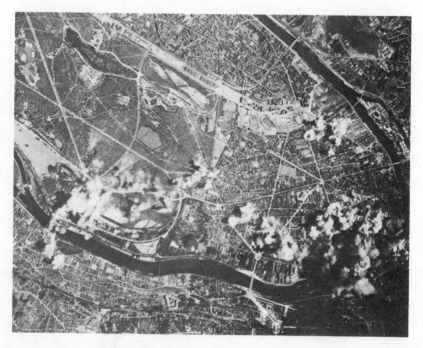

Lieutenant General James Doolittle addresses a unit that has completed one hundred missions. Seated *(left to right)*: Lieutenant General Carl A. Spaatz, an unidentified colonel, and Major General Curtis LeMay. *United States Air Force photo*

Aircraft 807 had its entire tail shot off at twenty thousand feet over Flushing, Netherlands, on August 19, 1943. Fate of its 305th Group crew is unknown. *Courtesy of 305th Group Memorial Association*

Major General Lewis H. Brereton *(left)* commanding general of the Ninth Air Force, and Lieutenant General Carl Spaatz, head of United States Strategic Air Forces, plan the invasion of Europe with General Dwight D. Eisenhower, chief of Allied forces in the European Theater.

Lieutenant Theodore A. Wilson of the all-black, Italy-based 99th Fighter Squadron rolls his parachute, having successfully bailed out of his P-40 after it was badly hit by enemy flak on May 3, 1944. *United States Air Force photo*

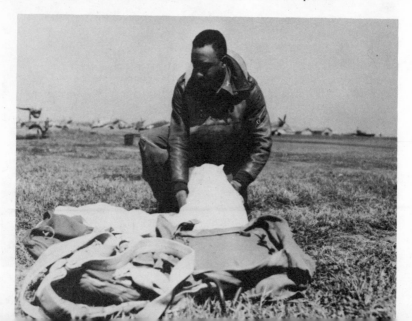

Germany's dreaded ME-262 jet fighter, deployed too late in the war to save the Reich. *United States Air Force photo*

Remarkable photograph taken during the July 15, 1944, raid on Rumania's Ploesti oil fields shows bombs falling past a B-17. Note flak burst (black smoke) ahead of the plane below. *United States Air Force photo*

The Normandy beachhead. Eisenhower's promise to give his invasion troops local air supremacy was fulfilled on June 6, 1944. Nevertheless, barrage balloons to

discourage German strafing are still tethered above a Channel black with
amphibious vessels. *United States Air Force photo*

German V-2 ballistic missile used against England and France. *United States Air Force photo*

Symbol of triumph. Nazi flag, flying over Schweinfurt when Major General "Lightnin' Joe" Collins and his 42nd "Rainbow" Division captured the city near the end of the war, was presented to the 305th Group, whose operations were typical of the Eighth Air Force's performance on the crucial Schweinfurt missions. Group Commander Colonel Henry Macdonald *(left)*, made the presentation to his men with Major George Schubert at his side. *Courtesy of Colonel Macdonald*

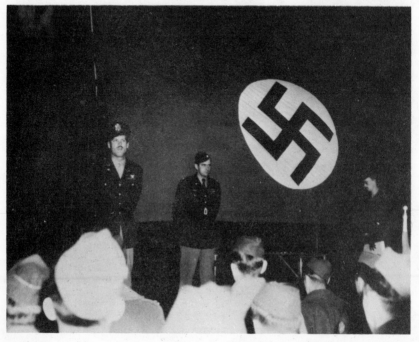

17

A HELL OF A FIGHT

It was a cold and foggy morning October 14 at Grafton Underwood when an Intelligence major strode to the front of the briefing room of the 92nd Group. He had fought as a fighter pilot in World War I with the Lafayette Escadrille and had volunteered to serve in another war. The men all called him pop and felt warm affection for him, knowing he had wangled his way to fly several rough combat missions, even though he was much too old for flying.

"Gentlemen, this morning we have quite a show," he said. He drew back the curtain while all eyes followed the heavy black yarn as it marked their route from Britain, across the Channel and the Low Countries, to a spot deep in Germany. "It's Schweinfurt again."

There were moans and curses as fliers stared at the dreaded target that had cost them so heavily in the middle of August.

The major said the First and Third Air Divisions would cross the Continent several miles apart, with the First Division taking off ten minutes ahead of the Third. "This has been done to confuse German fighter control, split his defenses, and prevent an overwhelming attack on either force. The Second Division will fly a more southerly route, and at a higher speed, which will bring them over Schweinfurt after the Third has bombed."

He freely discussed the hazards of the mission, reminding them that on the Münster raid German 109s and 190s had launched rockets from one thousand to seventeen hundred yards, and then reverted to their conventional roles as fighters. He said intelligence estimates figured there were five hundred German fighters in central and northern Germany, along with two hundred more in the occupied countries.

Next, the flak officer pointed to the red circles on the map along their route, saying that the three hundred flak guns reported around the target during the August raid had been doubled.

The Eighth's Fighter Command had hoped to sweep the target area with modified P-38s now that their radius of action had been increased, but they didn't become operational until the following day.

A message from General Anderson was read. "This air operation today is the most important air operation yet conducted in this war. The target must be destroyed. It is of vital importance to the enemy. Your friends and comrades who have been lost, and will be lost today, are depending upon you. Their sacrifices must not be in vain. Good luck, good shooting, and good bombing."

Colonel Budd J. Peaslee, from wing headquarters, had been assigned as First Division commander. He was scheduled to fly with the 92nd Group's operations officer Captain James K. McLaughlin. He spoke last. "If our bombing is good, and we hit this ball-bearing city well, we are bound to scatter a lot of balls around the streets of Schweinfurt. Tonight I expect the Germans will all feel they are walking around on roller skates." The laughter that followed was forced.

While four hundred B-17s and B-24s waited for permission to take off, a British Mosquito reconnaissance airplane flew over the target area to determine whether it was clear. Finally, the word was radioed back, "All of central Germany is in the clear."

General Anderson turned calmly to his aides. "Let the bombers take off."

Over 1,500 engines roared to life all across the Midlands shortly before 10:00 A.M. As bombers started to abort, the total came down to 377 forming over England, including 163 from the much-smaller Second Air Division. With most planes trying to form up in the clouds, the Second Division had difficulty assembling and was forced to cancel the mission except for twenty-four B-24s that were diverted to a secondary target in the Frisian Islands.

As the two B-17 divisions headed for the Continent, mechanical problems reduced their formations by another twenty-six bombers. It was not an auspicious start.

Anderson had issued strict orders that the mission should be aborted unless a complete wing formation was available to go over the target.

In the 40th Wing, one group had failed to join up, so it was short a third of its bombers. Its air commander, Colonel Peaslee, elected to go on and, breaking radio silence, told the following group to assume the lead because the 92nd was relinquishing it and would join them. He said that he would retain his command position in the high group.

Soon, friendly fighters weaved back and forth above them, and they were a welcome sight. They kept well out of range of trigger-happy gunners on the bombers. Then, at Aachen, they had to leave.

Their departure had been awaited by German fighters.

"Bogies!" called Peaslee's tail gunner, counting off as many as sixty German fighters.

Peaslee listened to the intercom as shrill voices tumbled over one another to announce attacks from all directions. He chewed them out for their lack of discipline, and the chatter died down.

Peaslee spotted so many German fighters that he soon lost count, sitting there in the copilot's seat, dreading every moment, knowing some bombers had already become victims along with their ten-man crews.

He was alerted to flashes that seemed to come directly at them, realizing quickly they were from 20 mm cannons as German fighters attacked head on. He marveled that they were not hit. Some fighters came so close that only a miracle spared fighter and bomber from collisions. He had been scared before, but nothing like now when he began to think they'd never survive such vicious attacks.

Peaslee acted quickly to check his formation and see how it was faring. Miraculously, all seemed to be with them. The plane's regular copilot, flying in the tail gunner's position, reported that airplanes to the rear of the bomber stream were in serious trouble. Two were smoking, he said, and one was falling back.

Guns roared again as fighters pressed their attacks at breathtaking speeds. Peaslee yelled at the gunners to save their ammunition. "Short bursts!"

"B-17 going down in flames," the copilot reported. "No parachutes."

Next, he called out that a formation of HE-111 light bombers and ME-210s were approaching at seven o'clock high. "My God! They've fired rockets!"

Peaslee could barely see the fighters as they came around in front on their breakaway.

Time fuses exploded the rockets and spread shrapnel like hail through their formation, some just fifty feet away. The rocket explosions revealed bright red centers like flak but blossoming to four times the size of antiaircraft bursts.

Fighter attacks now came from all angles. The gunners were making short bursts, Peaslee noted with relief, fully aware they'd need every round of ammunition if they were to have a chance of getting home. The interphone was quiet, the gunners were too busy to talk.

McLaughlin, sitting beside Peaslee, had been wounded, but he continued to fly the airplane. He pointed to a bomber in front that had been hit by a rocket. They both stared in shocked silence as the right wing folded upward, its propellers still turning, the fuselage slashed open as if a giant can opener had ripped it apart. While they watched, a man with one arm torn off hurtled out of the doomed bomber. The pilots still sat at their controls, fighting to keep their airplane in the air.

A glance to the right showed Peaslee their right-wing plane was falling back for no apparent reason. It suddenly disappeared. Other gaps appeared in the formation, and they were quickly filled by others who moved up from their own shattered formations. Everyone now wanted to be as close to the others as possible for mutual protection.

The formation plodded desperately forward. There was no evasive action against so many fighters; a maneuver might run them directly into the guns of the fighters. Commanders had learned it was best to stay in formation and fight it out.

As rocket attacks grew heavier, Peaslee authorized a shallow turn to the right to increase the deflection angle faced by German fighters. When rocket attacks ceased momentarily, formations slid back on course.

At the initial point, Peaslee was appalled to learn that his 92nd Group, which had started out with thirty-seven bombers, *now had only eight planes. The other group was down to six.* By radio, he quickly ordered the following group to join him and drop on their leader.

Peaslee interjected a word to their bombardier as he started to synchronize. "We've come a long way for this. Let's make it good."

Fighter attacks increased in intensity, and Peaslee was amazed to be still airborne. When flak from the ground burst all around, he was almost relieved, knowing fighters usually let up on formations at this point. Instead, German fighters ignored their own flak to continue their attacks. In the resulting melee, Peaslee had a moment to admire the extraordinary bravery of the German fighter pilots who had been ordered to stop the bombers or not come back.

After what seemed like an eternity, he felt the airplane lighten. At 2:40 he knew the bombs were away. A glance some moments later showed Peaslee that the bombs covered the target.

During the turnaway to the right, Peaslee glanced back at the formations still fighting their way in. They flew on relentlessly, even though they were under constant attack. Here and there a bomber burst into flames; Peaslee counted eleven columns of smoke rising from the wreckage of American bombers on the ground.

Without warning, ten members of another crew in his own formation hastily bailed out of the bomber to their right. To the rear, a bomber was hit in the center of its fuselage by an eight-inch rocket, and the resulting explosion sent debris hurtling like knives through the formation. There were no survivors.

The 305th Group, which had joined the wrong wing at assembly, had suffered terrible losses. Major G. G. Y. Normand responded negatively to a suggestion from his bombardier, Lieutenant John Pellegrini, that they make another run because they had been following the 91st Group and, he was convinced, were off target. He knew what Pellegrini did not know—there were only three B-17s left out of the eighteen that had departed Chelveston that morning. He said that if they went around to make another approach, they would be on their own and defenseless. He advised his bombardier to do his best, and their bombs were dropped on the center of the city. Normand was shocked again when another 305th plane fell back and headed down. Now there were only two left in his formation.

Lieutenant Silas Nettles, flying his second mission, was tail-end Charlie for the last wing of the Third Division. The original thirty-seven bombers in his group were down to sixteen as they headed on the bomb run. Nettles fought to keep his bomber in formation despite one engine shot out. He managed to do so until his bombardier, Lieutenant E. O. Jones, dropped their bombs. As he pulled away from the target, he kept dropping behind their formation until they were all alone over Schweinfurt. Then, with a horrible screech, one of the propellers started to run away. He quickly feathered it. With two engines out and flames shooting back from another, he ordered the crew to bail out. They obeyed the bail-out bell, and all ended up in a prisoner-of-war camp.

The First Division reached its rally point and assembled its depleted ranks. Despite smoke pouring out of the ball-bearing plants, it was feared they had not inflicted as much damage as they had suffered. Fighter attacks continued en route home, but they were halfhearted against Peaslee's wing because it maintained a tight formation. The Germans fell on the cripples, which were easier prey.

After touchdown, Wing Commander Colonel Howard M. Turner and 92nd Group Commander Colonel William Reid greeted Peaslee as he almost staggered out of the aircraft, hardly believing he was still alive. To their questions as to the rest of the group, Peaslee said, "You have just watched the group land. All that's left of it. We had a hell of a fight."

Turner and Reid were shocked. Only one squadron out of the 92nd's three had returned. They had been led to believe, through early reports, that the mission had been a milk run.

The Third Division reached Aachen in equally bad shape, hoping to pick up fighter escorts for the final leg of their journey. The P-47s were nowhere in sight; bad weather had grounded them in England.

The clouds were so thick that returning bombers landed at any base they could locate. When losses were tallied, it was learned that sixty B-17s had failed to return.

Arnold sent Eaker a cable indicating the alarm the heavy loss had aroused in Washington. "It appears from my viewpoint that the German air force is on the verge of collapse. We must not, repeat, not miss any symptoms of German air collapse. Can you add any substantiating evidence of collapse?"

Eaker replied the next day. "Yesterday the Hun sprang his trap. He's fully revealed his countermeasure to our daylight bombing." Eaker described the air battle, discussed the losses on both sides, and estimated the damage to the factories. "This does not represent disaster. The Eighth Air Force is ready to answer the enemy's challenge." He told Arnold that he could help by rushing replacement crews and planes, and send a large supply of 110- and 150-gallon drop tanks, which were desperately needed to extend the range of P-51 and P-38 fighters.

"We must show the enemy we can replace our losses," Eaker said. "He knows he can't replace his. We must continue the battle with unrelenting fury. This we shall do. There's no discouragement here. We're convinced when the totals are in that yesterday's losses will be far outweighed by the value of the enemy matériel destroyed."

Once he had more accurate information, he wrote Arnold a letter.

> I have within the past half hour seen the first strike photographs of yesterday's attack on Schweinfurt, and I shall be surprised if it is not classed as one of the best bombing efforts yet. Unless the strike photos are very deceiving, we shall find that the three ball-bearing factories are out of business for a long, long time.
>
> In regard to your personal cable regarding the German air force, yesterday's effort was not contrary thereto. I class it pretty much as the last, final struggles of a monster in his death throes. There is not the slightest question but that we have our teeth in the Hun air force's neck.

In conclusion, he pleaded with Arnold that he help to put more bite in those teeth by supplying the men and planes he desperately needed.

President Roosevelt told a press conference the Eighth Air Force could not afford to lose sixty bombers every day. He hastened to say that he wasn't implying that number had been lost over Schweinfurt when the press questioned him about the actual number.

He tried to get his foot out of his mouth as gracefully as possible, but he made matters only worse. He told his press conference that Germany's loss of one hundred fighters was a far smaller loss than sixty American bombers because fighters could be produced faster. The president tried to stress the importance of the loss of an important war plant, rather than the loss of the bombers, but newsmen were not convinced.

Arnold later spoke to the press, explaining why ball-bearing plants were so important to Germany, and tried to explain the difficulty of attacking a well-defended plant so deep inside Germany. He called the Schweinfurt raid an engagement between large armies, saying it was part of a major campaign. "In a few hours," he said, "we invaded German-held Europe to a depth of five hundred miles and crippled one of their most vital enterprises. We did it in daylight, and we did it with precision, aiming our explosives with the care and accuracy of a marksman firing a rifle at a bulls-eye."

Many in the news media remained skeptical, reflecting that the Royal Air Force had never lost sixty bombers on a single mission.

Arnold understood their reaction because he had private doubts that the target was worth such a heavy cost.

At another news conference on the 18th, he tried to explain again why such a raid was necessary. Unfortunately, newsmen came away from this conference believing that he had said that even a 25 percent loss rate would be acceptable. Since the number of B-17s sent out on the mission had never been announced, newsmen assumed that the loss rate was 25 percent instead of the actual 19 percent, which was bad enough.

German plant officials at first thought that the ball-bearing plants had been destroyed beyond salvage. Careful inspection showed that the very heavy machinery in the ball plant, located on the bottom floor of a two-story building and needed for the most important phase of the entire manufacturing process, looked awful but had not burned. Half of the machinery could be repaired. It was decided immediately to move the critical ball machines that night, though not to transfer operations of the rest of the plant.

Albert Speer realized the plants could be repaired only if the Americans did not continue their attacks, and he expected them to do so. He called Hitler from Schweinfurt. "All the factories have been hit hard, and oil baths have caused serious fires in the machine shops. Damage is far worse than after the first attack." He admitted that production had been cut 67 percent.

Göring told Hitler that they had been on the defensive for two years. He reminded the Führer that he had been asking repeatedly that one month's fighter production be assigned to home defense. Finally, Hitler gave home defense top priority for operations by the Luftwaffe.

Two days after Schweinfurt, Arnold ordered that the majority of P-51 production should be given to Eaker's Eighth Air Force, along with a third of all P-38 production. Later, on October 30, Arnold authorized that all long-range fighters be sent to Europe.

Eaker was relieved. He knew that the British Merlin-powered Mustang was more powerful at all altitudes than German fighters. And with its greater range, the P-51 could escort bombers to any place in Germany and bring them back. He wired Arnold immediately that these fighters would be fully employed.

British and American newsmen who believed the losses at Schweinfurt would prohibit further deep strikes into Germany were even more convinced when Eaker confined his strikes to targets within escort range of fighters. When B-17s bombed Düren on the 20th, many more were convinced that the Eighth Air Force had been reduced to impotence, and expressions by officials in England that deeper strikes into Germany could not be made due to bad weather were met with disbelief. Those who always had doubts about daylight bombing believed that such attacks had failed conclusively to achieve their objectives with acceptable losses.

Although Eaker and his officials didn't say so publicly, they knew that the sixty bombers lost over Schweinfurt plus the eighty-eight lost the previous week *were* a prohibitive depletion of frontline strength. They realized now, more than ever, that bombers on deep strikes must be escorted all the way to their targets.

General Hansell, the original top planner for the mission, said in analyzing the raid later that if the entire Eighth Air Force had been used on Schweinfurt in both raids, with larger bombs, the hoped-for results might have been achieved.

In regard to Speer's comments that incendiaries would have done more damage, Hansell said that, in his opinion, two-thousand- and four-thousand-pound bombs with delayed fuses would have penetrated to the factory's foundations and blown its machines apart. The use of five-hundred-pound bombs, he said, with instantaneous fuses, blew the roofs off the buildings, covered the machines with debris, but did not heavily damage them.

One direct result of the Schweinfurt raids was evident in the production of the Daimler Benz 603 engine. This new engine had to rely upon sleeve bearings for its crankshaft because ball bearings were no longer available. These bearings were not as reliable, and their use led to a large number of engine failures.

Göring addressed German day-fighter pilots in Holland October 23. He accused them of being tired and cowardly. He told them he was not at all pleased with their performance against American bombers. His uncalled-for remarks made a bad situation only worse, and fighter pilots resented him more than ever.

Generalleutnant Adolf Galland said after the war that his fighter pilots had flown 800 sorties that day, but had not shot down the 139 American bombers announced by the German press. He did say they had shot down more four-engine bombers than had ever been destroyed in a single engagement.

German losses were high with thirty-eight fighters lost and another twenty damaged. Five others were shot down that day, and possibly belong to the total. These losses were severe, but nothing like the estimated claims of 186 destroyed.

Sweden was the only country to benefit from the Schweinfurt raids. She was being paid a large sum of money by the Allies for not delivering ball bearings to Germany, while Germany was offering equally large sums in an effort to get them.

Arnold continued to criticize operations of the Eighth because Eaker was unable to send larger missions on a more regular basis. He said inadequate maintenance kept too many bombers on the ground, and they weren't being utilized to the fullest extent. Arnold was a victim of his own reporting system, which failed to consider the recuperative powers of the German air force or the ability of the German people to rebuild factories quickly and decentralize them with little loss of production.

Of greatest concern to air planners was the appalling cost in bombers and crews at a time when it didn't appear they were making much headway in reducing the effectiveness of the German air force. The Allies suspected, and after the war it was confirmed, that German fighter production actually increased during this period due to the recuperative powers of German industry.

With intensification of the Combined Bomber Offensive from the United Kingdom, the Germans fought back with everything at their disposal. They used air-to-air bombing, rockets, cannon, and coordinated attacks with various new weapons. Missions grew rougher and losses rose as heavy bombers penetrated farther into Germany without escorting fighters. With more damaged bombers, groups were rarely able to have half their bombers in commission for any one mission.

Eaker wrote Arnold that it would be his policy henceforth to conduct operations at such a rate that his command would always be growing and, therefore, a menacing force. "I will never operate at such a rate that I will be a diminishing and vanishing force."

He had known from the beginning that Arnold, Marshall, and many others were relying on them to destroy the German air force prior to an invasion of the Continent. All along, Eaker considered it his duty not to sacrifice his whole force by any unwise or hasty action. Earlier, he had resisted sending his first one hundred bombers on deep penetrations into Germany, knowing that he would undoubtedly have lost them all in ten days.

It had always been Arnold's understanding that the basic war-making industries of the Third Reich could be destroyed by 150,000 tons of bombs in a period of a few months. Actually, AWPD-42 called for dropping 200,000 tons of bombs on nine target systems in six months.* He had told Eaker that he wanted a third of these targets destroyed by the end of 1943. That was impossible to achieve with the numbers of aircraft and crews available to Eaker at the time.

The Combined Operational Planning Committee dropped Schweinfurt from its target list for the rest of the year, calling for priority to those industries directly supporting the German air force. The loss of 148 bombers and crews during a six-day period in the first two weeks of October indicated the Americans had lost air superiority over Germany. These losses created a crisis in operations until more—and longer-range —escort fighters became available.

British Bomber Command had not been idle. In a spectacularly successful raid on the night of October 22/23, most of its bombs were dropped on an aircraft production plant at Kassel. Earlier attacks on similar plants had been made with success at Mannheim and Hannover.

Once sufficient H2S equipment became available for all pathfinder aircraft, Harris wanted to try several heavy attacks on Berlin, despite failure in September to hit the center of the city.

Churchill had called for the bombing of Berlin as a defiant gesture in 1940, but only now in the fall of 1943 did Harris have sufficient bombers to make good the threat.

Harris sent Churchill a memo November 3. "We can wreck Berlin end-to-end if the USAAF will continue in on it. It will cost us between four hundred and five hundred aircraft. It will cost Germany the war." He reminded the prime minister that the Royal Air Force had virtually destroyed twenty cities, with nineteen others seriously damaged.

Churchill was still intrigued by the idea of bombing Berlin, which ranked with the Ruhr industrially but far outweighed it in the manufacture of precision instruments and electrical components. He didn't, however, share Harris's beliefs that these attacks would end the war.

On the night of November 18/19, the first of sixteen major British attacks (which would continue until the spring of 1944) was launched against Berlin. Sky markers had to be used most of the time to designate drop points; because of continual bad weather, few crews ever saw Berlin through the layers of clouds. Harris concentrated on the winter months for these attacks, knowing the long nights would give maximum protection to his bomber crews. These raids never achieved the spectacular

*Postwar records show a total of 557,000 tons of bombs were dropped on targets in Germany by American heavy bombers. Only 7 percent of this total, or 29,000 tons, were released in 1943, the rest in 1944 and 1945.

results of the Hamburg attacks, despite the greater number of bombers and the larger tonnage of bombs.

Harris stubbornly refused to admit defeat, sending out raid after raid through the rest of 1943 and into the spring of 1944. He kept saying that Germany could be forced to surrender if he could only launch fifteen thousand sorties against the Reich's major cities by April 1, 1944. Stubbornly, despite efforts by Portal to shift the weight of Bomber Command attacks to more lucrative aircraft industry targets, Harris continued his area bombing of cities. Although his command flew all but five hundred of the fifteen thousand sorties he had sought against major cities, there was still no sign in the spring of 1944 that Germany was ready to crack under the strain.

Meanwhile, in the fall of 1943, Portal grew more and more concerned, as did American commanders, once it appeared that the Battle of Berlin would end in failure. Harris absolutely refused to concede that Berlin was too large a city to destroy, or that it was too deep inside Germany to attack without prohibitive losses.

During the whole of 1943, one thousand British bombers were lost—three hundred of them in attacks against Berlin. The majority were shot down by German fighters. Despite attacks against major cities and targets in the Ruhr, German factories continued to operate. Bombing accuracy left much to be desired; only half the bombs dropped inside their target areas, the rest ranging up to three miles from their aiming points.

By the end of the war, 6,340 acres of Berlin had been devastated, and all but 1,000 of those acres were destroyed by the British, with American bombers accounting for the remainder.

While British bombers rode the night skies, heavy replacements of crews and planes were filling up the depleted ranks of the Eighth Air Force. By the end of October 1943, Eaker could put five hundred heavy bombers on a mission. If Arnold hadn't rushed over the replacements, Eaker would have been out of business three days after the second Schweinfurt raid.

British Bomber Command helped to destroy fifty-six V-1 flying-bomb sites in the Pas-de-Calais area and eight other sites on the Cherbourg Peninsula during the last month of 1943.

The subject of night bombing of French factories making arms for Germany was such a sensitive issue that Harris chose his 5 Group of experts to make such attacks with small formations.

Although Harris continued to advocate more area bombing of cities, Sir Charles Portal disagreed with Harris that it was necessary to destroy everything in a city to destroy anything of value. Portal understood Harris's reasoning that it was much easier to hit a city than a particular plant with the Bomber Command equipment at hand, but he was now more convinced than ever that it was an uneconomical method of attack.

As 1944 began, the German air force had one sixth of its fighter forces in the Mediterranean, a third on the Russian front, and the remaining half on the western front to defend German cities from Allied air attacks. The disproportionate number of German fighters assigned to the western front created a shortage everywhere else.

With the exceptions of the raids on Anklam, Marienburg, and Schweinfurt, operations of the Eighth Air Force during the fall of 1943 were inconsequential. They were the result of a frustrated command, short on crews and bombers—less than half the number called for in the plan for the Combined Bomber Offensive.

The second Schweinfurt raid caused far more damage than the first one because of fires in the machine shops. If the Allies could have followed up those two attacks, the ball-bearing crisis in Germany would have worsened. The Germans would have had to use up their reserves because their efforts to import bearings from Sweden and Switzerland had met with little success. Further American attacks had to be aborted until escort fighters became available. By then, it was too late. The Germans had dispersed their ball-bearing production throughout the countryside.

After the war, Speer said that if attacks against the ball-bearing industry had continued, the war would have ended a year sooner. This was another tragic case of Allied unpreparedness, and it cost hundreds of lives.

18

"THE DECISION
WE THERE MADE
WAS THE CORRECT ONE."

Despite increasing attacks, the German aircraft industry continued to grow during this period, posing problems in planning the invasion for the following spring.

The German ME-109 industrial complexes at Wiener Neustadt were within range of Doolittle's Fifteenth Air Force, while those at Regensburg and Leipzig were potential targets for the Eighth. The Fifteenth made its first contribution to the Combined Bomber Offensive November 2 when it made the seventeen-hundred-mile round trip and destroyed a large aircraft assembly shop and two hangars at Wiener Neustadt. German fighters were up in force, and flak was not only heavy but accurate, shooting down eleven bombers, or 10 percent of those on the mission. Despite the losses, the new air force had temporarily halted 30 percent of the total enemy single-engine fighter production. As a result, two hundred and fifty fighters were "lost" each month to the German air force for the next four months.

Arnold congratulated Spaatz, telling him the effects of this attack would save many lives in the air war.

Despite Churchill's perennial hope that the Italian invasion would expose a "soft underbelly," the Allied advance found the going tougher as the Allied Fifth and Eighth armies made little progress against stubborn German resistance. While bad weather limited air operations, ground troops repeatedly had to cross and recross the same winding rivers and fight through mountains against stubborn German resistance for every mile. When bomber attacks and tanks proved useless, tough Allied infantrymen gained their objectives the hard way.

The Fifteenth now had to devote most of its activities to ground support, particularly during the last fifteen days of 1943. Heavy bombers struck railroad lines and other targets in Brenner Pass and in northeastern Italy whose routes led to Austria and southern Germany. These attacks, which unfortunately diverted heavy-bombing efforts from strategic targets, brought about a heavy reduction in Italian rail traffic and kept troop reinforcements and military equipment from the Germans in the front lines.

The German air force in Italy proved more effective than at any time during the campaign, and Allied plane losses rose correspondingly. The percentage of combat crew casualties per thousand sorties that December rose spectacularly over those of the preceding month. Since the Italian invasion began, the casualty rate for ground troops averaged 6.33 per month for each thousand troops. The loss rate for airmen was 7.69 per thousand.

Officials of the Mediterranean Army Air Forces reported by year's end that German fighter factories had sustained "staggering" losses. Actually, German strength increased because there had been a limited number of strategic attacks against the fighter industry. More realistic airmen knew that unless extensive attacks were made against the German aircraft industry, further efforts in support of ground armies in Italy would be ineffectual. These men realized that top priority had to be given to further attacks on aircraft plants at Regensburg and Wiener Neustadt, as well as those at Erla in Leipzig, plus a small number of highly specialized component factories in Poland, southern Germany, and southeastern Europe. Such attacks were within their capability, but there had to be some restrictions on calls for ground support.

Arnold viewed the operations in Italy with growing uneasiness, emphasizing again that far too many missions were diversions from the main task. Eisenhower's staff assured him that they were aware of the problem. Arnold sought advance information of upcoming operations in order that better coordination could be achieved within all elements of the Combined Bomber Offensive.

The Mediterranean theater had an impressive 7,000 effective aircraft with 315,000 personnel. Units of the Twelfth and Fifteenth now had French and Italian squadrons, and even some Yugoslavians were flying B-24s in the 376th Group after training in the United States.

As Eaker had foreseen, Italian air operations posed a major problem in servicing airplanes, particularly new aircraft that had to be modified in the field.

Unknown to the Allies, the German High Command was so disturbed by Allied air raids that they called for further dispersal of the aircraft industry beyond the limits of the goals set the preceding summer. They delayed too long for dispersion to be truly effective, and it wasn't until the last part of 1943 that such plans got under way in earnest. German fighter production had increased throughout most of that year, yet lagged by a critical three months as 1944 began. After the war, the

United States Strategic Bombing Survey revealed that "the timing of this delay in fighter production at the close of the year contributed significantly to victory in the critical air battles during the winter of 1944."

The Germans later increased their production of planes, but their best pilots had been lost in air battles and they were irreplaceable.

Although the British had made ninety-six raids on twenty-nine different cities in the last nine months of 1943, these raids did little to reduce Germany's armaments programs despite British beliefs to the contrary at the time.

Behind the scenes in the Eighth Air Force, officials were thrown into a state of consternation when Eaker, now a three-star general, received a message from Arnold December 18 that he would be transferred to command of the Allied Air Forces in the Mediterranean. Spaatz, Arnold wrote, would command the United States Strategic Air Forces in Europe, and Doolittle would command the Eighth Air Force.

When Eaker read the cablegram, he could scarcely believe what he saw. He felt Arnold had let him down.

Eaker sent Arnold a handwritten message saying that his experiences during the last two years would be wasted if he was transferred, saying it would be heartbreaking for him to leave now that the Eighth was finally organized. If he was allowed any personal preference, he said, he would like to remain with the Eighth.

Eaker sent protest letters to Eisenhower, who soon would take over as Supreme Allied Commander, and to Spaatz also. He discussed the matter also with General Devers, commander of the European theater. Devers immediately cabled Arnold on Eaker's behalf.

Arnold's reply to Devers was polite, but he made it clear that he should mind his own business. "For retaining Eaker in command of the Eighth Air Force, all the reasons that you have given are those that you have advanced as to reasons why he should go down and be commander of the Allied Mediterranean Air Forces."

In his reply to Eaker, Arnold expressed his appreciation for his efforts, but refused to make any change in his decision to remove the Eighth Air Force's commander.

Eaker acknowledged defeat Christmas Eve. He wired Arnold, "Orders received. Will be carried out promptly January 1."

Eaker blamed Arnold for his relief, but that was only part of the story. There is no question that Eaker's continued explanations for failures irritated Arnold, who was interested in solutions, not problems. Moreover, Arnold had repeatedly criticized members of Eaker's original staff and Eaker's reluctance to make changes due to long-standing friendships. Perhaps Eaker's removal was influenced by Eisenhower, who had been told by Marshall upon his new appointment that he could have anyone he wanted to serve under him. The new Supreme Allied Commander had responded that when he came to London he would bring men with whom he had developed a close working relationship in the Mediterranean, and although Eisenhower had nothing against Eaker, Spaatz and Doolittle were the men who fit that category. Spaatz had become known as Eisenhower's air leader, and certainly he had more influence with him in aviation matters than anyone else. They had developed the kind of close personal relationship that Eisenhower insisted upon among his top commanders. Ironically, Eaker's virtues as a strategic air commander made him suspect to Eisenhower, who had named him as typical of officers who always wanted to go off somewhere and bomb distant industrial targets when the decisive contest was being fought out on the battlefield. Eisenhower saw himself as a great supporter of aviation—and constantly sought to use it in support of land battles.

Eaker often thought even Arnold had little conception of the problems of strategic air command in the field because the air forces chief of staff had never had a combat command. He recalled once getting a sarcastic letter from Arnold that compared the Eighth's combat hours with those of the training command in the States. Eaker knew such a comparison was unfair because the crews in the training command flew only in good weather, whereas his crews faced bad weather, either over the Continent or over Great Britain, on practically every mission and encountered bitter air opposition. He was aware, however, that his constant requests for more crews had irritated Arnold because the Second Air Force, which trained all crews, could accomplish just so much in the limited time they had before crews had to be dispatched overseas.

Arnold's universal impatience and habit of demanding the impossible of subordinates were undoubtedly two of the secrets of his success in running the air force in World War II. Personal relationships were difficult because Arnold hated excuses. When he decided on his next move, he wanted it carried out without further delay.

Doolittle always considered Arnold a "now" man. While he served as a top aide before coming to Europe, those on Arnold's staff jokingly said that if their chief got an idea while walking out his door, he'd give the job of carrying it out to the first man he met. There was some truth in that. General Giles, his chief of staff, told everyone to avoid the corridor outside Arnold's office lest the boss appear and give that person an order that he wanted carried out "right now!" Understandably, with Arnold's mind constantly full of top-priority tasks to be done, the man of the moment often got the job. The effect on orderly staff work could be chaotic.

Although Spaatz was closer to Eaker than he was to Doolittle, they had developed a good relationship in North Africa, and Doolittle, like Spaatz, had durable ties with Arnold. Never did Doolittle ask Arnold for more men or more planes while he commanded the Twelfth or Fifteenth air forces. He knew in his heart that he was getting enough to do the job and that anything additional would only deprive some other theater of vitally needed crews and planes. He realized that Eaker's situation had been entirely different and that Eaker had always been supplied with too little men and equipment to maintain Arnold's concept of strategic bombing.

Doolittle had had an uphill battle to convince Eisenhower that he was a professional airman. Many army professionals resented him because of his years in private industry between the wars, but what Doolittle may have lacked in longevity and theoretical strategy he more than made up for as a doer. He was an outstanding pilot, and he was willing to try anything once. His sense of humor and quick repartee irritated more conventional officers of lesser abilities, who considered him flamboyant. However, these were characteristics that Arnold admired and that undoubtedly influenced his decision to support Eisenhower's desires and replace Eaker with Doolittle.

Doolittle paid a price for Arnold's support. Eaker's staff was so loyal to their chief that many of them resented having to work under the new commander. Doolittle promptly approved their transfers.

His problems were not restricted to Eaker's staff members. The British, also, were cool at first, believing that Eaker, whom they had grown to admire, had been unjustly removed.

Through the early difficult days, Doolittle retained his characteristic aplomb, trusting that time would heal most of the wounds created by his elevation to command of the Eighth.

Eaker's British friends had set up a going-away dinner party for New Year's Eve. That afternoon, a British motorcycle messenger arrived at Eaker's home with a note that "Colonel Holt" would like to see him as he passed through Casablanca, if it was convenient.

Eaker called Portal and read him the telegram. Portal explained that Churchill used the pseudonym Holt frequently when he wished to remain incognito. "The prime minister is recovering from pneumonia," Portal said, "in the same villa in Casablanca where you talked to him last February and convinced him you should continue daylight bombing. He realizes you will pass through Casablanca going to your new command in Italy, and he wonders if you would have time to stop by and see him."

"Of course I'll stop by and see him. Send him a cable saying that I have plans to be in Casablanca for refueling, and would it be convenient for me to call on Colonel Holt?"

Eaker's plane landed next day at Casablanca, and he went to the villa where he had visited the prime minister almost a year before. Memories of that meeting returned vividly when he found Churchill in the same living room.

After they exchanged pleasantries, Churchill said, "I know that you are very disgruntled about having to leave the Eighth Air Force just when it is achieving its maximum effect in the war effort. As for your new assignment, I want to remind you that we are entrusting to you two of our favorite British units—the Balkan air force and the desert air force. If we didn't have great faith in you, we wouldn't put them under your charge. You'll also have the RAF Coastal Command, the French air forces, and your own very considerable Twelfth and Fifteenth air forces. All in all, it will be a much larger command, with more responsibilities than you had in the United Kingdom."

In parting, the prime minister said, "This gives me an occasion to tell you that your expressions regarding daylight and night bombing you made to me in this room last February have been and are being verified. Round-the-clock bombing is achieving the results you predicted. I no longer have any doubt that the decision we there made was the correct one."

Eaker was still upset over losing what he rightly considered the key command in the coming air war against Germany, but he was comforted by Churchill's words and by his thoughtfulness in meeting him at this critical juncture in his career.

Eaker's departure from his headquarters at Bushy Park had come just before operations over the Continent would dramatically prove his theories about strategic bombing. His leave-taking had been heartbreaking because it came just as the hard-won experience gained in 1943 with such limited resources was starting to bear fruit.

Before Eaker left England, he had been asked if he would accept a British officer as his deputy.

"Who do you have in mind?"

"Jack Slessor wants to go. What do you think of him?"

"I can't think of anyone that I'd rather have."

Sir John Slessor had been a planner on the British war staff at the start of the war. His authorship of the Casablanca Directive was perhaps the most crucial contribution to the endorsement of the strategic air offensive against Germany. An articulate man, who strongly supported American views, Slessor proved to be an outstanding deputy, and Eaker's association with him was founded on mutual respect and admiration.

Another outstanding British officer, Field Marshal Sir Henry Maitland "Jumbo" Wilson, was assigned as overall theater commander, with

General Jacob L. Devers as commander of United States forces. Eaker could take comfort in a continuing association with a friend who reciprocated his high regard.

Now that Feldmarschall Erwin Rommel's Afrika Korps had been destroyed in Africa, the Mediterranean war started to move forward.

19

READY FOR
THE JOB AHEAD

The Allies swept around the right flank of the Germans' Gustav Line in Italy on January 22, 1944, and landed two divisions thirty-three miles south of Rome, at Anzio and Nettuno. This was done in hopes of outflanking the Germans. The landings initially went well, but when the beachheads were not exploited the Germans reinforced their troops and almost drove the Allies into the sea.

A monastery built by Saint Benedict in the sixth century had a commanding view of the area. From its heights, German 88s and smaller guns pounded the advancing infantry. When ground commanders insisted the abbey had to be attacked from the air, Slessor talked to General Mark Clark, who shared his doubts that the Germans actually occupied the abbey.

Ground officers pressed for its destruction, however, and it was attacked and totally demolished. It was truly a tragedy because all evidence now indicates there never had been enemy occupation of the abbey itself.

Spaatz had taken over the strategic air forces on January 1, the same day Eisenhower established his Supreme Headquarters Allied Expeditionary Forces (SHAEF), in London.

Doolittle, who simultaneously took command of the Eighth, was never told why he had been selected. He thought Eaker had done a superb job, accomplishing much with very little. He also recognized that there had been a tremendous increase in available aircraft and crews shortly after he took over, which made his job that much easier. When Eaker left, Doolittle inherited a command of 185,000 men on a hundred bases. His most pressing problem, in fact, became logistic support—getting supplies to keep his men and planes constantly active.

The new commander was aware that he had a morale problem also, not only among staff officers who had elected to remain with him, but among some of the crews. A few of them believed that the much-publicized Tokyo mission in 1942 was a show-off affair, blaming Doolittle despite the fact that this first bombing of Japan was recommended by a navy captain, primarily as a morale booster for the American people, who had heard nothing but bad news until then.

One other assignment, the appointment of Major General Nathan F. Twining to head the Fifteenth Air Force, completed the changes Arnold had ordered to prepare for the aerial destruction of Hitler's Europe.

The upcoming invasion of the Continent now dominated all thoughts. Eisenhower, the senior American in England, was not only the theater commander whose authority embraced all United States Army personnel in England, but also the chosen Allied commander for the invasion. Naturally, he placed its success above all other objectives. The War Department General Staff had believed, since the start of the war, that only an invasion of occupied Europe would prove decisive for Germany's defeat.

Eisenhower immediately made it known that he wanted control of all air forces in the European theater, and that Tedder was his chief airman. There were several obstacles. The strategic air forces, both British and American, were still committed to the Combined Bomber Offensive and were operating under the Combined Chiefs with Air Chief Marshal Portal as their executive agent. Among other tasks, they had still to defeat the Luftwaffe, which Eisenhower himself considered absolutely essential to the success of the invasion. The Combined Chiefs had designated Air Marshal Sir Trafford Leigh-Mallory as commander in chief Allied Expeditionary Air Forces, but neither Harris nor Spaatz would work for him.

In Washington, Marshall was not pleased with some of the changes Eisenhower proposed. He believed Eisenhower was gutting the Mediterranean command of key personnel. He believed that the shifting of Eaker and Devers in particular would cause serious problems in the Mediterranean theater; he argued they should remain where they were, and that Spaatz should stay in the Mediterranean. Marshall also told Eisenhower that his chief of staff, Walter Bedell Smith, should remain in Algiers until February to help Wilson get oriented.

Eisenhower disagreed with everything the army chief of staff proposed. He insisted that he had to have Tedder and Spaatz as senior commanders because of their experience in the support of ground troops. He reminded Marshall that Eaker's experience had been solely strategic.

"The technique of air-ground cooperation is one that is not widely understood," Eisenhower said. "It takes men of vision and broad understanding to do the job right. Otherwise, a commander is forever fighting with those air officers who, regardless of the situation, want to send big bombers on missions that have nothing to do with the critical effort."

In conclusion, he said that with Spaatz and Tedder in England, Eaker would have nothing to do there.

Although Spaatz and Harris fully realized that the risks involved in a cross-channel operation were great and should have their full support, they still opposed total commitment of their bomber fleets.

Marshall understood Eisenhower's reasoning that if the invasion was to be a success, all resources should be applied to make it so. Eisenhower's experiences during the landings in Sicily and Salerno had convinced him that getting ashore and staying there could be extremely difficult. He insisted on getting a total commitment, and that meant use of big bombers.

Eisenhower expected trouble in securing the integration of all air forces. As European supreme commander, he theoretically was responsible for Spaatz's activities, but actually Spaatz was independent because he was still operating under the directive approved by the Combined Chiefs at Casablanca for a Combined Bomber Offensive against Germany. After Eisenhower became Supreme Allied Commander, he had only two air forces directly under him: the British Tactical Air Force, which had served under Marshal Montgomery, and the American Ninth Air Force.

During a visit to Washington, on January 5, Eisenhower discussed the situation with Marshall. He said Harris and Spaatz should be assigned to report to him several weeks before the invasion. The army chief of staff agreed, and so did General Arnold.

In a discussion with Arnold, Eisenhower said he had strong views on the subject of total air support for the invasion. Arnold agreed that all air forces should be under his direct command and promised to help in any way to achieve such control.

On February 9, Eisenhower told Marshall that a complete draft of an air plan for the invasion would be ready in a few days. Three days later, he presented a simple organization that would bring Harris's and Spaatz's organizations under his control. He reminded everyone again that destruction of the German air force was a required prerequisite before the invasion could be launched.

The reorganization plan for air support may have sounded simple to Eisenhower, but it unleashed a torrent of criticism, worsening the prospects for interservice cooperation.

Doolittle learned that each time he sent a big mission out, he could have a pretty good idea of how many crews he was likely to lose by studying actuarial tables. His most difficult decision was to weigh whether each mission would be worth its price over the long haul.

After studying records, it was apparent that his worst enemies in descending order were weather, German fighters, and flak.

He assigned a weather plane to report hourly on the weather two hundred miles out in the Atlantic. Weather fronts usually came from the west at a constant rate of about twenty miles per hour. Doolittle learned to figure the averages, but he found it was impossible to predict accurate weather conditions over Great Britain and the Continent. Sometimes a front would hit the coast of England and, for no apparent reason, speed up, slow down, or even stop. There were days when bad weather would start to move in quickly but, at the last moment, back off.

After Doolittle canceled three missions in a row, some of them after aircraft had started for Germany, Spaatz came to see him. "I understand you canceled three missions. Why?"

"The weather started to speed up faster than I anticipated. Although we had taken off and were partway to Germany, I believed there was a critical likelihood the fields would be closed before they got back, and we'd lose a substantial part of our force."

"If you haven't got the guts to run this air force," Spaatz said bluntly, "I'll get someone who can."

"Very well, sir. If I run it, I will have to use my best judgment."

"Come with me."

He crawled into Spaatz's plane fully expecting to be fired, and they took off for Spaatz's headquarters. After they had flown a half hour, the fog closed in, and their pilot had to make an immediate emergency landing in a large pasture that was hardly suited to B-17 requirements.

They climbed down from the airplane and stood in the fog. It was so thick they could not see beyond a few feet.

Spaatz turned to Doolittle. "Jim, I see what you mean."

That ended the matter, and Spaatz never questioned his judgment again.

Arnold had heard so much about weather problems in England that he turned to Dr. Irving Krick, whom he had known since the early 1930s. While Krick was a meteorologist at Cal Tech in California, Arnold asked him in October 1941 to give a series of lectures to Army Air Corps forecasters, which, after the war, was distributed throughout the service. Krick's theories involved analyzing current weather patterns in an area, then researching past records until he found similar patterns. His forecasts for a given period were based upon the type of weather that had appeared under similar conditions in the past. His theories were controversial, but they impressed Arnold because Krick's long-range projections proved remarkably accurate.

After war broke out, Krick was called to active duty by the navy because he had a reserve commission as a lieutenant. At Arnold's suggestion, he was assigned first to the Army Air Forces where he briefed Arnold's staff on the weather all over the world. The chief of the air force, meanwhile, talked to Admiral King and got his consent to get Krick reassigned as an air force officer. Once this was accomplished, Arnold sent him to England October 10, 1943, as a lieutenant colonel to join Baker's staff.

He was assigned to Fred Anderson and he soon learned that the command's weather forecasters were giving their bomber commander only bits of weather information without attempting long-range forecasts. Anderson's first comment was, "See if you can't cut these forecasts finer."

"I'll slice them as thin as you want," Krick replied, "but you'll have a few aborted missions. We can't be perfect."

Anderson understood, knowing that any improvement would be helpful.

When Spaatz took over the strategic air forces in January, 1944, he told Arnold that it was absolutely essential that he receive coordinated weather forecasts, including long-range forecasts. He said he had learned to appreciate Krick's work with Anderson's Bomber Command, and he told Arnold that Krick was the only one in the theater who was doing long-range weather forecasting.

Arnold approved Spaatz's recommendation that Krick and ten others from the Weather Information Branch be given top priority under Spaatz to coordinate weather information. Krick and Lieutenant Colonel Ben Holzman, whom he had trained at Cal Tech, were named as briefing officers.

Doolittle, who had to risk thousands of lives on accurate decision-making, at first viewed Krick with misgivings. He found him an excellent meteorologist, but one who had greater confidence in his weather forecasts than Doolittle believed was humanly possible. Clashes between two such disparate personalities were inevitable until each learned to appreciate the other's abilities.

During a mission in late January, Doolittle reported to Spaatz at his headquarters, and as Doolittle recalls it, Eisenhower dropped in to hear what he had to say.

"Why did you go to the alternate target?" Spaatz asked.

"I went because the primary was closed in," Doolittle said.

"Colonel Krick says the primary target was open."

"As usual, Colonel Krick is full of shit."

Eisenhower bristled. "What do you mean by that?"

"I have just had a report from an airplane flying over the primary target and another flying over the secondary target, and they report the secondary is open, but that the primary is not."

Doolittle was so new in his job and had so little faith in his weather forecasters that it took time for him to develop confidence in Krick. Eventually he learned to respect his judgment.

Doolittle decided to change one tactical doctrine that had irritated the Fighter Command since the war started: He would order Major General William E. Kepner, head of the VIII Fighter Command, to take on German fighters wherever he found them, and not merely to escort bombers. Times had changed since the Eaker days. Doolittle now had fighters available in quantities that Eaker had not.

When he told the general the change in tactics, tears came to the fighter commander's eyes. "You mean I can go on the offensive?"

"I'm directing you to do so."

Doolittle's division commanders told him this would needlessly sacrifice a lot of bomber crews. He replied that there might be some increase in losses temporarily, but going on the offensive would eventually give them control of the air.

Adolf Galland said after the war that "General Spaatz's decision" to take the fighters off the bombers and pit them against his Luftwaffe fighters lost the air war for the Germans. When Doolittle met him years later, he told Galland that it was he, not Spaatz, who had made the decision.

It was a wise move, and long overdue.

At the Casablanca Conference the previous year, the Combined Chiefs of Staff had decided to postpone the cross-channel invasion and concentrate on a Combined Bomber Offensive, while their victory in North Africa was followed up by an invasion of Sicily and Italy. Churchill had argued persuasively for such a strategy, but the Americans had clearly indicated their opposition. To allay any doubts about British resolution, Churchill had reiterated in November 1943 that the British had not weakened, cooled, or tried to get out of such an invasion of Europe. At the same time, he insisted that the cross-channel invasion should not become "a tyrant dictating all strategy, nor a pivot so firm that every opportunity in the Mediterranean would have to be ruled out."

The Russians, however, still pressed strongly for a definite commitment to an invasion of the Continent. At the Tehran Conference, Stalin suggested that Mediterranean forces be used to invade southern France. Such an invasion had already been considered by the British and Americans, so a strategy of invasion from the south and west was agreed upon while the Russians committed themselves to simultaneous large-scale offensives on the eastern front.

Spaatz was reminded again by Arnold of the indecisiveness of the American strategic effort. He told commanders of the Eighth and Fifteenth air forces just before the start of the new year, "This is a *must.*

Destroy the enemy air forces wherever you find them, in the air, on the ground, and in the factories."

Major General Kepner had developed the P-38 into a more effective fighter by the end of 1943. Also, with modifications the "B" version of the P-51 was made more maneuverable and its range extended to 850 miles. Of the P-51 Mustang, Kepner said, "It is distinctly the best fighter that we can get over here." (Kepner had a "fighting" heart. A handsome man in his forties, he flew with his pilots on too many missions for a man of his age. Short but sturdy looking, with clipped, graying hair and a florid complexion, he was one of the most liked commanders in England.)

With dramatic improvements in the versatile Mustang, it was proposed by Eisenhower's headquarters that all these fighters be assigned to the Ninth Air Force for tactical support of the coming invasion. Kepner objected because his Mustangs were needed for long-range escort of bombers prior to the invasion. Therefore, they were given a dual responsibility and all P-51s were assigned to the Eighth Air Force, while P-38s and all but one group of P-47s were transferred to the Ninth Air Force for invasion support.

When they had first arrived in England in the fall of 1942, medium bombers—whose crews had been trained specifically for low-level operations—started striking airfields on the coast of Holland. On the first mission, fifteen B-26s went out, and all returned safely, although many suffered battle damage. On the next mission, the same number went out, and not one came back! Tactics were changed immediately and medium bombers, teamed with Spitfire fighters, dropped bombs from medium altitudes of from ten thousand to fourteen thousand feet. They were so effective prior to the invasion, and afterward, that their bombing scores were the best of any bombers operating in the European and Mediterranean theaters. Since their penetrations were shallow, short-range fighters could give superb protection.

From the viewpoint of Allied leaders, the Combined Bomber Offensive in 1943 had failed to achieve any of its strategic objectives. Among some British and American military and political leaders, doubts about the value of such a great expenditure of assets were expressed again with growing insistence.

Following the war, when officials of the United States Strategic Bombing Survey interviewed German leaders, some surprising information was learned. Generalleutnant Adolf Galland, inspector general for the air defense of the Reich, said that when the United States Army Air

Forces started daylight heavy-bomber raids in August 1942, German fighter pilots had to devise new tactics. Those used against RAF bombers in daylight, attacking from above and behind formations, failed against B-17s because they were heavily armed against rear attacks.

Galland had been only thirty-three when he took over the air defense of his homeland, and he was one of the best and most courageous of all of Germany's fighter pilots.

Galland recalled an appearance before Hitler in January 1943 after American bombers had penetrated the Reich's defenses and bombed targets inside Germany. The Führer demanded to know what could be done to stop American bombers.

Galland told him that the quantity of day fighters would have to be increased to three or four single-engine fighters for each unescorted bomber. He said that if long-range escort fighters accompanied the bombers, his Fighter Command would have to be increased even more so that German fighters would be able to match their American counterparts one to one in addition to those committed to attack the bombers. With such numbers, Galland estimated that daylight attacks would become prohibitively costly for the enemy.

If bomber crews had only known with what apprehension German fighter pilots viewed attacks against them, they would have felt more reassured. At the time, it seemed to American crews that they were unable to reduce the throngs of German fighters that met them on each mission, while their own heavy bombers went down in flames.

Galland said the defensive firepower of American bombers was awesome—particularly against rear attacks, which his fighter pilots refused to make. Eventually, they learned that the early versions of the B-17 were vulnerable to head-on attacks, and they concentrated on them, often flying through the tightest formations—inevitably causing collisions.

Once escort fighters accompanied bombers all the way, Galland said, he devised new tactics. He ordered pilots to ignore the escorts and concentrate on the bombers. Such orders proved disastrous to pilot morale, and Galland said it was difficult to maintain air discipline because even his most experienced pilots developed what he called, "a fear of Allied fighters."

The commander of one of Galland's "Abbeville Boys," a fighter group based on the coast of France, was captured in January 1944. He had been through the entire combat period since heavy bombers made their first attacks against targets in France. He told how his group had suffered heavy losses against unescorted B-17 formations. He said rear attacks were so suicidal that they were forced to stop them and concentrate on more difficult but safer frontal attacks.

He told how Göring, embarrassed by his boast that the Luftwaffe would sweep American heavy bombers from the skies, directed German fighter pilots to continue to attack from the rear because it was an easier gunnery problem. He said his men tried such attacks again, but their losses were so terrible that they ignored Göring's orders and returned to frontal attacks.

The Luftwaffe chief threatened to court-martial pilots who disobeyed his orders, but they still refused. In a rage, he ordered Galland to assign observers to report those pilots who disobeyed him. Even such drastic action proved ineffectual and pilots refused to resume rear attacks.

Generalleutnant Johannes Steinhoff, a colonel during the closing days of the war and a member of the elite M-262 Squadron JV-44, said after the war, "The appearance of bombers in 1943 over the Reich was the turning point in World War II aerial warfare." He said there was no chivalry about the air war, such as there had been in the early days of the First World War. Now, he said, orders were to destroy or be destroyed. He described the air space over Europe as a battleground, and the Germans considered it their duty to stop heavy-bomber formations in any way possible. (His comments, he said, did not downgrade previous air battles such as the Battle of Britain, which would go down in military history as a classic example of a merciless battle between individual fighter pilots.)

Steinhoff, Germany's leading air ace with 176 confirmed victories, in describing the early battles against American bombers, said the first German attacks against them over Rouen, August 17, 1942, cost them a large number of fighters, and not one bomber was shot down.

He described his own first encounter with B-17 Flying Fortresses in April 1943. He said his group had been brought back from Sicily and it was difficult to get it back to operational readiness after heavy losses in the Mediterranean. Galland, he said, had given them instructions on how to attack a close-knit bomber formation by advising that it should be broken up, and attacks made on single bombers. In recommending the best approach to break up a formation, Galland advised a frontal attack right through the bomber formation. It had been proved, Galland told him, that fire should be withheld until the last moment, and then "fire from all buttonholes." He said his own attacks proved Galland knew what he was talking about.

After one particularly bad raid, Steinhoff told about a notice they received from the German High Command that one pilot from each fighter unit should be court-martialed for cowardice in the face of the enemy. He said every unit commander volunteered for court-martial, and Göring dropped the matter.

As raids continued through 1943, the Germans adopted a variety of innovative techniques in an intensive training program. One unit tried to break up a formation by releasing a thousand-pound bomb above it, and they were successful. Later, a few fighters were armed with similar bombs to repeat the attempt, but it proved impossible to figure the precise distance separating them and to drop the bomb with an accurate time fuse. Such tactics worked only once, and soon were discontinued.

The rocket launchers mounted beneath the wings of 109s and 190s and used to launch bazooka-type missiles were not accurate. Further, such airplanes were so heavy that these German fighters handled clumsily and seemed to take forever to climb to altitude.

Armor plating for FW-190s so increased their weight that pilots had difficulty getting up high enough to attack bombers. The 190s, equipped with extra pilot protection, were used to work close to bombers and even try to ram them. Ramming was tricky and had to be done perfectly if the pilot was to eject safely.

If Hansell and his First Bombardment Wing crews had only known the troubles the German air force faced in the first half of 1943, their morale would have been a lot higher.

With losses mounting week after week since those first months of 1943, surviving American crews played a morbid game of plotting their chances of survival on graphs that seemed to indicate that in three months they would all be dead. Mathematicians argued in vain that the loss line was a curve, not a straight downward projection, and that 20 percent would survive after three months. Crews didn't consider either curve very promising! After they were assured of twenty-five-mission tours, their spirits picked up, although even mathematicians agreed the chances of survival for a full combat tour were still only 20 percent.

There was little comprehension about the merits of strategic bombing in the minds of military men in the American, British, and Russian governments. They understood the possibilities inherent in an invasion of the Continent where, using age-old tactics, ground forces could come to grips with the German armies and defeat them in the conventional manner. But strategic air warfare was a new theory. Its decisive potential had never been demonstrated.

Arnold explained the situation to Secretary of War Stimson. "Our airpower in Europe had been built slowly because of the needs of other fronts, aircraft losses, and the sheer physical size and complexity of the bases required. At last we are ready for the job ahead."

20

BLOOD SEEMED
TO BE EVERYWHERE

As commander of all United States Strategic Air Forces in Europe, Spaatz differed with commanders in other services because he never believed the Combined Bomber Offensive was merely a prerequisite for a successful invasion of the Continent. To him, it was an alternative path to victory, but he had few backers outside his own ranks.

The Royal Air Force had been operating for some time, but, like the Eighth Air Force, only during the early days of 1944 was it possible to build up to full strength. The Eighth and Fifteenth air forces also did not until 1944 reach the strength originally envisioned by planners to complete the job of destroying Germany from the air.

Spaatz had consistently fought diversion of the strategic air war to support of ground operations in Italy. Although the Combined Bomber Offensive theoretically had top priority, theater commanders had been given discretionary powers to use heavy bombers when they considered a tactical emergency existed. Unfortunately, such emergencies seemed to erupt almost weekly. As a result, the Fifteenth was constantly being diverted from the bombing of industrial and military targets. When the Combined Chiefs directed that the Italian campaign must have priority over all other operations, the heavy bombers in the theater devoted most of their efforts to the assistance of ground troops.

Arnold's and Spaatz's fears that the Italian campaign might reach a stalemate and necessitate a permanent diversion of efforts by the Fifteenth almost came true. Churchill's "soft underbelly" had developed more muscle than anyone thought possible.

Spaatz had been planning raids against the German air force on a large scale for days, but it wasn't until January 11, 1944, that weathermen predicted a break in the bad weather over central Germany. To deal the German air force a crushing blow, Spaatz needed a week of good weather.

When the January 11 forecast looked promising, 633 B-17s and B-24s —three divisions—were sent out to attack the ME-109 production factory at Oschersleben, the JU-88 fighter production plant at Halberstadt, and the ME-109 parts and assembly plant at Brunswick. When the weather forecast didn't hold up, two divisions were recalled. The First Division and one combat wing of the Third Division continued to their respective targets, but only one group of P-51 fighters was available at the targets. They fought magnificently, shooting down sixty German fighters, but they were badly outnumbered. Fortunately, they lost none of their own fighters.

Lieutenant Colonel James H. Howard led his P-51 Group to support the Oschersleben attack. Just as his fighters joined the bomber formation, German fighters swept in. Howard quickly downed an ME-110 and found himself separated from others in his group.

A glance at the nearby bomber formation showed him that it was under heavy attack and that he was the only American fighter in the vicinity. In spite of such terrible odds, he immediately attacked a formation of thirty German fighters. Within thirty minutes, he single-handedly shot down three enemy fighters and probably destroyed or damaged others. With fuel running low and three of his guns out of commission, he continued to fight aggressively and warded off determined German fighter attacks against the bombers.

The First Air Division lost thirty-four bombers, but bombing was the best yet, and photo reconnaissance showed extensive damage to all three targets.

Earlier arguments to place Fifteenth Air Force heavy bombers in Italy because the weather was supposedly better than in England now failed to hold up. This year, Italy's weather was worse than England's.

Due to persistent bad weather, the plan for massive attacks against Germany had to be delayed until February.

The pressure to eliminate the German air force prior to the spring invasion rose in intensity. There were arguments about the selection of suitable targets to achieve this goal. Some planners recommended that primary targets be dropped and German air force targets be given top priority. Eaker and Spaatz were opposed because attacks of primary targets not only impaired the German capability to prosecute the war, but also brought up swarms of defending fighters, and with the superiority of American escort fighters, the ensuing air battles would serve to deplete the German air force. Spaatz pointedly reminded army planners that the war wouldn't end with landings on the beaches of France, and that it was equally important to continue attacks that would disrupt the whole of Germany.

After heated debate on both sides, a new directive was given to officials responsible for the Combined Bomber Offensive, which temporarily resolved the situation. It called for the "progressive destruction and dislocation of German military, industrial, and economic systems, the disruption of vital elements of lines of communication, and the successful reduction of German air combat strength by the prosecution of the Combined Bomber Offensive from all convenient bases."

Spaatz, using this directive as a guideline, revised priorities. For the present, German airframe and component production facilities would receive top priority, with installations supporting the German air force in second place. Other targets were not ignored, and V-1 German missile installations remained high on the list, as well as industrial areas for the RAF to attack at night. Area attacks would be made by the United States Strategic Air Forces whenever bad weather prevented visual bombing attacks, and drops would be made by radar.

The Allied Air Forces in the Mediterranean were given responsibility for targets in southeastern Europe.

The new directive dropped earlier language about "undermining the morale and fatal weakening of German willingness and ability to fight" —in other words, the area bombing of cities. Now, primary emphasis was placed on the defeat of the German air force, where actually it had been all along, and attack of primary targets was recognized as contributing to that objective.

There were no longer requests to attack submarine bases because the problem had been resolved by attacks at sea.

The directive did request that vital lines of communications be attacked, but details were lacking, which led to confusion.

Oil and rubber facilities were not listed for some unexplained reason. Failure to do so is inconceivable, since they were not formally canceled, but Spaatz and Harris kept oil targets on their own priority lists.

Weather over critical German targets didn't clear until the last week in February. Just when Spaatz's strategic forces needed every airplane to deal a lethal blow against the German air force, the Fifteenth was unable to take part because it was tied up in support of the Anzio operations in Italy.

When Twining was asked if the Fifteenth was prepared to cooperate in the coming aerial offensive, Eaker replied for him. He said the ground campaign at Anzio was in a critical stage, and that the beachhead was endangered. He told Spaatz that Lieutenant General Clark of the Fifth Army and Major General John K. Cannon of the Twelfth Army had requested full assistance, particularly on February 20, which they termed the crucial date for survival of the beachhead.

Spaatz went to the head of the Royal Air Force and tried to get Portal to release the Fifteenth Air Force, but he was told that Churchill wanted all available forces for beachhead support.

Eaker faced a dilemma because the decision had been left to him. He knew that failure to cooperate might result in a theater headquarters' decision to withdraw the Fifteenth Air Force from the Combined Bomber Offensive. He requested, therefore, that the Fifteenth not be committed on the 20th.

The Royal Air Force was ready to play its vital role and agreed night missions would be coordinated with Spaatz's day strikes.

Spaatz issued orders that immediate priority should be given to airframe and final assembly plants because such attacks would have a more direct impact on frontline German air strength.

There were doubts about the weather prior to the first scheduled attacks February 20. The weather projection for the target areas was good, but clouds hung heavy over English bases, and icing conditions were reported at several altitudes.

All during the night of February 19/20, weather planes checked conditions. Major General Anderson, Spaatz's deputy for operations, remained strong for making the attacks, although he was concerned about weather conditions at takeoff. He knew it would be necessary to take off before dawn because the hours of daylight were so short. After studying weather reports, noting heavy icing predicted during climb-out to get above the clouds at eight thousand feet, he realized that bombers would have to make the climb on instruments and assemble above the clouds in darkness.

Kepner, commander of the Eighth's fighters, was most concerned about the ability of his fighters to climb through the cloud layer. He thought his P-47s and P-51s could make it, despite icing conditions, but he wasn't sure of his P-38s, whose efficiency might be cut in half.

The risks were so great that Kepner and Doolittle refused to send their planes without a direct order from Spaatz. Brigadier General C. P. Cabell, who had just left his job as a combat-wing commander and happened to be at headquarters at Park House, met with Spaatz. Meanwhile, weather planes were sent aloft every hour to report on conditions. After serious discussion, Spaatz asked Cabell his opinion.

"In my judgment the mission, though marginal, is feasible."

Spaatz turned to General Anderson. "Let 'em go."

While American crews were assembling for an early-morning takeoff, the Royal Air Force struck Leipzig, one of the target areas for the day strikes.

Activity was intense before daybreak as sixteen combat wings of three air divisions, with over one thousand bombers, assembled high above East Anglia after penetrating deep cloud layers. In support of the massive effort were seventeen groups of escort fighters from the Eighth and Ninth air forces, plus another sixteen squadrons from the RAF Fighter Command. Brereton's Ninth Air Force mediums also joined in diversionary attacks.

Spaatz and his staff had selected twelve German aircraft factories as targets, two of them as far away as Posen, Poland. Most were in the Brunswick-Leipzig area where assembly plants were located, and ten wings were assigned to them. This central force was escorted all the way, and some American fighter groups refueled and flew two missions.

Six wings were allotted to attack targets in the Posen area in Poland and at Tutow in eastern Germany. They were unescorted because their northern routes lay beyond most Luftwaffe defenses.

Although the First and Third Division each had its own air commander, the Third was designated the lead division.

Colonel Henry Macdonald, commander of the First Division, positioned his Flying Fortresses abreast of the Third Division and flew on their wing until well into Europe. This compression of the entire force reduced the effectiveness of German fighter attacks.

For the Germans below watching the six hundred or more bombers overhead, it must have been an awesome sight, and one foretelling their ultimate fate. No single leader ever had so many bombers under his command on one mission, and that vast armada, including the two hundred or so Allied fighters "S-ing" overhead, was undoubtedly the greatest single formation of aircraft ever flown on one mission in the European theater.

During entry of the German radar screen, it was hoped that German fighters would concentrate on the bombers, preventing large numbers of German fighters from attacking the unescorted northern wings. In an endeavor to get maximum escort fighter support, this main force flew together over the same route until each wing had to diverge to make its specific attack. Evidently the Germans were misled by this tactic into believing that both the northern and central forces were headed for Berlin.

With good support of escort fighters and the fact that the RAF night raid had worn out German night fighters, losses were kept to a minimum over Leipzig. Actually, out of one thousand bombers dispatched that day only twenty-one were lost.

Lieutenant William R. Lawley, Jr., was relieved to see the clouds part as his 305th formation approached Leipzig February 20 to bomb one of the ME-109 Erla complexes. He had feared that the heavy cloud cover they had encountered during their flight across the Continent would prevent visual bombing.

While Lieutenant Harry G. Mason watched for release of the bombs from the formation's leader, he anxiously searched the sky for fighters. There were none in sight, but the antiaircraft fire grew in intensity as they reached the bomb-release point.

"Tail gunner to crew. Fighters at six o'clock!"

Lawley felt tension building as no further word came from his tail gunner. Unable to stand the suspense, in a soft voice with its unmistakable southern accent, he said, "What's going on?"

Tail gunner Sergeant Henry A. Malone chuckled. "They don't mean business. They're just playing around."

Lawley warned they would be back.

After the bombardier hit the salvo lever to drop his bombs on the leader, he leaned over his bombsight and noted with excitement that the formation's bombs covered the target. Then, with concern, he noticed his own bombs had failed to release.

Lawley's eyes followed a score of fighters moving in. He winced as his B-17 shuddered with the impact of 20 mm cannon shells that exploded in the cockpit, killing co-pilot Lieutenant Paul W. Murphy instantly.

He vaguely heard Mason shout, "We've got an engine on fire!"

Lawley fought desperately to control the crippled airplane with most of his controls shot away. After nervously brushing a hand across his face while the B-17 plummeted earthward, he realized the pains he had felt a moment ago resulted from wounds, because his hand was covered with blood.

His face was bleeding so profusely that he had difficulty seeing the instruments while the bomber continued its dive. Blood seemed to be everywhere, and the windshields were so spattered that he couldn't see out. He soon realized why he couldn't pull the airplane out of its dive. The copilot's body was slumped over the wheel on his side, and its weight forced the control forward. Reacting quickly, he fought his way to the right seat and removed Murphy's body.

Despite his own painful wounds and the sickening sight of blood splattered all over the flight deck, he slowly pulled the bomber out of its plunge and got it on a semblance of an even keel.

Mason had called to tell him their bombs hadn't dropped, and in their crippled condition, he knew the weight of those bombs only added to their problems. He called the bombardier, "Get rid of those bombs!"

Mason tried everything, but the bombs refused to release, and he told Lawley, "The racks must be frozen."

Lawley called all stations and found that eight crew members were wounded, so he decided their only hope was to bail out. But Sergeant Thomas A. Dempsey, the radio operator, called to tell him that two of the gunners were so seriously wounded they couldn't bail out.

Lawley gave no further thought to leaving the airplane himself, and he struggled to get his emotions under control. He did order, "All those who are physically able, bail out!"

Not one man chose to leave, even when fighters crowded around the battered bomber and set another engine on fire. Now it was a fight for survival, and the gunners fought back, keeping up such a continuous fire that the Germans abandoned their attacks.

Using fire extinguishers, Lawley finally got the engine fire out.

Lawley was so covered with blood that Mason was nearly sick just looking at him. When he told Lawley that he had finally salvoed the bombs, Lawley nodded weakly. Mason expected him to collapse any moment, but Lawley stubbornly hung on to the controls until he fainted from loss of blood and exhaustion.

Mason had been to primary flying school, but he had washed out as a pilot. He had had no experience whatsoever in handling the fifty-five-thousand-pound bomber, but he grabbed the controls and turned the airplane toward England. He thought he might be able to keep the bomber in the air, but he doubted he could land it safely. His only hope was to revive the pilot once they arrived over England, and help him land the airplane.

When they were over the coast, Mason spotted a fighter field. He shook Lawley into consciousness and told him of their predicament. Somehow, Lawley managed to take control.

When an engine stopped, with the prop windmilling, Lawley knew that engine was out of gas. He yelled thickly to Mason, "Feather it!"

On approach, another engine caught fire as Lawley desperately marshaled his last remaining strength and pointed the Fortress toward the end of the runway. It hit hard and went careening down the runway while fire trucks and ambulances roared to the place where the Flying Fortress ended its wild run.

Lawley received the Medal of Honor for his gallantry and intrepidity in action, which surely helped inspire the almost superhuman efforts of his crew.

Lieutenant Walter E. Truemper and Sergeant Archibald Mathies also won Medals of Honor on this date. The plane *Mizpah,* in which Mathies rode as engineer, was attacked near Leipzig by a squadron of enemy fighters and the copilot, Lieutenant Ronald E. Bartley, was killed instantly. Damage to the plane was so severe that Mathies was sure it was all over when his pilot, Lieutenant Clarence R. Nelson, was wounded and rendered unconscious.

Navigator Truemper, assisted by Mathies, managed to fly the airplane back to base and send a Mayday distress call to the flight tower. They asked permission to try and land the stricken bomber now that the rest of the crew had bailed out.

The 351st Group's commanding officer, Colonel Eugene A. Romig, after taking to the air and flying alongside the crippled bomber, decided the airplane could not be landed safely.

"Abandon the airplane," he told them by radio.

Truemper and Mathies told their commander that the pilot was still alive, and they would not abandon him.

Romig reluctantly agreed, fearing that their valiant attempt would be unsuccessful. His fears were justified because all three fliers perished when a third attempt to land ended disastrously.

These attacks at Leipzig resulted in good bombing accuracy, although machine-tool damage was not as severe as was thought at the time. Heavy damage was done to four plants which produced parts and assembled airframes for the JU-88. The Erla Maschinenwerke complex, produced 32 percent of all ME-109s in Germany, and suffered heavy damage. During strikes there forty complete aircraft were destroyed, and serious damage was done to a parts factory. Yet although the Allies were not aware of it at the time, a surprising number of machine tools survived these attacks because bombs blew roofs off factories but were not heavy enough to destroy machine tools. (Use of heavier bombs and incendiaries would have increased the damage.) Nevertheless, factory officials decided these plants had to be dispersed and this action resulted in a loss of production. The Kiepholtz airport was bombed accurately, along with several other airfields, when principal targets at Brunswick were covered by clouds. Heavy damage was done to the city, but none of these bombs hit aircraft factories.

It was an auspicious start to what later became known as "Big Week."

21

BIG WEEK

Weather for February 21 was predicted to be good, and prior to the all-out daylight attack by the Eighth Air Force against two ME-110 plants at Brunswick, the RAF went out at night with six hundred planes to hit Stuttgart, an important aircraft production center.

The Ninth Air Force found airfield targets in the Low Countries clouded over, so their part in the mission was canceled. The same was true of the Fifteenth Air Force because weather in Italy was so bad they couldn't even fly ground-support missions. All in all, the day's missions were not successful, with poor results from those that did bomb their targets.

When weathermen forecast that the weather over two important objectives at Regensburg and Schweinfurt, plus the Erkner ball-bearing plant near Berlin would be good, initial plans were set up for the twenty-second. After review of all considerations, it was decided that the deep thrust to Berlin should be canceled because it would spread the available force too thin. The word that the Fifteenth would send formations to Regensburg was warmly welcomed.

The final decision was to use the Eighth to attack aircraft factories at Schweinfurt, Gotha, Berburg, Oschersleben, Aschersleben, and Halberstadt. A small diversionary force with radar-jamming devices was assigned to fly to Denmark to bomb Ålborg airfield. Such strategy, it was hoped, would make it difficult for the Germans to spot the main force of bombers until it had formed over England and was on its way. It was also hoped that the Germans would be so misled by the intentions of the main attacking force that they would hold a number of their fighter squadrons in the north.

Often the best-laid plans go awry, and this time was no exception—

due to bad weather over East Anglia. LeMay's Third Division, headed for Schweinfurt, ran into difficulties during assembly, and there were several collisions over England. He canceled the division's part in the mission. Such a decision was understandable, but it left the Fifteenth to face stronger opposition in the target area.

The Second Division, bound for Gotha, was so strung out during the Channel crossing that it never did get formed properly and it was re-called.

When the Oschersleben force found their targets obscured by clouds, the leaders dropped on targets of opportunity.

Many of those headed for Halberstadt encountered the same problems and reacted the same way.

It was not a good day for the Eighth Air Force, and only 99 out of 466 bombers actually bombed primary targets.

The Fifteenth managed to attack the Messerschmitt factory at Ober-traubling, but due to bad visibility, the bombing results were poor. With formations of the Eighth and Fifteenth spread out, the Germans had a field day and downed 41 Eighth Air Force bombers out of 430. The Fifteenth lost 14 heavies out of 183, but escort fighters claimed 60 Germans shot down for a loss of 11.

Spaatz called off all Eighth missions February 23, and the crews were grateful. The Fifteenth managed to dispatch 102 bombers against an Austrian ball-bearing plant at Steyr and the plant, which turned out 15 percent of all German ball bearings, was 20 percent destroyed.

Weather opened up again on the twenty-fourth, and one of the princi-pal targets was the dreaded Schweinfurt. Five wings were assigned to the ball-bearing plant; three wings were designated for the Gothaer-Wag-gonfabrik A. G., largest producer of ME-110 fighters; while a third force of five wings was assigned aircraft factories in northeastern Germany and Poland that produced parts and assembled FW-190s. Formation leaders were told to bomb the city of Rostock if targets were cloud covered. And, finally, the Fifteenth was assigned the Steyr-Daimler-Puch aircraft plant at Steyr.

The mission was planned to protect the northern force, which because of the distance it had to travel, prevented fighter escort. Spaatz directed that the main units from the Eighth and Fifteenth air forces be assigned times over targets that, hopefully, would split German defenses.

This strategy worked for the northern force because the weather was overcast, but not for the others. Formations assigned Schweinfurt and Gotha, and fliers from the Fifteenth, ran into coordinated attacks by single-engine and twin-engine fighters, the latter using rockets. The Steyr formations lost seventeen bombers despite fighter support upon with-drawal. Gotha was even worse with thirty-five crews shot down after persistent attacks. The formations at Schweinfurt lost only eleven, but ten escort fighters were shot down. The Americans made the Germans pay a heavy price, claiming thirty-seven.

During the nighttime hours of February 24/25 the Royal Air Force dropped a much greater weight than the American bombers, and they were aided by fires set in daylight by 238 B-17s. The combined raids caused extensive damage to three out of four plants. The bombing by either side was nowhere near as good as on the October 14 mission. Schweinfurt's capacity, due to removal of machinery prior to the raid, which reduced its production, was down to 60 percent, so it was not as important a target as the Allies thought at the time.

At Gotha, practically every building was damaged, but machine tools emerged largely unscathed. Again, photographs of roofless buildings were misleading because they indicated more damage than was actually the case.

Postwar reports indicated a production loss of six to seven weeks, which was equal to 140 aircraft. The ever-efficient Germans, through wide use of slave labor, had the plant back in full production in two months.

Weathermen told Spaatz that the weather should be so good on the twenty-fifth that he could pick almost any targets in Germany. The Fifteenth was assigned the Messerschmitt parts facility at Regensburg-Prüffening, while the Eighth was given the Messerschmitt factories at Regensburg, a similar plant at Augsburg, the ball-bearing plant at VKF Stuttgart, and the Bachmann–von Blumenthal factory at Fürth, which made parts and assembled 110s.

These attacks were deep penetrations into Germany and the first coordinated attacks against similar objectives by the Eighth and Fifteenth air forces. Spaatz's advisers told him that such attacks would confuse the Germans, and that they came at a time when German pilots must be undergoing an unusual state of exhaustion after their day-and-night battles with Allied bombers and fighters. Spaatz was pleased with the operational plan because the targets were well concentrated and it would be easy to send the large force of bombers using a single line of penetration with heavy Allied fighter escort.

As it turned out, the Fifteenth was the most exposed because escorting fighters couldn't follow all the way to their targets. And due to the necessity of hitting rail yards and port installations in northern Italy in support of ground operations, the Fifteenth could only send 176 bombers for strategic strikes. The Foggia-based groups lost 33 bombers at Regensburg, or one fifth of all those attacking the target. The fighting was intense during final attacks and during withdrawal, while the Eighth also lost 31 bombers out of 738. These losses were a strong reminder to Spaatz that excessive losses could be expected any time day bombers had to fight their way through to a target against heavy German fighter opposition. German fighter pilots may have been suffering from fatigue, but it didn't affect their aggressive intentions.

Bombing results were good: especially so at Regensburg, center of ME-109 production, and at Augsburg and Fürth where there were heavy losses of completed fighters.

The raids against the Obertraubling factory on February 22 and 25 by the Fifteenth Air Force and by the Eighth against both factories on the twenty-fifth destroyed almost every building. According to plant records made available after the war, production fell from 435 planes per month in January 1944 to 135 in March. It took four months to get the Regensburg plant back in full production. The same was true at Augsburg where production capacity dropped to 35 percent after one third of the machine tools were damaged and 70 percent of stored materials was destroyed during the raids.

Damage assessment reports at the time failed to consider that the Germans had dispersed many of their manufacturing operations, so photographs were misleading. Manufacture of the Messerschmitt airplanes had been integrated into a system of small satellite plants, some concealed in forest areas near large assembly plants. These facilities were largely untouched by the raids. Also, the Allies were overconfident on machine-tool damage, which was usually slight unless incendiaries were used.

Despite overoptimism at the time, it really was a "Big Week." Postwar analyses showed that the almost ten thousand tons of bombs dropped on industrial targets damaged or destroyed 75 percent of the buildings that accounted for 90 percent of all aircraft production.

The German High Command viewed the damage to their aircraft industry with consternation and immediately ordered further dispersal. Responsibility was removed from Göring's air ministry to a new agency under Speer's ministry of armaments and war production.

It wasn't until after the war that the effectiveness of the attacks against Germany's ball-bearing industry became known. The attacks against Erkner, Schweinfurt, Cannstatt, and Steyr reduced the production of ball bearings to 29 percent, Speer revealed in *Inside the Third Reich*. He said the Allies threw away the success they had already achieved when such attacks ceased in April.

These "Big Week" raids were far heavier and more accurate than the attacks August 8 and during October 1943, but they were not as effective. The earlier attacks had cost the German aircraft industry three months of production.

Total impact of these February attacks on the German air force was catastrophic when actual air battle losses of more than six hundred fighters are considered along with plant destruction. It never again was able to get back to its previous ability because "Big Week" broke the back of the German air force.

The bombings denied hundreds of aircraft to the Germans at a critical point in the war and reduced their operational totals in the west when the German High Command was trying to build them up in preparation for the invasion.

During this week, the Royal Air Force dropped over 9,000 tons of bombs from a total of 2,351 bombers for a loss rate of 6.6 percent.

The Eighth and Fifteenth air forces launched 3,800 bomber sorties, 3,300 by the Eighth alone; the total tonnage during the week equaled that dropped by the Eighth during its first year of operations. The cost was high. A total of 137 bombers were lost by the Eighth and 89 by the Fifteenth, for an overall average of about 6 percent per mission. This loss, however, was below the RAF's loss during the same period.

Fighter escorts flew 3,673 sorties from units of the Eighth, Ninth, and Fifteenth air forces. Their losses of 28 were small in comparison to the number of missions, and only a fifth as large as bomber losses.

Spaatz's decision to launch "Big Week" was one of the great decisions of the war. In some ways, it was as crucial as Eisenhower's D-day decision. The tactical risks were enormous, and the strategic effects were decisive. The impact of "Big Week" on the German air force made possible the launching of the invasion and also opened the way for the "fatal weakening" of Germany by the Combined Bomber Offensive. In retrospect, if Spaatz had not made that decision, Eisenhower probably would not have had even a choice of decision to invade the Continent in June.

Spaatz's courage in making this vital decision stands with that which Eaker had shown in his battle to preserve daylight precision bombing. The two go hand in hand. If Eaker had not persevered when he was beset on all sides by grave misgivings by many American and British leaders, Spaatz would not have been able to institute "Big Week." If Spaatz had faltered, almost certainly there would have been no successful invasion of the Continent, and the destruction of the primary targets of the Combined Bomber Offensive might not have been achieved. Underlying both decisions was the inspirational courage of the bomber crews both generals commanded.

Spaatz's decision to launch the offensive directly against the German Fighter Command, in the air and on the ground, was made under the most adverse circumstances. He could have lost the war for the Allies if "Big Week" had failed.

When Spaatz gave the order to start that momentous week, he knew that with the icing conditions above the fields and the difficulties of assembling above the clouds, the mission posed a tremendous tactical risk. He was aware that if the weather at the bases did not improve as predicted, there was no assurance that *any* of the bombers would be able to get home safely.

He alone made the decision, one of the most crucial decisions any bomber commander ever had to make. If he had been wrong in his judgment, and the weather had worsened and failed to lift at the bases, the whole Eighth Air Force and most of the Ninth could have been lost in one afternoon. Quiet spoken, always decisive, Spaatz not only had courage but common sense. He had an uncanny knack for arriving at the best possible solution to a difficult problem.

Shortly thereafter, Eisenhower told Spaatz that he was concerned by the heavy bomber losses.

"What's that got to do with it? Are we getting control of the German air force? If we have to take the losses to control them, then we have to take them, that's all. You can't have a war and worry about that."

During a week that saw up to two thousand American aircraft over Germany at one time, air warfare grew more decisive. While the German air force remained a potent threat, it never again was able to challenge the Allies everywhere over the Reich. From now on, German fighters rose to fight bomber fleets only when priority targets were threatened or when local air superiority was possible.

Now that Hitler had lost faith in the Luftwaffe, he believed antiaircraft defenses would help to reduce the effectiveness of Allied air raids. Noting an increase in flak damage before the end of 1943, Spaatz had called for use of countermeasures to jam radar gun-laying equipment, but flak installations were a major concern for another year.

In Germany, Speer ordered fighter production increased fourfold in March, but actual output was less than in August 1941. Production fell even lower in April. Although fighter factories maintained a monthly production rate of 1,581 fighters during the first half of 1944, the German Fighter Command never recovered from those five days in February. It is interesting to note that Allied intelligence estimates that German fighter production was down to 655 per month were far off the mark. Again, they underestimated the ingenuity of German factory managers. Combat losses and lack of training, however, were taking their toll of the Luftwaffe.

Arnold knew the cost was high with total casualties of approximately twenty-six hundred men. What he did not reveal at the time was that his planners had warned him that up to two hundred bombers might be lost on a single mission. The commanding general of the Army Air Forces was convinced such losses were acceptable, and worth the price, if the German air force could be defeated prior to D day.

Fortunately, actual bomber losses for the week were far less, totaling 226.

These raids, and those to follow in the next few months, made it possible for General Eisenhower to say with conviction on June 6, 1944, as his troops prepared for the cross-channel invasion, "If you see fighting aircraft over you, they will be ours."

The Royal Air Force had been night-bombing Berlin since August 25, 1940. The Americans made their first drops on the Nazi capital March 4, 1944, when twenty-nine planes of the 95th and 100th groups made an unsuccessful attack.

Two days later, the entire Eighth Air Force went to Berlin with six hundred bombers.

While Lieutenant William M. Cagney sat with members of his 446th Group at Bungay, he listened to the briefing officers warn that the German capital was the most heavily defended city in all Europe. For the first time, they were told, they would come up against 140 mm guns, which were larger than any guns previously used against them. They were advised the Germans had a lot of them and an equally large number of fighters.

The group took off at 8:50 A.M. to lead the wing. Cagney's B-24 was number four in the lead section, and they had been assigned the Daimler Benz factory a few miles south of Berlin in the Erkner section.

On approach, Cagney could appreciate the lead bombardier's problems because the factory was camouflaged and could not be located.

Glancing around apprenhensively, Cagney noted that the Second Air Division was bunched as it zigzagged all over the sky, trying to locate a target. Allied P-51 fighter support was excellent, he noted with relief, as they finally headed for the heart of Berlin. There were dogfights all over the sky, but, as yet, no bomber had been shot down.

The flak hit just as their bombs started to drop. It was the worst he had ever seen, most of it from 105 mm guns, and they ran into it as they turned away from the target.

He felt the plane slow down, and listening to the intercom chatter, he heard they had lost their number-one engine. A shell had ripped through the engine housing, coming out through the top of the wing.

Lieutenant Melvin Beyer couldn't maintain his Liberator in formation with a feathered engine, and despite his desperate efforts, they fell out of formation.

Beyer pleaded for fighter support after two 190s closed in for the kill. "Why in hell aren't we being protected?" he shouted. There was no reply.

Just as their condition became more serious, four P-47s hit the German fighters from the right, while four P-38s struck them from the left.

One Focke-Wulf was quickly shot down, and the other pulled away at full throttle.

Beyer slowed to save fuel, knowing he had six hundred miles to fly to reach home base—the farthest distance any B-24 had ever flown on three engines. En route back, they were hit again by German fighters, so Beyer sent an SOS. They fought them off and continued slowly on their way. Beyer was bitter because his formation had refused to lower their ball turrets over the target, which would have helped to protect them. He knew pilots were reluctant to do so because lowering them upset the plane's balance and slowed a formation by ten miles per hour.

He finally landed the plane at home base, but only after they had had to go around twice because other planes had cut them out of the landing pattern.

The familiar Erkner ball-bearing factory was struck again March 8. The Germans proved they could still offer resistance, and thirty-seven out of five hundred bombers were shot down. So successful was the bombing that the plant was out of operation for some time. Bomber losses would have been heavier except for P-51 fighter escorts.

These raids provided a new shock for the German people. Göring said the appearance of large formations with escorting fighters was something he had never thought possible.

A final Berlin attack in March was ineffectual because the formations had to release through clouds using pathfinders.

These raids only managed to keep the Germans under pressure because bad weather prevented visual bombing in most instances. Industrial centers received attention, and V-1 sites along the coast were bombed.

The Fifteenth was unable to contribute to the strategic air offensive to any worthwhile degree because it was diverted to attacks against tactical targets in front of the stubborn German defense lines in Italy.

22

A VIABLE
ALTERNATIVE

Initially, plans had called for a combined bomber offensive to last six months at full force before Eisenhower's troops were scheduled to land in Normandy. Now, there were only three months prior to D day, and Eisenhower kept insisting that the air offensive be diverted from its primary strategic objectives to soften up German ground forces and inhibit movement of troops and supplies to the Normandy beaches.

Spaatz had objected ever since he returned to England. By April, his strategic air forces had sixty groups of heavy bombers and thirty-two groups of fighters, including those of the Ninth Air Force. His command at last was in reach of its goal of completing the destruction of the German air force and pressing on to the destruction of primary industrial targets in Germany.

Now he was asked to turn his command in to a supporting role for the invasion, but his bitter protests went unheeded.

Eisenhower had gone on record that he would not authorize an invasion of the Continent unless Germany's air force was destroyed. Sensibly, he made it an absolute precondition in discussions with military and political leaders of both Britain and the United States.

Spaatz, along with other air commanders, was a firm believer that once a powerful strategic air offensive was organized in depth, with sufficient support to maintain it for a period of time, and the enemy air defense had been seriously weakened, no nation could survive the onslaught. He believed that diversion of the strategic air effort now, at a time when air superiority had been achieved over much of Germany, would be catastrophic. He wanted his strategic air forces to make their maximum contribution to eventual victory, not merely to assist an early invasion of Normandy.

Eisenhower's concern, he told Spaatz, was the rate of buildup of

German divisions in the critical invasion area. His biggest problem, he said, was to transfer men and supplies across the Channel, over open beaches, and into the beachhead faster than the Germans could move their armies to resist them. He demanded that enemy movements be delayed by air attacks against railroads and other lines of communications.

Eisenhower's staff airmen had long advocated an air offensive against rail communications in France, with attacks against 110 railroad bridges, marshaling yards, and maintenance depots. In their words, airpower should make northern France a "rail desert" to hamper German army movement to the beaches.

The strategic air forces totally disagreed that all Allied airpower should be used for preinvasion support. Spaatz was not alone in his views; Air Chief Marshal Harris of the RAF Bomber Command, Eaker, and commanders of the Eighth and Fifteenth air forces supported him wholeheartedly. In contrast, they recommended a concentrated air offensive against Germany until mid-May when they would start an interdiction program in northern France. Spaatz argued with Eisenhower's officers that attacks should be concentrated on German oil resources and their production plants in order to dry up fuel resources for German aircraft and army ground units. He stressed such attacks would have the added benefit of keeping 490 single-engine and 322 night fighters in central Germany so that they would not be available for D day. He pointed out also that such strategic attacks into central Germany would force the German Fighter Command to come up and fight to preserve their precious fuel supplies, and their numbers would be reduced drastically as a result of air battles with Allied bombers and escort fighters.

His arguments proved fruitless even when he tried to convince Eisenhower's staff that German fighters were not concentrated in France and certainly would not fight for French railroads. He pleaded for just fifteen days of visual bombing for his Eighth Air Force, and ten for the Fifteenth, to prove what his command could do. Then, he told Eisenhower, three weeks before D day he would unleash his entire forces to destroy communications in France.

Adolf Hitler had realized as early as 1933 that Germany would be cut off from Venezuelan and Middle Eastern oil in the event of war with France and Great Britain, and he had resolved that Germany would become as self-sufficient as possible. He had authorized expansion of oil drilling in Germany, but most importantly, he started synthetic production of oil and gasoline from Germany's abundant coal resources. Aviation gasoline in Germany thereafter came almost exclusively from synthetic production.

From 1933 to 1939, production of natural petroleum in Germany increased by a factor of five. Synthetic production amounted to 16 percent of all oil products consumed by the country. This still left about 66 percent of oil needs that had to be imported.

At the start of the war, Hitler had reduced civilian use of gasoline to 10 percent of peacetime levels. Railroads and power stations were forced to shift from oil to more plentiful coal.

The ground so carefully laid for expansion of the synthetic industry was a lifesaver for Germany during the war when 84.5 percent of her aviation fuel, 85 percent of automobile gasoline, and all but a fraction of 1 percent of rubber production, and 100 percent of nitric acid and 99 percent of methanol, both basic ingredients in all explosives, were made synthetically.

Germany had only a third of her planned reserves of aviation fuel when World War II began, or 5.5 million tons. Without her synthetic industry, she would soon have become militarily impotent.

The synthetic process involved mixing coal and small amounts of oil under high pressure and temperature, followed by introduction of hydrogen. In 1926, the process developed originally in 1909 by German chemist Friedrich Bergius, and for which he received a Nobel Prize in 1931, became a reality when it was developed by I. G. Farben.

At the time, Standard Oil in the United States was interested in the process and considered a cooperative venture with the Germans. The American company lost interest when the Texas oil fields proved to have huge oil reserves that could be recovered at far less cost.

Hitler had been faced with a difficult decision at the start of the war to obtain sufficient amounts of these supplies for his war machine. His needs were so critical that he couldn't disperse operations in a number of small plants, but had to concentrate them in large factories, which proved to be extremely vulnerable to air attack. This critical shortage of vital reserves was one of the principal reasons why German military advisers had tried so hard to dissuade Hitler from going to war in 1939.

Arnold had endorsed Eisenhower's stand on use of the strategic air forces shortly after he was named Supreme Allied Commander. At that time, Spaatz had offered no objection to temporary use of his strategic bombers in order to ensure success of the invasion. He would never have agreed if he had known Eisenhower would want them so soon and would keep control of his command so long.

Spaatz did get from Eisenhower a concession that the strategic air forces would be permitted to initiate an early bombing campaign against oil targets.

Churchill and the British War Cabinet were dismayed by the possible civilian casualties in attacks against French targets, which analysts figured could cost as many as one hundred sixty thousand French dead and injured. The prime minister feared repercussions, knowing the French would consider such heavy attacks against their transportation systems an unnecessary and ruthless use of airpower against civilians.

Eisenhower said such casualties were unavoidable, and he insisted such attacks were necessary to secure a successful landing on the Continent to drive the Germans out of France.

Arnold had sent Eisenhower a letter shortly after he had assumed command in England that it was his wish that the Army Air Forces be under a supreme command, and offered his support.

Eisenhower replied, "I am perfectly willing to avoid terms and language that might startle anyone, but I want full power to determine missions and priorities for all forces without having to negotiate in the heat of battle."

Spaatz basically agreed with his views but only as they pertained to the crucial period of the invasion itself. During a luncheon with Eisenhower and Tedder in January 1944, Spaatz told Eisenhower that he was pleased with the agreement that had been reached whereby air operations would be controlled in the manner that had proved so successful in the Mediterranean.

Before Eisenhower set up his new command, with Tedder as Deputy Supreme Allied Commander responsible for Allied air operations for the coming invasion, Eisenhower had talked to Churchill about the chain of command, which put the British and American tactical air forces under Air Chief Marshal Leigh-Mallory and kept the bombers under Spaatz and Harris.

Tedder wanted all airpower under him, insisting that Churchill, who was still convalescing from pneumonia at Casablanca, had told him that he should have such overall control. When the matter was brought to the prime minister's attention, he thought the solution was quite simple: There should be only one tactical air force commander for the British and American tactical air forces, and that commander should be Leigh-Mallory, who would report to Eisenhower. He said also that Spaatz, serving under Eisenhower, should be told to obey Tedder. Bomber Command would also report to Eisenhower through Tedder. He thought there would be no difficulty between Tedder and Harris. "I do not like the idea of Tedder being an officer without portfolio," Churchill added.

The solution was not that easy. Sir Archibald Sinclair, British secretary of state for air, said if the Americans put Spaatz and Harris directly under Eisenhower, he was convinced that that would be a mistake. He reasoned that not even Tedder had any experience in conducting a bombing offensive. He said Tedder, if he was to be an effective deputy supreme commander, should not be involved in just air problems.

Churchill agreed, as did the British chiefs, that Tedder should exercise authority over all three services, even though Walter Bedell Smith's position as Eisenhower's chief of staff might become more difficult.

Tedder reminded them that he had been asked to be Deputy Supreme

Allied Commander by the Americans, and not just a substitute for Leigh-Mallory. He viewed his role as an adviser to Eisenhower on all air matters and authorized to speak in his name to all subordinates.

The British chiefs of staff and Sinclair were in agreement that the strategic air forces should be handed over to Eisenhower's control.

Churchill again interposed his views. It was his understanding, he said, that only those forces that had already been committed to Eisenhower should come under Tedder's control. In other words, Bomber Command should remain under Portal and the Combined Chiefs.

Churchill said that he did not consider Tedder any great authority on war in general, and certainly not in the use of armies and fleets. "He has, however, proved himself a master in the use of the air force, and this is the task I had hoped he would have assigned to him by the supreme commander in the same way that Alexander was entrusted in fighting the land battles in Sicily and Italy. If Tedder is only to be a sort of floating kidney, we shall be wasting him and putting more on Leigh-Mallory that [sic], in my opinion, he can carry."

Eisenhower brought the matter up again soon after he took over. He discussed the subject during many talks with Churchill because he was most worried about his relationship with Harris. Eisenhower considered the head of Bomber Command something of a dictator who didn't appreciate taking orders from outside his command. He told Churchill that Bomber Command had a responsible role to play in the invasion, and that if Harris proved difficult he could foresee endless friction between them.

Like Portal, Tedder was a scholar but without Portal's steadiness. He often had to lean on Portal in his relations with dynamic men like Harris and Spaatz. He tried to reassure a doubting Eisenhower that Harris would cooperate if he was given specific orders. As later events proved, Churchill's original view that Tedder and Harris would get along proved accurate.

Leigh-Mallory had taken over the two tactical air forces the previous November, but it became apparent after the first of the year that additional air support before and after the invasion would be required if successful landings on the Continent were to be made. Tedder remained convinced that the strategic air forces must be brought into the picture, despite Harris's lack of enthusiasm. Spaatz was openly opposed.

Harris put his views in writing. He said the only efficient support Bomber Command could give to the invasion was the intensification of industrial attacks on Germany. "To substitute for this process attacks on other targets such as gun emplacements, beach defenses, communications, or dumps would be to commit the irremediable error of diverting our best weapon from the military function for which it has been equipped and trained to tasks it cannot effectively carry out. Though this might give a specious appearance of supporting the army, in reality it would be the greatest disservice we could do them. It would lead directly to disaster."

Spaatz hastened to endorse Harris's comments.

Three days after Tedder wrote Portal conveying doubts that a unified air plan could be evolved if a number of disparate organizations were operating independently, Leigh-Mallory called a meeting of his tactical support committee. With him presiding, a so-called Transportation Plan, to consider attacks upon German rail communications on the Continent, was brought up for discussion. Leigh-Mallory said such attacks were vital to dislocate the enemy's rail network prior to and after the invasion. The thrust of his argument was that such attacks would restrict movements of troops and supplies over a period of many months, not just hamper movement of ten divisions to the invasion front at the last minute. Experts said such attacks would cripple the rail systems in France and Belgium, and that repeated attacks would prevent the Germans from repairing them.

Director of bomber operations, Air Commodore S. O. Bufton, had other ideas. Typically nonconformist, he urged that vital points be attacked around D day because it was impossible to bomb accurately over a period of months.

The Transportation Plan was the brainchild of Solly Zuckerman, a professor of anatomy who was one of thousands of British experts called upon to aid the war effort. He had planned the successful bombing of Pantelleria, and he had studied the results of the bombing of Rome's marshaling yards in July 1943. He believed strategic bombers could best be used to destroy the railroad networks in France and the Low Countries. He had easily convinced Leigh-Mallory that heavy bombers would make their most useful contribution to success of the invasion by bombing such targets, and he had adopted the plan as his own. Zuckerman next convinced Tedder of the validity of the plan and he, in turn, convinced Eisenhower.

Harris and Spaatz used every persuasive power they could to defeat the Transportation Plan. Harris pointed out that his heavy bombers were designed to fly at night and could not achieve the accuracy required to hit marshaling yards.

Harris said his bombers could not even get to precision targets by day because they had inadequate defensive armament. He believed that his heavy bombers should be used to destroy the enemy's interior lines of communication, which would permit a breakout later from the Normandy beaches. He argued that railroad tracks were very difficult to hit and could be repaired easily, but that marshaling yards were good targets because they included nearby repair shops and depots.

Tedder fought back. He accused Harris of juggling figures to show that his Bomber Command couldn't hit such targets. He said Harris seemed to forget that he had at least one group in his command that had been carrying out precision attacks quite successfully.

Eisenhower knew the Germans had a complete army, with many of their best divisions, and masses of armor to oppose the invasion. He was aware that these divisions, moving on interior lines of communication, could reinforce the beach defenses within a day or two. His basic problem, he reiterated, was to get his invasion forces ashore and supply them by sea in spite of inadequate landing facilities. He knew that any hope of securing a port on the French coast intact was wishful thinking. Then, after his troops were ashore, the next biggest problem was to achieve a breakout.

Eisenhower was faced with one of the most difficult and hazardous operations of any military commander in history. Many people advised him that the invasion could not succeed. He believed it could, but only if he could get total support from all branches of the services that could possibly be had, along with full control at all times. It was not an unreasonable request under the circumstances, but it posed problems for strategic air commanders.

Doolittle called the Transportation Plan a waste of effort. Much more serious was Portal's opposition. He reminded Eisenhower of a 1940 War Cabinet ruling forbidding air attacks on occupied countries if there was a serious risk of heavy loss of civilian lives.

When Leigh-Mallory sent a list of targets to the Air Ministry that he wished Bomber Command to attack, most of them were disapproved. When Eisenhower was informed, he referred the matter to the British chiefs of staff and Portal was told to examine the matter.

By the end of February, Portal decided the practicability of attacking railway centers should be put to the test. On the night of March 6, the railway center at Trappes was devastated by units of Bomber Command. Wing Commander G. L. Cheshire's 5 Group did an outstanding marking job by Oboe-equipped Mosquitoes and bombed blindly from an average altitude of seventy-five hundred feet. So heavy was the damage that Trappes was out of service for a month. Portal ordered additional attacks and it was quickly apparent from their success that Harris had underestimated the skill of his crews. After eleven similar attacks, Portal was convinced that the Transportation Plan was feasible.

Spaatz, however, refused to concede. He said strategic air's success in destroying aircraft factories and oil refineries not only would assure that the objectives of strategic airpower would be met, but also assist the invasion. He pointed out that by turning away from strategic targets to attack rail centers would allow German production to return to its former high rate. He convinced General Arnold, and the American air force chief of staff supported his views.

Spaatz moved quickly because he knew that his strategic forces would be engulfed by the Zuckerman program unless he came up with an alternative that would make a direct contribution to the invasion. His proposal was to give first priority to attacks on German oil targets, with special emphasis on plants producing gasoline. He said such attacks, in the long run, would immobilize the Germans far more than Zuckerman's Transportation Plan. In making such a proposal, Spaatz knew it would not have any immediate effect because the Germans had accumulated large stocks of oil in France in depots that were relatively safe from air attacks. Only after these stocks were used up would Spaatz's plan have an impact on frontline operations. Spaatz, however, refused to believe that the Transportation Plan would be of much help in keeping Germans out of Normandy, while his oil plan would be of major help later. That was the key point. Spaatz argued that the ground forces would have little difficulty getting ashore and staying there despite German opposition. Eisenhower disagreed. He supported the Transportation Plan because it promised some help, while, in his view, the oil plan offered none for the invasion itself.

Eisenhower pressed his arguments on Churchill. The prime minister was reluctant to give Eisenhower command of all RAF units in England. He was specifically opposed to release of the Coastal Command, which was charged with responsibility for the defense of the home islands. The prospect of Leigh-Mallory's command of Harris's heavy bombers disturbed Churchill also, because he didn't believe Leigh-Mallory understood how best to use them properly. Eisenhower patiently explained that he had no intention of taking over control of Coastal Command.

Leigh-Mallory's position was difficult, but he created many of his problems. A florid, good-looking man, with a trim military moustache, Leigh-Mallory had commanded 12 Group during the Battle of Britain. He was an experienced commander in air-ground support, but he could be egotistical and difficult at times. His frequent arrogance alienated not only many American commanders, but also some of his British colleagues.

When the Supreme Allied Commander met with Churchill February 28, he told him that he would issue an order giving Tedder authority over all existing air forces. He said Leigh-Mallory's position would not be changed in regard to forces already assigned to him, but those attached to the Supreme Allied Expeditionary Forces would not come under his direction. Therefore, command of all strategic air forces would remain under Tedder, and Leigh-Mallory would have no control whatsoever.

Eisenhower pressed his case when Churchill seemed to respond favorably, saying Tedder could be the aviation lobe of Eisenhower's brain. Just when Eisenhower thought he had won his case, Churchill said there could be no question of turning the RAF Bomber, Fighter, or Coastal commands as a whole over to the Supreme Allied Commander and his deputy. He said he was willing to assign forces from these commands to Eisenhower as the need arose, but he insisted that use of SHAEF airplanes must remain subject to approval by the Combined Chiefs of Staff. Eisenhower objected strongly to submitting his plans to the Combined Chiefs, and said flatly that anything less than complete operational control of the whole of Bomber Command and the United States Strategic Air Forces would be unacceptable. Eisenhower was very disturbed because it appeared to him that Churchill was reneging on what had previously been approved. He told Churchill that if the British refused to make a full commitment to the invasion, such as holding back part of the RAF Bomber Command, he had no alternative but to go home.

In a conversation with Tedder after the meeting, Eisenhower warned that the prime minister was very impatient, and he urged Tedder to hasten air plans for the invasion; otherwise Churchill will be "in this thing with both feet."

Churchill had second thoughts because he was upset by Eisenhower's threat to quit. He told the supreme commander that he would accept any plan that Portal and he agreed upon.

On the day of the Eisenhower/Churchill meeting, Zuckerman sent Tedder another memo. In it, he said it had been stated in recent meetings that diversion of the bombing effort from strategic air targets to invasion support would be a disaster because strategic air attacks were causing a crisis in Germany. He said Spaatz had wanted only twenty or thirty clear days to finish the war on his own, and that Harris, too, was saying Bomber Command raids on the heart of Germany could well be the winning factor. Zuckerman conceded there was some justification for such comments, but from SHAEF's point of view the vital factor was time. In reviewing all aspects of the proposed strategic bombing plan preceding the invasion, representing three months prior to D day, he said such attacks would not achieve more than a 7 percent loss in industrial output in Germany. Zuckerman completely discounted reports that such air attacks would destroy German morale.

Churchill intervened February 29. He called Eisenhower's command structure awkward and protested because no final air plan as yet had been agreed upon. In an attempt to provide guidelines, he said Eisenhower should be Supreme Allied Commander of all invasion forces, and that Tedder should command all air forces permanently or temporarily assigned for the invasion in a manner that would best fulfill the Supreme Allied Commander's overall plan.

Under such a proposed organization, Leigh-Mallory would execute Eisenhower's orders, which would be channeled through Tedder as deputy. In effect, Tedder would have the authority to issue orders in Eisenhower's name to Spaatz and Harris, and also to Sir Sholto Douglas, who had just taken over Coastal Command.

Tedder and Portal were in constant contact during the first nine days of March, struggling to reconcile differences. Eisenhower's insistence that he must have complete control of all heavy bombers, and Churchill's insistence that Fighter, Bomber, and Coastal commands *not* be turned over to Tedder to use as he wished, created wide differences. Eisenhower was well aware that the title Supreme Allied Commander did not mean the Combined Chiefs would turn all their authority over to him, or that the British chiefs of staff would ever give him total control of all British air forces if a serious emergency developed on the home front through attacks by "V" weapons.

Eisenhower met with his staff March 10. He found himself in basic agreement with Portal and Tedder that the best method of employing strategic air forces in the three-month period prior to the invasion would be in attacks first to destroy the German air force and second against the French transportation system.

Within two days, two memos were circulated. One came from the air forces, the other from the Air Ministry. Both provided arguments against the Transportation Plan, but they used inadequate information and were not in accord with facts. It was stated in one that the French and Belgian railroad systems were not fully utilized, and that German ability to repair them quickly was almost unlimited. It was argued that only a small part of the rail systems in both countries would be needed to be kept in operation.

Eisenhower called a meeting March 25 and requested that Portal, Spaatz, Leigh-Mallory, Tedder, and Harris attend. He would act as chairman and listen to both sides of the dispute.

23

EISENHOWER
THREATENS TO GO HOME

Leigh-Mallory spoke first, saying that the strategic air forces had offered only to participate in an interdiction program to begin shortly before D day, and concentrate on railroad yards to prevent the Germans from moving reinforcements to the beachheads.

Tedder rose in protest, saying it was a matter of concentration of effort, and cited a military axiom to back up his words. "If the air forces would have their way," he said, "Spaatz would have his bombers flying over Germany making precision attacks against oil targets. And Harris would be engaged in area drops against cities." Then, he cited the advantages of the Transportation Plan over such attacks.

Spaatz was next. He knew it was a crucial moment for strategic airpower and his wide, hard-set mouth was cast in stern lines. He was an officer of the old school, graying at the temples, with a distinguished moustache. His listeners were attentive because he had proved his extraordinary proficiency in two world wars, and they respected his incisive mind. "The Transportation Plan will not work. At best, the Allies could reduce by twenty percent the present efficiency of the enemy railroads, which is hardly sufficient. The Germans could make up that loss by cutting down on the food carried for the civilian population. On the other hand, fourteen synthetic oil plants produce eighty percent of all German petrol and oil. By concentrating on them," he said, "the Eighth Air Force can practically dry up the German supply." He went on to recommend continued destruction of the German air force and an all-out attack against Axis oil production.

In regard to tactical support of the invasion before D day, he said such attacks should be made in great strength against communications and military installations of all kinds to assist to the maximum the initial phases of the invasion.

To cap his arguments, he gave them copies of an order that a German quartermaster general had sent to his high command headquarters that stated that motor fuel was so short that every unit should economize wherever possible.

When Spaatz completed his presentation, Portal said he had heard that German stocks of fuel in France were plentiful, and "if that was so, would your oil plan be effective?"

Spaatz admitted that his plan to bomb refineries would have little effect on frontline operations until four or five months after the invasion.

Harris turned against Spaatz's oil plan. He said he preferred to continue attacks against German cities at night.

Eisenhower stood up. He reminded them that they should never forget that one of the fundamental factors that led to the decision to invade the Continent was the conviction that the Allied Air Forces would make such an operation feasible; otherwise it would be extremely hazardous, if not foolhardy. "No one has a greater stake in the success of this operation than the French. It would be sheer folly to abstain doing anything that can increase in any measure our chances for success in Overlord."

Eisenhower reiterated again his strong conviction that it was essential to take every possible step to assure that the troops get ashore and stay ashore. "The greatest contribution I can imagine the air forces making to this aim is that they should hinder enemy movement."

After the meeting, Eisenhower admitted to Churchill that the arguments against the Transportation Plan had been strong, but that he was convinced it would increase his chances of success. "Unless it can be proved to be an erroneous conclusion," he said, "I do not perceive how we can fail to proceed with the program." He reminded Churchill that the French people were at present slaves and would benefit from success of the invasion. In his opinion, he said, it would be sheer folly to refuse approval of the Transportation Plan.

Churchill promised to meet with Portal and Tedder. When he did, Portal told the prime minister he had been against the Transportation Plan, but that he had been impressed by the arguments advanced by Eisenhower and Tedder, as well as Zuckerman's comments about the results achieved by bombing in the Mediterranean campaign. He told Churchill that if the railways were dislocated just one week to delay the arrival of nine divisions, this might well turn the scales. He said he had always been convinced of the value of systematic air attacks against communications targets, and the plan had his approval.

Churchill reluctantly agreed to the plan, although he insisted that Tedder be responsible also for security of the British Isles against robot bomb and rocket attacks, and that such attacks, if they started, should have precedence over all other priorities. The prime minister got Eisenhower's reluctant agreement also that the command organization would be reviewed once the Allied armies were established on the Continent.

Arnold, in Washington, insisted on a provision that gave the Combined Chiefs of Staff power to approve the final plan for strategic air forces participation in invasion plans before they went into effect. The arguments concerned use of certain words and their interpretation. The British wanted the agreement to read that Eisenhower would be charged with the responsibility for "supervising" air operations. Eisenhower insisted on "command of." Arnold decided the words "direction of" should be used.

The compromise was not satisfactory to all, and the United States Strategic Air Forces under Spaatz disliked the fact there was only one American officer on Tedder's nine-man council. In the past, there had been breakdowns in communications between the council and his headquarters.

Prior to this agreement, Arnold had considered naming Spaatz commander of all United States Army Air Forces in Europe, which would have given him a position practically equivalent to Eisenhower's.

When Eisenhower heard of this proposal, he asked Spaatz not to press for such a change because he was negotiating with the British for inclusion of the RAF's Bomber Command in his invasion plans. Spaatz agreed and discouraged Arnold from making the proposal. Later, he regretted his decision after units of his command were ordered on missions by a variety of headquarters.

Eisenhower had been so upset over failure to obtain agreement earlier for a total air commitment to his invasion plans that he had confided to his diary, "If a satisfactory answer is not achieved or reached, I'm going to take drastic action and inform the Combined Chiefs of Staff that unless the matter is settled at once, I will request relief from this command."

After the British chiefs announced their acceptance of the Transportation Plan, with reluctant agreement by American air leaders, he added a postscript, "I was told the word direction was acceptable to both sides of the house. Amen."

Eisenhower wrote General Marshall, "I must say that the way it is shaping up I am far happier than I was a week ago."

Spaatz gave in graciously, feeling he had at least been given a fair hearing.

Although Harris refused to admit it, the Battle of Berlin had ended in failure. There is no question that Bomber Command had inflicted heavy damage to Berlin and other major German cities, but the German people fought on and dashed Harris's hopes that his bomber offensive would destroy their morale and will to continue the fight.

"Berlin won," the head of 5 Group, Sir Ralph Cochrane, said, "because it was just too tough a nut."

Bufton, as director of bomber operations, accused Harris of doubling up on each losing throw of the dice.

Harris fell back on the explanation that Bomber Command's assignment to aid the upcoming invasion caused the failure of his war-winning plan to bring Germany to her knees in abject surrender. It was as good an excuse as any, but it just was not true.

Eisenhower won the argument about use of all airpower in support of the invasion because Portal and Tedder agreed with him. It seems likely that if they had joined forces with Spaatz and Harris, Churchill would not have accepted the plan.

Few serious arguments are settled for good. When Leigh-Mallory, in late March, exercised his jurisdiction over Ninth Air Force P-47s and transferred them from bomber escort duty to strafing railroads in France, Spaatz exploded. He still believed it was premature to attack targets in support of the invasion because the Germans would have time to repair the damage. He complained to Eisenhower that without the P-47s as bomber escorts, deep penetrations into Germany would result in greatly increased losses. He reminded Eisenhower that reduction of bomber attacks would cost them many opportunities to deal punishing blows to the German air force.

Eisenhower called Spaatz and Leigh-Mallory into his office. He listened first to Leigh-Mallory, who argued that paralysis of the French railway network could not be achieved in a week or two. He said unless the job was done properly, there would be little advantage in doing it at all.

Spaatz used the familiar arguments that it was too early to start the plan, reminding them that, for security reasons, many important bridges should not be attacked until D day.

Eisenhower supported Spaatz and gave him first call on fighters for escort duty for the present.

During April, Churchill continued to voice doubts about attacks on French rail centers and the civilian casualties that would result. He sent repeated notes to Eisenhower that the Transportation Plan should be revised so that attacks would be made only against rail centers where the casualties would not exceed 100 or 150 French. His last protest was sent April 29 following a meeting of the War Cabinet.

Eisenhower told Tedder to reply, giving the usual rebuttals.

When the War Cabinet met May 2, Churchill gave copies of his reply to members. "Care should be taken not to add unnecessarily to the burdens of the supreme commander, but I have never realized that airpower would assume such a cruel and remorseless form. . . ." He said he feared the Transportation Plan would smear the Royal Air Force across the world.

Eisenhower and Tedder remained adamantly opposed to any changes in their plan for attacks against the rail systems in France. The Supreme Allied Commander wrote Marshall that the British were trying to change his mind. "I've stuck to my guns because there's no other way in which this tremendous air force can help us."

Churchill recommended that a member of Eisenhower's staff should discuss the matter with the Free French. Walter Bedell Smith, Eisenhower's chief of staff, talked to Major General Pierre Joseph Koenig. The French general shrugged. "This is war, and it must be expected that people will be killed. We would take the anticipated loss to be rid of the Germans."

Churchill was still disturbed. He decided to take the matter up with President Roosevelt so that the Americans would have to share responsibility. He wired the president that to kill ten thousand Frenchmen prior to D day very likely would have a serious effect on relations with the French government. Churchill said he realized that a successful invasion would shorten the war and save the lives of possibly millions of conquered peoples, but that the War Cabinet was unanimous in its anxiety that these French slaughters, as he called them, should be avoided by resorting to other methods. "Whatever is settled between us, we are quite willing to share responsibilities with you."

Roosevelt replied that military considerations must dominate. "No possibility of alleviating French opinion must be overlooked, always provided our effectiveness against the enemy is not reduced at this crucial time. However regrettable the attendant loss of civilian lives is, I am not prepared to impose upon, from this distance, any restriction on military commanders that, in their opinion, might militate against the success of Overlord, or cause additional loss of life of Allied forces of invasion."

Roosevelt thereby ended a dispute that had agitated men on both sides of the Atlantic. Churchill dropped the matter. Fortunately, French casualties were far less than feared, and sealing off the Normandy beaches from German reinforcements by railroad may have been the greatest contribution that Allied bombers made to the success of the invasion.

After the war, it was learned that Generalleutnant Adolf Galland had told his Nazi superiors in April that his day-fighter arm had lost more than one thousand pilots, including their best squadron and group commanders. Furthermore, each heavy attack by the British and the Americans cost them an average of fifty pilots. He told top officials of the Luftwaffe, "The time has come when our force is within sight of collapse."

In one of the most badly planned and executed raids ever flown by British Bomber Command, 999 British and 10 American bombers took off the night of March 30 to bomb Nuremburg. Eighty crews quickly aborted the mission for a variety of reasons, and those that carried on to the target found the bright moonlight an open invitation to swarms of German night fighters. As crews tried to locate their aiming points in the cloud-covered city of Nuremburg, silhouetted by the rays of a full moon above the clouds, German fighters attacked. One hundred eight Allied intruders and bombers fell to their guns. Lancasters and Halifaxes bore the brunt of the losses, and despite savage air battles in the eerie moonglow, only ten German night fighters succumbed to the bombers' guns.

Pilot Officer Cyril J. Barton, a quiet, deeply religious twenty-two-year-old, was shocked to come under such savage attack even before they reached the target area. The 578 Squadron's Halifax was quickly riddled by cannon fire. All turrets were shot out, and shells penetrated the fuel tanks, forcing him to shut down an engine.

When he tried to call on the intercom to get reports of damage, he found he had no radio communications with his crew. In trying to reach them by calling out, the bombardier, navigator, and radio operator misunderstood his orders and bailed out.

Despite the loss of these vital members of his crew, Barton chose to fly to the target and drop his incendiaries, even though the condition of his airplane would in fact have justified a bail-out order.

Somehow he managed to get the badly crippled airplane to the bomb-release point and the incendiaries were dropped, although his flight engineer later said he thought they were dropped on another city.

Barton knew his chances of getting back to England on three engines without a navigator and radio operator to guide him—not to mention the loss of a large quantity of his fuel from leaking tanks—were slim. Still, he figured a heading he hoped would get them back to their East Anglia base.

Over the Channel, clouds were so heavy that he judged they must have missed the coast of England, so he turned north, seeking any place to land. His fuel supply was an ever-present worry, and he ordered the jettisoning of everything movable to reduce fuel consumption.

He finally spotted the coast and headed in, still not knowing where he was. Just as he crossed land, his fuel supply was exhausted and he had to land immediately. He put the plane into a dive after ordering his two gunners and flight engineer to their crash positions on the main spar. Ahead, he saw he was headed for a row of cottages, so he desperately pulled back to clear them. His Halifax roared above them, but slammed into the ground on a slope, tearing itself apart.

Miraculously, the gunners and flight engineer survived, but Barton was killed instantly as the nose of the bomber collapsed on him.

For "gallantly completing his last mission in the face of almost impossible odds" Barton was awarded the Victoria Cross.

The loss rate of 13 percent on this mission was bad enough, but equally depressing was the fact that because of heavy clouds over the city, bomb damage to Nuremburg was slight.

Lieutenant William M. Cagney, whose B-24 had survived a direct hit over Berlin on March 6, was flying in a wing position, gazing down at the city of Brunswick on April 8 as it rapidly succumbed to immense fires. He noted that the lead bombardier of his formation had decided to drop his 446th Group's bombs on a huge plant alongside the river. Cagney couldn't see how he could miss. It was the biggest thing in sight —at least a mile long and as wide.

The lead bombardier directed the formation to make a 180-degree turn and placed his bombsight's cross hairs on the target just as they pulled out. The synchronization looked perfect. He bent over his sight to spot the impact. To his consternation, only one bomb hit the huge plant, and all others exploded in the river. Later, Cagney realized that the centrifugal force of the turn was still with them, and they had been sliding sideways enough to throw the bombs away from the target.

On another 446th Group mission, Cagney released his bombs on a V-2 missile site. The gunners called to say that one five-hundred-pound bomb was hung up, *and hanging nose down with the arming wire pulled out.*

Cagney waited until the plane got over the English Channel, to avoid killing innocent German civilians on the ground, and decided to manually trigger the bomb's release.

They were at ten thousand feet, so Cagney crawled back to the bomb bay with the doors wide open and sat on the middle catwalk. The air that tore through the compartment was thin and freezing cold. There was little to hold on to as he leaned over to check if any ships were in sight. He did not want to bomb a British ship in the Channel and possibly cause serious casualties. He hung on for dear life as he peered in all directions as far as he could see. When he was satisfied there were no ships in sight, he reached out with a screwdriver and tripped the shackle.

The bomb released. With his legs wrapped around the catwalk, he watched its descent. It seemed as if it would never disappear from sight, but it finally was lost to view about one thousand feet above the Channel.

Then, to his horror, Cagney spotted a two-thousand-ton ship coming into view ahead of them, right in the bomb's trajectory. The bomb hit almost alongside the ship, creating a huge waterspout, but far enough away to prevent any damage. He could imagine the crew shaking their fists, saying, those stupid Americans are trying to sink us. We're the only ship in the area, and they try to bomb us. And miss . . .

A thousand heavy American bombers were sent out April 11 to destroy six FW-190 assembly plants in central and eastern Europe. Spaatz ordered the mission as a double thrust into the Reich to disrupt enemy defenses.

Lieutenant Edward S. Michael, in a 305th Group formation east of Berlin, noted that both his primary and secondary targets were covered by clouds. He instructed his bombardier, Lieutenant John L. Lieber, to pick a target of opportunity.

Just then his copilot Lieutenant Franklin A. Westberg yelled, "Fighters!"

Dozens of them swept toward the formation, some flying right through it.

When bullets slashed through the bomber, Michael realized they were singling out his plane. He watched in amazement as the Germans recklessly tore through the formation, ignoring their own ground fire and the bomber escorts, and his B-17 shuddered as it was riddled. He lost control, and the aircraft was forced out of formation. It plunged sickeningly toward the ground while Nazi fighters spiraled down with it, bearing in for the kill.

When a cannon shell exploded in the cockpit, he noted with concern that his instruments were gone and his side window had been shot away. Struggling to regain control of the plunging bomber, he had a moment to look at Westberg, his copilot, who signaled that he was all right, although there was a look of intense pain on his face as blood welled from deep wounds.

To add to their problems, Michael realized that the hydraulic lines had been cut, and along with heavy smoke that filled the cockpit, hydraulic fluid covered the windows so that he could see nothing through them.

His altimeter had been destroyed along with the rest of his instruments, but he knew they had to be close to the ground. Using every bit of his remaining strength to pull back the wheel, he was relieved when the nose of the plane started to rise.

The radio operator, noting cannon shells had ignited some of the incendiaries, yelled, "There's a fire in the bomb bay!"

Michael was sure they faced disaster, expecting fire to engulf the bomber and detonate the fuel tanks.

He urged Lieber to try everything possible to release the bombs, but the bombardier was unable to do so.

Michael reached a decision. "Bail out! We're on fire!"

Seven crew members did so quickly, but Michael noted that Lieber was still firing his nose guns, and he called for him to get out immediatley.

Lieber dropped his guns and reached for his parachute, noting with shock that it was riddled by shell fragments. He crawled up to the pilot's compartment and showed it to Michael.

The pilot dropped any further consideration about bailing out. Meanwhile, fighter attacks continued, and despite wounds that bled profusely with excruciating pain, he finally evaded the German fighters in a cloud bank. While these attacks were going on, Lieber managed to salvo the smoldering bombs.

He was now down to treetop level at the mercy of flak towers, which poured a steady stream at the riddled airplane, but he continued flying across France hoping to make a safe landing at the first field he found.

Blood lay in pools beneath Michael's seat, and Westberg could see that he could not last much longer. When Michael lost consciousness, the copilot took over the controls and flew an uncertain course toward England. When he saw an RAF field near the coast, he headed directly for it.

Michael regained consciousness at this moment and insisted on taking control of the B-17 despite his weakened condition. Westberg looked at him doubtfully, but Michael assured him that he could handle it. The copilot described the plane's condition, telling him the gear was useless, the bomb bay doors were jammed open, but that the bomb bay fire was out.

Michael nodded, comprehending the desperate situation he was in, particularly with all his flight instruments out. As he approached the field, he learned that the landing flaps were not going to come down, either.

Westberg watched with growing disbelief as Michael somehow managed to bring the airplane in, belly-landing successfully just off the runway. Michael's heroic action was recognized when the president of the United States hung the Medal of Honor around his neck at a later ceremony.

In Italy, meanwhile, Lieutenant Raymond L. Knight volunteered April 24 to lead two other fighter-bombers against the heavily defended air base at Ghedi.

In the target area, he told his companions to cover him while he attacked. He skimmed the ground through a deadly curtain of antiaircraft fire to reconnoiter the field, and located eight German aircraft hidden beneath heavy camouflage.

He rejoined his flight and described conditions on the ground by radio. They joined him in attacking the aircraft through a withering hail of fire and managed to destroy five of them.

After they returned to their own field, he volunteered to lead three other fighter-bombers in an attack against Bergamo airfield.

Again he left his comrades in the sky while he explored the field by flying his Thunderbolt through an intense barrage of ground fire that seriously damaged his P-47. His courage was rewarded by the sight of a squadron of camouflaged airplanes and he led his men to attack at low level.

After the first strafing, he returned alone and made ten deliberate passes against the field despite two more hits on his plane. In these strafing runs, he destroyed six fully loaded twin-engine aircraft and a fighter plane.

His plane was so seriously damaged that he had to return to base.

Next morning, Knight led three other pilots back over Bergamo. Upon arrival, he spotted a plane on one of the runways. They roared down in a blistering low-level sweep through vicious antiaircraft fire that damaged Knight's plane so seriously that it was virtually unflyable, but three more German planes were destroyed on the ground.

Knowing how seriously short his unit was in planes, he refused to consider bailing out to save himself. He decided to try and reach his home base and might have done so but for treacherous air currents over the Apennines that hurled his plane into the ground.

Knight's self-sacrifice in helping to eliminate the German aircraft, which were poised to wreak havoc on Allied forces pressing to establish the first bridgehead across the Po River, was recognized by a grateful nation in awarding him a Medal of Honor posthumously.

Harris's bombers had attacked the city centers of Brunswick, Munich, and Schweinfurt during the latter part of April, using Mosquito crews from 5 Group who dive-marked with red flares after the aiming points were identified visually. There were times when 5 Group's Lancasters had to also lay down sky markers through use of H2S radar under control of a master bomber by radiotelephone.

Four 617 Squadron Mosquitoes led by Wing Commander G. L. Cheshire, with Squadron Leader D. J. Shannon, Flight Lieutenant G. E. Fawke, and Flight Lieutenant R. S. D. Kearns, went to Munich April 24. They had to dive through intense flak while searchlights followed them during the laying of red spot-flares. With incredible bravery, they lit up the aiming point within a hundred yards and permitted a devastating attack on the city. Remarkably, all returned safely, and Cheshire was singled out for special recognition and was presented with a Victoria Cross.

Schweinfurt was hit on the twenty-sixth, although the attack wasn't anywhere near as successful even though some bombs were placed well.

These raids proved that 5 Group's leaders were correct that precision bombing could be done at night, although they still were not as precise as the best of daylight attacks.

Cochrane had long pressured Harris to permit his 5 Group to demonstrate that low-level marking could be accomplished effectively and with no increase in casualties.

Air Vice-Marshal Donald Bennett, commander of 8 Group, openly disputed Cochrane's claims, saying it was impossible to locate targets at one hundred feet, and above that altitude marking planes would be annihilated by flak.

Cochrane pointed out that his 617 Squadron had accomplished such a feat successfully when it had destroyed two Ruhr dams from sixty feet. He conceded failure in the winter of 1943 to knock out the Dortmund-Ems Canal, but pointed out that the previous December 16 nine of his Lancasters had achieved an error of less than three hundred feet when they bombed the V-weapon launching site at Abbeville with the new automatic bombsight.

Cochrane had reminded Harris in early 1944 that Wing Commander Leonard Cheshire had successfully marked the Gnome and Rhone engine factories at Limoges from a height of only two hundred feet, and that 617 Squadron then was able to demolish the plants.

Harris was convinced that Cochrane should be given a chance to prove what 5 Group could do with Mosquito bombers. Much to Bennett's fury, he ordered him to transfer his 8 Group's 627 Mosquito Squadron, plus 83 and 97 Lancaster squadrons, to Cochrane's 5 Group. He told Bennett that they would remain under his jurisdiction for administrative purposes, but operate under Cochrane's orders.

Bennett was furious and, for a time, considered resignation. During a stormy session at High Wycombe, Bennett demanded to know where 8 Group would get more Mosquito bombers after Cochrane's were all shot down.

Unfortunately, the rivalry between these two great airmen became more and more bitter.

Cochrane devised a marking plan that was unique. No bomber was permitted to drop its bombs until a master bomber approved the marking of targets. Inevitably, delays over targets became common, and the tactic could be used only when the target was clear. Perhaps the technique was most successful because it was used during a period when German air defenses were declining and ground defenses were deteriorating. There's little doubt that such attacks against heavily defended targets would have been foolhardy.

Cochrane's prestige rose as the achievements of 5 Group eclipsed those of Bennett's 8 Group. On invasion targets, the unique marking reduced civilian casualties and helped to destroy many vital targets. When targets were not visible, due to smoke, Cochrane devised offset methods so that the bombsight could be used to synchronize on a predetermined point in the clear and the bombs were offset into the target with accuracy levels below nine hundred feet.

Sir Charles Portal's growing resentment of Harris's stubbornness about area targets versus high-priority targets like aircraft plants might well have led to his replacement by the imaginative Cochrane, but Portal was aware that Churchill would never stand for Harris's removal at this stage of the war.

24

PREINVASION STRIKES
OPEN THE DOOR

By the end of April, it was too late to hope that the RAF and the United States Strategic Air Forces could be combined into one organization, despite the efforts of an operational planning committee authorized by Spaatz and Portal. Each air force had basic philosophical differences for the conduct of the air war. Many American officers disliked serving under British commanders, and the reverse was also true. Spaatz's attempts to integrate American and British commanders was done primarily to get all airpower out of the hands of ground commanders. On this, at least, the aviators could agree.

Arnold told Eisenhower that no command changes would be requested until after his invasion forces were established in France. By then, the organization set up by Eisenhower had proved so effective that field commanders ignored requests for changes in command structure. Spaatz, however, remained unhappy about constant demands for use of his heavy bombers for support of ground troops long after Eisenhower's armies really needed them.

This unwieldy chain of command succeeded because American and British commanders worked in harmony, knowing that the invasion had to succeed. When Eisenhower needed air support for ground troops, orders quickly got down to supporting units.

Spaatz's battle to throw his heavies into action against Germany's oil resources was granted a grudging single concession by Eisenhower to get Spaatz's agreement to early preinvasion support. An attack on the synthetic plants was launched with devastating effect May 12, but oil targets weren't given first priority until June 8, and even these attacks were sporadic.

The German High Command dreaded such attacks and were astonished that it took two years before they were undertaken in force. Defenses were formidable at the hydrogenation plants that produced aviation gasoline. Repair crews stood by at all hours, and extensive camouflage and smoke screens were used. Barrage balloons were used to prevent low-level attacks, and German fighters were told to concentrate against bomber formations headed for any of these plants. Hitler even ordered decoy plants to be built, hoping to confuse Allied bombardiers.

Following the first strong raids May 12, Speer told postwar interrogators, "On that day the technological war was decided. Until then we had managed to produce approximately as many weapons as the armed forces needed, despite their considerable losses. But, with the attack by nine hundred thirty-five daylight bombers of the American Eighth Air Force on several fuel plants in central and eastern Germany, a new era in the air war began. It meant the end of German armaments production."

"The enemy has struck us at one of our weakest points," he told Hitler at the time. "If they persist at it this time, we will soon no longer have any fuel production worth mentioning. Our one hope is that the other side has an air force General Staff as scatterbrained as ours."

Efficient repair crews had the plants back in production within two weeks, but they suffered far worse damage May 28 when they were attacked by four hundred bombers along with plants at Zeitz and Magdeburg. This was the day that the Fifteenth struck a devastating blow at Ploesti where refinery production was cut in half.

Diversion of the bomber fleets to aid in the invasion of Normandy prevented further continuous attacks, although by June 22, 90 percent of synthetic aviation gasoline production was halted.

While Eisenhower continually called upon the heavy bombers as his armies ran into obstacles in their march across France, the Germans worked frantically to restore synthetic production.

When Eaker could release his Fifteenth Air Force bombers for further attacks, the strikes against synthetic oil production were renewed, and again production dropped to 10 percent of normal despite heroic and often nightmarish efforts by German work crews to get the plants back into operation.

Production dropped to 5.5 percent in September. Speer told Hitler the Luftwaffe and the army's mechanized forces would have to rely upon fuel reserves as long as they lasted. After they were gone, he knew, the fuel situation was hopeless. He asked Hitler for permission to exercise total mobilization power of all resources and give Edmund Geilenberg, his head of repair efforts, authority to confiscate materials and allocate skilled workers to maintain synthetic oil production. Hitler refused.

Fuel was so short that pilot training was now reduced to one hour a week, and combat units were often grounded. Ground forces were equally short, and there were even reports that some trucks had to be pulled by oxen.

Destruction of oil plants, if it could have been done earlier, would have shortened the war. Spaatz always contended that Germany could be defeated by airpower if sufficient resources were made available to the strategic air forces. This conviction was reinforced in the fall of 1944 because it was now apparent that the oil offensive was more conclusive in achieving decisive results than any of the strategic air operations. Destruction of synthetic plants, he pointed out, not only reduced the German air force to impotence and thwarted ground campaigns as tanks and trucks went dry, but these synthetic plants also decreased production of nitrogen and methanol, also made at these plants, and which were necessary to manufacture explosives. Ninety percent of the stocks of these chemicals were destroyed by airpower.

Regardless of the unavoidable delays in attacking oil targets, a basic strategic objective of the Combined Bomber Offensive was eventually achieved. If heavy bombers had been available in sufficient quantities to be decisive in November 1943 and not diverted to less important targets, the Germans would have been completely out of aviation gasoline by May 1944. The German army would also have been in an equally impossible situation.

Even Allied air planners of the period did not appreciate fully the need to make continued, heavy attacks against such plants if production was to be stopped completely. The Zeitz plant was kept out of production only because a thousand tons of bombs were dropped on it in five major raids. The great Leuna plant had to be attacked twenty-two times to keep it out of production.

The postwar United States Strategic Bombing Survey reached the conclusion that Germany's defeat was inevitable after it was deprived of the bulk of its fuel and ammunition production by strategic bombing of oil targets in the last full year of the war. The Nazis' fate was sealed when they could neither manufacture nor capture any more appreciable quantities of liquid fuel.

The Germans fought back with limited resources. There is no question but that the big air battles in the first part of 1944 had cost the Germans more heavily than attacks against their aircraft factories. Speer made herculean efforts to increase production, and indeed produced a surplus of aircraft, but the German air force suffered painfully from inadequately prepared pilots because there was not sufficient fuel to train them properly.

Göring said after the war that Luftwaffe losses were about one third of those claimed by the Allies, but he admitted also that by April 1, 1944, the German air force had been defeated.

While the Eighth Air Force continued to attack targets in Germany, the Ninth Air Force prepared for its primary role of supporting the amphibious landings in Normandy, and cooperating with ground commanders once a breakout was achieved from the beachheads. The spectacular growth of the Ninth was due to remarkable leadership, which transformed it in seven and a half months from a plan on paper to the world's largest tactical air force.

In July 1943, Brigadier General Hansell had drafted a detailed plan for tactical support of the invasion. It proved a useful guide for organization and employment.

Arnold had ordered the Ninth Air Force under Major General Lewis Brereton transferred to the European theater from the Middle East where Brereton had earned the reputation of being an aggressive man of action. His combat and service units were given to the Twelfth Air Force. Therefore, Brereton was faced with a huge training job in a short time because most of his men and equipment came directly from the States.

By the end of April, the Ninth Air Force was prepared to meet its obligations for the invasion from eleven bomber bases located in Essex, northeast of London, and its fighter bases, which were located in Hampshire, extending south to the coast. All Tactical Air Command's seven groups were located southeast of London opposite Pas-de-Calais, and Troop Carrier Command's fourteen bases were scattered throughout the area.

Until the first of May, the Ninth had supported the Eighth with escort fighters and had done much of the bombing against missile sites, but now it was a full-fledged tactical air force responsible only to Eisenhower, and it had to train and prepare for its vital role in support of the invasion.

The Ninth's mission was spelled out in three phases. In the first, from D minus fifty to D minus thirty, it would perform reconnaissance and attack German air force bases in France. The second phase, from D minus thirty to the day prior to D day, its principal attacks were to be made against the German air force, strategic railroad centers and bridges, selected coastal batteries, and airfields within a 130-mile radius of Caen. The night before D day, the Ninth would drop American paratroopers on the Cotentin Peninsula. British paratroopers would be dropped between the rivers Orne and Dives. And, finally, on the big day, Ninth fighters would protect the beaches and the invasion fleets.

After assault troops were dug in, the Ninth was assigned, along with other air forces, the responsibility for conducting bombing operations behind the lines, attacking German troops, and helping to destroy the Luftwaffe. Specific duties were to delay enemy reinforcements to the combat areas, provide air transport, air support for ground troops, attack formations of troops, and provide continuous reconnaissance for ground commanders.

Brereton hoped that forty days after Allied landings he could base 116 fighter squadrons in France. Hansell's plan called for 3,467 American and British heavy bombers available for D day, along with 835 light and medium bombers, 565 fighter-bombers, 2,250 day fighters, and 170 night fighters. It was anticipated that the Germans might be able to bring 1,950 combat aircraft of all types to bear. This prediction proved much too high; "Big Week" had taken care of that.

Ninth Air Force attacks against transportation targets in April caused enormous damage. Thirty-three thousand tons of bombs were dropped on railroad centers and bridges despite heavy flak; then targets were attacked repeatedly to keep these choke points out of service.

Later in the month, the Ninth started its campaign to bomb transportation routes into Normandy. So successful were these attacks that by D day fifty-one out of eighty railroad centers had suffered major damage, with most completely knocked out. Fortunately, French and Belgian casualties were kept to a minimum thanks to the skill of the crews who maintained a high level of accuracy and suffered only light losses.

Railroad traffic in the west of France dropped significantly by May 19, meeting predictions of a one-third reduction.

Leigh-Mallory authorized fighter sweeps against moving trains the following day. During the next two weeks, 475 locomotives were damaged; French train crews fled as Allied planes dropped fuel tanks on trains and then strafed them to set them on fire. The Germans now had to rely on their own crews, and after May 26 railroad traffic in daylight was reduced sharply.

At first, attacks against bridges were not considered effective. Such doubts disappeared May 7 when eight P-47s each dropped two thousand-pound bombs on a 650-foot railway bridge over the Seine near Vernon and demolished it. Brereton assigned B-26 bombers May 24 to continue attacks against Seine River bridges and it wasn't long before crossings over the river were limited.

Despite massive daily strikes, the transportation network was not destroyed according to plans. German energy and efficiency in repairing bridges reduced the effectiveness of these attacks. After Brereton ordered last-minute attacks on Seine bridges just prior to D day, all those south of Paris became impassable, but repeated bombings had to be made to discourage repair crews.

It was while the Ninth was active in its invasion-support role that Spaatz received permission May 12 to give first priority to oil targets. Analysts listed eighty-one targets, of which twenty-three were synthetic plants. Spaatz had finally convinced Eisenhower that a sharp reduction in Germany's oil supply would not only affect operations of the Luftwaffe, but seriously curtail ground operations of the German army.

May 12, fifteen hundred bombers from the Eighth and Fifteenth air forces smashed a dozen refineries and synthetic plants. Hitler was so concerned about these attacks that he moved twelve thousand antiaircraft guns to the sites, while Göring advised air commanders to ignore most Allied air attacks unless they were headed for oil targets. Thus, German fighters were pinned down in eastern Germany defending the oil supply, far from the beaches of Normandy.

The German High Command faced a catastrophe as these raids cut the supply of German fuel and lubricants almost in half just at a time when it was faced with a large-scale Russian offensive in the east and an invasion in the west. Despite the greatest economy, their oil reserves dropped to a dangerous level.

Attacks rose to a crescendo three weeks prior to D day, and approximately 100 airfields within 350 miles of the coast of Normandy were attacked repeatedly to keep the Luftwaffe from using them. Even the Eighth Air Force's heavy bombers joined in during the final hours.

Allied radio monitors heard a Paris commentator say May 23 that the French railway system was in complete chaos. The Allies, he said, had successfully pulverized all marshaling yards, countless locomotives, and made most railroad stations unusable. In conclusion, he said, saboteurs completed the job by blowing up railway tracks and attacking rolling stock.

By D day, only three marshaling yards were working at full capacity in France. One of these was at Le Bourget outside Paris. Several others were working at only 2 percent of capacity, while some were able to operate at 10 percent.

Fighter Commander Adolf Galland said after the war that most airfields were so bombed that he couldn't use them for his German aircraft, relying on fields farther inland. He said he was not able to bring in sizable reinforcements before and right after D day.

German coastal batteries along the French coast had concerned Allied planners from the start. The Ninth had attacked them frequently, and the Royal Air Force dropped the largest tonnage, along with the Eighth, while the invasion forces were getting organized. The constant attacks did lower the efficiency of German gun crews, but few emplacements were destroyed.

All along, air commanders had worried about the possibility that Allied bombers and fighters might be grounded on D day because of bad weather. Generals Spaatz, Doolittle, and Kepner privately agreed in advance to send their air fleets out regardless of the weather even if they were all lost.

One unusual group, known as the "Carpetbaggers" because they originally had dropped leaflets over France in 1943, later made a unique contribution to the war effort by delivering espionage agents and vital supplies to underground organizations on the Continent and in Norway, as well as retrieving interned airmen from neutral Sweden. Their stripped-down B-24s, camouflaged in black nonreflecting paint, either operated as electronic countermeasures aircraft, or served in reconnaissance roles or as pathfinders.

Colonel Bernt M. Balchen, a legendary airman of Norwegian ancestry who later became a naturalized American citizen, led the group. He had earned a Medal of Honor in 1932 for his pioneering work as chief pilot of the Commander Richard E. Byrd Antarctic Expedition. A quiet, unruffled man known for his exceptional skills in handling diplomats of many countries, Balchen was the ideal officer to command such an outfit.

During its most active period, from January to May 1944, twenty-five of the group's fifty B-24s were shot down, and eight others had to be scrapped because of heavy battle damage.

The group had several designations throughout its service life, but it is best remembered as the 492nd Bombardment Group, although it operated under such a designation in name only. Its nonbombing missions, in collaboration with the Eighth Air Force and the Royal Air Force, were performed in the strictest secrecy. Its Liberators were highly modified, with all but the top and tail turrets removed. The ball turret was replaced by a shroud ring that was covered in flight by plywood. This ring, called a "Joe-hole," served as an exit for agents parachuting from the aircraft.

Balchen's group brought 4,304 Norwegians, American internees, and nationals of at least six other countries from Sweden to the United Kingdom. His planes were the only dependable means of communication between the American Legation in Stockholm and the outside world. Actually, they provided the basic means by which supplies and equipment could be sent to United States air crews there, thus permitting repair of nearly two thirds of all American aircraft forced down in this neutral country. Through the surreptitious assistance of Swedish officials, who often agonized over what the Germans might do in retaliation, vitally needed supplies were taken to Sweden and then transshipped to Norway for the underground. Planes often returned with Swedish ball bearings and other critical items for the United Kingdom.

Only an experienced all-weather pilot like Balchen could have trained such a group of young aviators to the degree of flying skill required to perform such difficult tasks. Few other World War II organizations ever achieved such perfection in flying techniques, and no one will dispute that the group's expertise was due primarily to this extraordinary pilot.

German day fighters were now no match for the combination of large numbers of American bombers and long-range fighters. The reverse was true at night because the British were faced with a rejuvenated German night-fighter force that was on the verge of winning a major victory against British Bomber Command. For a time, it appeared that day strikes might become safer than night attacks.

The long-awaited invasion of the Continent of Europe was about to be unleashed to establish a second front. On the Allied side few realized —aside from air leaders like Arnold, Spaatz, Portal, and Harris—that a second front had been in existence in the skies over Fortress Europe for more than a year.

The Germans knew it. After the war, Feldmarschall Erhard Milch said that the combined British and American air effort had forced Germany to tie up nine hundred thousand men in the west to defend the Reich from Allied bombers as early as 1943. He was speaking of the men in the fighter forces, the antiaircraft battalions, the fire fighters, and the large number of men who were needed to repair damaged factories.

As always with the offense, even the relatively small force of bombers available in 1943 tied up large numbers of antiaircraft units because the Germans had to provide defenses for all areas of the Reich, never knowing where bombers would strike next. As the bomber commands increased their efforts in 1944, it took almost a million Germans to man antiaircraft defenses alone. So great was the drain on Germany's manpower to defend their country from bomber attacks that the Soviet Union profited enormously from the diversion of German effort and was able to survive and launch offensives.

Although the Germans used a slave-labor force of six million workers from conquered countries under the supervision of Gestapo chief Heinrich Himmler, this restive force had to be controlled by German military manpower. Despite tight, often brutal control of slave laborers, there were frequent factory fires and attempts at sabotage. Certainly, the turnover of a German cryptographic machine and its secrets to the Allies by Polish workers was invaluable in enabling the Allied Ultra Process to intercept and decode German communications about their plans and contemplated actions. In retrospect, the Germans would have been wiser to mobilize women to increase the work force in their factories, as was done in the United States and Great Britain.

During preinvasion strikes, thirty-seven railroad centers had been allotted to the Royal Air Force and forty-two to the Eighth Air Force. So successful were strikes against all but four of these centers that in the days preceding the invasion all attacks by heavy bombers were called off and light bombers were used to destroy the few remaining buildings.

Lieutenant Colonel Leon R. Vance led a heavy-bomber formation June 5 against coastal positions near Wimereux, France. His plane was hit repeatedly as it made its bombing run; Vance noted that the pilot was dead and that several members of the crew were seriously wounded. His own right foot was practically severed.

From the copilot's seat, he continued to lead the formation over the target, despite excruciatingly painful injuries. As they pulled away, the radio operator helped him to apply a tourniquet to his leg.

With only one out of four engines functioning and the bomber in danger of stalling, he struggled to an upright position on the floor and feathered the dead engines. He had to keep the plane in a constant shallow dive to maintain flying speed to reach the English coast. There, he ordered the crew to bail out, knowing he had an unexploded bomb hung up in the bomb bays. Over the interphone, he was led to believe one crew member was unable to jump because of his injuries.

Grimly, he stayed with the plane. He decided to ditch it in the English Channel and hopefully save the injured crew member. Because his foot was still trapped under the seat, he was unable to use the rudder, so, using only ailerons and elevators for control and the side window for visual reference, he ditched the airplane.

Once in the water, the plane started to sink, and he was still trapped. Then an explosion blew him free of the cockpit and he landed in the water, surrounded by parts of the shattered airplane. With his last remaining strength, he reached a piece of floating debris, clinging to it until he could inflate his life jacket. He searched frantically for the crew member he thought was still in the wreckage. Actually, all those who were left alive after leaving the target had bailed out safely.

Vance was picked up fifteen minutes later by an air-sea rescue plane and after several weeks was awarded a Medal of Honor for his exceptional bravery.

The original date set for the invasion had to be postponed because of bad weather, while 150,000 men and 1,500 tanks stood by with 4,000 ships ready to take them across the Channel. Air commanders at bases all over the south of England waited expectantly to send out 8,000 airplanes to cover the invasion fleet, drop paratroopers in Normandy, and provide bombers of all kinds to attack targets far behind German lines in France.

Forecasters earlier had predicted that the moon, tide, and the hour of sunrise would be suitable for the invasion on June 5, 6, and 7. American weather officers Lieutenant Colonels Krick and Holzman and four British forecasters from the Air Ministry were selected to form a team to advise Eisenhower on the precise date when there would be no winds to raise a heavy, running swell in the Channel, and a period when the skies would be clear for air operations. The British officers insisted that a five-day forecast in advance of the operation was impossible. Krick and Holzman did not agree, and actually presented such a forecast June 3 that predicted sea-and-air conditions would be suitable for the invasion from June 4 on. Despite their optimism, the Normandy invasion was canceled June 4 and 5.

By the morning of the fifth, the British forecasters began to have doubts about their original pessimistic forecast for this period, and tended to agree with Holzman and Krick, who had remained steadfast in their beliefs. At a conference, it was agreed to recommend to Eisenhower that the invasion should proceed the following day.

Meanwhile, Spaatz talked to Eisenhower, saying he had learned to trust Holzman and Krick, and recommended that he should go along with their optimistic forecast for the following day.

Eisenhower pondered the reports from the weathermen, facing one of the toughest decisions any military commander ever had to make. His principal commanders offered divided counsel. His naval commander, Admiral Sir Bertram Ramsay, said the waves on the beaches were too high. His air commander, Leigh-Mallory, said cloud cover would impair air support. His army commander, Montgomery, advised him to go ahead. Finally, he turned to his staff the night of June 5. "Well, we'll go."

Now it was up to the ground forces of the Allied nations to storm a hostile shore where the Germans had erected the most ingenious defenses ever devised by man. Most of them were impossible to destroy by airpower. At best, as Spaatz told Arnold later, the preinvasion strikes "opened the door for the invasion"—the dreaded Luftwaffe did not put in an appearance. What was left of it was guarding the vital targets in central Germany.

Generalleutnant Werner Junck, who commanded German fighters in the region, said later he had 160 aircraft available on D day, but only 80 were operational despite Hitler's order to resist the invasion with 1,000 fighters. The Germans launched less than 300 sorties, the Allies more than 13,000. Furthermore, in the coming months, Junck was given only 600 planes to contest the massed airpower of the Allies, which enjoyed air superiority throughout the period.

Allied air commanders had hoped for such a situation, but even they had not realized that German aircraft losses in combat, destruction of factories, oil refineries, and other industries had reduced the once-mighty Luftwaffe to such impotence.

After the war, Sir Norman H. Bottomley, who had been deputy chief of the Royal Air Force's Air Staff, in speaking of the effectiveness of the air war against Germany, said, "In the building up of a situation of air superiority which was an absolute prerequisite for the projected land assault of Europe, the greatest contribution made by any force was that made by the strategic air forces, and particularly those of the United States."

Prior to the invasion, British Bomber Command had devoted three fourths of its missions to attacks against railway targets in France and the occupied countries. Harris knew such attacks were needed, but he was upset because they reduced the bombing pressure on Germany.

In the spring, Bomber Command had a daily average of more than 1,000 bombers available for missions. This total increased to 1,600 by war's end. In the same period, the Eighth Air Force had an average of 1,049 bombers, a figure that was doubled by the spring of 1945.

The increase in availability of British bombers came at a time when German night fighters were especially effective against the RAF's night bombers. Although German day fighters had been largely overwhelmed, due to the supremacy of the P-51 and the growing immunity of American Flying Fortresses and B-24 Liberators to fighter attacks, German night fighters were still undefeated. Actually, no effective defense was ever conceived against German night fighters, although British Bomber Command established a measure of control after the invasion of the Continent. It was not until Allied ground forces were able to push to the Rhine that a drop in casualty rates was noted as German night fighters lost the support of their ground-control systems.

General Arnold, speaking of the failure of the German air force to contest the amphibious landings on Normandy, said, "D day should have been a field day for a strong Luftwaffe. Thousands of ships and boats and landing craft crowded the Channel. A dominant German air fleet could have created incalculable havoc."

The cost in ground troops was still high, and the amphibious landings June 6 resulted in 10,700 casualties—about half the number suffered by fliers prior to the invasion.

25

D DAY

The night before invasion, two squadrons of Lancasters—including those of the highly skilled 617th—performed an unusual service to confuse the Germans about the exact destination of the invasion forces and to convince them that the Allies planned to land near Boulogne and Cape Antifer instead of Normandy.

A special type of foil chaff "window" was dropped in bundles from a precise height so that these metal strips would simulate a large number of ships on German radar screens. So precise was the dropping along previously established flight paths that they simulated a convoy crossing the Channel at seven knots.

Lancasters circled the Channel for five hours, flying a series of precise overlapping paths, each series coming closer and closer to the Normandy coast. This was a remarkable navigation feat and gained the Allies valuable hours to make their prescribed landings. The Germans were completely taken in by the ruse.

Other RAF bombers joined those of the Eighth Air Force to jam German early-warning radar, while a third force of British bombers from 1 Group patrolled in the direction from which German fighters might be expected to attack the convoys. The latter had special equipment to jam the radios of night fighters so that they could not maintain contact with their ground controllers.

Still other British forces from 3 Group released bundles of "window" to simulate a much larger force than the Allies actually had, even dropping dummy parachutists and machines that made noises like rifle fire and battle sounds as a diversion from the real airborne landings in Normandy.

While a huge armada transported five divisions of troops and their equipment across the Channel for landings on the shores of Normandy, between Caen and the Cherbourg Peninsula, thousands of Allied air missions were flown in support of Eisenhower's troops.

Although the Luftwaffe flew three hundred separate missions that day, not one reached the beachhead in daylight. Despite earlier doubts at all levels about the effectiveness of the German air force, it was now evident that the Luftwaffe was powerless to oppose the landings. In effect, air-power had achieved one of the main goals of the Combined Bomber Offensive.

The Royal Air Force's Bomber Command had concentrated on German coastal batteries prior to the invasion, then shifted its night bombings to the Cherbourg peninsula to prepare the way for troop-carrier operations transporting three airborne divisions. They were assigned to cut off rear-area communications and block German reinforcements to the beach areas. American sky trains with 17,000 men of the 82nd and 101st Airborne divisions and their equipment assembled over England in 900 planes and 100 gliders of the IX Troop Carrier Command in the waning hours of June 5. The Germans were alerted six minutes before midnight by RAF night fighters and intruders that went in advance of the troop carriers to attack enemy guns and searchlights.

Although they were unopposed, pathfinders had difficulty identifying drop zones, and formations either overshot their zones or released too soon.

If the Americans were confused in the air, the Germans were even more so on the ground. They finally got their wits about them and some Allied elements underwent heavy fire during landings.

Eisenhower had told commanders that airborne operations behind the front lines were essential to success of the landings at Utah Beach. While small units assembled on the ground, they were able to accomplish most of the vital missions despite dispersal from assigned areas. In spite of the confusion and mistakes, losses were far below expectations.

The Eighth Air Force sent three bomber divisions to hit coastal batteries and shore defenses on Omaha Beach and those the British were preparing to assault. The big bombers took off as late as 5:29 A.M., dropping their bombs right up until ten minutes before the troops landed. Medium bombers started operations at 3:43 A.M., but beaches east of Omaha were not hit, and the V Corps suffered heavy losses as a result.

The combined sea-and-air bombardment shook the entrenched Germans as nothing had done before. Weather and beach conditions had been so unfavorable that the local German High Command actually reduced the state of alert, assuming that no one, even Americans, would be so foolish as to launch a hazardous invasion under such circumstances. They were stunned by the attacks.

The situation at Omaha Beach was so serious that the IX Bomber

Command was assigned rear choke points and bridges to prevent reinforcements, and these attacks were helpful.

Utah Beach landings went more smoothly, and by day's end, most of the beachhead had been secured by 155,000 Allied troops occupying eighty square miles of France.

Destruction of the railway system proved crucial because it took the Germans several days before troops and supplies could be brought into the Normandy sector from other parts of France.

Lancasters of 5 Group used twelve-thousand-pound, medium-capacity bombs, developed by British scientist Dr. Barnes Wallis, capable of penetrating twelve feet of concrete, on a railroad tunnel at Saumur. This tunnel was on the main line leading north to Normandy from the interior of France. Bombs dropped on the night of June 8/9 broke through the roof of the tunnel and also created enormous craters in the cut leading up to the tunnel. The line was effectively blocked.

German officials said they had forty reserve divisions available to move up to the front, but it was impossible to move them rapidly because of such attacks, and some could not be moved at all to meet Allied troops.

Despite bad weather, strikes against railroads and key roads continued. One day, the British received an urgent request to destroy a large fleet of E-boats and other light German boats in the Channel. While continuing night attacks, Harris sent bombers out by day with fighter cover to Le Havre and Boulogne where more than 60 boats, practically every one in these harbors, were sunk. Actually, later attacks destroyed virtually all light naval and auxiliary craft, for a total of 130.

Once the troops were off the beaches and pushing inland, close support by fighters and bombers proved more difficult because of the problem of determining the front lines. Fighter-bombers were used most effectively as they blasted enemy strongpoints and denied the Germans use of roads and rail transportation for supplies and men. One German soldier spoke for the majority when he said, "The American fliers are chasing us like hares."

Eisenhower called for major air support as General "Lightnin' Joe" Collins and his VII Corps prepared for the final assault on Cherbourg. Allied air turned out in mass and helped to isolate the battlefield by destroying German lines of communications. They were so effective that the railroad system in northwestern France could not be used, and even the roads could be traveled safely only at night. As a result, fuel and ammunition for German tanks soon became critical. Cherbourg was captured June 27.

Now that the beachhead was secured, the Ninth Air Force and the Royal Air Force's Second Tactical Air Force would have been sufficient to maintain control of the air and eliminate enemy opposition. Together they were far larger than the entire Luftwaffe, which was fighting on five fronts. Spaatz suggested that his strategic air forces be permitted to return to their campaign of destruction of targets inside Germany, but Eisenhower flatly refused.

The Germans proved they were far from powerless when the first German pilotless aircraft flamed across the night sky June 13 from Pas-de-Calais and landed on a railroad bridge in the center of London. A new era in warfare began as V-1s, or aerial torpedoes with wings, began to shower on London. They would be followed later, in September, by the fourteen-ton V-2 rockets.

British intelligence had been aware that Hitler was developing retaliatory secret weapons since the latter part of 1942. Now, the British government demanded that all efforts be undertaken to counter these missiles, which were causing great damage in England.

Leigh-Mallory called upon the strategic air forces to take over the job of bombing the "V" sites, despite Arnold's resistance. The RAF's chief of staff had shown remarkable foresight. He had had "V" sites built on a test range in Florida and had experimented with various types of bombers to attack them. The tests indicated that attacks by low-level fighter-bombers or medium bombers with two-thousand-pound bombs had proved most effective against these hardened sites. Test results showed conclusively that heavy, high-altitude bombers were least effective.

Major General Grandison Gardner, who had conducted the tests at Eglin's proving ground, was sent to England to explain the results to Leigh-Mallory. The air chief marshal, with typical stubbornness, refused to believe him and insisted on using heavy bombers. It took weeks of constant prodding by Arnold to get him to try the techniques developed in Florida, while heavy bombers attacked the sites with little success and other strategic targets of top priority were downgraded to third place.

Meanwhile, the Germans were also hard at work on rocket-propelled V-2 ballistic missiles. The Germans had gained valuable knowledge for their "V"-weapons program from experiments in the field of liquid-propelled rockets, which had been conducted by the American scientist Robert H. Goddard. Although Goddard was ridiculed in his own country, the Germans took him seriously, with devastating results.

German scientists were first to develop pilotless strategic weapons. Initially, Hitler was not impressed because their production would interfere with other vital production programs. When Speer took over responsibility for all German war production in March 1943, he had tried to revive the program but Hitler adamantly refused.

Generalmajor Walter Dornberger, who had been in charge of military missile and rocket development in Germany since 1931, and Professor Wernher von Braun, the man most responsible for the V-2 rocket, joined Speer in urging Hitler to reactivate the program. The Führer later did so reluctantly, but two vital months were lost.

Hitler conceded later how tragic for Germany his original decision had been. For one of the few times in his life he admitted he had made a mistake. He told Dornberger, "If only I had had faith in you earlier! In all my life, I have owed apologies to two people only, Feldmarschall Walther von Brauchitsch, who repeatedly drew my attention to the importance of the A-4 [V-2] for the future, and yourself. If we had had the A-4 earlier and in sufficient quantities, it would have had decisive importance in this war. I did not believe in it."

Speer gave the program top priority as soon as Hitler approved it. Plans called for dropping a million tons annually on England, or about the same tonnage the Allies dropped on Fortress Europe in their most successful year. Despite the priority emphasis, many in the German High Command refused to believe the program could be effective even after Hitler was told by the brilliant designer Willy Messerschmitt that one hundred thousand V-2 rockets could be produced each month.

In April 1943, Churchill's son-in-law and aide, Duncan Sandys, had told the British War Cabinet that the threat posed by these German secret weapons should be taken seriously. After launching sites were spotted, they were kept under constant surveillance. The experimental site at Peenemünde, hidden on the Isle of Usedom in the Baltic Sea, received the greatest number of reconnaissance flights. The Royal Air Force sent 597 bombers to attack it on August 17, causing some damage to buildings and resulting in the deaths of many German technicians. The loss would have been greater except that the Germans had already started to transfer their equipment elsewhere.

The Eighth Air Force had struck the same site ten days later, and throughout the fall and winter of 1943–44, attacks continued against Peenemünde and newly discovered launching sites along the French coast. Some American and British leaders had scoffed at these sites, saying they were hoaxes and set up only to frighten Allied leaders into postponing the invasion.

A pattern of attacks by heavy and medium bombers continued into the spring of 1944. Although larger sites were conspicuous, hitting vulnerable spots called for precision bombing and proved difficult for heavy bombers. Arnold had tried to tell the British the lessons he had learned in Florida, but they refused to listen.

Not only were these attacks futile, but they cost the Allies 771 airmen and 154 bombers. The postwar bombing survey said these attacks may have delayed the launching of the V-1s by three or four months, but that they didn't consider them effective.

Photo surveillance in early June 1944 indicated no sign of offensive activity, so by the twelfth the Allied command assumed air attacks had overcome the threat. They were sadly disillusioned the next day, when the first V-1 hit London.

In the next few months, V-1s killed 6,000 Londoners and wounded approximately 40,000 others. The populace screamed for protection. Before the threat was eliminated by occupation of the coastal sites, 75,000 buildings were destroyed in extensive but not crippling damage to London.

Fighters of the Royal Air Force quickly became adept at destroying these 400-mile-an-hour cruise missiles, and only 2,420 out of 8,000 of those fired from coastal sites actually caused any damage. The first of Britain's Gloster Meteor jet fighters was effectively used in such defense tactics.

Arnold had long sought permission from the Russians to use their bases to fly shuttle-bombing missions. Once such bases became available in late May 1944, targets hitherto beyond the range of Italian and British bases could be attacked. Spaatz was particularly interested in the Heinkel works at Riga, and another at Lwów, Poland.

When he proposed to the Russians that they furnish bases so that these targets could be bombed, their General Staff opposed such a move without giving any reasons. They asked that targets in Hungary and Romania be bombed instead. Spaatz refused because they were too minor for consideration.

W. Averell Harriman took Eaker to Moscow to carry on the battle with Stalin, but he wasn't successful until the end of May.

They stayed on into June and Harriman received a message to tell Stalin that Eisenhower had crossed the Channel on D day, but the premier already knew about the invasion.

Stalin turned to Eaker, saying he would like him to confer with his air chiefs. Eaker was eager to do so and, at 4:00 A.M., met with Colonel General Aleksandr Novikov who asked him a number of questions about American strategic bombing operations.

"We've found it is better to destroy German tanks in the factory, rather than meet them on the battlefield," Eaker said. "I've been wondering why you haven't engaged in strategic bombing?"

"That's a good question," the general said. "We've observed your very successful knocking down of a lot of factories. We know about it, and we applaud it because it's helping us, too. When the Germans invaded our motherland, we took full stock of our resources. We thought we might stop them if we put every resource we had into stopping these vast land armies. So, we devoted all our air effort to support of our ground forces. Now that we've stopped them, we've got them on the run. Now, we're beginning to think about some strategic operations. I've prepared a memorandum for your Ambassador Harriman for four hundred Liberators."

Eaker's experience in Moscow quickly taught him that lower-level Russian commanders were friendly, but once one got to those at the higher levels who had been politically indoctrinated, the same was not true.

The request for four hundred bombers was later turned down because the Americans and British believed they could reach all necessary targets in Germany from their own bases, and it's possible the transfer of such a large number of bombers to Russia was considered an unwise move.

Once permission was granted to use Russian bases, Eaker went along with his Fifteenth Air Force crews to fly over Yugoslavia and bomb the Debrecen marshaling yards, and then fly on to Russian bases. One of the bombers unaccountably exploded over the target, although no fighters or flak were seen.

Eaker had his men land at Poltava and they were welcomed by a large crowd of dignitaries. To his surprise, he was given permission to bomb the Heinkel factory at Mielec—a go-ahead he had sought for some time.

Weather prevented the attack for several days, and Eaker decided to bomb Romanian airfields June 6 instead. After several more days of inclement weather in Poland, Spaatz cabled Eaker to remain in Russia for a few more days. The weather failed to clear, so they returned home June 11, bombing a Romanian airfield en route.

The Eighth Air Force set up its first shuttle run to Russia June 21 when a synthetic oil plant south of Berlin was bombed. Unnoticed by the crews, a German He-177 followed them back to Poltava. Within five hours, German bombers and fighters swept the airfield without loss. While German fighters strafed the flight line, 110 tons of bombs added to the destruction. The loss on the ground was heavy with forty-three B-17s destroyed, another twenty-six damaged, and fifteen P-51 fighters destroyed, plus some Russian airplanes. Russian defenders refused to permit American fliers to expose themselves on the ground fighting numerous fires.

Spaatz insisted on American night fighters, but the Russians refused, saying they could defend their own airfields. For a time, Harriman thought he had gained Stalin's approval for night fighters, but permission was never forthcoming. Several fighter-bomber missions were carried out from Poltava after that, and the Germans returned several times, but each time the Americans had already departed. Without night-fighter support, Spaatz refused to risk American bombers and the program was canceled.

Despite diversions of a large part of Allied airpower to attack the V-1 sites, German troop and supply movements were kept to a minimum due to air superiority over Normandy.

After the war, Germans said the complete paralysis of the railroad network, along with destruction of all bridges over the Seine below Paris, and the inability of their own air forces to function effectively were the principal causes of their defeat after the amphibious landings. Feldmarschall Gerd von Rundstedt, commander in chief of German forces in the area, said air attacks against French railroads and vital roads were maintained on such a "clockwork" basis that they were more effective than attacks on frontline troops.

Freiherr Heinrich von Luttwitz, commanding general of the second Panzer Division, said in a top secret report July 14, "The Allies wage war regardless of expense. In addition, they have complete mastery of the air. They bomb and strafe every movement, even single vehicles and individuals. They reconnoiter our area constantly and direct their artillery fire. The feeling of helplessness against enemy aircraft has a paralyzing effect, and during barrage bombing the effect on inexperienced troops is literally 'soul shattering.'"

The invasion that Eisenhower said was "aimed at the heart of Germany and the destruction of her armed forces" ended its first phase in mid-July after the battle of the beachhead was won. A breakout, Eisenhower believed, would require all-out support by air units, but it had to be delayed until weather made air operations feasible.

After the Germans started to retreat from the coast, they left behind a series of fortified channel ports whose commanders were told by Hitler to fight to the death.

As the British Second Army prepared to advance south of Caen on July 18, Bomber Command dropped most of the 6,800 tons of bombs needed to clear a path at three strategic points. These and later carpet bombings, resisted by Harris at first, caused Field Marshal Montgomery to award his command a commendation for the results they achieved. Within hours, the British could launch one thousand bombers that could drop bombs equal in weight to the shells of four thousand guns. It would have been impossible for the British and the Americans to have assembled that many guns at a given point on such short notice.

Spaatz had also protested use of his heavy bombers and increased his arguments against their use to Eisenhower when a formation July 24 mistook its aiming point and its bombs killed sixteen soldiers and wounded sixty others in the American 30th Infantry Division. Spaatz now ruled that heavy bombers should never release bombs unless bombardiers could sight visually on targets. Despite this, a formation of Eighth Air Force bombers dropped a load short of the German lines and killed Lieutenant General Lesley J. McNair and 102 other soldiers, most of whom were with the 30th Infantry Division.

Eisenhower remained steadfast in his insistence upon heavy-bomber support, claiming long after the battle that the Saint-Lô breakout was possible only because of direct support by the Eighth and Ninth air forces.

After the war Von Rundstedt agreed with Eisenhower, saying the heavy strikes in support of the Saint-Lô breakout July 25 were "the most effective as well as the most impressive tactical use of airpower in his experience." He cited the bombing as one of the factors most meaningful in contributing to the Allied victory. He praised also the initiative of Allied armor and infantry divisions, but said that the weakness of his German ground forces played a part in the outcome.

Short bombing pointed up the need for better radio contact between ground controllers and aircrews. Colonel Elwood R. Quesada recommended that an air-support party be assigned to each armored column and be equipped with two-way radios using air forces channels. General Omar Bradley liked the idea, and thereafter each advancing column was covered at all times by a four-plane flight to maintain close contact with ground forces. Fighter-bombers were used to strike enemy tanks in advance of Allied armor, and proved effective tank destroyers.

For his airborne forces, which had not proved as effective in the invasion as he had hoped, Eisenhower decided in June that an aviator should be placed in command. Therefore, Brereton was named to head the First Allied Airborne Army, and Major General Hoyt S. Vandenberg was given the Ninth.

Sir Henry Maitland Wilson had suggested to Eisenhower on June 19 that the best way to force the Germans to withdraw divisions from the French front was to attack in Italy and force the Germans to defend a line between Venice and Verona by the end of August. Then, Wilson said, they should strike eastward toward Trieste and the Ljubljana Gap in conjunction with an amphibious operation against the Istrian Peninsula.

Marshall believed there were sufficient air forces available for an all-out offensive in Italy, as well as an invasion of southern France. He was opposed by Alexander and Wilson who believed an invasion of southern France up the Rhone Valley would run into serious opposition, that overwhelming air superiority would be needed there, and that it could not be achieved in both countries simultaneously. Eaker and Slessor also believed such moves were unduly optimistic.

A week later, Eisenhower insisted on an invasion of southern France on August 15 to support the operations in western Europe. He said such an invasion would prevent the Germans from massing to meet his armies. When Churchill realized that Roosevelt and all the American senior military men supported the invasion of southern France, he gave in reluctantly.

In the middle of July, Wilson discussed a new directive with Eaker and Slessor prior to a visit by Marshall and Arnold.

Slessor said he believed they should avoid a letdown in the offensive in Italy and should continue to drive the Germans into the Alps. Then, he said, we should strike east to Zagreb to turn the enemy's right in the Balkans, or drive into southern Austria. Wilson said he would like to see the Americans and British on the Danube before the war came to an end.

When Marshall and Arnold arrived at Eaker's headquarters, they asked him which operation—the one through southern France or the advance through the Adriatic—his air forces could support most effectively.

"It would be easier for my air forces to support such an operation through the Adriatic because——"

Marshall interrupted. "You've been with the British too long!" He said it in such an exasperated tone that Eaker was taken aback.

"Well, general, would you listen to my reasons?"

"Go ahead."

"From the airdromes where we are now located, we easily have the range to support the operation through the Adriatic. It's purely a matter of geography and distance, and I realize very well the contention between the British and the Americans. I know why the prime minister wants us to go through the Adriatic, but I'm not in the political field, and I'm not motivated by political concerns. You simply asked me from an operational standpoint which is most feasible, and I've given you the right answer. It will take some time to change my bases and logistics, as you well know. We'd have to move our bombs and gasoline, in addition to moving our units."

Marshall had listened intently. He and Roosevelt believed that first jobs should come first. In other words, clearing the Germans out of France and destroying the German armies should have first priority over any other operation regardless of how interesting it might be.

Eaker was relieved that, in parting, Marshall seemed to understand his views better after they were explained.

There was no doubt in Eaker's mind, however, about the Adriatic venture. It was definitely out of all planning, despite Churchill's argument that the Allies should try to parallel the Russian advances through the Balkans and beat the Russians to Berlin in order to keep them from advancing into western Europe.

Marshall revealed one interesting fact. He said there were some forty to fifty American divisions ready but still awaiting deployment to Europe from the United States. He said they could not be brought to France until more channel ports were opened.

General Charles de Gaulle visited Eaker's command at Caserta, Italy, at the latter's request to decorate members of his Mediterranean air forces.

Eaker was embarrassed to find that de Gaulle had an exaggerated opinion of himself, along with a deep-seated hatred of the British and American leadership he thought was responsible for failing to give him the full partnership he thought he deserved in the war. Eaker was relieved when he finally bid him good-bye.

Colonel Budd J. Peaslee, too old at forty-three to be a fighter pilot at the start of the war, now piloted a P-51 Mustang July 16 above Munich twenty minutes ahead of the 1st Bombardment Division's bomber stream. This was his first mission as an air scout, a concept he had promoted in the previous summer while he was a bomber group commander. He had often been frustrated flying missions inside Germany only to find targets covered by clouds and their efforts thwarted.

His idea was to use fighters to scout the route ahead and report weather conditions to the bomber commander so that he would have reliable information upon which to base his decisions. He'd had a long battle to convince higher-ups of the plan's feasibility. . . .

He finally got an appointment with First Division Commander Robert Williams and described what he had in mind, telling him the P-51 Mustang now had proved it could go anywhere over Germany, and that it would make a fine scouting aircraft if precise plans were drawn up for its use.

Williams had agreed. "It looks solid to me, and we need it badly. Take it to Doolittle and tell him I recommend approval of the project."

Peaslee reported to Doolittle the next morning, described his plan, and mentioned Williams's endorsement.

"What do the other division commanders think of your plan?" Doolittle said.

Peaslee said he did not know because he had no authority to talk to them.

"You have authority now," Doolittle said. "Go see Partridge and LeMay. If they approve, come back here and give this plan to my staff for action. Good luck."

Partridge and LeMay both liked the plan, so he was told to form the

1st Scouting Force (Provisional). With full authority, he procured a staff and eight bomber pilots, each of whom were volunteers who had completed their duty tours as formation leaders.

After moving to Steeple Morton, 355th Group base, and briefing their commander, Colonel William Cummings, who gave his wholehearted support, the pilots checked out in the Mustang. . . .

On the Munich mission, the faster fighters had taken off after the bombers so that they would arrive over the target twenty minutes before the First Air Division. Weather reports had indicated excellent weather over England and the Continent.

The air scouts intercepted the bombers and Peaslee made contact with their formation commander. His group had been given the code name "Buckeye Red." On the radio, he asked the division commander if he understood who he was and what his role in the mission was.

"Roger," came the reply.

Peaslee quickly learned the weathermen were wrong in their forecast. Above him and parallel to their course was a wall of clouds, while other clouds spread beneath them.

Prior to takeoff, bomber pilots were advised to make a right turn after hitting the target to get them over France as quickly as possible. Peaslee saw such a turn would bring them into the cloud mass.

He called the commander, "You'll have to bomb by instruments. Do not, repeat, do not turn off the target as briefed. Turn in the opposite, repeat, opposite, direction."

Back came immediate acknowledgment. "Roger. Thanks, Buckeye."

At critiques it was learned that Peaslee's advice had been heeded and there were no losses in the First Division, whereas other divisions without air scouts lost nine aircraft.

The concept was so successful that officials of the Second and Third Bombardment Divisions visited their base so that they could establish their own air scouts. Many scouts were killed later, but their deaths were not in vain because bombers improved in accuracy, and there were far fewer losses and aborted missions.

Air scouts performed many other missions such as helping air-sea rescue efforts of downed bomber crews in the North Sea, reporting smoke screens at targets, revealing the times enemy fighters took off from their airfields, and often guiding crippled bombers safely home. Equally important, scouts reported weather conditions at English bases to bombers coming home, thereby reducing losses that were at times heavy.

Peaslee flew nineteen missions with the scouts during a six-month period. There is no question that he and the others who flew these vital missions were of inestimable value to the success of bomber operations.

GERMAN OIL PRODUCTION
DROPS TO 23 PERCENT

Allied air continued to pound rear areas in support of ground forces during August. Normandy and points east received priority attacks.

With most of the bridges over the Seine destroyed, the strategic and heavily defended L'Isle Adam railroad bridge was in heavy use moving German troops, supplies, and equipment to Paris. Captain Darrell R. Lindsey led thirty B-26 medium bombers on August 9 to try to knock it out.

Shortly after reaching enemy territory, his formation encountered heavy flak. Just before starting his run on the bridge, Lindsey's plane was shot full of holes and his right engine caught fire. His plane was hurled out of formation by the blast, which damaged the engine, but he maneuvered it back into lead position and continued the run. With fire streaming from his right engine and his right wing half enveloped in flames, he led them on and they dropped their bombs on the bridge.

Pulling away, he yelled to his crew, "Bail out!"

He remained at the controls as the plane descended and the crew bailed out, although he knew that his bomber could explode any minute.

The bombardier was last to leave, offering to lower the wheels so that Lindsey might escape through the nose. He refused because he knew the procedure would endanger the bombardier's chances of exiting the plane. Shortly after the bombardier bailed out, the plane exploded before Lindsey could save himself. In recognition of his courage, he was awarded the Medal of Honor.

By now, the whole of Germany's synthetic fuel output was reduced to 490 tons a month, an amount sufficient to operate only about eighty German bombers.

With little fuel to fly fighters and bombers, crews were drafted into the infantry. Many training schools were closed and their personnel similarly treated.

Albert Speer tried to shield his refineries with blast walls that protected the most critical elements, and deep shelters were dug to protect repair crews. His heroic salvage efforts worked for a time, largely because the strategic air effort was directed against other targets, and by November, the fuel tonnage was up to thirty-nine thousand.

American air continued to support operations in Brest and around Mortain and in the Falaise-Argentan area, but capture of the citadel at Saint-Malo in Brittany August 17 resulted from actions by ground forces alone.

Ground actions south of the Loire and around Breton ports received air assistance, but it was all part of the campaign in northern France. Allied Air Forces were helpful in maintaining the strong drive eastward after the Falaise-Argentan gap was closed.

It was an exhausting time for all units of Allied Air Forces as the pressure increased against marshaling yards, bridges, airfield installations, and supply dumps behind the German lines.

In late summer, while General George S. Patton was driving across France, some strategic bombers were hastily converted to transports to keep his army supplied after he had outrun his logistical support.

As necessary and important as these missions were to support Eisenhower's drive inland, Spaatz tried to get permission to resume all-out strategic bombing in a systematic air assault that he believed would destroy Germany's war-making capabilities. He now had adequate resources in crews and planes because the Eighth Air Force had grown to 2,100 heavy bombers, with another 1,200 assigned to the Fifteenth. In addition, there were 1,100 heavy bombers available to the Royal Air Force for night bombing. Eisenhower had earlier agreed that Spaatz and Harris could resume the strategic bombing campaign and that the United States Strategic Air Forces could attack the heart of Germany "any time it was not needed for battle emergencies and for missile-site attacks." That was the problem. Ground commanders seemed to be forever announcing emergencies and calling for air attacks whether they were needed or not, and with the V-1 situation still causing concern in England, large numbers of bombers were used to attack these missile sites.

During the spring, any time discussion came up about bombing the thirteen refineries around Ploesti, the Americans got involved in a dispute with the British who claimed that the German war economy could be made impotent by limiting movement of matériel instead of trying to destroy refineries.

To get around the question of priorities, Colonel Charles Young, intelligence officer for the Fifteenth Air Force at Bari, Italy, agreed with the command's operations officer, Brigadier General Charles Born, that the marshaling yard at each refinery should be the aiming point. Thus, during the early spring raids, the yards were bombed, but each run was set up so that bombs would spill over into the powerhouse complex that was the heart of each refinery.

While the third attack on the oil refineries at Ploesti was under way June 23, Lieutenant David R. Kingsley of the Fifteenth Air Force's 97th Group tried to ignore the exploding antiaircraft fire as he prepared to drop his bombs. He knew his B-17 Flying Fortress had been damaged severely by the intense flak while approaching the target, forcing him to leave the formation and make the run alone.

After bombs away, three ME-109s attacked and the battered bomber limped along, trying to stay in the air.

When Kingsley learned that the tail gunner had been wounded seriously and had been brought to the radio compartment, he hurried back to lend assistance. He removed the gunner's parachute harness and heavy clothes, and, after applying first aid, covered the wounded man with blankets.

Eight ME-109s attacked, wounding the ball-turret gunner, who crawled to the radio compartment so that Kingsley could help him.

The plane was in such dire straits that the pilot ordered everyone to bail out. All exited safely but Kingsley, who was last seen by crew members standing on the bomb bay catwalk while the aircraft continued to fly on automatic pilot until it nosed over and crashed. For his action in saving the life of the wounded gunner, his government honored him with the Medal of Honor.

Just after bombs away over Ploesti July 9, Lieutenant Donald D. Pucket felt direct hits from antiaircraft guns. One crew member was killed instantly, and six others were seriously wounded. The airplane was badly damaged, he knew, with two engines out, control cables cut, the oxygen system on fire, and the bomb bay awash with gasoline and hydraulic fluid.

Once he regained control of the airplane, he turned it over to his copilot. Attending to the wounded crew members, he proceeded to administer first aid while he surveyed the damage. When he found the bomb bay doors jammed shut, he manually cranked them open to let the gasoline escape.

After the plane started to lose altitude, he ordered all guns and equipment jettisoned. Still they lost altitude, so he ordered the crew to abandon the airplane. When three of the crew, in shock or out of control due to fright, refused to leave, Pucket stayed behind despite entreaties by the rest of his crew. The flaming bomber careened into a mountainside a few minutes later. Pucket, who gave his life in an attempt to save the lives of three comrades, earned his Medal of Honor.

Despite Royal Air Force opposition, Spaatz had issued orders June 8 that all strategic air forces under his command would have as their primary mission the denial of oil to Germany's armed forces. He gave the Fifteenth responsibility for refinery targets around Ploesti, Vienna, and Budapest, along with synthetic plants in Silesia, Poland, and in the Sudetenland. Eaker assigned the Royal Air Force's 205 Group in southern Italy the task of continuing to mine the Danube in order to obstruct oil shipments to the Reich. Synthetic oil plants in central and eastern Germany were given to the Eighth Air Force as top priority targets, and the Royal Air Force's Bomber Command bombed plants in the Ruhr Valley.

Spaatz developed almost an obsession about oil production targets, although the Royal Air Force opposed such a priority. Even when the Eighth and Fifteenth air forces caused vast damage to Ploesti, the RAF stubbornly refused to support Spaatz.

Elements of Spaatz's command had been released two weeks after D day to resume attacks against oil targets, and they were successful in knocking out nine tenths of the production of aircraft fuel by June 22, according to Speer. By July 21, he said, such Allied attacks had reduced production of aircraft fuel to 2 percent, although valiant German efforts were able to get production up when Allied bombers were diverted again to assist the ground campaign.*

Berlin was bombed June 21 in the largest attack yet by American fliers against the capital, and the British tried to convince Spaatz that the German capital should be area-bombed in retaliation for the V-1 bombing of London. Spaatz refused. He believed terror bombing was not effective in undermining German morale and served no useful military purpose. He believed also, and postwar interrogation proved him right, that terror attacks, although they disrupted the labor force and often affected production, stiffened German resistance. When the British increased their pressure for such attacks, Eisenhower supported Spaatz and so did Arnold in Washington.

---

*Albert Speer, *Inside the Third Reich*.

In June, after the Allied armies had moved inland, Spaatz had sent twenty-five hundred heavy bombers against aircraft factories and other strategic targets. Harris had to withdraw his Bomber Command because fighter units, which might have supported him, were needed to aid ground troops. Despite loss of forty-four United States bombers, most targets were hit and twenty-two German fighters were destroyed in the air.

Postwar interrogators were surprised to learn that Hitler had been so convinced that the war would be short that he did not order complete mobilization until late in 1944. Even increased calls for more military production after Soviet Russia regained the initiative in the winter of 1941– 42 had not changed the one-shift-a-day economy. There were remarkably few women in factories, unlike in the United States and Great Britain where women were in the majority. Interrogators now understood something that had baffled strategists during the war. Germany was able to withstand massive strategic bombing because she was undermobilized to begin with, and there were so many unused tools available that they could be used in hidden factories to continue production.

The Germans had earlier concentrated upon producing fighters, achieving by November 1944 a rate of four thousand fighters a month. This almost unbelievable production rate was possible because manufacture of all bombers and reconnaissance aircraft was stopped. It was still a remarkable feat because the work was done in primitive workshops under conditions that were almost impossible. Quality was sacrificed, however, and technical defects caused many planes to crash.

Practically until the end, machines and production tools were plentiful and were never used to their full capacity. Foreign slave labor helped to repair bomb-damaged plants, and there was always a plentiful supply of German labor to meet one-shift requirements.

In spite of all this, the Luftwaffe had suffered irretrievable losses in trained pilots. Göring's authorization to transfer most of the German Training Command to transport and combat units in a desperate effort to save Feldmarschall Friedrich Paulus's army at Stalingrad was a stupid misuse of instructor flying personnel. Training Command never recovered, and ill-trained German pilots were thrust into combat and quickly destroyed by seasoned Allied airmen.

Despite numerous attacks against the aircraft industry, the results of both American and British raids, amounting to only 2 percent of all missions, were too few in number to cause appreciable damage. How poor the Allied air effort was in destroying the German aircraft industry at this time can be seen by the fact that 39,807 planes of all types were delivered by German factories in 1944, compared to 8,295 in 1939 and 15,596 in 1942.

If Hitler had listened to his top scientists, some of whom had pressed for production of jet aircraft as early as 1941, the air war would have turned out differently. The Führer disallowed production because he believed the war would be won before they could be produced in quantity.

Hitler had changed his mind in January 1944, but directed that the ME-262 jet fighter be converted into a bomber to retaliate against England. The jet fighter had to be extensively redesigned as a bomber, with a new landing gear, bomb-releasing equipment, and so forth. There still was no satisfactory bombsight, and the jet bomber was limited to one five-hundred-pound bomb. Although the ME-262 was superior to any Allied fighter, it was almost worthless as a bomber.

In its fighter configuration, the 262 was armed with four cannon. It had an extremely thin wing, with a round aerodynamic shape, and used a tricycle landing gear. On the ground, its six-ton weight made it difficult to maneuver, so it had to be towed. The Germans quickly learned that its fuel requirements were double those of conventional twin-engined fighters, and if it was not towed into position by a tractor, taxiing would use up half its fuel—an amount equal to one and a half to two hours in flight depending upon altitude.

Hitler's intransigence lost Germany her last chance to gain control of the air.

Speer said in *Inside the Third Reich* that Hitler had closed his mind about the ME-262 as a fighter because he wanted to increase planned retaliation against England, initially programmed at thirty rockets a day carrying twenty-four tons of explosives. Such a total was equivalent to the bomb load of twelve Flying Fortresses, and much too small an amount to be effective. At that time, Speer said, Allied bombers were dropping an average of three thousand tons of bombs on Germany each day.

During the first week of August, Eisenhower issued orders that Montgomery's British and Canadian forces should hold a "hinge" at Caen, while Patton's armored forces swung south and eastward to try and surround the main German army.

The Germans counterattacked before dawn August 7 from the town of Mortain and headed toward Avranches on the sea. Although Patton completed his end run, Montgomery failed to move quickly enough from Caen and the Germans escaped through the Falaise-Argentan Gap.

During the drive across France, Eisenhower called for daily maximum air support. The Eighth Air Force, therefore, spent most of its time bombing German airfields, destroying bridges, bombing railway installations, and carrying emergency supplies. These were jobs best left to fighter-bombers, medium bombers, and transports, but Spaatz was helpless to do otherwise.

He had a chance August 4 to send his bombers to attack ten major oil refineries. These strikes, along with attacks against the experimental rocket works at Peenemünde, were the only strategic air operations permitted his command.

In the same period, the Fifteenth Air Force in Italy set an impressive record by making twenty daylight attacks against Ploesti, while the Royal Air Force made four night raids from their Italian bases. These attacks against oil refineries and synthetic plants in the occupied countries to the east caused the Germans the loss of 1.8 million tons of crude oil, aggravating an already serious crisis of petroleum products. They were so devastating that most refineries were either destroyed or seriously damaged as the Russians closed in on Romania. The attacks were kept up, however, so that plant equipment could not be removed to Germany.

The Fifteenth sent four hundred bombers against four aircraft factories in southern Germany August 3 at a time when practically all strategic attacks from England had ceased for the time being.

When Allied troops landed in southern France August 15, opposition was so weak that Eaker did not have to take much time off from strategic attacks to assist the invasion.

On August 24, all operations at Ploesti ceased.

After departure of the Germans, and three days before the Russians occupied the Ploesti area, Colonel Young, intelligence chief for the Fifteenth Air Force, sent his chief target specialist, Lieutenant Colonel Bradley Magill, to survey the damage to the refineries. Magill got along so well with everyone, including the Russians, that he was selected to be the American representative for the Romanian military government.

Eaker also went to Ploesti, observing that the sustained bombing of the installations had been most effective in destroying them. The cost had been high with 350 bombers lost on all raids. Fortunately, the Russians rescued 1,162 fliers.

And still the Fifteenth's oil offensive rolled on with five hundred bombers seriously damaging refineries in Poland and Czechoslovakia. Regrettably, bomber losses were high because the Germans had concentrated antiaircraft guns on the ground, and the weather was generally bad. Losses in July totaled 318 bombers for the Fifteenth, but August was worse. Eaker estimated that 30 percent of the crews who were sent out on a mission were shot down. His losses actually exceeded the number of men lost in ground fighting by the Fifth and Eighth armies.

Royal Air Force losses also were high. Harris admitted that casualties exceeded those of the British Second Army for several weeks after the Normandy invasion.

In late summer, due to the loss of Germany's early-warning network in the occupied countries and a huge increase in the number of available bombers, British Bomber Command achieved air superiority at night against the German air force.

Such superiority was due, in large part, to achievements of British technology, which made it possible for Bomber Command to develop new marking techniques so that bombing accuracy often exceeded day accuracy. Night-fighter support by 100 Group proved valuable, plus the extensive use of countermeasures.

In the past, Harris had resisted daylight attacks, particularly beyond the Rhine, because his bombers could not fly formation above eighteen thousand feet, and he knew that at that altitude antiaircraft fire would be prohibitive. Now British daylight operations increased, and by August, they accounted for more than half of all bombing missions. With growing air superiority, losses were kept to a minimum; even though Bomber Command sent out three times as many aircraft in September as it did in June, it suffered only two thirds as many losses.

Harris authorized the first major daylight operation against a German target for August 27, when 216 Halifaxes from 4 Group and 27 Mosquitoes and Lancasters from the Pathfinder Force hit an oil plant at Homberg in the Ruhr. With an equal number of Spitfires in support, this most heavily defended target in the Ruhr was attacked without the loss of a single plane. Only one ME-110 rose to defend the target and was driven off.

Harris quickly authorized more attacks on Emden and oil plants at Kamen and Castrop-Rauxel. They were bombed visually by using target indicators laid by pathfinders. Two-ton bombs caused heavy damage.

Attacks against oil refineries and synthetic plants, along with the loss of Ploesti, brought Germany's fuel situation to a catastrophic shortage by September. At the time, it was estimated by Allied experts that German oil production was 32 percent of the level it had been prior to these concentrated attacks. Actually, production was only 23 percent. Such fuel losses had an effect on the battle fronts. Allied commanders at Caen noted that the Germans had to use their fuelless tanks as small forts dug into the ground. As Allied armies swept France, German armor and trucks were found everywhere with dry fuel tanks.

Early in the bomber campaign against oil targets, Albert Speer had charged Edmund Geilenburg with the reconstruction of bombed plants and their dispersal whenever possible. To keep the plants repaired, Geilenburg developed a force of three hundred fifty thousand men who worked day and night.

Spaatz and his commanders were concerned about crew morale, which had sagged noticeably because of the intensity of operations and the consecutive pace of daily operations. Morale came back a little in the Eighth after sufficient crews became available to assign two crews per airplane, but the Fifteenth was unable to achieve such a rate until December.

If Spaatz thought he had a morale problem, it was nothing compared to the one faced by the German air force. The Luftwaffe was losing an average of three hundred aircraft each week, despite the fact that the number of flying personnel had grown to forty-four thousand from a total of thirty-one thousand in the summer of 1941. In that three-year time span, the losses totaled thirty-one thousand German aviators.

The 492nd Group, commanded by Colonel Eugene Snavely, had a special problem: Its losses since May 1, 1944, had been staggering. When the group prepared to take off July 31 to bomb the marshaling yards at Ludwigshafen, Lieutenant Harry Orthman, one of the group's more experienced leaders at only twenty-one years of age, was told to watch over Lieutenant David O'Sullivan's plane, which would fly on his wing. O'Sullivan was flying his last sortie, and to date, not one crew member had survived to complete his missions and be rotated home.

At first, it appeared the strike would be a milk run, with some flak but no fighters. Then, shouts crackled through the intercom systems as an ME-262 jet fighter came from below and streaked through the formation. It was the first of the new fighters Orthman had seen, and he, like the others, was shaken by the suddenness of the attack, even though it did no damage. They stared with disbelief as the jet fighter climbed almost vertically through their formation.

On turns, Orthman tried to get O'Sullivan to stay as close as possible, and all appeared well. They were now heading in toward the target and had flak damage to several aircraft, but they had still suffered no loss. A quick glance to Orthman's right showed him that O'Sullivan's plane was still tucked in. Then their bombs were away and they turned for home, getting reports that the yards had been hit.

After a safe landing at North Packingham, O'Sullivan was mobbed by Group Commander Snavely and everyone else as champagne corks popped and toasts were made to the first man of the 492nd to complete his missions. Each, in his own heart, hoped the jinx was broken.

Heavy losses continued, however, and after three months, the Eighth Air Force disbanded the group because it was down to only twenty-two crews out of the seventy-two that had come to the theater. This was the only group in the Eighth Air Force to gain this dubious honor, and remaining personnel were assigned to other organizations.

The 492nd was an unlucky group, and some of the reasons for its demise could be traced to the B-24 itself. Some thought losses were due to the fact it was the first Liberator group to fly silver airplanes. Previously, all other bombers had been painted in camouflage colors. That reason appears invalid when one considers that huge formations were going over the Continent at a time when German fighter attacks had been drastically reduced. Actually, the B-24 had to be modified so much to permit it to survive over Germany—armor plate surrounding the crew and the vulnerable wing tanks, plus more turrets for protection—that its performance at altitude suffered severely. Whereas B-17s flew at twenty-five thousand feet, B-24s had to fly five to nine thousand feet lower. Such altitudes made them sitting ducks for German fighters, and they came into range of 88 mm antiaircraft guns, which were most effective at these bombing altitudes.

Flying Fortress crews kidded that B-24s were the best fighter escorts they could get because German fighters concentrated on them at their lower altitudes.

The Liberator was also a difficult plane to fly in formation, and pilots had to keep on top of it all the time because its thin wing was not efficient at high altitudes.

Air Marshal Harris's Bomber Command had yet another morale problem. He had written Portal July 1, "I think you should be aware of the full depth of feeling that is being aroused by the lack of adequate, or even reasonable credit to the Royal Air Force, in particular, and the air forces as a whole for their efforts in the invasion. I have no personal ambition that hasn't years ago been satisfied in full, but I for one cannot forbear a most emphatic protest against the grave injustice which is being done to my crews. There are more than 10,500 aircrews in my operational squadrons. In three months, we have lost half that number. They have the right that their story should be adequately told, and it's a military necessity that it should be."

Bomber crews enjoyed none of the glamour conferred on fighter pilots in the public's esteem, so it was inevitable that they were never to receive the acclaim they deserved.

In late summer, most of the ground campaigns were progressing well. The Russians were rapidly ousting the Nazis from the Balkan states, and the Allied invasion of France had progressed through territory between Normandy and the Moselle River. The Germans now had been driven back to their own borders.

The advance in Italy had been stopped below Cassino in the spring, until a triphibious operation was launched to establish the Anzio beachhead. After May, the Allied armies had made a three-pronged advance with the Fifth and Eighth armies sweeping past Rome in less than a month. In August, the battle line lay from Arno to Florence, beyond Perugia in the center, and above Ancona on the east coast.

While pressure was maintained on all fronts in Italy, the Seventh Army had crossed the Ligurian Sea and landed in southern France on August 15. In a month's time, this force had moved up the Rhone Valley and joined forces with Patton's Third Army.

Paris fell on August 25, and the Germans retreated toward their Westwall along the German border.

During this period, four squadrons of the Twelfth and Fifteenth air forces earned undying fame despite handicaps that would have reduced lesser men to self-pity.

In one of the most unhappy examples of racism in American history, blacks were turned down as flying cadets in the years prior to 1941 despite the fact that most who applied were college graduates. After the war broke out, they were encouraged to enlist—in all-black units with white officers and instructors. Segregation forced these black pilots to train at Tuskegee, Alabama, because the white bureaucracy would not permit them to be quartered or trained with whites.

These "Lonely Eagles" were not only destined to train alone, but to fight alone. Members associated with the 99th, 100th, 301st, and 302nd squadrons shamed many white outfits with their superior flying abilities and esprit de corps. During their combat operations in the Mediterranean, they shot down 260 German planes, sank a Nazi destroyer, and wrecked hundreds of military vehicles in strafing runs against fleeing German ground units. The Germans learned to respect them, calling them the black birdmen. Blacks called their outfit the "Spook Waffle."

There were many outstanding fighter pilots in the group, including Frederick Hutchins, Alexander Jefferson, William Melton, and Herman "Ace" Lawson, to name only a few. These outstanding squadrons suffered high casualties, and sixty-six of their pilots were killed in action.

Antwerp had been occupied by the British Second Army on September 3 without significant resistance, but the Germans continued to occupy Walcheren, an island in the Netherlands at the mouth of the Scheldt. Walcheren is mostly below sea level, and a two hundred-foot-thick seawall prevented flooding of the surrounding countryside. The Germans had installed gun batteries on the wall and elsewhere around the area, so a parachute or glider attack was almost impossible.

Airborne divisions tried to force a crossing of the lower Rhine at

Arnhem and Nijmegen in October but failed, and they were surrounded.

Brussels fell to the Allies September 3, and among the first airmen to join the populace to celebrate the event was the crew of *Shoo Shoo Baby II* piloted by Lieutenant Lewis A. Huston, Jr.

His 487th Group plane had been hit over Magdeburg, Germany, on September 12 and knocked out of formation. With one engine out, Huston nosed the plane down, hoping to land at a friendly air base. When a second engine failed and he couldn't feather the propeller, he spotted an airfield inside Belgium. He headed for it, hoping it was in friendly hands. Luckily it had recently been occupied by Allied troops.

There were no facilities there for his crew, so Huston led them into Brussels where they were mobbed by wildly cheering crowds. Women grabbed them, kissing them first on the left check, then on the right, then starting over again.

They walked around in a daze. Somehow, they found themselves with five quarts of champagne and countless offers to dinner. In one cheering group of almost hysterical Belgians, the men gave away their service ribbons, insignia, and other uniform items, which the civilians begged to have in remembrance of this historic occasion.

From the balcony of their hotel that night, the airmen watched the great city go wild with joy all over again now that the Germans had been driven out. It was an experience none of them would ever forget.

Next day they were flown home. *Shoo Shoo Baby II* had to wait until repairs were completed, but eventually it also returned to base.

Harry Orthman, recently promoted to captain, and now with the 44th Bombardment Group, was one of those assigned to make resupply drops of food and ammunition to the parachutists and glider crews surrounded at Arnhem and Nijmegen. After practicing at treetop levels in England, they set out to make their drops in Holland at Nijmegen.

At five hundred feet, Orthman headed toward his drop point while Dutch people rushed out of their homes waving flags and jumping up and down in their excitement. Some of them thought the war was over. Orthman was quickly reminded by flashes from German guns that it was not.

It had been a difficult navigation job to pinpoint the drop area due to their low altitude levels over the flat terrain, but they soon saw fields jammed with gliders. Orthman wondered how they had all got in, so tightly packed were they between hedgerows.

While P-47s ripped flak towers apart, his group dropped their supplies and headed home. The mission was not without its cost. Two bombers failed to return, while others limped back to base with tree limbs and pieces of fences jammed into their underbellies.

Later, British Bomber Command attacked the German batteries on the seawall, and Fortresses breached the wall in a number of places.

Inevitably, the sea flooded the land, and even more breaching was needed on either side of Flushing and on the northeast coast to reduce the German garrison. This unfortunate flooding of valuable crop land removed the Germans from control of the mouth of the Scheldt November 6. After Walcheren was captured shortly afterward, the first Allied ships could be unloaded at Antwerp November 26.

Darmstadt, for one reason or another, had been spared the annihilation treatment, but September 11, 5 Group bombed it with 218 Lancasters and 14 Mosquitoes. The raid virtually destroyed the city, leaving it so saturated by bombs that the destruction resembled Hamburg's. Almost twelve thousand civilians died—a tenth of Darmstadt's population.

By mid-September, Eisenhower's armies were running out of supplies. With winter approaching, he decided to consolidate his positions and clean up pockets of resistance in the Low Countries.

27

GERMAN DEFEAT
INEVITABLE

While the Combined Chiefs were meeting for the second time in Quebec, Spaatz had reported to Eisenhower on September 2 that it had been agreed that strategic bombers would be taken away from Eisenhower's control and returned to that of the Combined Chiefs of Staff so that the Combined Bomber Offensive could be resumed.

Despite his original commitment to return the strategic forces after he was established on the Continent, Eisenhower immediately wired Marshall that such a move would be a serious mistake. He said all available forces should be kept under one command. He claimed that there had been no clashes of policy or even sharp differences of opinion on the proper use of air forces since the issue had been resolved in early spring. He said both Spaatz and Harris were happy with the present arrangement, but he knew better than that, particularly in regard to Spaatz.

In the hope of enlisting Arnold's aid, Eisenhower wrote him that the basic conception underlying his whole campaign was the possession of an overpowering air force. He said it had destroyed the German air force, disrupted communications, neutralized beach defenses, and made possible the breakout from the beachhead. He said that the strategic air forces had been committed to the greatest possible extent to the destruction of German industrial and oil targets. His front lines had moved so far forward, he said, and construction of new airfields on the Continent was so far behind schedule, that only heavy bombers could reach targets in the forward areas. He added, to separate the big bombers now from SHAEF would make coordination difficult, if not impossible.

Although Spaatz was willing to go along with Eisenhower, the Combined Chiefs reassumed control of Bomber Command and the United States Strategic Air Forces with Portal and Arnold in charge. Arnold delegated Spaatz to exercise Combined Chiefs' authority over the strategic air forces on his behalf. Eisenhower retained the right to call upon heavy bombers in an emergency. He accepted the situation, believing that the goodwill of those involved and the fact that his operations would be supported when necessary would assure a smooth transition. Actually the change made little difference in operations because Eisenhower continued to call on heavy bombers, claiming 50 percent of their efforts. No one on either side was completely pleased with the arrangement, and the only reason it worked was the special relationship between Eisenhower, Spaatz, and Harris. They understood one another, and could work cooperatively, despite disagreements.

Eisenhower had been pleasantly surprised by Harris, who had helped enthusiastically and became exceedingly proud of his membership on the Allied team. Harris put some of his feelings into words when he wrote Eisenhower how delighted he had been to be of service, and assured the Supreme Allied Commander that he would support him in the future. In conclusion, he said, "I wish personally on behalf of my command to proffer you my thanks and gratitude for your unvarying helpfulness, encouragement, and support, which has never failed us throughout the good fortunes and occasional emergencies of the campaign."

After the war, Eisenhower acknowledged he had held on to the strategic air forces much too long.

With the German army out of France, German air defenses started to crumble because they had lost their early-warning system. The Allies now moved their own ground stations for navigational aids to the Continent, which extended the range of all their equipment.

The Americans and the British were desperately short of bombs; more tons of bombs were dropped on Germany than had been released during the whole of 1943. By the end of the year, the Royal Air Force alone had devastated or seriously damaged 80 percent of all German cities with prewar populations of one hundred thousand or more.

The Ruhr was kept under constant attack to prevent rebuilding of previously damaged factories. This key industrial area relied upon its own internal transport for survival, and it had its own gas and electricity grids. So great was the aerial destruction of lines of communication by the Royal Air Force that production came to a halt in many places even though the area abounded in coal mines. Due to continued autumn bombing, the Ruhr was rapidly reduced to a wasteland of devastated cities and factories.

Wing Commander Willie Tait's 617 Squadron added to the destruction greeting Eisenhower's armies by breaching the Kembs Dam on the Rhine in order to prevent the Germans from controling the river's level and perhaps flooding the valley when the Allies tried to cross the river.

He personally led thirteen Lancasters in spectacular drops of "Tallboy" bombs, special weapons developed by Dr. Barnes Willis.

The Dortmund-Ems and Mittelland canals, indispensable to the Germans for transport of coal, ore, and heavy equipment to and from the Ruhr, were bombed repeatedly by the British so that canals would be kept drained despite German efforts to repair them. Most missions were flown by 617 Squadron using Wallis's twelve-thousand-pound thin-case bombs. One bomb could breach a bank and flood the countryside.

Wing Commander Tait led 11 Lancasters of his 617 Squadron, loaded with Tallboys, against the Dortmund-Ems Canal aqueduct near Münster. Another 125 Lancasters of 5 Group with smaller bombs and 5 Mosquitoes for markings also participated in the raid. Their intent was to breach the banks of the canal, which were above the level of the countryside at this point, and drain it.

Their bombs were aimed so well that six and a half miles of the canal were drained, beaching many barges carrying vital cargoes. The Germans promptly repaired the banks in the coming months, but the British went out each time and breached them again.

After these raids, made especially dangerous by fog and mist at low levels, 617 Squadron was down to six crews. As a result of these attacks and other strikes against rail centers, coal production between the middle of August and February of the following year was cut in half. With coal strictly rationed, locomotives were idled because there was no coal to run them. With rail lines disrupted, factories ceased producing. The million and a half people thus forced out of jobs were put to work to repair breaches in the canals, but their efforts proved fruitless.

As Eisenhower prepared to push into the heart of Germany, he agreed with Spaatz about placing German transportation targets in first priority. Such a recommendation was approved by the Joint Chiefs of Staff and the combined strategetic target committee. All-out air attacks against communications to complete the disruption of the German industrial system and also to sever the Rhine front from the rest of the Reich were pressed by the strategic air forces and were supplemented by the tactical air force.

After the Dortmund-Ems Canal was drained, the most vulnerable communications targets were railway bridges and the Bielefeld Viaduct near Bremen, which was the main link between the German armies defending the Ruhr arsenal and the industrial centers of northwest Germany.

The viaduct proved a tough nut to crack. After three thousand tons of bombs failed to breach it, Wallis's Tallboy bombs, and one of the ten-ton Grand Slam bombs, knocked it down. The Grand Slam exploded one hundred feet below ground, sending out shock waves so severe that the viaduct's foundations and arches collapsed. Several more Grand Slams were later used to destroy railroad bridges.

These Grand Slams were so powerful that two of them penetrated twenty-three feet of reinforced concrete to explode in the tunnels of the submarine pens at Brest.

In an action that boosted Allied morale, the battleship *Tirpitz* was finally sunk in November 1944, after she was moved to Tromsö Fjord in northern Norway. Group Commander Donald Bennett was killed in the raid. The sinking followed two unsuccessful attempts that had cost the lives of many crews. In retrospect, it appears that the *Tirpitz* might just as well have been left alone to stagnate in the Arctic Circle until the war ended.

The Allied ground war in Italy bogged down for several reasons. First, the invasion forces in southern France had priority over men and materials. Moreover, the Allied armies had paused at the Arno River to regroup and did not renew their offensive until August 26. The much-vaunted Gothic Line was breached by September 21, but the Apennines in northern Italy proved a far more formidable barrier, and the action ground to a halt.

Earlier, Eaker had recommended to Arnold that the Twelfth Air Force be permitted to move to France because it would only stagnate if left in Italy. Then the ground situation improved in Italy, and Eaker withdrew his recommendation.

The air effort caused only a slight reduction in the scale of V-1 operations, and the British contemplated all-out war on Germany with every means at their disposal. Proposals ranged from saturation bombing of German cities to the use of poison gas. The latter was quickly discarded because use of gas would result in German retaliation. Then the last V-1 fell in Kent September 1, as the last launching sites fell into Allied hands, and British military chiefs called off further attacks on September 7, believing all danger from V weapons was past. Duncan Sandys announced to the press on that date that the "Battle of London" was over, although he thought there might be a few more firings.

While the newly liberated people of Paris were eating dinner the next day, the first fourteen-ton V-2 rocket exploded in the city. The hypersonic forty-six-foot missile, carrying a ton of explosives, came without warning and struck the city at thirty-six hundred miles an hour after attaining a peak altitude of sixty miles in its trajectory.

London was hit a few hours later. Actually, the V-2's warhead caused less blast damage than the V-1. At first, the Allies did not believe the Germans had V-2s in significant numbers, so the Royal Air Force did not embark on massive retaliations. It was believed that Allied advances on the ground would quickly overrun these bases.

When more and more V-2s came over England, causing thousands of casualties and destroying hundreds of buildings, Eisenhower called for emergency priority to attacks against these sites. Until these installations, too, were overrun, eleven hundred V-2s were launched against England. They caused extensive damage, but they arrived on the scene too late to alter the war's outcome.

Allied armies were forced to stop their advances by the middle of September because they were too far ahead of their sources of supply. The drives across France and Belgium had brought them to or near the borders of Germany. Most of France and Belgium was in Allied hands, as were nearly all of Luxembourg and even a small part of Holland in the Maastricht region. The United States First Army had penetrated Germany for ten to fifteen miles after breaking through the outer defenses of the Siegfried Line in the vicinity of Aachen on the Belgian border.

The Germans had suffered heavily, but Eisenhower knew they were still a formidable threat and would be even more so the farther the Allies pushed into the German homeland. While the tempo of the air war increased during the fall of 1944, the ground war remained in a state of stagnation.

The German High Command's decision before the war to use the German air force primarily for support of ground operations was a strategic error that may have lost them the war. Failure to develop a long-range bomber command, similar to those in the United States and Great Britain, and to provide greater range for their fighters probably cost them the Battle of Britain, and with it the last chance at a quick and decisive victory. Failure to build up the Luftwaffe in the same manner and degree as they built up their land and sea forces undoubtedly made their ultimate defeat inevitable. Although German scientists were the first to develop missile and rocket systems successfully, their weapons arrived too late to be decisive. Hitler and most of his top generals share the blame for failing to understand that these systems, along with jet aircraft, were war-winning weapons that might very well have changed the outcome. Similar attitudes prevailed in many high American and British councils. Fortunately, there were men like Spaatz, Eaker, and Arnold to fight for their beliefs, and a superb and open-minded chief of staff in George Marshall; otherwise the Allies might have failed to build up massive airpower and thus have lost the war.

In spite of Allied concentration on aircraft assembly plants, the Germans succeeded in producing twenty-five thousand single-engine fighters during 1944. Postwar investigation indicates that destruction of aircraft engine plants would have been more effective. But the Luftwaffe's inability to train pilots because of the fuel shortage and the loss of training instructors to fill depleted combat ranks did far more to cripple the German fighter command than the early attacks against the aircraft industry when Allied bomber forces were small. Now that bomber forces were up to full strength, attacks against aircraft plants in the fall of 1944 would have been more devastating, but continued requests for ground support prevented them.

German fighter strength actually rose to twenty-two hundred in 1944, but the quality of pilots was so low that their effectiveness could not be measured by numbers. Due to the destruction of the synthetic oil plants and the attacks on Ploesti, new pilots had only enough fuel to fly three and one half hours a week in training. The German air force was defeated not due to any shortage of planes, but because of the depreciation in the qualitative standards of its pilots. Newly trained pilots survived an average of seven missions, an attrition rate of 14 percent per mission. Once control of the air was lost in early 1944, the Germans were never again able to regain it.

The heavy attacks against petroleum targets caused a drastic reduction in operations of conventionally powered aircraft. Now, however, jet aircraft appeared that could fly on low-grade fuels and did not require highly refined aviation gasoline.

German submarine *production* actually increased during the year despite extensive USAAF and RAF attacks—not counting midget submarines; the Germans built 1,158 submarines from 1935 until 1945 —but the number *in operation* by 1944 had declined. The disastrous losses of Allied merchant ships in early 1943 were not repeated. American attacks against submarine pens proved fruitless, and only the RAF's Tallboy bombs were able to penetrate the concrete-reinforced pens.

A new type of U-boat, which would have better underwater efficiency, had been proposed by Admiral Karl Doenitz in 1943. When the idea was presented to Speer, he recommended these undersea ships be constructed in sections at various inland factories and then shipped to three shipyards for final assembly and launching. His plan was explained to the German navy July 5, and production started in November. The first new submarine was not delivered until early in 1944, and only 180 were built by the end of the war because air raids destroyed a third of them during final assembly. The proposed rate of forty a month, which would have been disastrous for Allied sea commerce, proved impossible to attain because of strategic air attacks.

The Royal Air Force had concentrated on the German tank industry the fall of 1943, but this top-priority program of Hitler's suffered no serious setback. During a series of attacks, approximately seven hundred to eight hundred tanks were destroyed or damaged, but there was never a shortage of tanks in the front lines. Instead, the basic problem was a shortage of fuel to run the tanks.

The first coordinated attacks against the truck industry, which produced nine thousand vehicles each month, were started in July 1944. Actually, the disruption of the railroad industry, which caused a loss of truck parts and assemblies, did as much as anything to reduce truck production by March of 1945 to less than a quarter of its peak rate.

Eisenhower never fully understood strategic airpower, and the effect of bombing selected industries or systems meant little to him. He could comprehend the contribution made by air forces in support of ground troops, but the broader philosophy that strategic airpower by itself could be decisive ran counter to his beliefs and everything he had been taught about military strategy. It was a weak link in an otherwise strong military campaign.

Air Marshal Tedder, his senior airman, had similar views; in fact, that was the main reason for his selection. Therefore, Eisenhower supported him instead of Spaatz and Arnold. Eisenhower's views on the use of strategic airpower were more parochial than one might have hoped for in a Supreme Allied Commander.

After Spaatz lost the battle for control of strategic airpower prior to the invasion, he was concerned that refusal to use the strategic air forces to the best advantage would result in disaster for the Allied cause. He told Eisenhower that if he persisted in refusing requests to attack strategic targets, it would be best for him to find another air commander.

Eisenhower had relented somewhat, permitting a fourth of the strategic effort to be directed against oil targets. Those earlier attacks May 12 and 28 had proved so disastrous to the Germans that Spaatz's case was proved beyond the shadow of a doubt, but Eisenhower still refused their continuance on a sustained basis.

After the Allied landings in Normandy, Hitler had at first issued orders that all fighters from central Germany should be transferred to the front to resist the invaders. Just as Spaatz had predicted, Speer and Galland insisted they be retained instead to defend oil facilities and other vital industrial plants. Under the force of such arguments, Hitler had reluctantly backed down. His decision proved critical because the Germans quickly lost air superiority over the battle lines.

Eisenhower did not really need the Royal Air Force Bomber Command or the strategic air forces, at least not after the breakout from the beachheads. For support of his troops, there were 1,520 bombers and 3,160 fighters available from the USAAF and the RAF directly assigned to him. They were more than sufficient to isolate the battlefield and provide close support for ground troops. Eisenhower's use of strategic bombers for ground support was a serious error of conservatism that was compounded when he continued to demand their support long after his armies started to spread out from the beachheads.

Meanwhile, the German air force was declining at such a rate that its very existence was threatened. Between June and October, the Luftwaffe had lost thirteen thousand fliers. The American air forces would be able to claim by the end of 1944 that it had destroyed more than thirty-seven hundred German planes in daylight operations alone.

28

RAF'S CHIEF OF STAFF
BACKS DOWN

With France virtually free of German troops by September and the limited American offensive against oil targets showing remarkable success, Portal insisted that absolute priority should be given to Germany's fuel industry.

In early July, when he had asked what oil targets had been given to the British Bomber Command, he had been surprised to learn that Harris had issued no governing directive for such attacks, although a few strikes had been made. Air Commodore S. O. Bufton, director of bomber operations, told him that most of these attacks had been made by small Mosquito forces. On two occasions, however, three or four hundred heavy bombers had participated. Bufton admitted that only the attack against the Nordstern plant at Gelsenkirchen had been a success.

Bufton further explained that he personally was anxious to start an oil offensive, particularly against targets in the Ruhr, but the Air Staff had never given Harris specific directives, even though they professed to believe such targets should have priority.

Portal was not happy with this state of affairs because he had directed formation of a Joint Oil Targets Committee back in July to coordinate bomber strikes against Germany's oil industry. They had reported later that month that their analyses indicated Germany would be unable to continue the war past December if the fighting continued on all three fronts and the aerial war was stepped up. Their report said that German consumption of oil exceeded production by three hundred thousand tons as of August 1. The committee report said that every hydrogenation plant in Germany had been damaged, but that the Germans had given the highest priority to their reconstruction.

Portal enjoined the Air Staff to consider an all-out effort to wipe out

Germany's oil production, and they called for attacks against oil targets in the Ruhr in preference to strikes against urban centers.

Meanwhile, Russian advances neutralized the principal oil fields in Poland and started to seal Romanian distribution centers in late August. The British Air Staff reported to Eisenhower's headquarters that "we are presented with an exceptionally favorable opportunity in the next few weeks of imposing on the enemy a critical situation in his war economy that, if exploited to the full, may prove decisive to our efforts."

The Air Staff stressed again that oil targets must be attacked on a sustained basis or the plants would be back in production. They pointed out that German salvage operations made any but concentrated attacks worthless.

The Royal Air Force Air Staff by now had abandoned its early support of area bombing, although Harris felt as strongly as ever that it was the only way to bring the Germans to their knees. Therefore, the staff adopted three categories for the final air offensive. The oil campaign received first priority, followed by attacks against communications targets, then attacks against the German air force.

Once Portal regained some measure of control over Bomber Command in September, he held a number of meetings with Allied air leaders to establish the final air phase, which culminated in a plan to start September 25. Communications targets would be attacked deep inside Germany to destroy vehicle production, while other large strikes would be made against German rail and water systems, and attacks against tank factories and ordnance depots.

Despite the wishes of the Air Staff, Harris remained convinced of the value of urban attacks. His command dropped twice as many bombs during October as any previous month. Duisburg received about the same tonnage of bombs during a twenty-four-hour period as the Germans dropped on London during the entire war. Interestingly, about a quarter of these British attacks were made in daylight.

At the end of the month, Portal told Churchill that even daylight operations were made with a loss rate of less than 1 percent, and they included attacks on industrial areas, communications targets, and synthetic oil plants. Yet despite the September directive issued by the Air Staff, Harris continued to make most of his attacks against cities instead of concentrating upon oil and communications targets.

The Combined Bomber Offensive, authorized by the Casablanca Directive, had been controlled by Sir Charles Portal until Eisenhower had preempted his authority for six months prior to and following D day. Now, the chain of command became more cumbersome because control was shared by Portal and General Arnold in Washington and their delegates Sir Norman Bottomley and General Spaatz.

Such an arrangement made it necessary to establish a Combined Strategic Targets Committee in order that a weekly priority list could be given to Bomber Command and the United States Strategic Air Forces for guidance. A major problem had developed as to how much bombing effort should be diverted to tactical support of Eisenhower's armies. Portal understood from his American friends that General Marshall was considering measures that might end the war in 1944. In such an event, the ground war would be escalated, and the strategic bombers would be needed for an even greater role in support of increased ground actions. Portal was disturbed about greater diversion of his bombers from their strategic targets and he told Tedder October 22 that he would not welcome such a policy. He told Eisenhower's deputy that he realized armies should have whatever air support was necessary, particularly during an offensive that might be decisive, and where success would be unlikely without it. He stressed, however, that the proper application of the strategic bomber forces to targets behind the front lines would do more to shorten the war than operations in support of the battlefields.

He expressed his concern that constant application of bomber forces to support land battles, when it was not essential and its only purpose was to reduce casualties, would eventually lead to demoralization of the army. "If one division captures an objective with strong heavy-bomber support and loses only a few men, other divisions will naturally be reluctant to attack without similar support." Sooner or later, he said, they would reach a stage where almost the whole of the bomber effort "will be frittered away in small packets if the army is to attack at all."

In reply, Tedder admitted that the army was "drugged with bombs," saying he agreed with Portal and that demoralization was already evident. "It is going to be a difficult process to cure the drug addicts," he said, "particularly since the troops are undoubtedly getting pretty tired."

Tedder freely admitted to Portal that he was uneasy about the conduct of the main ground offensive but said that his views would not be acceptable in some quarters. Airpower should work toward a common goal, Tedder said. "I believe airpower will be decisive—and quickly."

He told Portal that he considered there were two ways to win the war. One was by military invasion, and the other by strategic bombing. One does not conflict with the other, he said, and they are not alternatives. He said he was not satisfied that airpower was being used most effectively, and that various types of operations should fit into one comprehensive pattern. "At present," he said, "I feel they are more like a patchwork quilt."

Bottomley and Spaatz issued a new directive November 1 that varied little from the earlier ones; oil was again given first priority with communications in second place, with the emphasis to be placed on targets in the Ruhr.

Harris's continued opposition to concentration on oil targets caused a serious split in his relationship with Portal. In the past, Portal had considered their disagreements a matter of opinion, but now Harris's open flouting of Air Staff directives reached the stage where Portal seriously considered Harris's removal as head of Bomber Command. Sadly, while the dispute dragged on, the effectiveness of Bomber Command was reduced. Few fliers ever saw Harris because he remained in his headquarters, but to them he represented the spirit of Bomber Command—the one man who, through strength of character and prestige, had forged a mighty aerial weapon against Nazi Germany that had achieved great successes. Harris was a legend in his own time—an officer who was sometimes ruthless and who demanded absolute obedience. This remote figure had become so strong in the minds and hearts of his men that Portal hesitated to take the step of removing him during the war's final phase. Harris's men held him in awe, but no less strong was their affection for him. Then, too, Harris and Churchill had established an unusual rapport, shared by few other British leaders. It is understandable that Portal hesitated to take an irrevocable step whose consequences he could not foresee.

Despite Harris's contributions to the war effort, his judgment at times had been erratic. At first, he had opposed incendiary bombing, creation of the pathfinder force, and development of the bombs that destroyed the Möhne and Eder dams. He had grudgingly conceded that his bombers could be used effectively against rail transportation targets only after he was forced to try such attacks. Yet Harris had the kind of courage that few top leaders ever demonstrate. The Cologne raid was an early case in point, but there were many others. His own courage to stand by strong convictions, despite attacks on all sides, boosted the spirits of his command. His men knew they had a leader who would fight—for them.

He wrote Tedder November 1, complaining about the number of cooks now engaged in stirring the broth, saying that conflicting demands were being made by "panacea mongers." In particular, he condemned the British Admiralty, which he accused of reviving the U-boat threat, and the Special Operations Executive. Harris insisted again that he would continue his attacks against German cities, claiming that Bomber Command had "virtually destroyed" forty-five out of the sixty leading German cities during the previous eighteen months.

He said that he had succeeded in maintaining a destruction rate of two and a half cities a month and started the destruction of many others, despite what he called "invasion diversions."

"Are we now to abandon this vast task that the Germans themselves have long admitted to be their worst headache, just as it nears completion?"

He told Tedder that all that was required was to destroy cities such as Berlin and Hannover, which as yet had not been damaged enough to cause serious deterioration of their economic viability.

Harris's letter was in response to Tedder's memorandum which outlined targets for the remainder of the war. If Harris continued to avoid oil targets, Tedder and Portal knew, the oil plan would not succeed, and they perceived that he was challenging them.

Portal responded November 5. "At the risk of dubbing me another panacea merchant, I believe the air offensive against oil gives us by far the best hope of complete victory in the next few months." He called the oil campaign a battle between destruction and repair. "In the oil campaign, I do not believe that the bombers can afford to give a single point away over and above the many that we shall be compelled to give away in direct support of the land forces, and in deference to the Admiralty's uneasiness about the coming U-boat offensive.

"In light of available intelligence, I feel that the whole war situation is poised on 'oil' as on a knife edge, and that by a real concentration of effort at this time we might push it over on the right side. Failure to concentrate in this manner might well prolong the war by several months at least."

Harris replied the next day, grudgingly admitting that there was a justifiable urgency for developing an effective oil plan. He said he regretted Portal's apparent impression that he did not understand the importance of the oil plan, because "that is entirely wrong."

Portal was not satisfied with Harris's words; he knew that Bomber Command's actions were quite to the contrary. In a letter on the twelfth, he told Harris that he felt it was his duty to remind his subordinate that Bomber Command must not lose any opportunity of attacking primary targets approved by the Air Staff's directives.

In reference to Harris's November 1 letter, in which he discussed the destruction of sixty German cities and claimed that their annihilation was the most effective way of bringing about the collapse of Germany, Portal told the commander in chief of Bomber Command, "I must confess, at times I wondered, whether the magnetism of the remaining German cities has not in the past tended as much to deflect our bombers from their primary objectives as the tactical and weather difficulties which you described so fully in your letter. I would like you to reassure me that this is not so. If I knew you to be as wholehearted in the attack on oil as in the past you have been in the matter of attacking cities, I would have little to worry about."

In the face of such direct orders, Harris assigned a considerable portion of his November efforts to the oil campaign. But he remained unconvinced that such attacks were worth the effort, and renewed his arguments in December.

Portal faced the issue squarely. He told Harris that the immediate task facing Allied strategic bomber forces was "to put out, and keep out of action, the eleven synthetic plants in central Germany." He reminded Harris that these plants were still producing 70 percent of Germany's surviving supplies of aviation and motor fuel. In blunt words, he told Harris, "There is no doubt in my mind that their immobilization, and the continued immobilization of the remaining major producers, would represent by far the greatest and most certain contribution that our strategic bombers could make to the achievement of an early decision in the German war.

"If you allow your obvious doubts in this direction to influence your conduct of operations, I very much fear that the prize may yet slip through our fingers. It is difficult for me," Portal wrote, "to feel that your staff can be devoting its maximum thought and energies to the accomplishment of your first priority task if you, yourself, are not wholehearted in support of it."

Harris remained stubbornly opposed to the oil plan. In a letter to Portal December 28, he said he resented Portal's suggestion that his lack of belief in the plan was being reflected in the conduct of operations.

Portal had enough justification to fire Harris for insubordination, but he could not bring himself to take the irrevocable step. He continued to try to change Harris's views. He warned his bomber chief that his failure to destroy the Schweinfurt plants to achieve a drastic reduction in Germany's war-making capabilities had been similar to his present failure to proceed with top priority in the oil campaign.

Portal believed Harris's area offensive had become a self-defeating policy and, after German air defenses had ceased to be effective with the advance of Allied ground troops, a policy whose reason for being no longer existed. He told Harris that his general area-bombing campaign had become a vicious circle, effective only because of the effectiveness of the American daylight-bombing campaign and the invasion. He said development of precision techniques by Bomber Command made such area attacks unnecessary and nonproductive.

It was a frustrating and difficult situation for both men because no common ground of understanding was possible. The charges and countercharges caused dissension in the ranks that could have been avoided if Harris had been more tractable on this issue. Instead, he played his trump card: Harris told his chief that it might be appropriate to replace him.

The chief of the Air Staff backed down. Portal wrote Harris January 20, 1945, that he would accept his assurances that he would do his utmost to follow the policies of the Air Staff. "I am very sorry that you do not believe in it, but it is of no use my craving for what is evidently unattainable. We must wait until after the end of the war before we can know for certain who is right, and I sincerely hope that until then you will continue in command of the force which has done so much toward defeating the enemy, and has brought such credit and renown to yourself and the air force."

29

BATTLE OF THE BULGE

While the ground war continued to stagnate through the early part of November, the tempo of the air war picked up, and many German targets still proved to be well defended.

The nose of the plane in which Lieutenant Robert E. Femoyer was the navigator near Merseburg on November 2 seemed to explode as three antiaircraft shells slashed through it. He twisted in agony as shell fragments ripped into his back and side.

When a crew member tried to inject morphine to ease Femoyer's extreme pain, he refused it, knowing that he had to have all his wits about him if he was to navigate the shattered bomber back to England.

Even though he was unable to sit up, Femoyer asked to be propped on the floor so that he could see his charts and instruments. For two and a half hours, despite heavy loss of blood and excruciating pain, he gave the pilot precise directions on how to fly a course to home base.

Only after the plane was safely on the ground did he permit injection of a pain-killer. He died shortly afterward, but his heroism and self-sacrifice were rewarded by posthumous bestowal of the Medal of Honor.

A week later, Lieutenant Donald J. Gott of the 452nd Group felt his bomber shudder as antiaircraft fire exploded all around it just before bombs were released on the marshaling yards at Saarbrücken November 9. After a call to members of the crew to report damage assessments, he learned that three engines were damaged beyond use, with flames from one of them shooting back to the tail.

With great effort, he held the airplane in formation until their bombs were dropped. Now some flares had ignited in the cockpit, and slashed hydraulic lines spurted fluid all over them.

To make matters worse, the interphone system failed. Just before it did, Gott learned that the engineer had been wounded in the leg, and the radio operator's arm was severed below the elbow. So intense was the operator's pain that he lapsed into a coma while a tourniquet was being placed on his arm.

Gott discussed the situation with his copilot, Lieutenant William E. Metzger, Jr., knowing they faced an explosion any second. Something had to be done quickly to save the radio operator's life. Gott decided that their best chances were in flying the flaming aircraft to friendly territory and attempt to crash-land.

The bomber somehow managed to survive, despite its crippled condition, and once over Allied territory, Gott told all those able to bail out to do so. Metzger elected to remain to assist Gott in landing the plane.

Gott turned the bomber in a shallow bank toward the side of his one good engine, but a hundred feet from the ground the plane exploded and all three were killed.

Gott's and Metzger's posthumous Medal of Honor citations referred to their loyalty to their crew and their knowing performance of their last services to their country as examples of valor at its highest.

General Eisenhower had tried to be tolerant of Field Marshal Bernard Montgomery's comments about his alleged failures to press harder against the Nazi armies in the fall of 1944, and even of his public disagreements with some Allied strategists, but he finally decided he would take no more. He prepared a cablegram for President Roosevelt that said, "I have reached the end of my limits. It's me or Montgomery. One of us must go. Now!"

Major General Francis W. De Guingand, Montgomery's chief of staff, was appalled by the rupture. "General Eisenhower, let me take this to Monty. I'll be back before twenty-four hours. But let me have twenty-four hours to talk to Monty."

Eisenhower agreed, and the proposed cablegram was shown to Montgomery. "All right," he said. "Showdown! If it comes to a showdown, Churchill will back me up."

De Guingand said, "Yes, he certainly will, Monty, but he hasn't got the marbles. If it comes to a showdown between the president and Churchill, I can assure you that you have lost your command."

This information completely deflated Montgomery. He wrote Eisenhower a most conciliatory note, and signed it, "Your obedient servant, Montgomery."

As the Allied armies continued to push eastward through Holland and Belgium toward Germany, the RAF's Bomber Command was called upon more often to carry out daylight attacks against tactical targets in support of ground forces.

November 16, Flight Lieutenant Doug McKinnon sat with his crew while 50 Squadron at Lincolnshire was briefed for an attack against the town of Düren, an important road and rail center between Aachen and Cologne. Other groups, they were told, would bomb the town of Jülich to the north.

Later, crossing the coast near Dunkirk, McKinnon's Lancaster was part of a long stream of bombers flying in the same manner as at night. Below, a pocket of German troops still held out, and McKinnon noticed a small amount of flak around them. He was not concerned at first, but then his number-four engine began acting rough. Flight Engineer Robert Bell called out that the oil pressure was dropping and the engine's temperature was rising.

"S" *Sugar* was an older Lancaster, but she had earned a good reputation by somehow always managing to bring her crew home safely. McKinnon had faith in her as he feathered the bad engine. Presently, two squadron aircraft flew alongside, with their crews making thumbs-up gestures, so McKinnon ignored their problems and concentrated on the job ahead.

As they ran up to the target, McKinnon was shocked to see what appeared to be smoke pouring out of a right engine of the Lancaster ahead of them. The "smoke" disappeared as suddenly as it had appeared, and McKinnon realized that it was not smoke at all but fuel. Evidently a bomb dropped from a German aircraft above them had hit the bomber's starboard wing, rupturing the main fuel tank. What at first appeared to be a pending disaster was quickly rectified by the skill of Pilot Officer William Drinkell.

After bombs were dropped, they all turned for home. They crossed the coast of England at dusk, so navigation lights were turned on.

Just as it appeared they were "home free," McKinnon was startled by the loud hammering of the hydraulic accumulator. Flight Engineer Bell reported that the piston was rising and falling even though no hydraulic circuits had been selected. Worse, Bell said there was no pressure in the accumulator. This meant they had lost all their hydraulic fluid; they would be unable to lower the undercarriage normally, but would have to rely upon emergency compressed air.

Over Lincolnshire, McKinnon called the tower to advise them he was on three engines, without hydraulic power and unable to lower his flaps. This meant he would be coming in "hot"—at a higher rate of speed than safety allowed.

The tower told him to keep clear of the approach pattern for thirty minutes until all other aircraft had landed.

McKinnon acknowledged, and uneasily circled the field. Once he had permission to land, he blew the undercarriage down with compressed air and started his approach. Directly ahead was the magnificent Lincoln Cathedral, so he was unable to come in as shallowly as he would have wished. He came down steeply, desperately trying to keep the speed as low as possible and get on the ground before his fuel ran out.

He quickly saw he was much too high and coming in much too fast, so he decided to go around, while the tension mounted and he fought to keep his emotions under control.

Before he could attempt another landing, the tower told him to go to Carnaby, eighty miles distant, where he could make a long, low approach over the sea. He knew his fuel supply was low, so he was concerned about those extra miles, but he decided to try. At last, he was near Carnaby and started his approach from the sea. With consummate skill, McKinnon set the Lancaster down, and so high was its rate of speed that it took every foot of the six thousand-foot runway to stop the bomber. Just as he turned off the airstrip, all the engines quit. "*S*" *Sugar* had come home again, but it almost did not make it this time.

Flight Lieutenant Ron A. Pickler settled into his seat at 10:00 A.M. November 27 in the briefing room of 514 Squadron at Waterbeach in East Anglia. Once the doors were closed, the curtain covering the large map of Europe on the wall above the podium was drawn back and Pickler's eyes anxiously followed the black tape as it ran from their base to Cologne.

Until recently, heavy-bomber squadrons of 3 Group had confined their operations to night attacks. Now, on Pickler's twenty-first mission, they were going again into the heart of Germany in daylight. At first, British day missions had been restricted to France until aircrews gained experience. This was not Pickler's first experience on a long daylight mission because his plane had taken part in the raid on Essen a few weeks before, and it was the best-defended target in the Ruhr.

He gathered his crew together after the briefing and they went out to their Lancaster on the flight line at 11:50.

Warrant Officer B. A. "Cliff" Clifford, their bomb aimer, had already completed one operational tour of thirty trips and was only required to make twenty trips on his second tour. This was Clifford's twentieth, and he had already decided to stay on with the crew and complete a third tour of ten more trips. Once the armorers completed the loading of the last bomb, Clifford carefully checked the one 4,000-pound "cookie" blockbuster, and the fifteen 500-pound general-purpose bombs.

Pickler started engines at 11:55 and taxied out fifteen minutes later. He was grateful for the good weather as they took off and began to climb routinely to nine thousand feet to pick up their wingmen.

Sergeant Laurie Woodroofe checked out a new device called "Gee-H," a modified form of the Gee navigational aid, which his squadron was first to acquire. It was designed specifically for bombing through heavy cloud cover. Woodroofe was the best Gee-H man in the squadron, so Pickler's crew usually was given the dubious honor of leading the squadron. This time three other Lancasters from a nearby base at Wichford joined them, and the rest of the bomber stream fell in line as they climbed to twenty thousand feet.

Pickler was given a course by Woodroofe as they crossed the English coast south of the seaside town of Aldeburgh. He led his formation over the North Sea, crossing the coast of Belgium northwest of Brugge. At Halle, he turned northeast to a point ten miles north of Hasselt, then flew east to Wassenberg, and finally southeast for the run to Cologne.

Pickler watched for their P-51 Mustang escorts, and as the American fighters joined them at Wassenberg he felt reassured.

As they approached the target, Woodroofe turned on the Gee-H set, but it promptly burned out. Fortunately, there were no clouds, so they could bomb visually.

Cologne's huge marshaling yard appeared directly ahead, just as German flak exploded around them. Flight Sergeant G. "Brook" Coulson, in the rear turret, commented that the flak was getting close, while in the upper turret, Flight Sergeant "Doug" Craig used a few choice expletives to deride the poor accuracy of the German gunners.

Pickler headed straight for the target without evasive action. A glance to either side was reassuring; the bomber stream now had bunched up, and Lancasters were all around them.

Sergeant Norrie Coultous, the wireless operator, momentarily popped his head into the astrodome above his radio. He shouted, "Skip, they're on to us!"

Simultaneously, the Lancaster shook from a blast that seemed to come from just under the tail.

There were brief outbursts of "Christ!" and "What the hell was that?" which stopped instantly when bombardier Clifford called, "Left, left!" as he guided them to the release point.

No one spoke for thirty seconds. Then, Pickler felt the familiar shudder and heard Cliff's "Bombs gone!" at precisely 3:00 P.M.

Pickler was concerned about the gunners, although the Lancaster seemed to be flying normally. Coulson reported that his rear turret had suffered a lot of damage and that his hydraulic system was out, but that he was unhurt.

Craig, in the upper turret, said simply, "I'm hit."

Norrie Coultous called that he was OK and going back to help Craig.

Up front, Pickler noted with relief that no one had been hit.

Coultous reported that he had Craig out of his turret and onto the rest bed. Blood was streaming from under his helmet, but otherwise he seemed unhurt. Removing Craig's helmet, Coultous found several pieces of metal sticking out of the back of his head. It had been drummed into them many times during training that under no circumstances should they attempt to remove anything that was deeply embedded because they might not be able to stanch the flow of blood from the wound. Coultous, therefore, covered the wounds with a shell dressing and made Craig as comfortable as possible.

The planned route away from the target called for them to continue another thirty miles into Germany before returning home by a round-about route. Pickler was so concerned about Craig's condition that he turned out of the bomber stream and headed straight for home base.

He had hardly left the bomber stream than a flight of P-51s drew level and Pickler ordered the firing of a red flare to alert the American fighter pilots of their situation, hoping they would understand and escort them home. Pickler was upset when they turned away.

He had started a slow descent to increase their airspeed and they were down to seventeen thousand feet when the flight engineer, Sergeant Alf Gair, checking the rear fuselage for damage, reported that he had found some broken control cables. Almost simultaneously, the nose of the aircraft pitched up violently and the bomber went into a near-vertical climb, its airspeed dropping alarmingly. Clifford, who had been standing beside Pickler, threw his shoulder against the control wheel while Wood-roofe jumped up behind Pickler's seat and, reaching around the armor plate, put both his hands over the pilot's and pushed with all his might.

The three of them got the nose down enough to avoid stalling, and Pickler wedged his right knee behind the control column to get sufficient leverage to bring the aircraft level, wincing with the pain as bolts on the column pressed into his kneecap.

Pickler lowered the landing gear, which reduced their airspeed and thereby relieved some of the strain. Coultous went looking for a piece of rope and found one that was normally used to stop the rubber dinghy from floating away when it was thrown overboard following a ditching. He tied the rope around the control wheel, passing it under the instrument panel, while Clifford, Woodroofe, and Craig went down into the bomb-aimer's compartment in the nose and, by pulling forward on the rope, managed to take a lot of the pressure off the pilot's knee.

Pickler relaxed momentarily, but then the bomber started to yaw from side to side. There was no rudder movement, so he decided the rear turret must be swinging. Repeated calls to Brook Coulson brought no response, so Norrie Coultous went aft to see what was going on. He found Coulson in the turret, which was swinging erratically, and he noted that the oxygen-supply hose to the turret was severed. Coulson was unconscious due to lack of oxygen. Somehow, the five-foot, 120-pound Coultous dragged the much heavier tail gunner in his heavy, bulky flying suit out of the turret and plugged him into an emergency oxygen bottle. In a few seconds, Coulson regained consciousness and came forward to take his turn applying pressure on the rope in the pilot's compartment to keep the Lancaster from pitching up.

Coultous returned to his radio set and began to transmit Mayday signals, and the Lancaster reached the Belgian coast without further incident. There, they were greeted by the welcome sight of a Warwick Air-Sea Rescue aircraft, complete with underslung lifeboat, homing in on them.

The Warwick escorted them across the North Sea to Woodbridge, an emergency field on the English coast a few miles northeast of Ipswich. Woodbridge was one of three emergency airfields constructed specifically for damaged aircraft returning across the North Sea. The single runway was actually three runways side by side, and it was double the length of the normal RAF field with long, unobstructed undershoot and overshoot areas.

Pickler had a problem lining up with the runway because the rope attached to the pilot's wheel prevented him from using the ailerons. And with one knee jammed behind the column to prevent it from moving backward, he was unable to operate the rudders. Finally, Pickler managed to achieve directional control by varying the throttles of the four engines.

Pickler anxiously watched the rate of descent. It was uneven because he could only control it by alternately pulling and releasing the rope.

The Lancaster touched down smoothly at 180 miles an hour, and Pickler was grateful for the extra runway length.

Craig was rushed to the hospital by an ambulance while the slightly hysterical crew inspected the damage to their aircraft. The rear turret looked as if it had been battered by a massive sledgehammer. The canopy was shattered, and the floor was covered with shrapnel. There were more than thirty holes in the aft fuselage and horizontal stabilizer. Two of them were large enough to crawl through. The mid-upper turret looked like a colander, and the floor of the fuselage was littered with shrapnel and spotted with blood.

They soon found the cause of their near-fatal stall: The elevator trim tabs were jammed in the full-down position, which had forced the elevators hard-up!

When they got to the mess, they were surprised to find Craig already there, awake and with a large bandage around his head. It turned out that the pieces of flak were not deeply embedded after all, although the fact that he later found three more pieces stuck in his helmet persuaded him that he was indeed a very lucky bloke.

After dinner, a truck took them back to Waterbeach where they learned they had been reported shot down, having been seen to "explode over the target" by none other than Pickler's roommate.

As they parted at the mess, Clifford turned thoughtfully to Pickler. "I guess that's it, skip. I won't be doing that next ten trips after all."

Pickler, knowing that Clifford had just completed a second tour, said, "I don't blame you."

Pickler had a vivid reminder of their near-tragedy—as if one were needed. While his right knee had been jammed against the control column, two bolts located just below the wheel had pressed into his knee so hard that he carried their impression for weeks.

Attacks against Germany's railroad systems in the fall of 1944 had proved more effective than was realized at the time. Critical materials, destroyed or delayed by air attacks, caused shortages of all munitions and weapons by the start of the new year, frustrating the German High Command.

In *Inside the Third Reich,* Speer said, "Signs of total anarchy loomed before us. Coal trains no longer reached their destinations but were stopped en route by Gauleiters who confiscated them for their own needs. Moreover, available rail capacity for economic traffic in Germany was reduced to a point that could not hope to sustain, over any period of time, a high level of war production. The loss of transportation facilities completely disorganized the flow of basic war materials, components, and semifinished materials, and production was no longer possible."

The original Air War Plans Division plan had envisioned just such an occurrence because transportation was the lifeblood of the German nation. If coal was not available to fuel the trains, then more coal could not be delivered by trains to steel plants and power stations. When coal stocks dropped to an eighteen-day level in October of 1944, then to a four-and-one-half-day supply in February of 1945, and to less than a day's supply in March, orderly production of all manufactured goods was brought to a halt.

Due to the original slack in the mobilization of Germany's economy for war, production did not fall away appreciably as factories were hit. Revitalized under the genius of Albert Speer from 1941 to September 1944, production actually trebled. During this period, the strategic air offensive likewise had not really started in force. Then, in four months, massive air attacks caused the fully extended German production to collapse.

The lull in the ground war was rudely shattered by Hitler's surprise initiative on December 16, when he sent his armies through the Ardennes. Hitler hoped to sever the communications lines of the United States First and Ninth armies and the Twenty-first Army Group, and possibly destroy twenty to thirty Allied divisions.

While clouds covered the front, grounding Allied airpower, the Wehrmacht drove a sixty-mile wedge through thinly held American lines in the Ardennes forest in an action later dubbed the "Battle of the Bulge."

When the weather cleared December 23, the full weight of Allied tactical and strategic air forces was thrown into the battle, and the German offensive was stopped.

Brigadier General Frederick W. Castle, assistant commander of the 4th Bombardment Wing, led a large number of heavy bombers against German airfields on Christmas Eve. En route to Germany he was forced to relinquish command because of failure of one engine. Knowing they were over Allied troops, he refused to permit jettisoning of his bombs, although he realized the flight back to base would be difficult on three engines.

After he turned for home, his aircraft was jumped by German fighters, whose shells ripped open the left wing of his bomber and set the oxygen system on fire. A quick check of the crew revealed two of his men were wounded. For a moment he thought they might elude German fighters without further damage, but attacks persisted, starting fires in two engines, and Castle knew the bomber would explode any moment.

"Bail out!" he yelled.

The airplane was practically out of control, but he stayed at the controls so that his men could leave the aircraft safely. Just as the last man left the stricken bomber, fighters swept in and their cannon fire exploded the fuel tanks in the right wing. Castle had lost his last chance to escape, and he rode the plunging bomber to his death. His Medal of Honor citation said his willing sacrifice of his life to save members of his crew was in keeping with the highest traditions of the service.

The Germans were forced to abandon their drive toward the Meuse River by the end of the month and elected to concentrate their strongest forces against Bastogne to widen the salient along the III Corps's front. Brigadier General Anthony McAuliffe's famous reply to a demand from the Germans that he surrender his men surrounded at Bastogne was a contemptuous "Nuts!"

The battlefield was in such a fluid state there was confusion everywhere at first, compounded by Germans in American uniforms infiltrating the Allied rear. The heroic defenses put up by Allied troops at Saint-Vith and Bastogne, both important highway-network hubs, plus massive air raids, doomed the offensive.

During the first week of January 1945, the lines seesawed back and forth while bad weather impeded the movement of General George S. Patton's armored corps.

After Patton's breakthrough, and under pressure from four American corps against the German southern and northern flanks, with the British

30th Corps exerting pressure on the center of the line, the Germans were forced to retreat, but they withdrew slowly, with fierce rear-guard actions that set up roadblocks, booby traps, and obstructions in a disconcertingly efficient manner.

The Germans launched their last counteroffensive in the Sixth Army sector on New Year's day. While GIs, British Tommies, and other Allied soldiers fought well, the back of the Ardennes offensive was broken by tactical and strategic airpower that virtually paralyzed all traffic west of the Rhine River and caused a critical supply problem for the German armies.

Eisenhower committed heavy bombers to carpet-bomb towns believed used by the Germans as ordnance centers. Tragically, Malmédy, which was occupied by Allied troops, was bombed by mistake and heavy casualties resulted.

After delaying the Allied timetable six weeks, German troops fell back, drained of vitality, with the loss of irreplaceable reserves.

Once the last German resistance had collapsed, Allied superiority in tanks, men, and combat aircraft brought an end to Hitler's desperate gamble, prompting Churchill to say that the "greatest American battle of the war" was won.

The setback caused disillusionment in high Allied military circles about an early end to the war, and advances were made with more caution.

General Omar Bradley said later that after the Ardennes offensive, both the Russians and the Allies in the west were able to continue a war of movement because Allied air attacks had denied oil to the Germans. He said the German retreat from the Ardennes was slow and costly to them because supply trucks had to be drained to fill the tanks of fighting vehicles.

Bradley told officials of the United States Strategic Bombing Survey, "The withdrawal of the Sixth SS Panzer Army, begun in daylight on 22 January 1945, was marked mainly by success of the United States fighter-bombers against its tanks and trucks. When the Allies' threat shifted north of the Aachen sector, the enemy was unable to sidestep his mobile formations to meet it in the measure he sought—again for lack of gasoline. When the Allied breakthrough followed west of the Rhine in February, across the Rhine in March, and throughout Germany in April, lack of gasoline in countless local situations was the direct factor behind the destruction or surrender of vast quantities of trucks and tanks and thousands upon thousands of enemy troops."

On the eastern front, German forces, restricted by lack of gasoline, were unable to cope with the Russian onslaught. At Baranov bridgehead, two hundred German tanks, which had been massed to hold the position, were immobilized because they had no fuel and were overrun by the Russians.

Speer and General Alfred Jodl told postwar interrogators that the Russians could not have broken out of the Baranov bridgehead and captured Upper Silesia if it had not been for the fuel shortage. Even Marshal Stalin, who had often spoken slightingly of Allied airpower's effects on the war's outcome, said that the strategic air offensive against the German's oil resources played a vital part in making Russian victories possible in the east.

American insistence on precision attacks against strategic targets, instead of the British concept of area bombing, had paid off according to prewar plans.

AWPD-1, the plan developed prior to America's entry into the war, had expressed serious doubts about the effect of mass bombings on German civilian morale. It was believed that to be truly effective, such efforts would have had to utterly destroy Germany's cities.

During the war, 25 million Germans were subjected to bombing attacks; 305,000 civilians were killed and another 780,000 injured. There's no question that the suffering of the German population was intense, not just from the effects of the bombing, but due to dislocation of five million more people. Toward the end, their suffering was so abject that their emotions were primarily those of anger, not only against the Allies, but against their own leaders.

In retrospect, it seems apparent that British attacks would have been far more useful if it had been possible to direct them against selected targets vital to Germany's war-making potential rather than on the cities of the Reich. It must be understood, however, that British bombers and escort fighters were unable to sustain themselves in early daylight attacks because they were not armed and armored sufficiently to withstand heavily armed German fighters. Therefore, they had no choice but to engage in night area attacks against cities. Unfortunately, the British most of the time were unable to distinguish and destroy selected industrial targets at night. Such a failure was not due to any lack of courage or diligence among the fliers involved, but to the limitations of equipment developed by British scientists to assure accuracy under all conditions.

In early 1945, Germany was all but defeated, but her true situation was not known to the Allies. Even Arnold had doubts about the effectiveness of the air war. He had noted reports that seemed to indicate factories all over Germany had been destroyed, yet the Germans still appeared capable of resistance on the ground and even of mounting an offensive like the recent one in the Ardennes.

He wrote Spaatz, "We have a superiority of at least five to one now against Germany and yet, in spite of all our hopes, anticipations, dreams, and plans we have as yet not been able to capitalize to the extent which we should. We may not be able to force capitulation of Germany by air attacks, but, on the other hand, with this tremendous striking power, it would seem to me that we should get much better and much more decisive results than we are getting now. I am not criticizing, because frankly I don't know the answer, and what I am now doing is letting my thoughts run wild with the hope that out of this you may get a glimpse, a light, a new thought, or something which will help us to bring this war to a close sooner."

Spaatz was equally pessimistic, fearing that a secret Nazi weapon might be thrown into the war. He had heard intelligence reports about a new gun with a five hundred-foot barrel that could fire explosives a long distance. And he was aware that new and more deadly German submarines had appeared in the Atlantic. His most crucial anxiety stemmed from reports of new jet fighters that might well prove disastrous to his bomber fleets.

His concern about jet fighters was not new. Back in September 1944, he had directed that factories producing these new jets should have priority just under that for oil targets. Harris, however, believed jet fighters posed no threat to his night bombers because their great speed would be a handicap at night.

Conventional German fighter production had almost doubled from September to November, and production of twin-engine fighters rose from 675 to 855. The Luftwaffe started to concentrate most of its attacks on Allied bombers. Precious gasoline had to be hoarded, but when Allied formations had struck the synthetic oil plant at Merseburg November 2, four hundred German fighters surprised bomber crews by rising to challenge them after a lapse of several days. One formation was attacked from the rear by sixty German fighters, and twenty-six bombers plummeted to earth.

Spaatz wired Arnold that more bombers would have been lost except for almost perfect Allied fighter cover.

Air commanders were concerned not only about jet fighters, but also German use of heavier-caliber explosive shells and incendiary bullets, which, if fired from outside the range of the .50-caliber guns in American bombers, might easily make Allied daylight raids even more costly.

Doolittle expressed concern because the Eighth Air Force had insufficient escorts—only one for every two bombers—when a one-for-one ratio was desirable. He was so concerned about Eighth losses that he had told his staff in mid-November that the Eighth might have to drop its other strategic objectives and concentrate on defeat of the German air force all over again.

Spaatz was equally concerned about the likelihood of a German air force resurgence. He had told Arnold in December that the Germans had a very formidable fighter strength, admitting that though less effective, plane for plane, it was numerically larger than it had ever been.

The Germans learned that air-to-air missiles were most effective against American bomber formations. Generalleutnant Johannes Steinhoff, who fought the big bombers all during 1943 and 1944, found them useful after he activated Germany's first jet fighter wing with the ME-262. Twenty-four 50 mm missiles were attached beneath each jet fighter's wing; when all were fired in salvo, results were good up to one thousand meters. At close range, these missiles seldom failed to make a kill. Unfortunately for the Germans, by this time the skill of their fighter pilots had declined due to losses of the most experienced ones, and morale was at a low ebb. Jet fighters, too, were not available in sufficient quantities to be potentially decisive until early in 1945.

These new fighters, knowing there was no American or British fighter available that could shoot them down, gave Doolittle fits. Some ME-262s were destroyed while landing, but not one was shot down in the air. Propeller-driven fighters were simply no match for them.

In advance of massive raids, the Eighth sent twelve-plane formations to drop "window" to "snow up" German radar. On one mission, ME-262s concentrated on these formations, and all aircraft dispensing "window" were shot down.

The British and the Germans had started almost simultaneously to design jet engines, but both suffered delays due to bureaucratic and political bias. In Germany, Messerschmitt and Milch had been to see Hitler to urge production of a new experimental jet engine in the fall of 1941, while the great German drive on Moscow was in full swing. Hitler asked how soon it could be operational. When he was told it would take two years, he vetoed the project. It would not be necessary, he said, because the war was already won. The British also failed to respond to the same urgent recommendations, despite pleas by Sir Frank Whittles who developed the first workable jet engine in England.

In the spring of 1943, the ME-262 had proved itself after a period of intensive testing. It was the first airplane to be powered by a turbojet engine, and even Göring was impressed by its performance. Hitler was not convinced, insisting upon a retaliatory jet bomber, and the project was denied a production priority.

After Hitler finally gave a production go-ahead to the fighter version, 1,433 were built, but only 100 were used in combat. They proved deadly adversaries, flashing through bomber formations with four 30 mm cannons blazing away, and out of sight before most gunners could get their wits about them. In a short time, thirty B-17s were shot down.

Spaatz worried even more about German jet fighters after the first of the year when more of them put in an appearance. He feared they might upset the Allied balance of power. He even told Arnold that he was also concerned about some kind of a German death ray, or a motor-stopping beam of which he had heard rumors from Allied intelligence sources.

Attacks against jet-fighter production facilities had been hampered during the fall of 1944 by bad weather, and radar bombing had to be employed even though it was far less accurate.

Spaatz would have been relieved if he had known how hopeless the situation was considered by the average German pilot. They often had to fight far from their bases and frequently became so disoriented in bad weather they picked the first field they could find, so that aircraft were scattered all over the countryside. Navigational aids became so unreliable they were of little use.

There was only a limited number of seasoned German pilots as 1944 ended. The majority were very young and inexperienced. With the desperate fuel situation, new pilots were trained in a few hours and put into the cockpit of a combat fighter.

Adolf Galland had been using his limited fuel reserves to concentrate on certain missions. By refusing to dissipate his fighter strength in futile attacks against all Allied air attacks, he hoped to destroy as many as four hundred bombers at a time by using his entire fighter command on one mission.

Göring continued to make outrageous and impossible demands. He raged at his commanders, calling them cowards and threatening to transfer them to the infantry. Toward the end, Galland was removed as commander of fighter forces and he returned to head a combat group.

Against this rather desperate backdrop, the Germans were developing the Komet, the first rocket fighter. This egg-shaped aircraft was still in the experimental stage in late 1944. It was difficult to fly and had a tendency to explode on landing because its two-wheel takeoff dolly had to be dropped after the plane left the ground and a skid used to land. Its flight time was restricted to ten minutes because it quickly exhausted its fuel supply. It could climb rapidly toward a bomber formation and make a quick pass with guns blazing, but was then forced to land. It was a deadly weapon, but fortunately for the Allies only a few were operational before the end of the war. One rocket pilot proved how lethal the interceptor could be by shooting down three Flying Fortresses in rapid succession.

The Komet was used first in August 1944 against Allied bombers raiding Leipzig. Its crash rate was extremely high because it could not be maneuvered while being rocket propelled. Once its maximum speed was reduced, however, it was very maneuverable. It could glide better than a conventional fighter because it was so light, and it could outmaneuver any other fighter at low speeds. Some were shot down as they glided in for landings.

Development of these weapons was hindered by the German High

Command, which had always been oriented to ground warfare. Alexander M. Lippisch, who designed the Komet, had an additional problem. He and Wilhelm "Willy" Messerschmitt, who had designed the jet fighter, did not get along. The brilliant Messerschmitt refused to back a design that had not originated with him, so the rocket fighter came too late to help Nazi Germany in her final hours.

Premier Stalin increased his demands on the American and British leaders to provide more strategic air support for his Russian armies, which now were threatening the heart of Saxony. He had long accused the western powers of relaxing their attacks in the east to favor their armies on the western front.

Prior to the Yalta Conference of February 4 –11, Churchill believed some kind of action should be taken by the Allies to convince Stalin that they were providing all-out support for the Russian drive in Saxony. At the conference, it was agreed that Portal's and Spaatz's bomber commands should attack Dresden, the main center of communications in that eastern area. Neither Harris nor Spaatz was happy with the order, believing that destruction of such a city—an architectural wonder—at this late date was unnecessary, although they did not resist it. The plan that was worked out by the Combined Operational Planning Committee called for Spaatz's Eighth to attack the rail center in daylight, while Harris's Bomber Command attacked the city at night.

Dresden's population had doubled to 1.3 million people by the night of February 12/13, many of whom were homeless women and children fleeing the advancing Russian armies. Most of them had never heard an air-raid siren.

Harris sent 244 Lancasters out first with crews expert in starting urban fires to create a fire storm and attract fire brigades from the surrounding areas. The fire storm was started, proving so intense that it engulfed eight square miles and sucked many victims into the heart of the fire. Bodies of human beings shriveled to half their size on scorching pavements. Then another wave of 550 Lancasters came over, causing a havoc that no other city had ever endured as the result of one raid.

While British night crews were being debriefed in England, Flying Fortresses of the First Air Division approached the stricken city in daylight to bomb the rail yards. The Americans bombed the city instead because the rail targets were obscured by smoke and clouds, thus heaping more hell onto a city already tortured beyond imagining. It took the 450 B-17s only eleven minutes to destroy another eight hundred acres of the once-beautiful city. Later, P-47 fighter-bombers attacked key crossroads.

Destruction of Dresden was an unnecessary tragedy, and all Allied military and political leaders must share the blame. Certainly Portal and

Spaatz should have been more forceful in their opposition to the raid. After resisting many of Stalin's demands throughout the war, there was no need—nor was this the way—for Churchill at this late date to appease the Russians.

While Dresden was being battered, Harris had sent 717 bombers to hit Chemnitz, and four hundred others made diversionary raids. Chemnitz was saved from Dresden's fate by bad weather.

Arnold's headquarters in Washington sent an immediate inquiry following the raid. "Does this represent a change from American policy of bombing selected industrial structures to one of bombing cities?"

Spaatz wired back, emphatically denying any such change in strategic air policy.

As the world recoiled in horror over the destruction of a city with the war almost over, Churchill had second thoughts. He sent a memorandum to his military aide, General Sir Hastings Ismay, and Portal. "It seems to me that the moment has come when the question of bombing German cities, simply for the sake of increasing the terror, though under other pretexts, should be reviewed. The destruction of Dresden remains a serious query against the conduct of Allied bombing. I feel the need for more precise concentrations on military objectives such as oil and communications behind the immediate battle zone, rather than on mere acts of terror and wanton destruction however impressive."

He was rather late in coming to that conclusion.

30

GERMANY
MADE IMPOTENT
BY AIRPOWER

Any thought the Germans may have had of prolonging the war was dispelled in February 1945, when strategic air attacks reached their greatest intensity. Despite weather conditions that rarely permitted visual attacks, improved radar-bombing procedures made possible an attack against the primary targets on 80 percent of all missions. A series of raids against oil targets prevented any resurgence of production in this vital industry. Of the forty-seven attacks made by Harris's Bomber Command in 1945, more than half were against such targets.

The 305th Group was deep inside the Ruhr on February 10 when Lieutenant D. C. Shoemaker ordered Tokyo tanks shut off at 11:00 A.M. over their initial point. These auxiliary fuel tanks, which permitted long-range flights, were routinely shut off for fire safety after fuel was transferred into the plane's main tanks. Shoemaker turned the controls over to his copilot, Lieutenant R. P. Moullen, while he checked his instruments and ordered "window" dispensed to confuse ground radar operators who were directing antiaircraft guns.

Moullen was tense as he made a 360-degree turn between the initial point and the target in order to avoid another group, which was slipping in ahead of them.

At 11:05 A.M., they started on their bombing run while vicious flak burst around the group ahead. Antiaircraft bursts surrounded them just before bombs were released, and Shoemaker winced as the plane shuddered with the impact of shells in the tail section.

"Oh, God, I'm hit!" the tail gunner cried, and waist-gunner Sergeant R. K. Buckley rushed aft to give him medical aid. He was appalled to find that one of Sergeant G. L. Snyder's legs had been shot off at the knee and hung only by tendons and skin.

The top turret position was hit hard, and Sergeant I. Roisman noted with shock that there was a flak hole in the top of the dome where his head had been seconds before.

Shoemaker's concern grew as damage reports came over the intercom, noting there were sixteen holes in the radio compartment, and the operator, Staff Sergeant R. J. Benton, had three wounds in his left leg. He heard also that one shell had gone through the right wing, between the engines.

Despite continuous attacks, Buckley gave first aid to Snyder in the tail. Radio operator Benton dressed his own wounds while surveying the extent of the damage to his compartment. He was dismayed to find that his oxygen system was shot out and his radio set was so damaged as to be useless. In the tail, Buckley found that the morphine syringe in the first-aid kit was frozen, and he had to warm it before he could give the tail gunner a quarter grain to deaden his pain. While the morphine was thawing, he applied a tourniquet to Snyder's thigh to stop the bleeding.

To his relief, Shoemaker found all engines were functioning; but just then a shell exploded outside, flak tore through the pilot's windshield, and he slumped over.

Moullen checked him anxiously and, after finding no apparent wounds, decided the pilot was only stunned. After Shoemaker recovered, he went into the nose section to keep warm because the icy blast roaring through the shattered windshield was almost incapacitating.

Moullen maintained the plane's position in the formation as it swung over the coast to the North Sea and started to let down from twenty-four thousand feet. Just as he leveled off, the wheel was jerked from his hands as the plane was caught in the prop wash of the one ahead. The left rudder cable snapped, forcing Moullen to drop to a lower level to join another squadron. Despite his efforts, he found it impossible to hold pressure on the right pedal, so he called Sergeant Roisman to assist him. Even with their combined efforts, the airplane could not be controlled.

Shortly thereafter, smoke filled the pilot's compartment, and they noticed fire coming out of the right wing through a flak hole. Moullen watched with fear as the fire grew in intensity and the wing's skin started to curl from the heat.

"Bail out!" someone yelled.

The engineer reached behind the pilot's seat to get his parachute and handed Moullen his chute. A quick glance into the nose showed that the still-stunned Shoemaker was already wearing his. Roisman jettisoned the navigator's escape hatch. Then he noticed that the navigator, Lieutenant E. L. Pinkley, and the bombardier, Sergeant A. O. Cantue, were huddled in one corner and making no move to get out. He struck Cantue and motioned him to bail out, but the bombardier did not move.

"Let's ditch the damn thing!" Shoemaker yelled.

Moullen returned to his seat while the engineer fired distress flares. Meanwhile, the radio man and one of the gunners were at the waist hatch, the door to which was gone because gunner Buckley had bailed out.

Moullen started to slip the plane down to the North Sea as pieces of the wing flew off. He feathered numbers two and three engines because they were running away and he feared the propeller blades would spin off and slash through the fuselage. Shoemaker, still in a state of shock, stood between the pilot and copilot's seats but sat down just before the airplane hit the water at 90 miles an hour.

They had to evacuate immediately before the plane sank, and the radio operator and flight engineer worked frantically to open the top hatch, which had stuck. They knew that with both lower hatches open, the plane would fill rapidly with water.

The top hatch finally released and Roisman climbed out, noting the right dinghy was in the water but was only half inflated. The left life raft never did release. The pilot joined Roisman on top and the copilot quickly followed him.

Ball-turret gunner Sergeant Q. A. Bastanzi shouted, "Get away from the ship——!" Before anyone could stop him he jumped over the dinghy into the water. He went under and never resurfaced.

The navigator started to swim away, but his harness caught on the airplane; the copilot helped to free him.

Roisman yelled to Shoemaker, "Get in the dinghy!"

The pilot ignored him and, with blood streaming down his face, just stared dazedly into space.

The tail gunner never got out, and the bombardier panicked and refused to leave.

Roisman pulled the dinghy close to the pilot, but he would not get in. The copilot, meanwhile, tried to release the right dinghy, but he could not budge it. When the plane started to submerge, a piece of the tail section hit Roisman on the head and pulled both him and the dinghy beneath the surface as the plane went down nose first.

Roisman desperately fought his way up, finding the surface of the sea littered with debris.

Moullen searched for the pilot and tried to free the dinghy from the tail section before it, too, sank. Once it was freed, he climbed in and, using his hands, paddled over to help Roisman. After he had the engineer in the dinghy, he paddled over to the radio operator who, he could see, was in a bad way. His face was cut open on the left side, his lips were purple, and his eyes were glassy. Moullen got him to the side of the dinghy and struggled to haul him in, but Benton was dead.

Moullen spotted another body floating nearby while a Wellington rescue plane circled above. He helped Roisman to remove his parachute just as another "Wimpy" dropped smoke markers and flares. On the next swing, the Wellington dropped a lifeboat by parachute, but it drifted away from them. They managed to paddle to a line about forty-five feet away, and Moullen latched on to it. Now, a rescue boat arrived and they were picked up. Roisman was in such a bad way that he was taken to a Royal Navy hospital. The experiences of Shoemaker's crew showed again that the war, though winding down, was no less deadly.

Germany's rail system was under such a heavy strain by March that the Combined Chiefs of Staff gave first priority to all transportation targets. The effects of attacks against rail and waterway systems was immediate in the Saar and Ruhr regions. Attacks on the four major waterways severed traffic on the Rhine and north German canals. Through traffic to the Ruhr came to a standstill, and eventually the movement of coal by barges to south Germany ceased altogether. Rail traffic was reduced to the point that car loadings had dropped 76 percent by March 3.

Eisenhower now approved plans to destroy the eighty-two battered German divisions on the western front, which, actually, had suffered so many casualties that only twenty-seven were at full strength. Three thrusts were planned toward the Rhine, with Montgomery's 21st Army Group in the north split so the Canadian First and British Second Armies could strike southeast toward the Ruhr. Meanwhile, the United States Ninth Army was ordered to move northeast. The strategy was to drive the Germans out of the region between the Meuse and the Rhine and clear the west bank of the Rhine, which faced the Ruhr basin, of all German troops. General Bradley's 12th Army Group, which included the United States First and Third armies, was assigned to drive north of the Moselle and, with the help of Patton's Third Army, reach the Rhine near Koblenz. In the south, Lieutenant General Devers's 6th Army Group, consisting of the United States Seventh Army and the French First Army, was to attack a German force near Colmar and drive the Germans across the west bank of the Rhine from Strasbourg to the Swiss border, and then link up with Patton's army.

The British and Canadians ran into strong opposition in the Reichswald forest, and their progress was impeded by heavy rains, which slowed tank operations. After the Ruhr River was deliberately flooded by the Germans, the United States Ninth Army was delayed two weeks by stubborn German rear action. Progress in the south went more smoothly; Devers's 6th Army Group destroyed a large German force and linked up with Patton.

During their retreat across the Rhine, the Germans methodically destroyed practically all bridges. Eisenhower's ground forces were surprised, however, when a platoon of the Ninth Armored Division found the Ludendorf railroad bridge over the Rhine at Remagen still standing. Troops seized it minutes before the Germans were scheduled to blow it up.

In the next ten days, before the bridge collapsed under intense German air and artillery barrages, five divisions moved across and immediately set up a twenty-mile bridgehead so that still more troops could cross the Rhine.

Since the start of 1945, General Marshall had called for widespread attacks on communications targets all over Germany. British Bomber Command devoted its major attacks to the Ruhr to help isolate it from the rest of Germany. Such attacks had long been advocated by Tedder.

Before Eisenhower's armies crossed the Rhine, British attacks were concentrated on railway centers because eight out of the seventeen main centers were still in operation. Although Portal and Spaatz feared such attacks might divert effort from the oil offensive, by the beginning of April the principal parts of the oil and communications plans had been executed. Speer told Hitler on March 15 that "the German economy is heading for an inevitable collapse within four to eight weeks."

There was no doubt that the end was in sight. With the Russians moving toward Vienna and Berlin, and Eisenhower's troops crossing the Rhine on a wide front, it was only a question of time until Germany collapsed.

The advancing armies reported unbelievable devastation everywhere, and even Spaatz was surprised at the magnitude of the destruction his planes had helped to wreak.

Eaker received a cable from Marshall in March, telling him to meet Marshall in the south of France.

He and Spaatz arrived at their hotel at the same time.

"Where the hell are you going?" Spaatz said, with his customary impishness.

"Suppose I'm going to the same place you are. Up to see General Marshall."

Spaatz nodded. "That's right."

Brigadier General Frank McCarthy, Marshall's aide, met them upstairs. All he said was, "The general's asleep."

The three of them decided to have dinner.

When they met later with Marshall, he said, "I've had you two join me here because Arnold is sick, and I'm going to send him to the hospital to save his life." Eaker was reminded again of the selflessness that was so characteristic of Marshall.

Marshall continued, "One of you is coming home to be his deputy and run the Army Air Forces until he gets well."

Eaker rightly suspected he was that man, knowing that Eisenhower would not permit Spaatz to leave and, moreover, that he was the junior man.

Eaker returned to Washington, and Marshall called him in. He said that with the war in Europe nearing an end, he wanted him to see MacArthur and General George Kenney in the Philippines, fly to India to see Major General George Stratemeyer, and then return to Europe to discuss with Eisenhower and Spaatz how much of the Army Air Forces in the European theater should be transferred to the Far East to defeat Japan.

It took Eaker twenty days to complete the circuit and file his report with Marshall. By then, he knew, the war in Europe was drawing to a close.

The Allies claimed almost complete air supremacy over Germany, but Lieutenant Lloyd Flanigan had his doubts on March 28 when his 303rd Group was over Berlin.

While the lead bombardier synchronized on the Brenden-Burgische Motorenwerke, Technical Sergeant Beresford Gilkes manned the top turret. He winced each time a shell slammed into the fuselage, knowing they were getting badly mauled by ground fire.

He listened as Flanigan called the navigator. When he got no response, Flanigan continued to call him. Gilkes could not understand why Flanigan kept using the "call" switch because he knew Flight Officer Edward Heaney was not on the interphone.

Gilkes decided to investigate. He dropped out of his turret and saw Flanigan, half out of his seat, trying to fly formation with one hand while fighting off the wounded copilot, Flight Officer James Wokersien, with the other. The copilot was covered with blood, his body having taken a burst of flak through his side of the cockpit, and Wokersien had such a desperate grip on the control column that the airplane was being thrown out of control despite Flanigan's efforts. All the pilot had been able to manage was to hit the interphone button under his left thumb and call for help.

Gilkes helped to remove Wokersien from his seat and lay him on the floor. First aid was given promptly, and Flanigan landed at an advanced Ninth Air Force fighter base in Belgium hoping to saving Wokersien's life, but the copilot was dead.

The plane, *The Greenhill Belle,* was flown back to England, but the main wing spar was so severely damaged that the bomber had to be junked. It was proof again, if any were needed, that Allied airmen could still die in the skies over Germany.

Portal warned on April 7 that further destruction of German cities would only magnify the problems of occupying forces. Therefore, area bombing by the Royal Air Force was discontinued, and Spaatz issued his last formal directive April 13. Strategic bombers thereafter were used only to provide direct assistance to Eisenhower's ground troops.

Spaatz sent a personal message to Generals Doolittle and Twining April 16. "The advances of our ground forces have brought to a close the strategic air war waged by the United States Strategic Air Forces and the Royal Air Force's Bomber Command. It has been won with a decisiveness becoming increasingly evident as our armies overrun Germany."

Production of oil and lubricants in Germany had ceased, and there was no fuel to fly airplanes or drive vehicles of any kind. The German air force was—at last—totally destroyed.

Germany's transportation system had been attacked so successfully that her railroads and canals were practically useless. It was apparent to airmen that Germany could not have continued the war even if Allied armies had not invaded the Reich.

The Germans in Italy surrendered unconditionally May 2. Six days later, the Reich surrendered, and Americans and Russians drank captured champagne at the Elbe to celebrate the occasion.

Colonel Henry Macdonald stood in front of the personnel of his 305th Group in Hangar 2 at Chelveston. He was smiling, because all eyes were not on him but on the eight-by-fifteen-foot Nazi flag draped on the wall behind him.

To his right, the group adjutant, Major George Schubert, looked around the packed building. "It's a damn good thing you're a loud speaker."

The throng quieted down as Macdonald started to talk. "This flag behind me was flying over the city of Schweinfurt when the Forty-second 'Rainbow' Division captured the German ball-bearing center with only sixty casualties."

He looked at them with pride, especially now that they had received still another very personal recognition of their efforts. In his own mind, and the minds of the other old-timers, he recalled those greatest of all air battles when the 305th had twice fought through fighter-filled skies to help destroy the vital plants. Macdonald recalled the terrible October 14 mission best because the 305th had lost thirteen out of the fifteen bombers it had sent out on the mission.

He told them how the army commander there had remembered the Eighth's sacrifices, and realized their destruction of the strategic plants was directly related to the feeble opposition the Wehrmacht presented when the "Rainbow" Division captured Schweinfurt.

"Major General Collins, commander of the Forty-second, decided the captured emblem would be a fitting symbol of triumph for the Eighth's air warriors. Accordingly, he sent the flag to General Spaatz, who selected the Three-oh-fifth because our operations were typical of the Eighth's performance on the crucial Schweinfurt missions."

"I'm sure you all join me," Macdonald said, "in thanking the 'Rainbow' Division for this trophy, which is the first of its kind to be given to an air force in this theater."

The colonel pointed to a corner of the flag. "The inscription reads, 'To the Eighth Air Force. The 'Rainbow' has avenged your losses at Schweinfurt.' "

Macdonald realized later how strong their pride in the 305th really was when many of them, most of whom could have gone home to their families after VE day, chose to remain and take part in the difficult mapping of the Continent, including parts of North Africa, Iceland, and Greenland—for which they characteristically received another unit citation.

General Doolittle sent Macdonald and all other group commanders a letter May 10. It said, "There was never a time when I called on my commanders for anything that I didn't receive more than I asked."

31

IN A POSITION
TO KNOW THE TRUTH

The original strategic air plans had as their central purpose the total weakening of Germany, calling for defeat of the German air force, destruction of the German sources of usable petroleum products, and disruption of the German transportation system. Although German electric power systems were included in the first two American plans, in the field they were given too low a priority to make attacks on them decisive.

These plans originally called for full-strength attacks by the strategic air forces before a decision was made about the necessity for an invasion of the Continent. For reasons already noted, such massive attacks were delayed for more than a year. Eisenhower, who had demanded control of the strategic air forces three months before the invasion of Normandy, gave Albert Speer and his munitions organizations a vital temporary respite while bombers were diverted to communications targets in France.

After bombing attacks at full strength were carried out between mid-January 1944 and January 1945, Germany was totally weakened.

Attacks on the petroleum industry were one of the most dramatic success stories achieved by strategic bombers. Aviation gasoline production plunged to 40 percent in one month after the initial attacks, and to only 10 percent in September 1944.

Attacks on the synthetic oil industry also caused a drastic plunge in production of rubber and nitrogen. With almost all explosives dependent on nitrogen, a by-product of the synthetic oil industry, production of explosives dropped so low in early 1945 that the Wehrmacht faced the possibility of being out of ammunition of all kinds. Food production, likewise highly dependent upon nitrogen as fertilizer, also suffered.

Heavy attacks against transportation systems were late in developing, but once they were started in September 1944, they undoubtedly contributed more than any others to cripple the munitions industry, and manufacturing in general. Officials of the United States Strategic Bombing Survey said that the loss of transportation facilities almost completely stopped the flow of basic war materials, components, and semifinished materials, and often even production was no longer feasible. Speer repeatedly had reminded the Führer that Germany faced total anarchy.

Strategic attacks against rail and water transportation achieved the results that the strategic plans had predicted. They prevented ore transport to steel plants, and coal could not be moved to the electric power stations. Eventually the shortage of coal prevented trains from running because there was not even enough to fire the locomotives.

In January 1944, Germany's frontiers had been still intact. Her transportation system, as vital to the corporate life of a modern state as the flow of blood is to the human body, was functioning almost normally. By fall, air attacks had completely changed her industrial life. The level of coal stocks for railroads dropped to eighteen days in October, and to four and one half days in February 1945. Steel output in the first quarter of 1945 dropped to 11 percent of the nine million tons produced in the first quarter of 1944.

Under the industrial genius of Albert Speer, German production of ammunition actually trebled prior to the start of heavy bombing in September 1944, but once Allied bombers were unleashed in force, munitions output plummeted, and Speer could do nothing about it. This effect was achieved despite the fact that Eisenhower still demanded ground support for his armies, and more than half of all bombs dropped by the strategic air forces from mid-September 1944 to mid-January 1945 were released on targets in support of his armies.

The United States Army Air Forces in Europe had flown 755,000 sorties and dropped 1.4 million tons of bombs. A million of those tons were dropped by the Eighth and Fifteenth air forces. About three fifths of these bombs were released on targets specified by the Combined Bomber Offensive, including close support of the Normandy invasion. The remaining two fifths were dropped in France in support of land campaigns after the breakout from the beachheads, and in Italy and the Balkans. Only 551,000 tons were dropped on Germany.

The United States Strategic Air Forces lost 9,949 bombers during its 756,124 attacks against the enemy, averaging one bomber lost for every 76 dispatched on a mission. In addition, the Americans lost 8,500 fighters. The death toll was 64,000 fliers.

In contrast, the Royal Air Force's Bomber Command lost 11,965 bombers in 678,462 sorties, or a rate of one lost out of every 57 bombers dispatched. Earlier British arguments that night missions were less costly than United States strategic daylight operations failed to bear up, and British losses of planes in strategic operations exceeded American losses by approximately one third (due also, of course, to the fact that the British were over Germany two years before the Americans were).

British crew losses under Harris alone were 44,000 killed, with half that many wounded, and another 11,000 taken prisoner. Eight thousand other men and women lost their life on the ground in dangerous jobs for which they received little or no recognition. There were never more than 250,000 people in Bomber Command at any one time, so these casualty rates were high. (The number lost was below that of the Americans because B-17s and B-24s carried much larger crews.) Of the 57,143 British fliers who died in the war, 41,548 have no known graves.

British Bomber Command, once the only command engaged against the enemy in almost daily combat early in the war, now reaped an unwelcome harvest. As reports from Germany told the world of the awesome destruction of Germany's cities, revulsion set in and some people were quick to forget Nazi Germany's transgressions. Now, more than ever, Fighter Command received the plaudits of victory, while the men of Bomber Command were regarded with ambivalence or even castigated for the destruction they had caused.

The man who had built up this magnificent fighting organization and created a second front long before one was possible on the ground now was rejected by his former superior, Winston Churchill. Harris was denied further employment in the Royal Air Force, and the prime minister refused to recommend him to King George VI for a peerage at a time when men like Tedder were being so honored.

Harris was dedicated to the defeat of Nazi Germany, and out of this single-minded purpose came decisions made with iron resolution. He never felt guilty about attacks against German cities because he had witnessed the London blitz and he never developed the short memories of some British politicians about the Nazi extermination camps, the atrocities against Allied fliers, soldiers, and sailors, and the devastation wrought by German bombers and V weapons in England and the occupied countries long before the Allied air offensive became effective. Yet, throughout the criticism, Harris maintained his sense of humor, falling back upon a fund of stories to enliven postwar associations. He had a rare ability to relate his experiences charmingly; even his "racy" stories were temperately told.

Today, many students of World War II decry as immoral the bombing of German cities, discounting the justification that Germany had started a war of aggression that eventually engulfed the whole world, causing the death of at least 52 million people. Some British writers, as well as many

Americans, tend also to denigrate the effectiveness of strategic air warfare.

On the other hand, most World War II fliers—who certainly learned to hate war because they saw it at first hand in all its horror—are not disposed to denounce the campaign, authorized as it was by their governments for the express purpose of saving lives by shortening the conflict.

Many British critics who have expressed strong disapproval of the bombing of Germany's cities are the same ones who were responsible for Great Britain's failure to develop strategic bombers that could survive over a hostile country in daylight and thereby destroy Hitler's war-making capabilities without resorting to the area bombing of cities. The death of tens of thousands of young Allied fliers can properly be ascribed to their shortsightedness.

Undoubtedly many British leaders, including Harris, deluded themselves about the efficacy of bombing urban areas. There is no question that the bombing was pursued long after there was any reason, or excuse, for such action. On the other hand, despite such errors in judgment, the bombing campaign unquestionably played a vital role in the defeat of Hitler's Germany. Area bombing during the early war years can moreover be seen as a reaction to Hitler's use of terror attacks against Great Britain and other countries on both the eastern and western fronts.

Significantly, there was no other strategy open to Bomber Command, given the equipment available during the war. Harris's determined approach to bombing Germany's cities cannot be viewed apart from Bomber Command's inability to bomb precision targets by daylight in all but the final six months of the war.

Winston Churchill not only supported such attacks, but insisted on even more of them, almost to the end of the war. Dresden is a good case in point. Then, as some people recoiled at such total destruction of Germany's cities, Churchill dissociated himself from Harris and the men who had done his bidding at great personal sacrifice. In Churchill's postwar writings, the greatest accolades went to the men of Fighter Command. The men of Bomber Command, who had served him just as faithfully, were almost ignored. This stands in stark contrast to his statement in the fall of 1940 that "the fighters are our salvation, but the bombers alone provide the means of victory."

Churchill's refusal to approve a campaign medal for Bomber Command upset Harris more than anything else. He no longer cared that Churchill had turned against him, but he felt deeply that thousands of young men who had served their country with such devotion and courage did not deserve to be so casually passed over. For six years the men of Bomber Command had engaged the Luftwaffe in the skies over Europe in a bitter duel to the death, carrying the war deep into Germany while the British army and navy—though with equal valor—all too frequently were losing one battle after another. Churchill's refusal to honor these brave men adequately is to many of them today inexplicable.

German experts agreed with American air strategists after the war that daylight attacks against selected industrial targets were more effective than night raids by the British Bomber Command, whose planes carried heavier bomb loads but were not as sturdy nor well-armed as American bombers and hence not suited to daylight operations. United States Army Air Forces leaders had learned other lessons, too, which they hoped would be useful in planning the final phase of the air war against Japan.

The United States Strategic Bombing Survey repeatedly commented on failure of American bombers to drop their bombs more accurately, along with the fact that 14 percent of all bombs that were dropped never exploded. It is interesting to speculate, through extrapolation, that the lives of nine thousand American fliers might have been saved if all bombs had exploded properly.

Further, fliers had learned that attacks frequently had to be repeated to keep plants out of production. Three major plants were studied by survey teams to analyze bombing attacks, and even Spaatz was shocked when the word came back that only 3 percent of all bombs released on these targets actually damaged them.

Officials cited as reasons that too many small bombs were used and nowhere near enough incendiaries. Far fewer missions and lower bomb tonnages would have been needed if these shortcomings had been appreciated and corrected.

General Hansell, who had drawn up the plan to use American airpower in Europe, said after the war that an undeviating application of airpower, unhampered by constant diversion for support of ground troops, would have contributed to an earlier victory. Years later he added, "The strategic objectives of air warfare, described in the original plans, were actually attained. If strategic air warfare could have followed the plans, mortal wounding of Germany probably could have been attained in June 1944 rather than March 1945.

"The strategic air plans were not closely followed, and their effect was considerably diluted," Hansell says today. "In my considered opinion, this dilution had a tragic effect in prolonging the war with attendant loss of life. I believe the general air strategy devised by the Air War Plans Division, and described in AWPD-1, AWPD-42 and the plan for the Combined Bomber Offensive, was correct and sound."

On the German side, General Walther Wever, who served as the first chief of staff of the Luftwaffe, strongly endorsed the concept of strategic bombers despite Hitler's opposition. In 1934, he had called for development of a four-engine bomber whose radius of action would extend far out over the Atlantic so that Britain's sea-lanes could be attacked, and that would be valuable in attacking distant targets in Russia. Five prototypes of the Do-19 and the J-89 were developed in 1936. Although underpowered, both bombers showed promise.

On June 3, 1936, Wever was killed in an airplane crash. After his death, no one else believed as strongly in the role of strategic bombers and the General Staff dropped further heavy-bomber development. Germany thus entered World War II without heavy bombers for strategic warfare even though she had one of the most modern air forces in the world.

There was another school of thought that professed equal enthusiasm for airpower but believed that it was a vital adjunct to land power and should be employed to provide maximum contribution to land operations. Principal adherents were Eisenhower and MacArthur and the latter's South Pacific air commander, General George Kenney, on the American side, and Tedder and Leigh-Mallory on the British side. American admirals Ernest King and Chester Nimitz strongly embraced the use of airpower in furtherance of sea missions, but stopped short of the belief that airpower could be the primary influence against an enemy.

Among the United States Joint Chiefs of Staff, General Marshall stood alone as a nonpartisan, espousing the employment of forces in what he perceived to be the best distribution for meeting national objectives, regardless of service prejudices, doctrines, and enthusiasms. In the tug-of-war between competing factions, theater commanders often prevailed in diverting strategic air forces to support of surface campaigns. Arnold and Spaatz, a minority in the higher councils, were at even greater disadvantage when confronted by President Roosevelt, a navy man, and Prime Minister Churchill, who initially supported but later lost confidence in the British Bomber Command's ability to force the Germans to surrender through air attacks.

The concept of strategic air warfare was one from which Arnold, Spaatz, and Eaker never willingly departed, though they had to throw their full weight into support of the invasion when a failure to bring all available forces to bear could have involved disaster on a major scale. Once the beachheads were secured, they urged resumption of the air offensive against Germany, and only Spaatz's threat to resign persuaded Eisenhower to grant him permission to start a campaign against oil targets.

The original air plans had shortcomings, and General Hansell speaks candidly about them—particularly the omission of escort fighters and the exaggerated effectiveness of small bombs. In his opinion, development of the P-47 and the P-51 long-range escorts proved crucial to the success of the strategic air offensive. He says early bomber losses were also due in large measure to inadequate training in flexible gunnery.

He says one of the most important modifications of AWPD-1 was to transfer large numbers of fighters from hemispheric defense to fighter escort and tactical air force roles. Fighters in a dual role of fighter-bombers proved immensely effective in support of ground operations. He says they quickly absorbed the role medium bombers played in interdiction and battlefield support. Medium bombers, operating at limited range, under escort at ten thousand to twelve thousand feet, could deliver a bomb load comparable to a B-17 with much better accuracy.

AWPD-42 had called for a strategic air strength of 3,000 heavy bombers in Europe and the Mediterranean by November 1943. Actually, there were only 1,100 heavy bombers in the fall of 1943, and in May of the following year there was still only an average of 1,750 aircraft available for any one mission, or 58 percent of the strength called for in the plan. Allied Expeditionary Forces were able to make a successful invasion of Normandy because of local air superiority, but the German state was far from being "fatally weakened" prior to the invasion as implied in the Casablanca Directive.

Failure to follow the AWPD-1 and AWPD-42 guidelines about the importance of electric generating stations and substations, which were extremely sensitive to attack by air, was another unfortunate error. The bombing survey says that destruction of such installations would have had a catastrophic effect on Germany's war production.

The Germans agreed that disruption of these systems would have contributed as much to winning the war as the campaign against oil. Both American plans had given top priority to such targets, but the Committee of Operations Analysts dropped electric installations to thirteenth place because they believed there were not enough forces available to disrupt them.

Speer told survey officials, "According to estimates, a loss of sixty percent of total power production would have sufficed to lead to a collapse of the whole power network. Destruction of power plants would have been a most radical measure as it would at once have led to a breakdown of all industrial and public life. It was the only field, besides gas, where no reserves could be stored which were likely to postpone the effect for some months."

In retrospect, it might have been possible to destroy the German electric power system before the invasion, if the strategic air forces had been built up on schedule, without lessening air attacks on the German air force and the oil industry. It certainly could have been accomplished shortly thereafter.

Eisenhower had never forgotten how a small number of German aircraft had disrupted Allied landings on the beaches in Sicily, so for the Normandy invasion he demanded and got assignment of all air units—

at the expense of delaying the Combined Bomber Offensive. Actually, he had had sufficient tactical airpower to do the job, and most heavy bomber missions were wasted (or worse, when some bombs were dropped short on Allied lines). Eisenhower's other staff members had similar views about airpower, including Lieutenant General Walter Bedell Smith, his chief of staff, who refused to listen to arguments by strategic air leaders. He made it clear that he did not understand their theories about objectives of strategic air warfare and told them their comments were not appreciated.

Despite mistakes, unavoidable shortcomings, and the late start of the strategic air offensive, one of the world's most powerful military nations was finally made impotent by airpower.

In General Hansell's views, the Combined Bomber Offensive could have brought fatal chaos to internal Germany before the invasion, but the decision to invade North Africa and later Sicily and Italy was too great a diversion of strategic air strength. This political decision was resisted by American military leaders at the time, and their opinions should have been respected. These Mediterranean adventures absorbed enormous resources and contributed little to the defeat of Germany. Although Italian bomber bases were useful, they were not needed to provide the final knockout blows to the Third Reich.

It is true—and it is often pointed out—that strategic airpower did not destroy Germany soon enough to avoid an invasion. The fact that it could have done so, given the resources of men and planes earlier in the war, was borne out three months later when Japan capitulated almost as a direct result of strategic airpower. Although it was not recognized at the time, Japan was substantively defeated by August 1, 1945, before the atomic bombs were dropped. Her navy had been almost eliminated by the United States Navy, while ships of her merchant marine were either destroyed or confined to harbors after extensive aerial mining. Most of Japan's cities were in ruins following bombing attacks by Twentieth Air Force B-29s.

After the Japanese surrender, Prince Fumimaro Konoye said, "Fundamentally the thing that brought about the determination to make peace was the prolonged bombing by the B-29s."

Of the reasons for Japan's surrender, Prime Minister Kantaro Suzuki said, "It seemed to me unavoidable that, in the long run, Japan would be almost destroyed by air attack, so merely on the basis of the B-29s alone I was convinced that Japan should sue for peace."

The atomic bombs gave the Japanese an excuse to surrender, but it is now apparent that airpower would have forced them to the same conclusion no later than November 1, 1945.

Equally revealing was Albert Speer's statement that the war in Europe could have been decided in 1943 if the vast but pointless area bombing of targets had instead been concentrated on centers of armaments production. When he was interrogated by officials of the United States Strategic Bombing Survey after the war, Speer was emphatic in saying that bombing could have won the war without an invasion. During his years of watching the troubled skies over Fortress Europe, he was in a position to know the truth.

After VE day, Colonel Henry Macdonald's veteran 305th Group assumed its task of mapping the European continent.

For the first time, Macdonald and members of his group had a chance to observe the destruction of Germany caused by the Allied Strategic Air Forces. Poststrike photographs had revealed only a small part of the story. Now, as the 305th's bombers flew back and forth across the countryside on their mapping runs, free at last of intereference by German fighters and antiaircraft guns, the full extent of the Allied bombing was visible. They could see in awesome detail the shattered cities of the industrial Ruhr, which had received the worst bombing of all. During the war, any time weather was bad over Germany, Allied bombers dropped their bombs on the Ruhr because it was so heavily industrialized that it was almost impossible to miss a target even on a radar run.

The Ruhr's utter destruction sobered the men of the 305th, who realized the same thing could have happened to their own country if they had not helped to turn the tide of battle in Europe. The bleak rubble in the key center of Aachen seemed to symbolize a Third Reich that had finally been rendered helpless under Allied might and airpower.

Macdonald took off one day in a P-51 fighter to make a personal tour and see for himself. He flew low over Hamburg, noting that only a small section of the city remained standing, while a few inhabitants moved aimlessly through their blackened city. Later, over Cologne, he saw the same degree of destruction, except that the city's magnificent cathedral stood miraculously amid the ruins, appearing structurally sound, although its windows had all been blown out.

The autobahns that crisscrossed Germany were empty because of the heavy damage caused by ground and air forces. He spotted only a few vehicles that still were able to travel, noting they had to use the fields to get from one city to another.

The crumpled Siegfried Line, the rubble of Germany's factories and cities, and the huge prison camp on the Rhine swept beneath Macdonald's plane, tragic monuments to the consequences of the German people's support of Adolf Hitler and his vision of world conquest.

Macdonald headed back to base, recalling how close the Allies had come to defeat in the air, and how thousands like him in these now-empty skies had helped to turn early disaster into victory. His sense of horror at the destruction he had just witnessed was tempered by his personal knowledge of how thin had been the Allied margin of victory. He realized now more fully that had Nazi leaders not made some major airpower mistakes, his flight over Germany might well have been duplicated by a Nazi air leader over a devastated England and United States.

BIBLIOGRAPHY

Ambrose, Stephen E. *The Supreme Commander, the War Years of General Dwight D. Eisenhower.* New York: Doubleday, 1970.

Andrews, Allen. *The Air Marshals.* New York: Morrow, 1970.

Arnold, General H. H. *Global Mission.* New York: Harper, 1949.

Brickhill, Paul. *The Dam Busters.* London: Evans Brothers, Ltd., 1951; New York: Bantam Books, 1979.

Coffey, Thomas. *Decision over Schweinfurt.* New York: McKay, 1977.

Committee on Labor and Public Welfare, United States Senate. *Medal of Honor 1863 – 1968.* Washington, D.C.: Government Printing Office, 1968.

Craven, W. F., and Cate, J. L. *The Army Air Forces in World War II.* Chicago: University of Chicago Press, volume 1, 1947; volume 2, 1949; volume 3, 1951.

Galland, Adolf. *The First and the Last.* New York: Holt, Rinehart and Winston, Inc., 1946; New York: Bantam Books, 1978.

Gibson, Guy. *Enemy Coast Ahead.* London: Michael Joseph, Ltd., 1946; New York: Bantam Books, 1979.

Hansell, Major General Haywood S., Jr. (Ret.). *The Air Plan that Defeated Hitler.* Atlanta: Higgins-McArthur Longine and Porter, Inc., 1972.

Harris, Sir Arthur, GCB, OBE, and AFC. *Bomber Offensive.* London: Collins, 1947; New York: Macmillan, 1947.

Hastings, Max. *Bomber Command.* New York: The Dial Press/James Wade, 1979.

Ilfrey, Jack, with Max Reynolds. *Happy Jack's Go-Buggy.* Hicksville, N.Y.: Exposition Press, 1979.

Middlebrook, Martin. *The Nuremburg Raid.* New York: William Morrow, 1974.

Morrison, Wilbur H. *The Incredible 305th: The "Can Do" Bombers of World War II.* New York: Duell, Sloan and Pearce, 1962.

Peaslee, Colonel Budd J. (Ret.). *Heritage of Valor*. Philadelphia and New York: J. B. Lippincott, 1964.

Reynolds, George A. *ETO Carpetbaggers*. Birmingham: privately published, 1977.

Slessor, Sir John. *Central Blue: The Autobiography of Sir John Slessor*. New York: Frederick A. Praeger, 1957.

Speer, Albert. *Inside the Third Reich*. New York: Macmillan, 1970.

Tedder, Lord. *With Prejudice: War Memoirs of Marshal of the Royal Air Force Lord Tedder, GCB*. London: Cassel, 1966.

United States Strategic Bombing Survey. Washington, D.C.; Government Printing Office, 1946 – 47.

Webster, Sir Charles, and Frankland, Noble. *The Strategic Air Offensive Against Germany, 1939–45*. London: Her Majesty's Stationery Office, 1961.

Wolff, Leon. *Low Level Mission*. New York: Doubleday, 1957.

INDEX

Aaron, Sgt. A. L., 135
  Victoria Cross awarded to, 135
Abbeville, 49
  V-weapon site at, 224
Abel, Lt. Dunstan T., 144
Aircraft
  A-20 Boston, 2, 90, 91
  B-17 Flying Fortress, 8, 10, 34,
    47–49, 51–57, 59, 60, 73–75, 85,
    100, 106, 108, 109, 116, 117, 119,
    125, 137, 138, 140–145, 147, 149,
    157, 160–163, 165, 166, 181, 186,
    189, 192, 194, 221, 222, 236, 243,
    251, 254, 258, 260, 289–291, 303,
    307
  B-17G, 156
  B-24 Liberator, 8–10, 34, 53,
    56–59, 62, 89, 127, 129, 131, 133,
    134, 157, 160, 172, 189, 202, 203,
    232, 236, 243, 258, 303
  B-26 Marauder, 73, 139, 184, 230,
    249
  B-29 Superfortress, 8, 51, 65, 308
  B-36, 8
  DC-3, 33
  DO-19, 306
  HE-111, 103, 129, 161
  HE-177, 243
  JU-88, 33, 69, 189
  JU-89, 306
  P-38, 56, 69, 106, 118, 135, 156,
    160, 164, 165, 184, 191, 202
  P-47 Thunderbolt, 106, 107, 114,
    118, 135, 140, 145, 156, 163, 184,
    191, 202, 217, 222, 223, 230, 260,
    291, 306
  P-51 Mustang, 59, 60, 105, 118,
    164, 165, 184, 189, 191, 202, 203,
    236, 243, 247, 248, 281, 282, 306,
    309
  YB-40, 117
  Armstrong, Whitworth Whitley, 28
  Avro Manchester, 20, 25, 28
  Beaufighter, 119
  Blenheim, 14, 15
  Focke-Wulf 190, 22, 49, 56, 57, 63,
    69, 74, 139, 140–142, 159, 187,
    197, 202, 203
  Gloster Meteor, 242
  Halifax, 20, 119, 219, 256
  Hampden, 14, 17
  Handley Page Halifax, 28
  Komet, 290
  Lancaster, 20, 25, 28, 30, 40, 112,
    119, 219, 223, 224, 237, 239, 256,
    261, 264, 279, 280, 283, 291
  ME-109, 116, 129, 137, 141–143,
    145, 159, 171, 187, 251
  ME-110, 20, 21, 49, 74, 109, 110,
    141, 156, 189, 197, 256
  ME-210, 161
  ME-262, 186, 254, 257, 289
  Mosquito, 96, 97, 136, 160, 210,
    223, 224, 256, 261, 264, 270
  Short Stirling, 20, 28, 29
  Spitfire, 43, 47, 49, 56, 73, 139, 144
  Typhoons, 139
  Warwick, 283
  Wellington, 14, 20, 21, 28, 69, 119,
    296
  Whitley, 14
Air Divisions (numbered)
  First Air Division, 117, 138, 139,
    141, 142, 145, 149, 150, 159, 160,
    163, 189, 192, 247, 248, 291

London, 18, 33, 34, 40, 43, 52
  bombing of, 123, 265, 303
  first V-1 dropped on, 240
Longfellow, Col. Newton, 47
  Brig. Gen., 73, 85, 89, 104, 110
Lovett, Robert A., 105, 110
Luftwaffe, 9, 13, 14, 19, 25, 30, 38,
  50, 66, 82, 87, 102, 103, 118,
  136, 165, 179, 185, 186, 192, 201,
  218, 227–231, 235, 236, 238, 240,
  253, 257, 266, 267, 288, 297, 304,
  305
Luttwitz, Gen. Freiherr Heinrich von,
  244

MacArthur, Gen. Douglas, 10, 40,
  66, 298, 306
Macdonald, Maj. Henry G., 90
  Col., 146, 192, 299, 300, 309
Macdonald, Wing Com. J. C., 29
McAuliffe, Brig. Gen. Anthony, 285
McCallum, Robert, 137
McCarthy, Brig. Gen. Frank, 297
McCollum, Maj. Loren G., 140
McCord, Lt. Lawrence, 146, 147
McElwain, Lt. R. F., 147
McKee, Lt. Ralph D., 115–117
McKeegan, Lt. Rothery, 147–149
McKinnon, Flight Lt. Doug, 279, 280
McLain, S/Sgt. Robert, 147, 148
McLaughlin, Capt. James K., 160
McNair, Lt. Gen. Lesley J., 245
McNarney, Lt. Gen. Joseph T., 71
Magill, Lt. Col. Bradley, 255
Malone, Sgt. Henry A., 193
Mannstein, Feldmarschall Erich von,
  43
Manser, Flight Officer Leslie T., 29
  Victoria Cross awarded to, 29
Marienburg, 102
  bombing of, 157, 170
Marshall, Gen. George C., 3–8, 11,
  12, 38–40, 44, 45, 48, 51, 54, 67,
  82, 92, 100, 126–128, 134, 152,
  154, 155, 167, 174, 179, 180, 216,
  218, 245–247, 262, 267, 272, 298,
  299, 306
Mason, Capt. C. C., 34
Mason, Lt. Harry G., 192, 193, 194
Massachusetts Institute of Technol-
  ogy, 100
Mathies, Sgt. Archibald, 194
  Medal of Honor awarded to, 194
Mathis, Lt. Jack W., 97
  Medal of Honor awarded to, 98

Medal of Honor, 98, 126, 134, 138,
  155, 194, 222, 223, 232, 234, 249,
  251, 252, 277, 278, 285
Melton, William, 259
Memphis Belle (B-17), 137
Merlin (engine), 59, 60, 106, 165
Messerschmitt, Wilhelm, 241, 289,
  291
Metzger, Lt. William E., 278
  Medal of Honor awarded to, 278
Michael, Lt. Edward S., 221
  Medal of Honor awarded to, 222
Middle East, 23, 43, 44, 67, 70, 83,
  84, 91
Midway, Battle of, 2, 42, 43, 79
Milch, Feldmarschall Erhard, 24, 31,
  151, 232, 289
Miller, George R., 133
Mitchell, Maj. Curt, 146
Möhne Dam, 112, 113, 273
Mölders, Gen. Werner, 24
Montgomery, Marshal Bernard, 82,
  180, 235, 244, 254, 278, 296
Morgan, Flight Officer John C., 124,
  125
  Medal of Honor awarded to, 126
Morgan, Maj. Robert K., 137
Morocco, 67, 68
  plans for invasion of, 67
  invasion of, 68
Moscow, 242, 243
Moullen, Lt. R. P., 293–296
Munich, 223, 247, 248
Murphy, Lt. Paul W., 193
Murphy, Robert, 68
Murphy, Lt. Thomas E., 140, 142
Münster, 20, 157, 159, 264
Murray, T/Sgt. Charles L., 148
Mussolini, Benito, 96, 126, 152
  overthrow of, 127

Naples, 153
Nelson, Lt. Clarence R., 194
Nettles, Lt. Siles, 163
Newall, Sir Cyril, 18
Nimitz, Adm. Chester, 66, 306
Normand, Maj. G. G. Y., 162, 163
Normandy, 33, 204, 211, 218, 227,
  229–231, 234–237, 239, 244, 249,
  255, 258, 268, 301, 302, 307
Norstad, Brig. Gen. Lauris, 149
Norway, invasion of, 15
Novikov, Col. Gen. Aleksandr, 242
Nuremburg, 218, 219, 220

Timoshenko, Marshal Semën, 44
Tobruk, 8, 44
Torch (invasion of North Africa), 59, 70
Towers, R/Adm. John H., 40
Transportation Plan, 209, 210, 211, 213, 214, 216, 217
Trenchard, Lord Hugh, 122
Trident Conference, 95
  Combined Bomber Offensive approved at, 95
Truemper, Lt. Walter E., 194
  Medal of Honor awarded to, 194
Turner, Col. Howard M., 146, 163
Twining, Maj. Gen. Nathan F., 179, 190, 299

U-boats, 57
  success of, 58, 60, 63
  offensive against, 96
  new type of, 267
Udet, Ernst, 24, 136
U.S. Army Air Corps, 4, 106
U.S. Army Air Forces, 7, 9, 10, 37, 42, 43, 46, 53, 54, 66, 79, 82, 100, 105, 106, 118, 153, 168, 182, 185, 201, 207, 267, 269, 298, 302, 305
U.S. Navy, 9, 34, 39, 40, 43, 46, 60, 65, 79, 94, 308
U.S. Strategic Air Forces, 95, 173, 188, 190, 212, 216, 226, 250, 262, 272, 299, 302
  see also Spaatz and Eaker
U.S. Strategic Bombing Survey, 104, 173, 184, 228, 286, 302, 305, 309
Utah Beach, 238, 239

V-1, 136, 169, 190, 203, 242, 244, 250, 252, 265, 266
V-2, 136, 220, 240, 241, 265, 266
Vance, Lt. Col. Leon R., 234
  Medal of Honor awarded to, 234
Vandenberg, Maj. Gen. Hoyt S., 245
Vandevanter, Col. Elliott, 140
VE day, 300, 309
Vegesack, 89, 97
Versailles Treaty, 13
Victoria Cross, 16, 21, 29, 113, 135, 219, 223

Walker, Col. R. R., 56
Wallace, Col. James, 74

Wallis, Dr. Barnes, 112, 113, 239, 264
Walter, Lt. Donald A., 49
Ward, Sgt. James, 20
  Victoria Cross awarded to, 21
Weaver, Sgt. Tyre C., 124
West, Lt. Henry A., 56, 57
Westberg, Lt. Franklin A., 221, 222
Westover, Maj. Gen. Oscar, 50
Wetzel, Lt. William, 116, 117
Wever, Gen. Walther, 305
White, Maj. Thomas D., 6
Whittles, Sir Frank, 289
Widdowson, Sq. Leader R. F., 20, 21
Wiener Neustadt, 153, 171, 172
Wilhelmshaven, 14, 19, 89, 100, 108
Williams, Lt. David, 145
Williams, S/Sgt. Frank E., 147, 148
Williams, Brig. Gen. Robert, 89, 117, 118, 141, 145, 149, 150, 247
Wilson, Field Marshal Sir Henry Maitland, 176, 245, 246
Winant, Amb. John G., 41
Wings (numbered)
  1st Wing, 73, 77, 92, 143, 144, 187
  2nd Wing, 73, 140, 141, 146
  3rd Wing, 73, 77, 117, 140, 141, 143
  4th Wing, 93, 105, 146
  40th Combat Wing, 146, 160
  101st Wing, 147
Wittans, Col. Edgar, 143
Wokersien, Flight Officer James, 298
Wood, Col. Jack, 130, 132
Wood, Sir Kingsley, 14
Woodroofe, Sgt. Laurie, 280, 282
World War I, 17, 44, 83, 106, 159, 186
Wray, Col. Stanley, 73, 77, 144
Wright Field, 75, 106
Wurzbach, Lt. Col. Clemmons L., 146
Wycombe Abbey, 33

Yalta Conference, 291
  Dresden attack approved at, 291
Yankee Doodle (B-17), 47
Young, Col. Charles, 251, 255

Zemke, Col. Hubert, 140, 141
Zuckerman, Prof. Solly, 114, 209, 211, 212, 215